D1490492

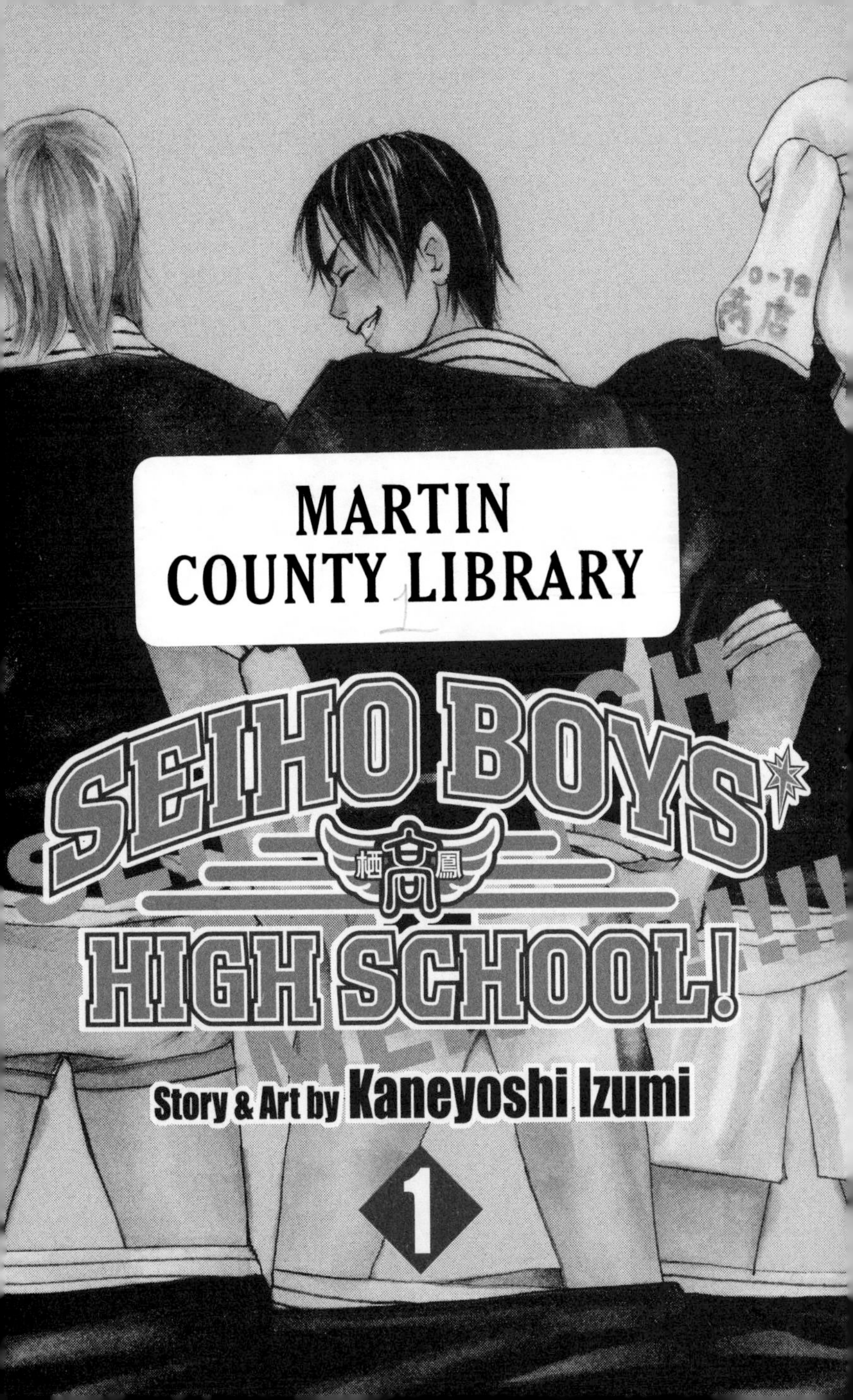
SEIHO BOYS
栖高鳳
HIGH SCHOOL!
Story & Art by Kaneyoshi Izumi
1

SEIHO BOYS' HIGH SCHOOL!

1

CONTENTS

SEIHO BOYS' HIGH SCHOOL ♠CHAPTER 1♠

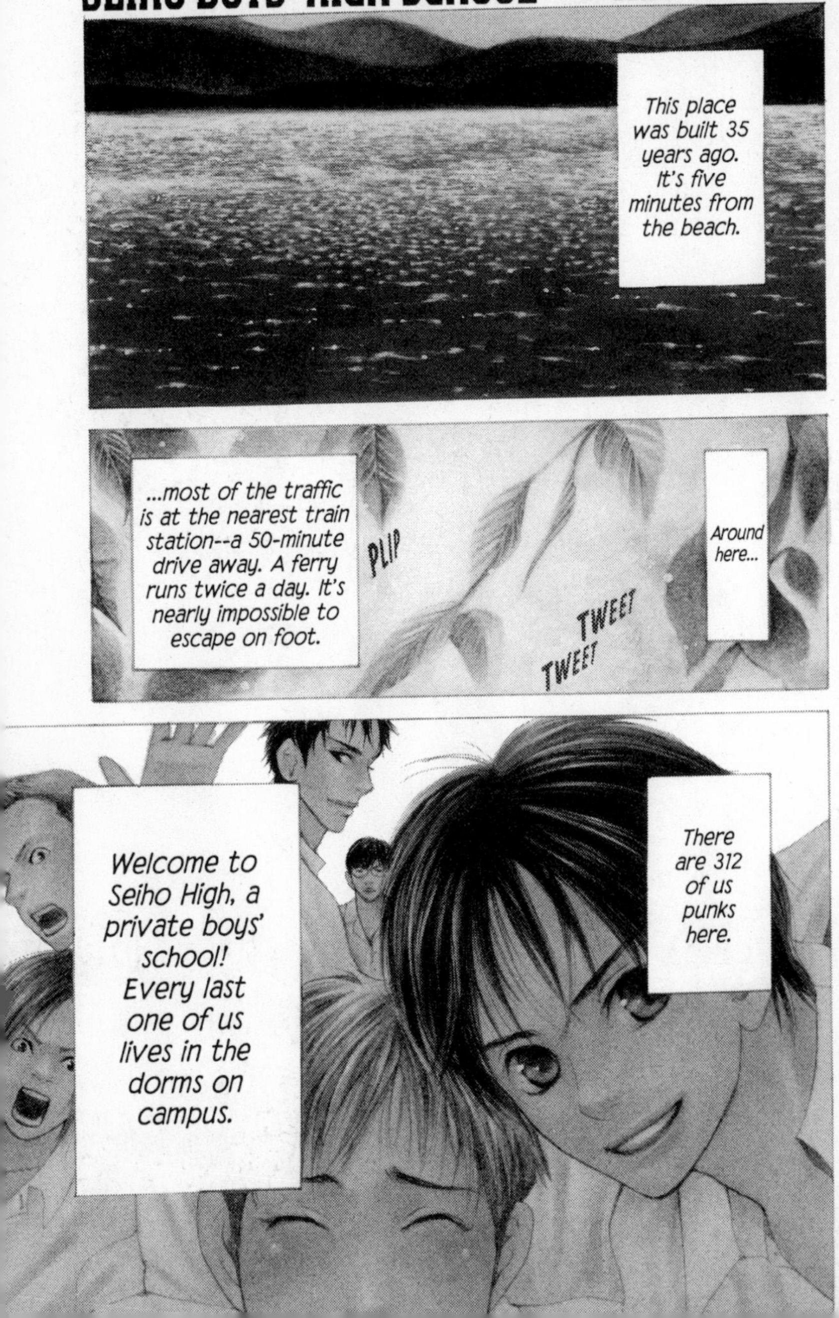
This place was built 35 years ago. It's five minutes from the beach.
Around here...
...most of the traffic is at the nearest train station--a 50-minute drive away. A ferry runs twice a day. It's nearly impossible to escape on foot.
TWEET
TWEET
PLIP
There are 312 of us punks here.
Welcome to Seiho High, a private boys' school! Every last one of us lives in the dorms on campus.

SEIHO BOYS' HIGH SCHOOL!

♠ CHAPTER 1 ♠

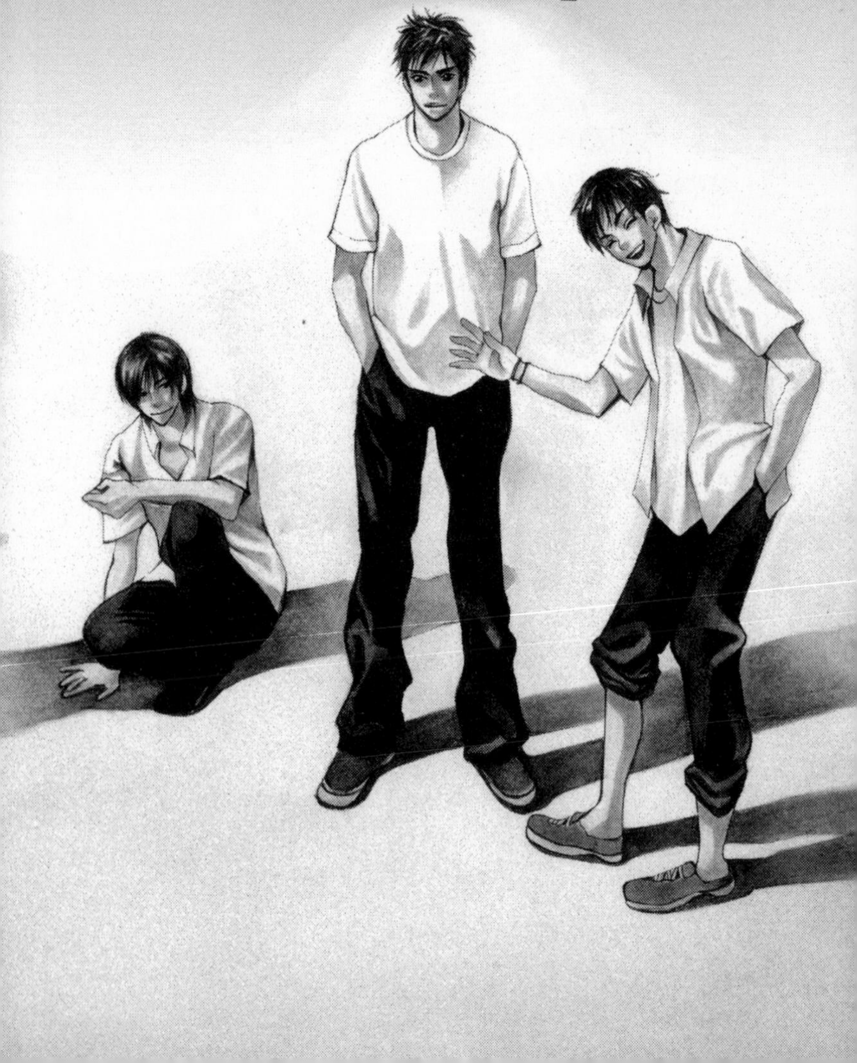

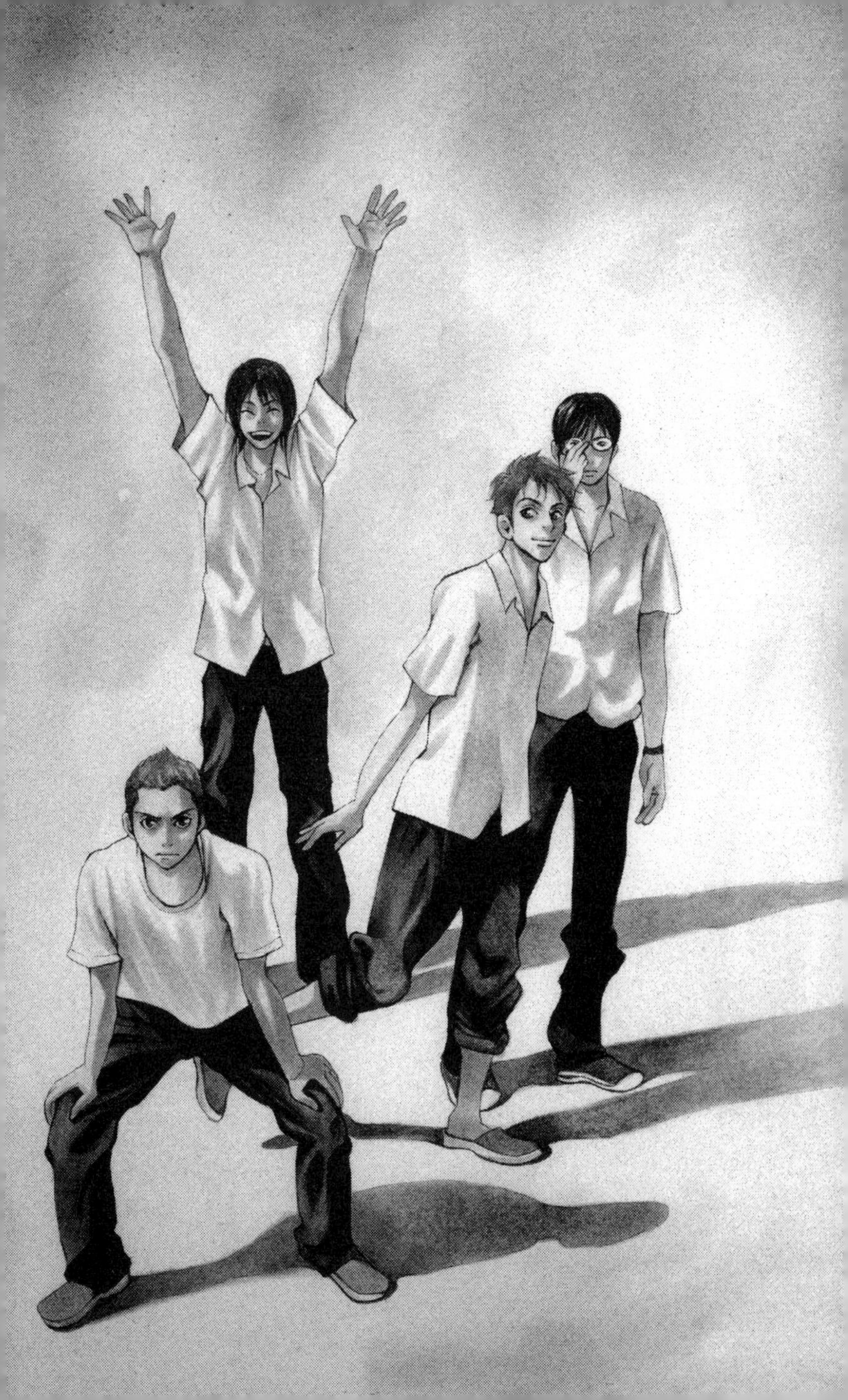

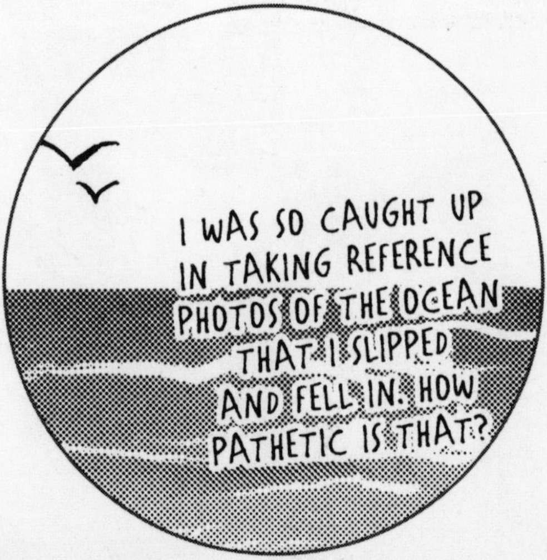
I WAS SO CAUGHT UP IN TAKING REFERENCE PHOTOS OF THE OCEAN THAT I SLIPPED AND FELL IN. HOW PATHETIC IS THAT?

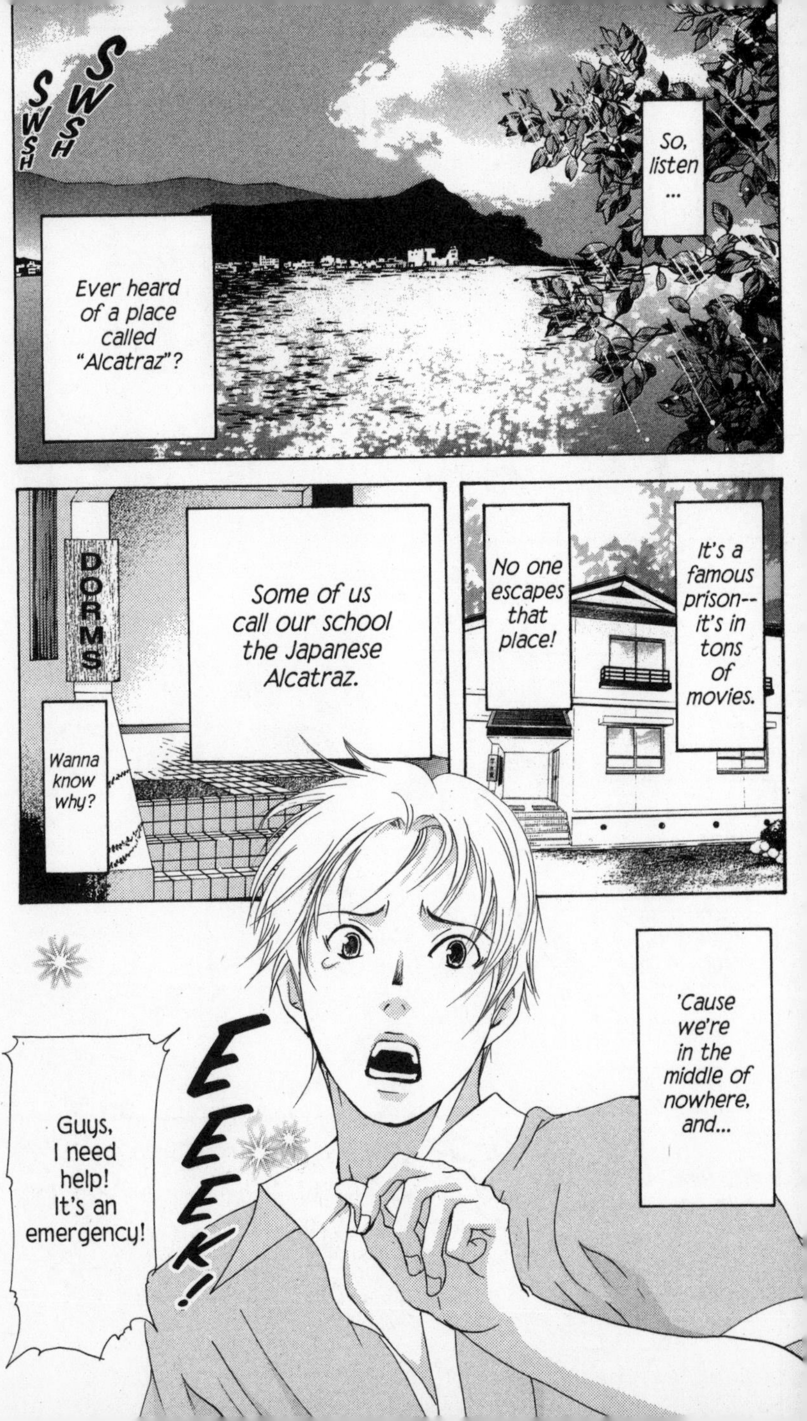
So, listen ...
SWSH SWSH
Ever heard of a place called "Alcatraz"?
It's a famous prison--it's in tons of movies.
No one escapes that place!
Some of us call our school the Japanese Alcatraz.
DORMS
Wanna know why?
'Cause we're in the middle of nowhere, and...
EEEEK!
Guys, I need help! It's an emergency!

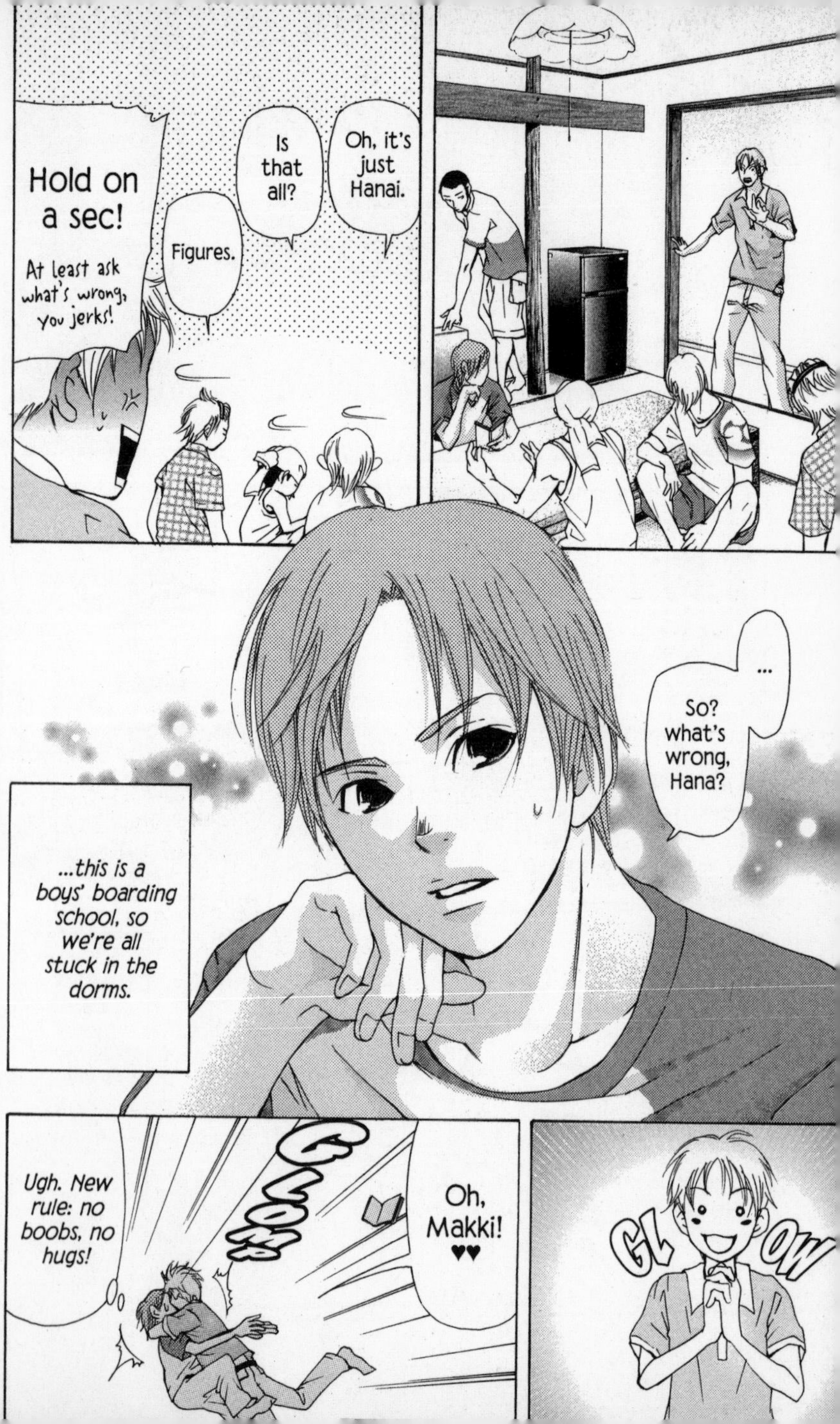
Oh, it's just Hanai.
Is that all?
Figures.
Hold on a sec!
At least ask what's wrong, you jerks!
...
So? what's wrong, Hana?
...this is a boys' boarding school, so we're all stuck in the dorms.
GLOW
Oh, Makki! ♥♥
GLOMP
Ugh. New rule: no boobs, no hugs!

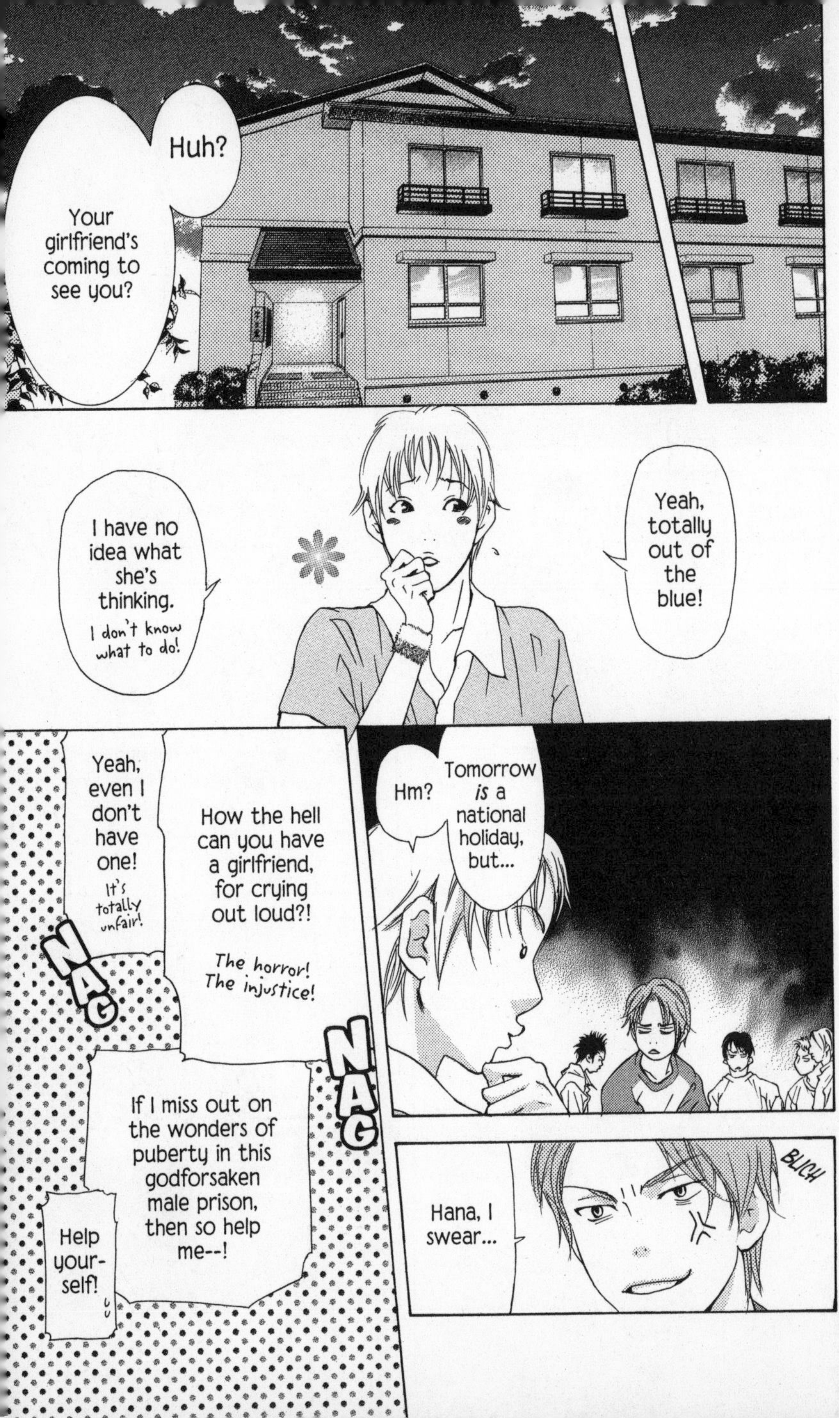

Huh?
Your girlfriend's coming to see you?
Yeah, totally out of the blue!
I have no idea what she's thinking.
I don't know what to do!
Tomorrow *is* a national holiday, but...
Hm?
BLICH
Hana, I swear...
How the hell can you have a girlfriend, for crying out loud?!
The horror! The injustice!
Yeah, even I don't have one!
It's totally unfair!
NAG
NAG
If I miss out on the wonders of puberty in this godforsaken male prison, then so help me--!
Help your-self!

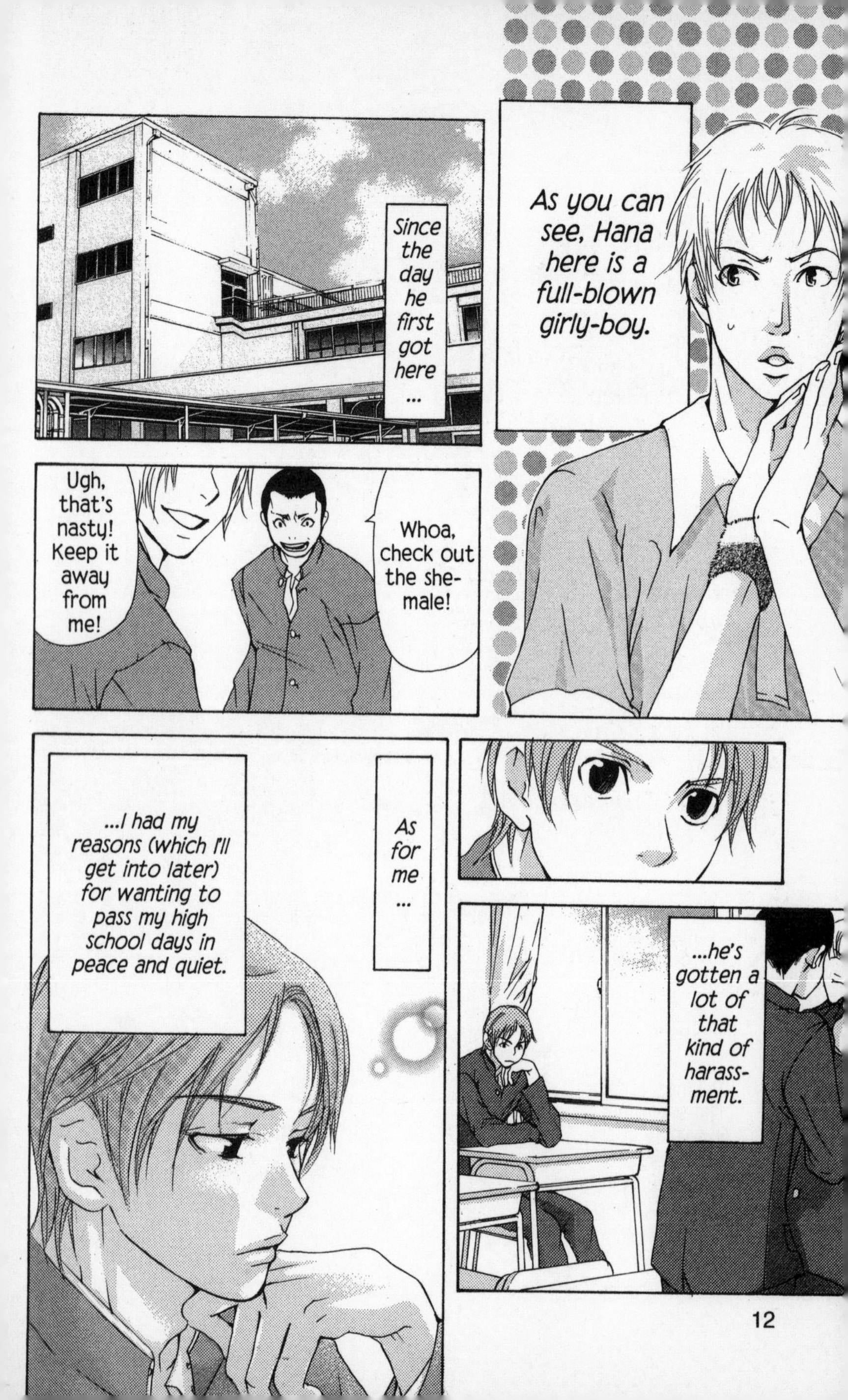
As you can see, Hana here is a full-blown girly-boy.
Since the day he first got here...
Whoa, check out the she-male!
Ugh, that's nasty! Keep it away from me!
...he's gotten a lot of that kind of harassment.
As for me...
...I had my reasons (which I'll get into later) for wanting to pass my high school days in peace and quiet.

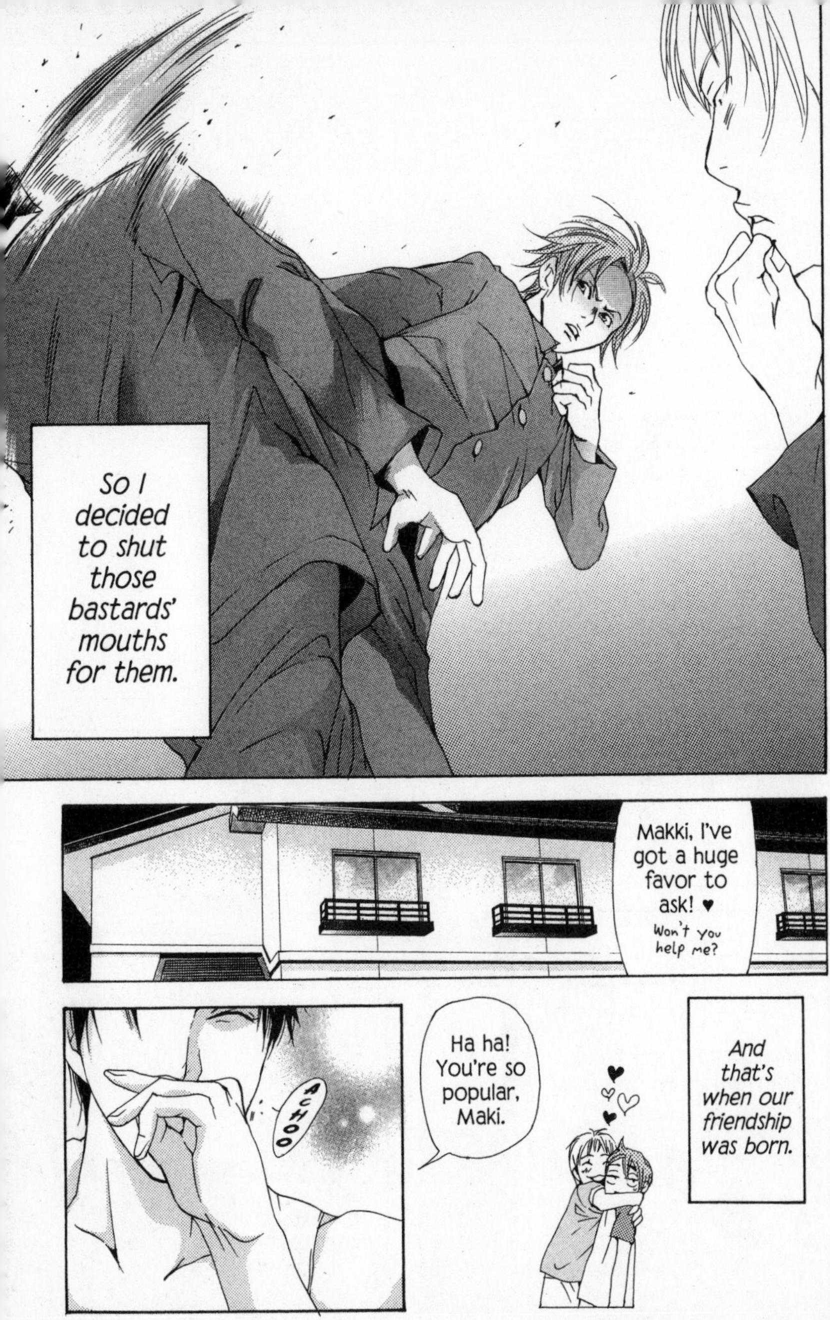
So I decided to shut those bastards' mouths for them.
Makki, I've got a huge favor to ask! ♥
Won't you help me?
And that's when our friendship was born.
Ha ha! You're so popular, Maki.
ACHOO

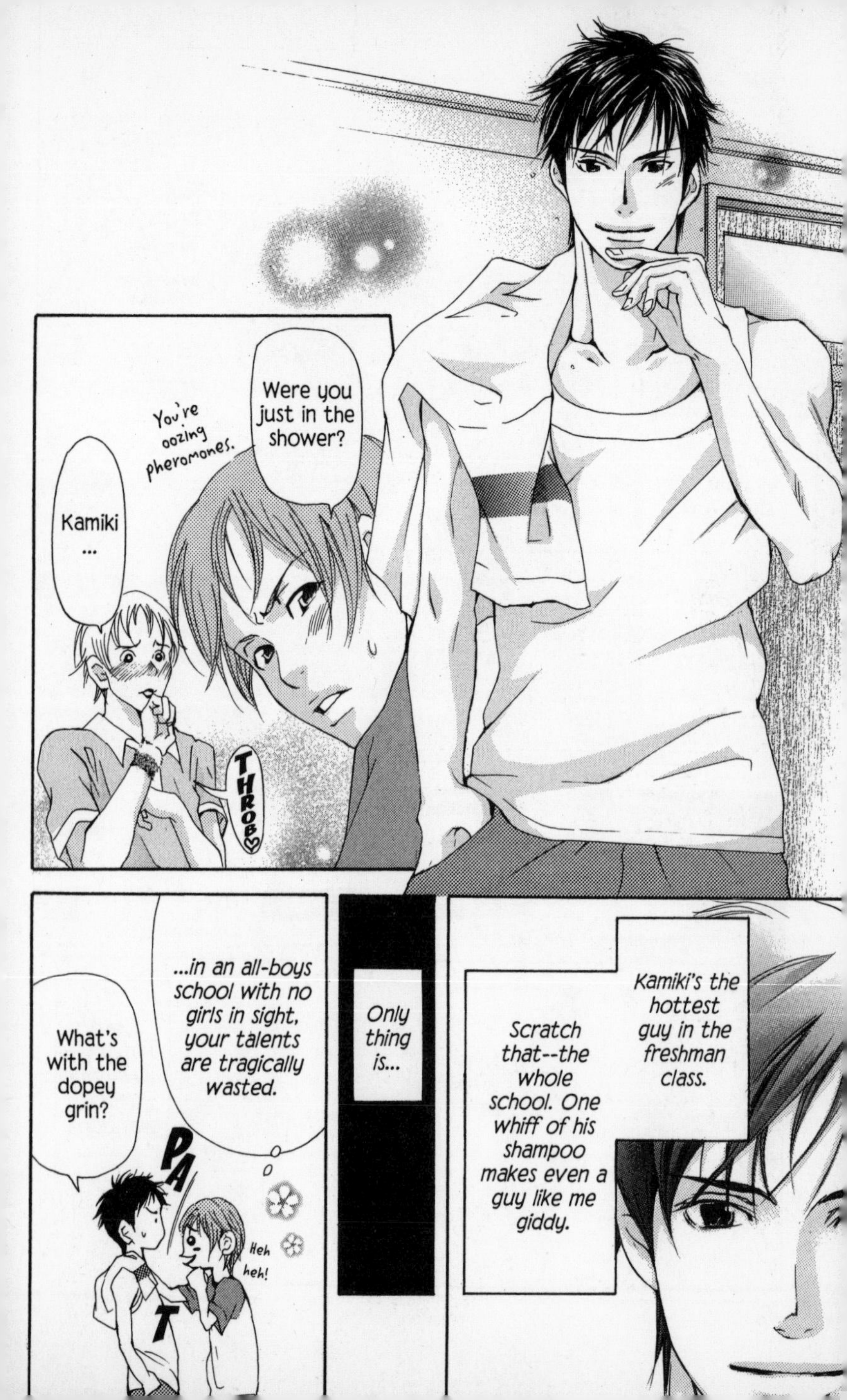

Were you just in the shower?
You're oozing pheromones.
Kamiki...
THROB
Kamiki's the hottest guy in the freshman class.
Scratch that--the whole school. One whiff of his shampoo makes even a guy like me giddy.
Only thing is...
...in an all-boys school with no girls in sight, your talents are tragically wasted.
What's with the dopey grin?
PAT
Heh heh!

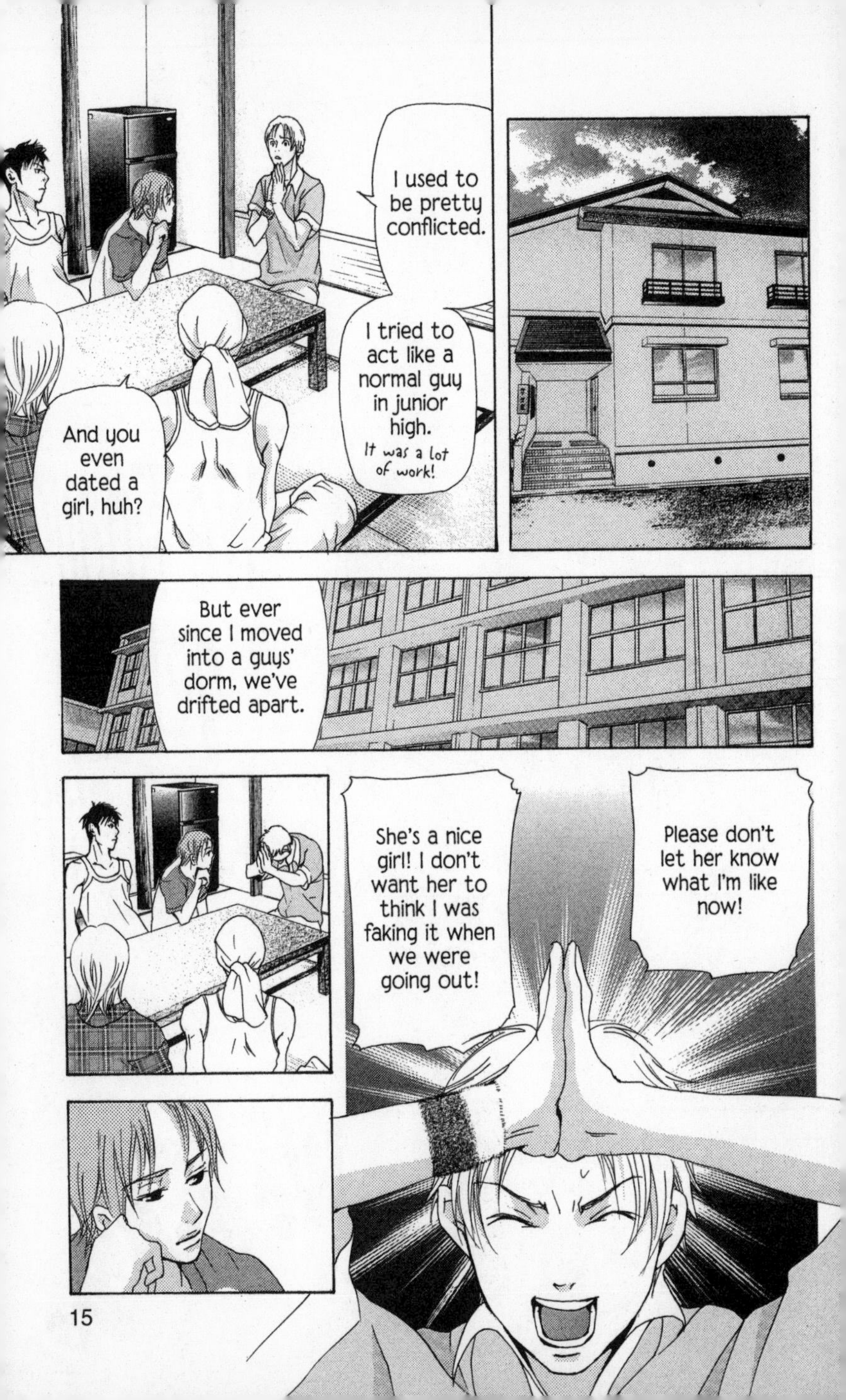
I used to be pretty conflicted.
I tried to act like a normal guy in junior high.
It was a lot of work!
And you even dated a girl, huh?
But ever since I moved into a guys' dorm, we've drifted apart.
Please don't let her know what I'm like now!
She's a nice girl! I don't want her to think I was faking it when we were going out!

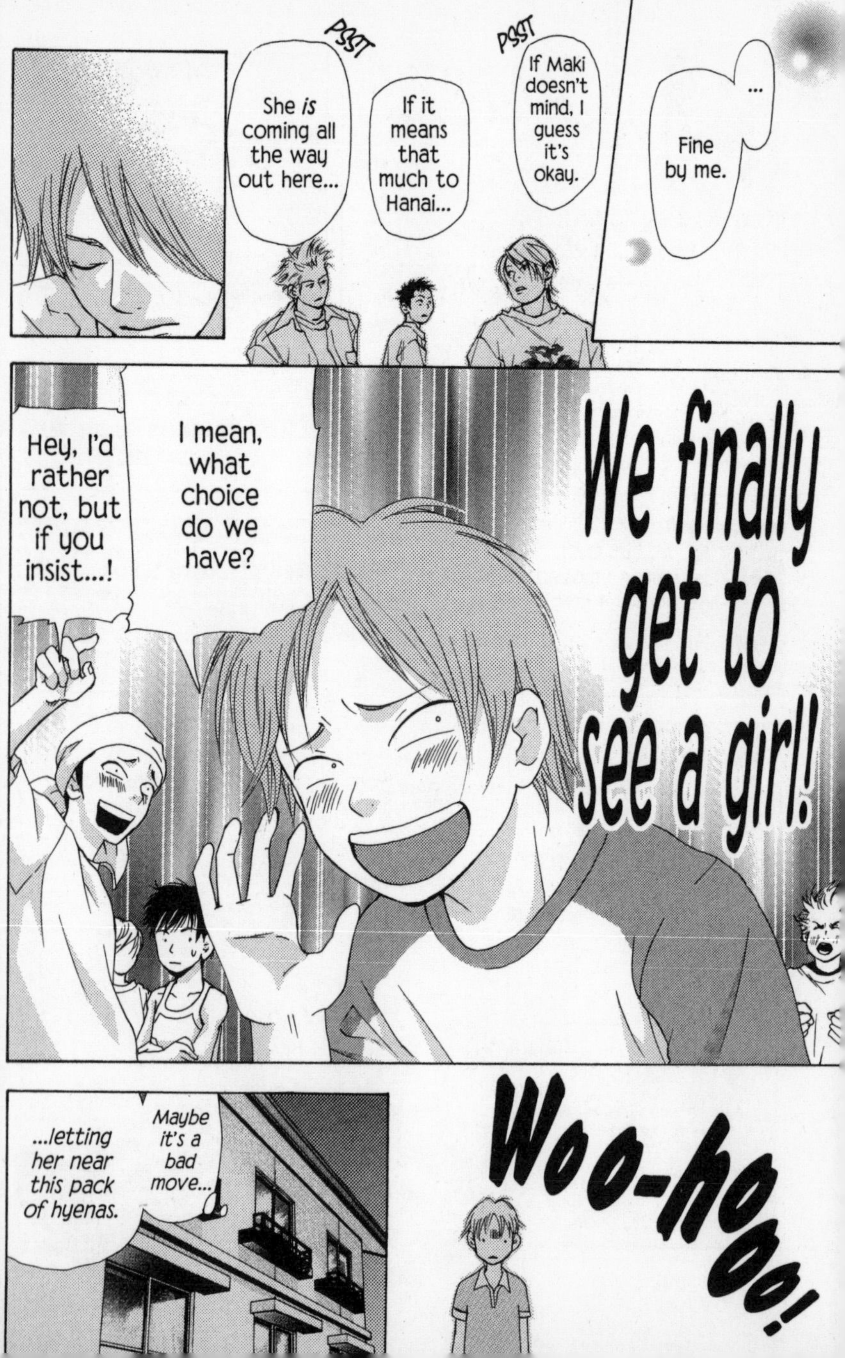
...
Fine by me.
PSST
If Maki doesn't mind, I guess it's okay.
If it means that much to Hanai...
PSST
She *is* coming all the way out here...
We finally get to see a girl!
I mean, what choice do we have?
Hey, I'd rather not, but if you insist...!
Woo-hooo!
Maybe it's a bad move...
...letting her near this pack of hyenas.

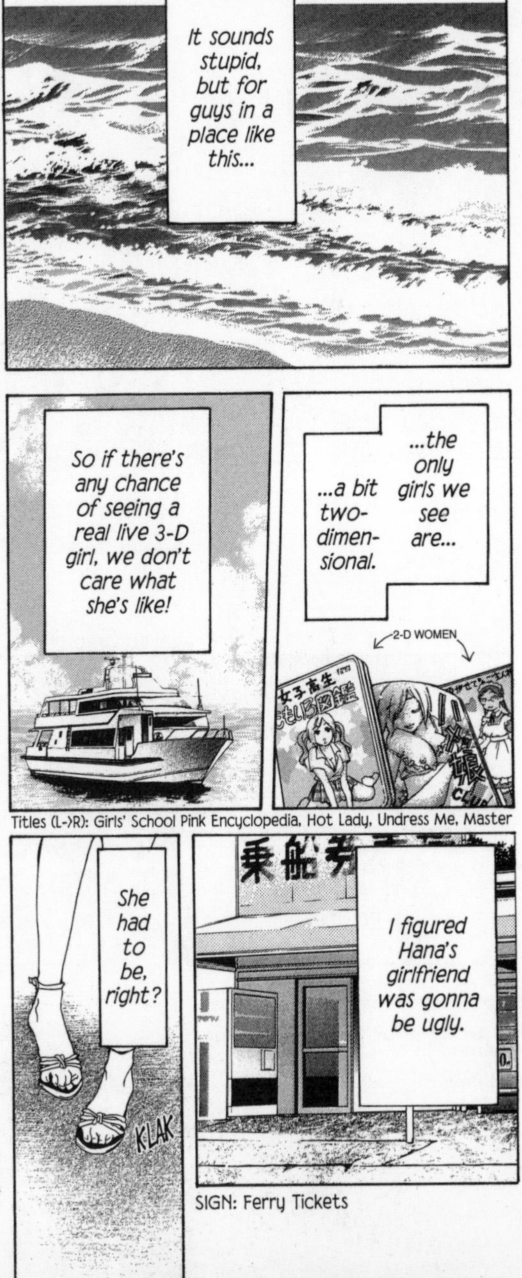
It sounds stupid, but for guys in a place like this...
...the only girls we see are...
...a bit two-dimensional.
2-D WOMEN
So if there's any chance of seeing a real live 3-D girl, we don't care what she's like!
Titles (L->R): Girls' School Pink Encyclopedia, Hot Lady, Undress Me, Master
I figured Hana's girlfriend was gonna be ugly.
SIGN: Ferry Tickets
She had to be, right?
KLAK

1/3 Half-Assed Space Filler

Introducing gifts I don't appreciate!

The so-called "No thank you souvenirs." ©Jun Miura

I appreciated the thought, but I **don't know what to do with them!** This is the second feature on these wretched things!! (The first installment is in an earlier book of mine. See what I mean about "half-assed"? Sorry...)

#1
From: Kanazawa City

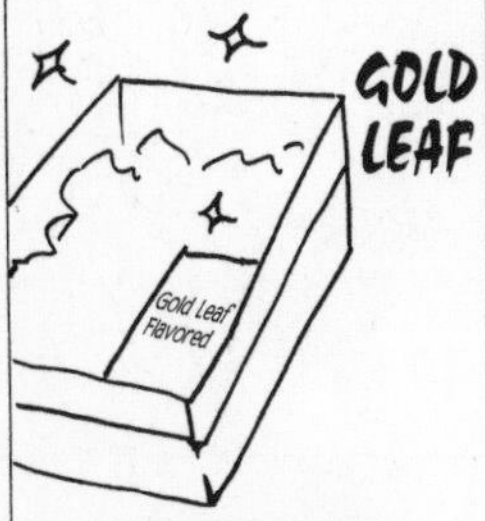
GOLD LEAF
Gold Leaf Flavored

I seriously don't know what to do with it.

The box says "Enjoy these sparkles and dreams wrapped in gold," but I have no idea how I'm supposed to enjoy them...

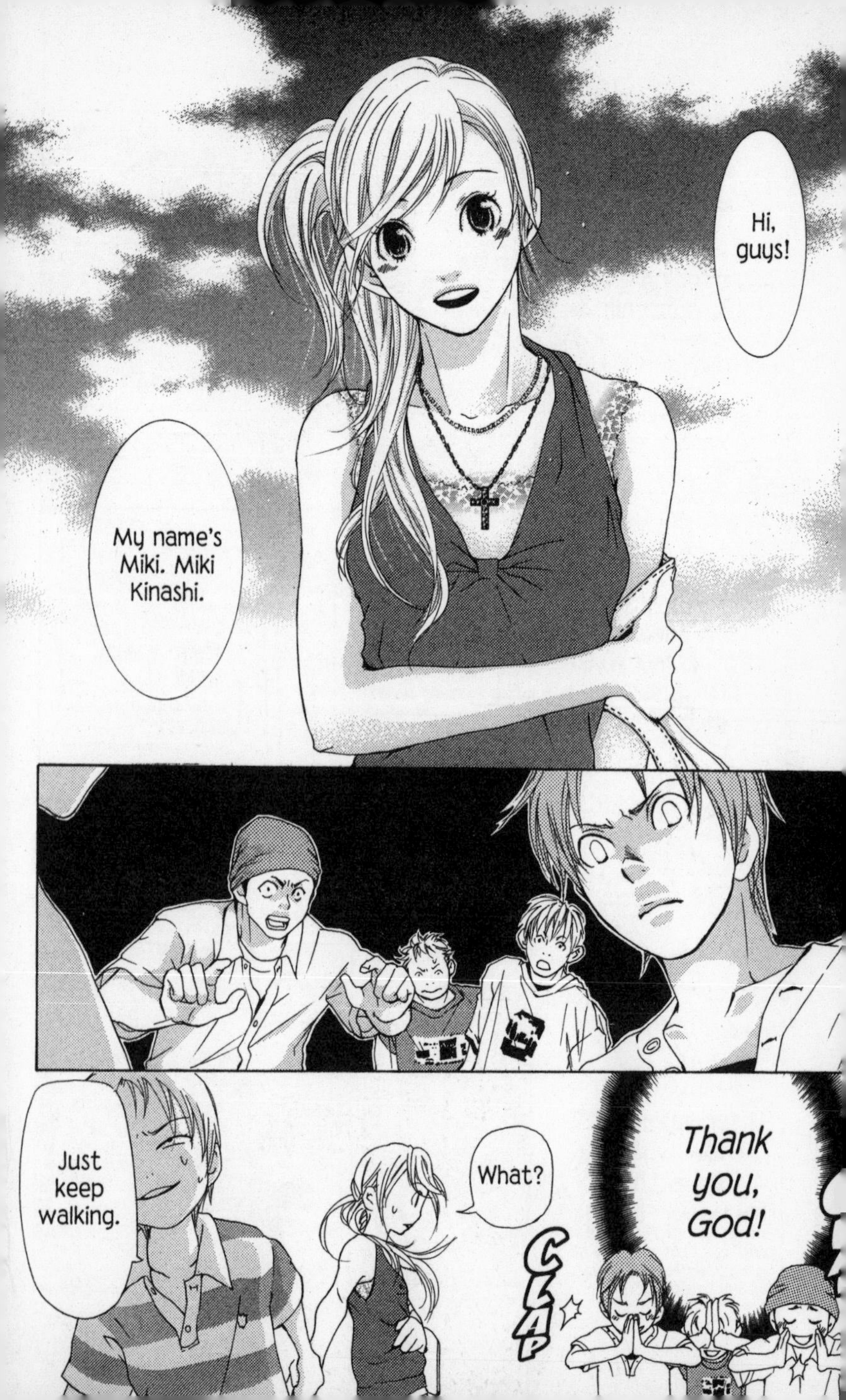
Hi, guys!
My name's Miki. Miki Kinashi.
Thank you, God!
CLAP
What?
Just keep walking.

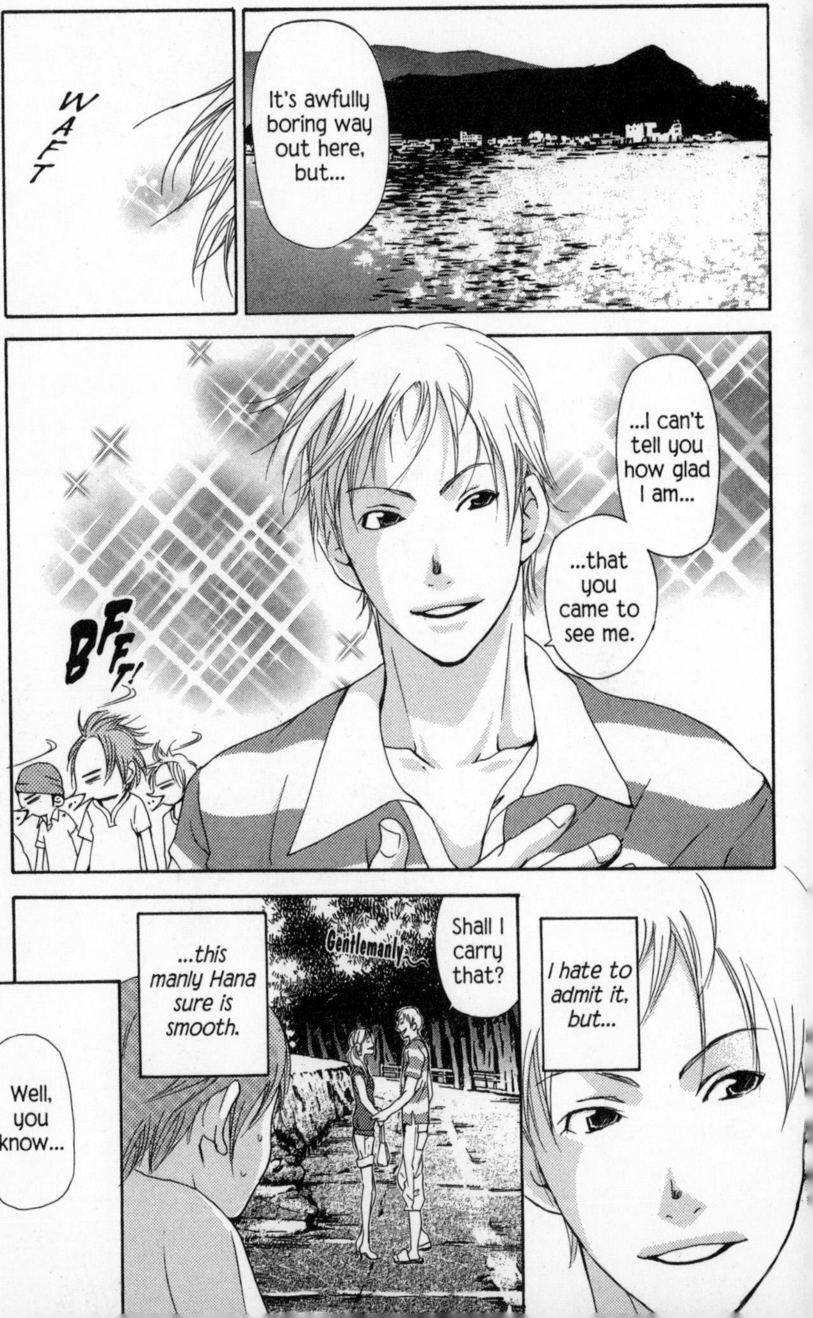
It's awfully boring way out here, but...
WAFT
...I can't tell you how glad I am...
...that you came to see me.
BFFT!
I hate to admit it, but...
Shall I carry that?
Gentlemanly
...this manly Hana sure is smooth.
Well, you know...

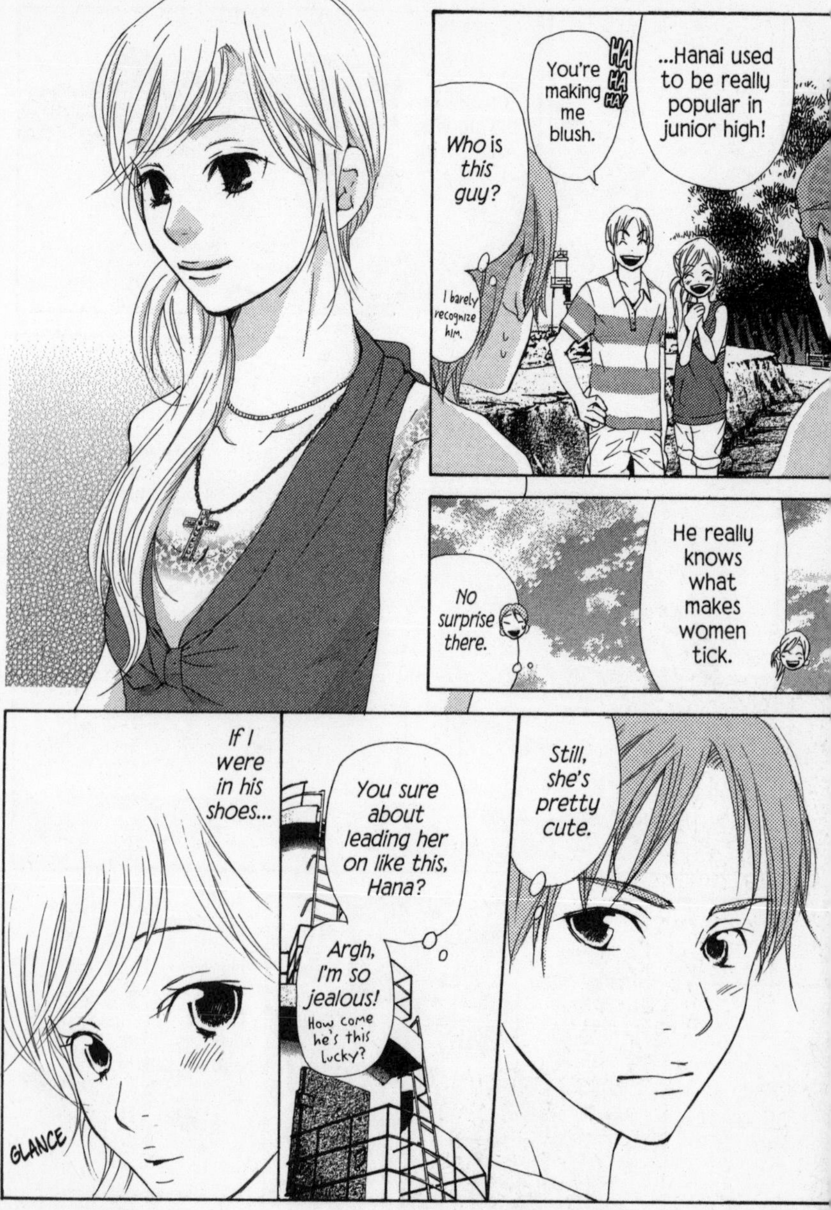
...Hanai used to be really popular in junior high!
HA HA HA!
You're making me blush.
Who is this guy?
I barely recognize him.
He really knows what makes women tick.
No surprise there.
Still, she's pretty cute.
You sure about leading her on like this, Hana?
Argh, I'm so jealous!
How come he's this lucky?
If I were in his shoes...
GLANCE

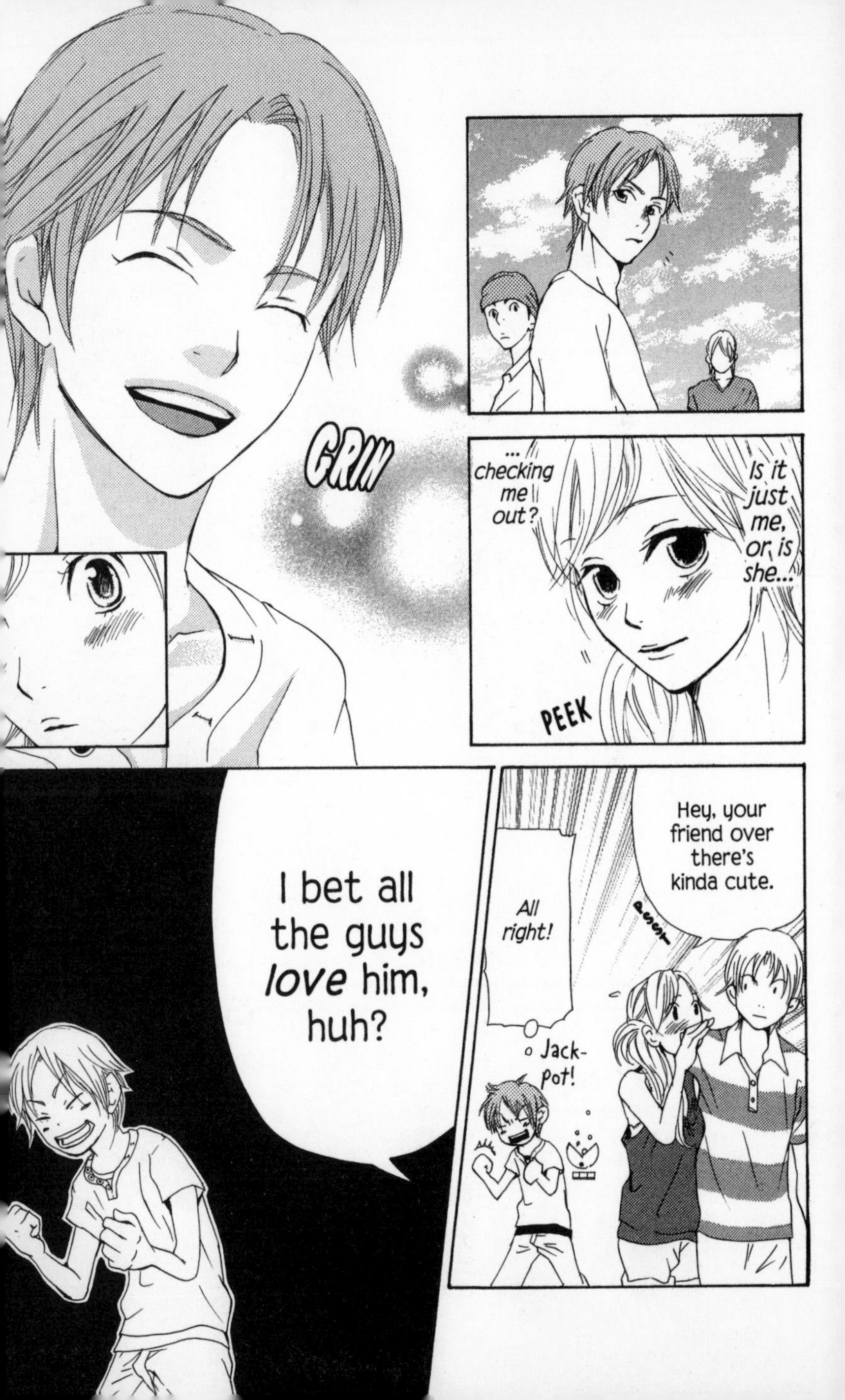
Is it just me, or is she...
...checking me out?
PEEK
GRIN
Hey, your friend over there's kinda cute.
All right!
Jack-pot!
I bet all the guys *love* him, huh?

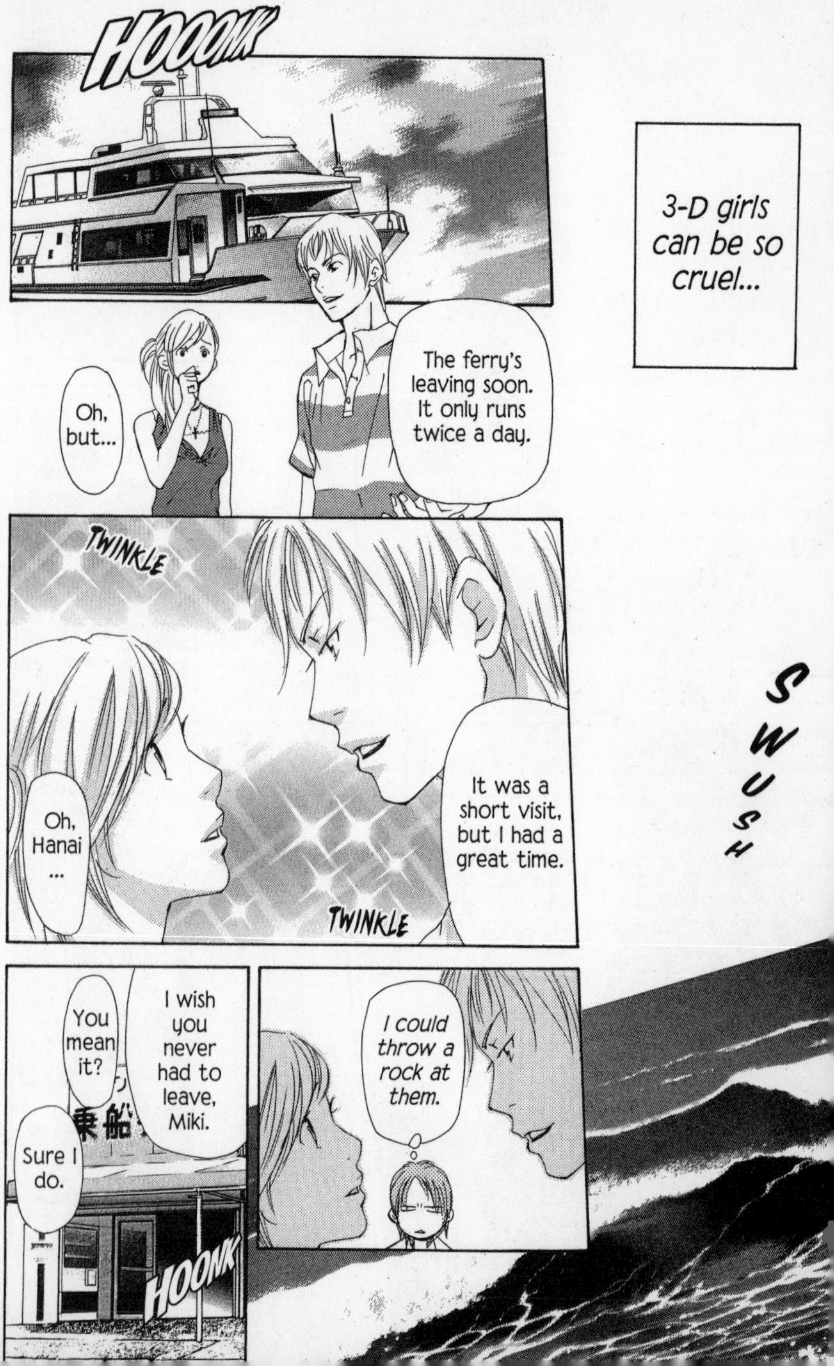
3-D girls can be so cruel...
SWUSH
HOOONK
The ferry's leaving soon. It only runs twice a day.
Oh, but...
TWINKLE
It was a short visit, but I had a great time.
TWINKLE
Oh, Hanai ...
I could throw a rock at them.
I wish you never had to leave, Miki.
You mean it?
Sure I do.
HOONK

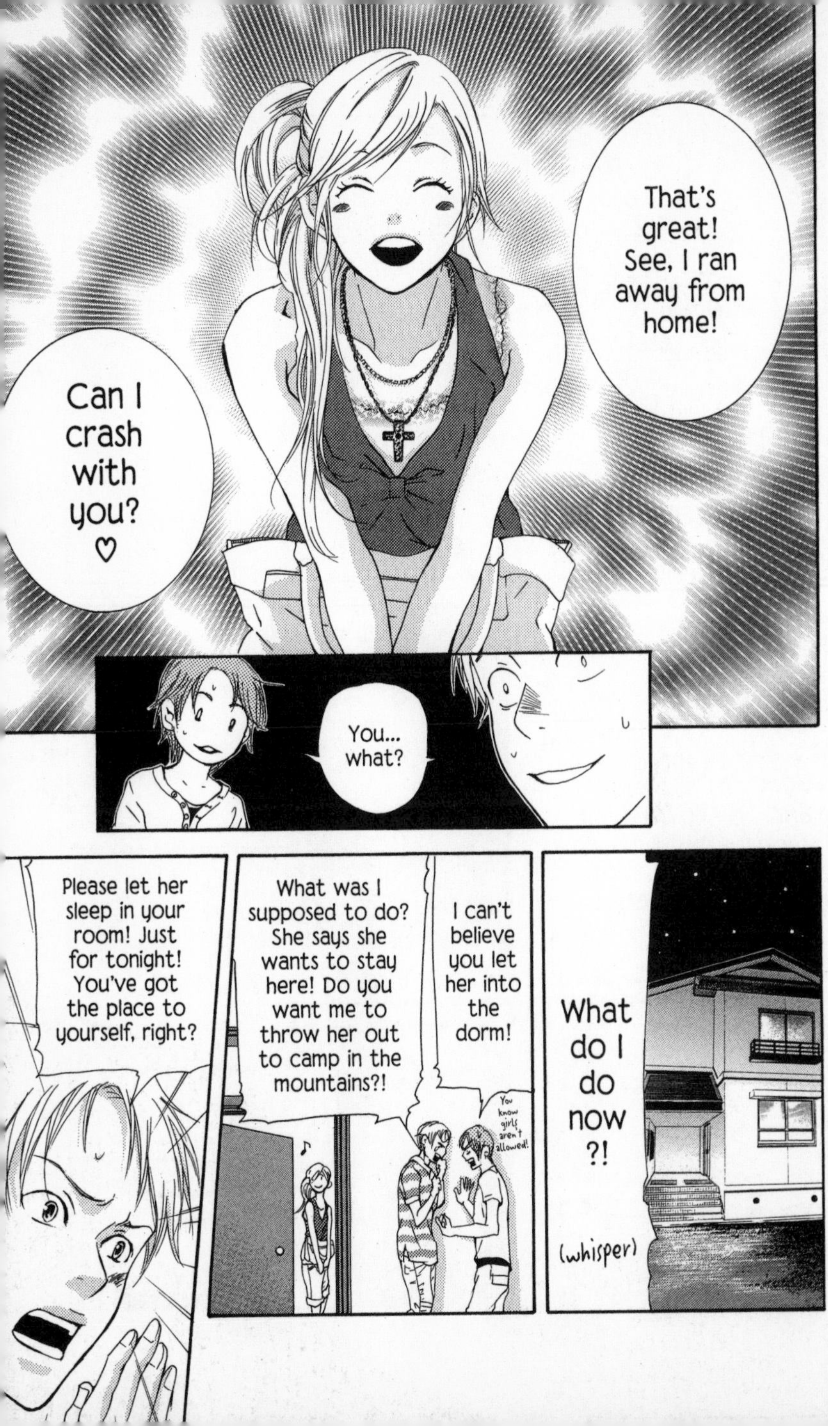
That's great! See, I ran away from home!
Can I crash with you? ♡
You... what?
What do I do now?!
(whisper)
I can't believe you let her into the dorm!
You know girls aren't allowed!
What was I supposed to do? She says she wants to stay here! Do you want me to throw her out to camp in the mountains?!
Please let her sleep in your room! Just for tonight! You've got the place to yourself, right?

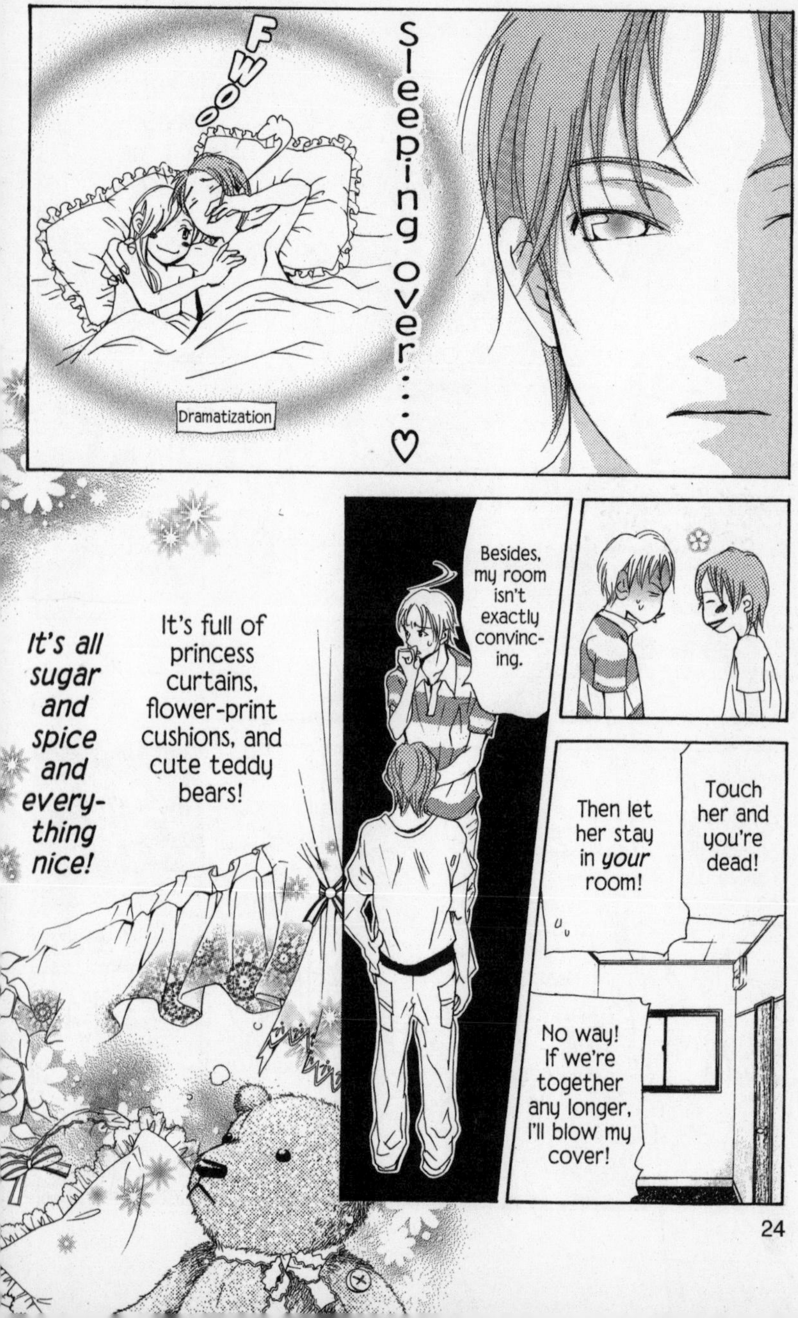
Sleeping over...♡
FWOOO
Dramatization
Touch her and you're dead!
Then let her stay in *your* room!
No way! If we're together any longer, I'll blow my cover!
Besides, my room isn't exactly convinc-ing.
It's full of princess curtains, flower-print cushions, and cute teddy bears!
It's all sugar and spice and every-thing nice!

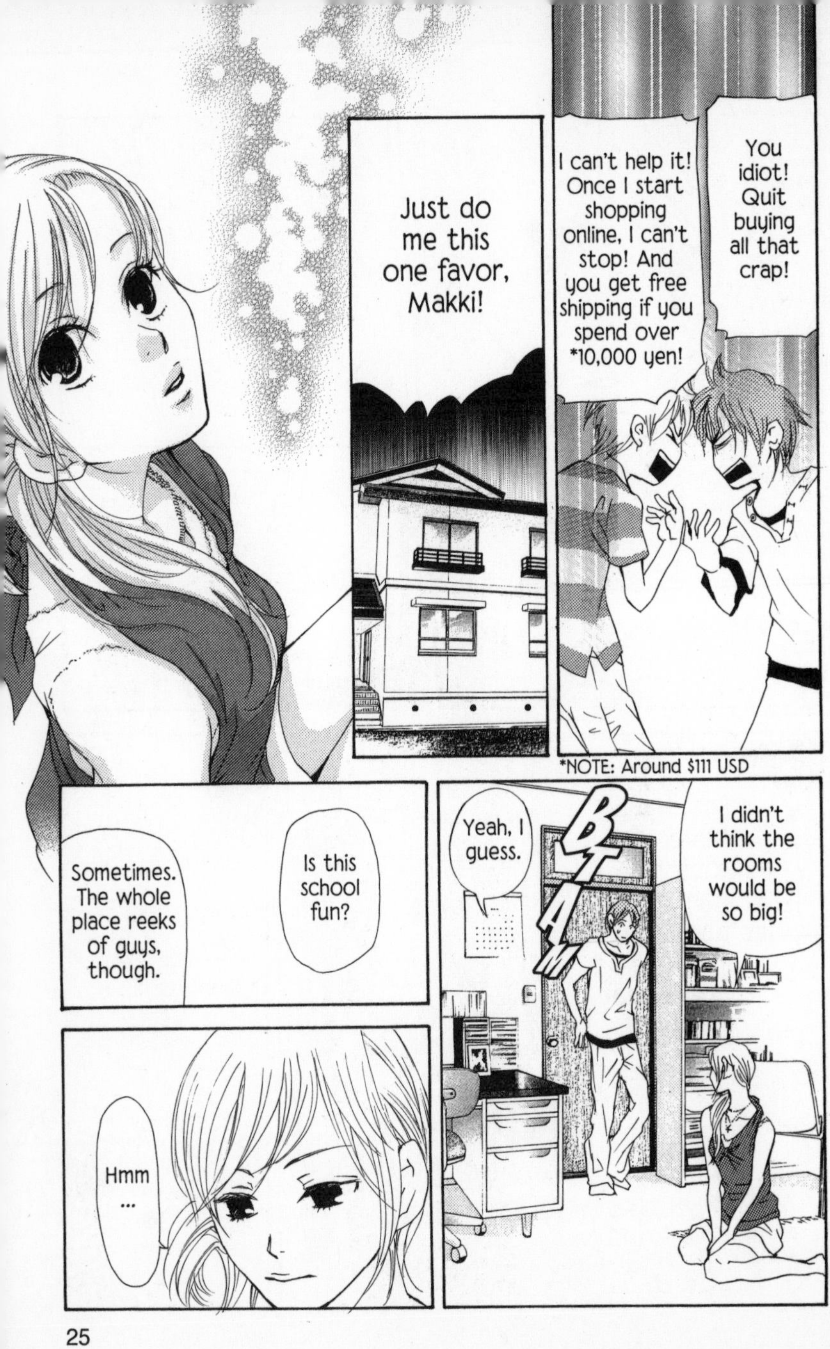
You idiot! Quit buying all that crap!
I can't help it! Once I start shopping online, I can't stop! And you get free shipping if you spend over *10,000 yen!
Just do me this one favor, Makki!
I didn't think the rooms would be so big!
BLAM
Yeah, I guess.
Is this school fun?
Sometimes. The whole place reeks of guys, though.
Hmm ...

*NOTE: Around $111 USD

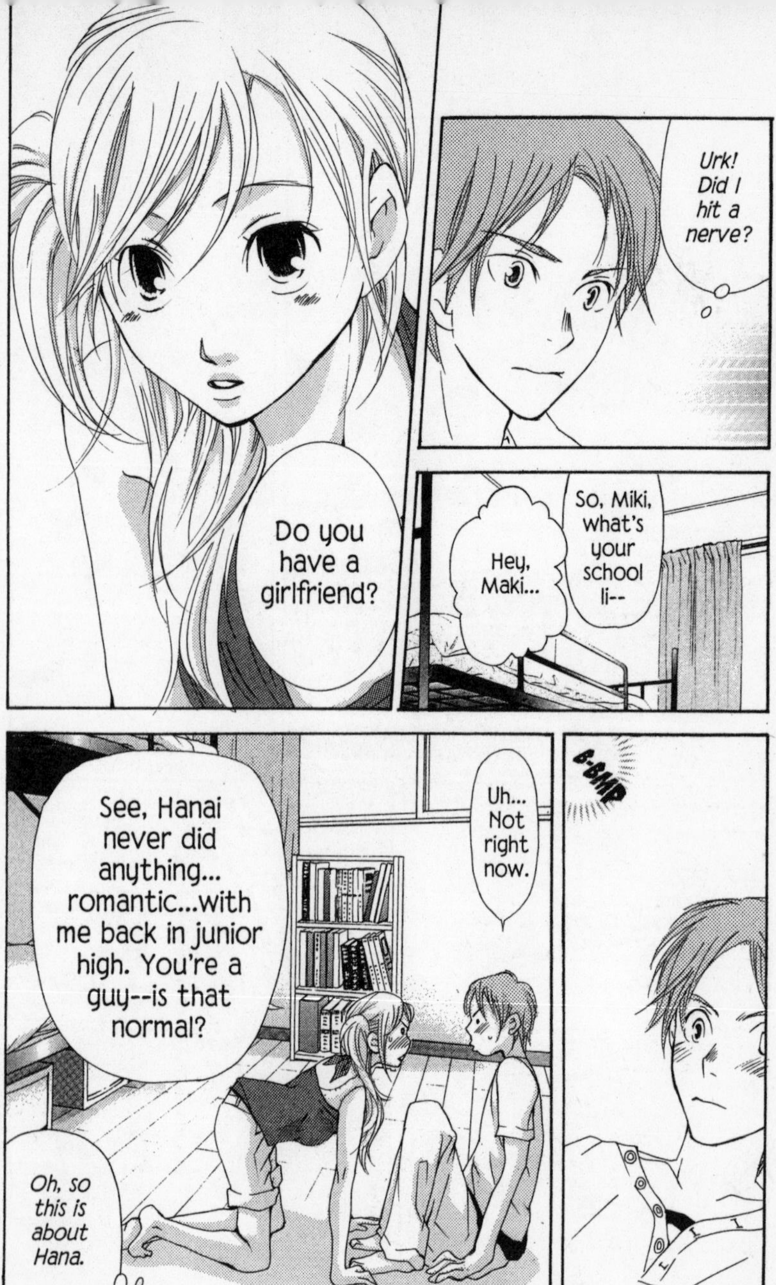
Urk! Did I hit a nerve?
So, Miki, what's your school li--
Hey, Maki...
Do you have a girlfriend?
B-BMP
Uh... Not right now.
See, Hanai never did anything... romantic...with me back in junior high. You're a guy--is that normal?
Oh, so this is about Hana.

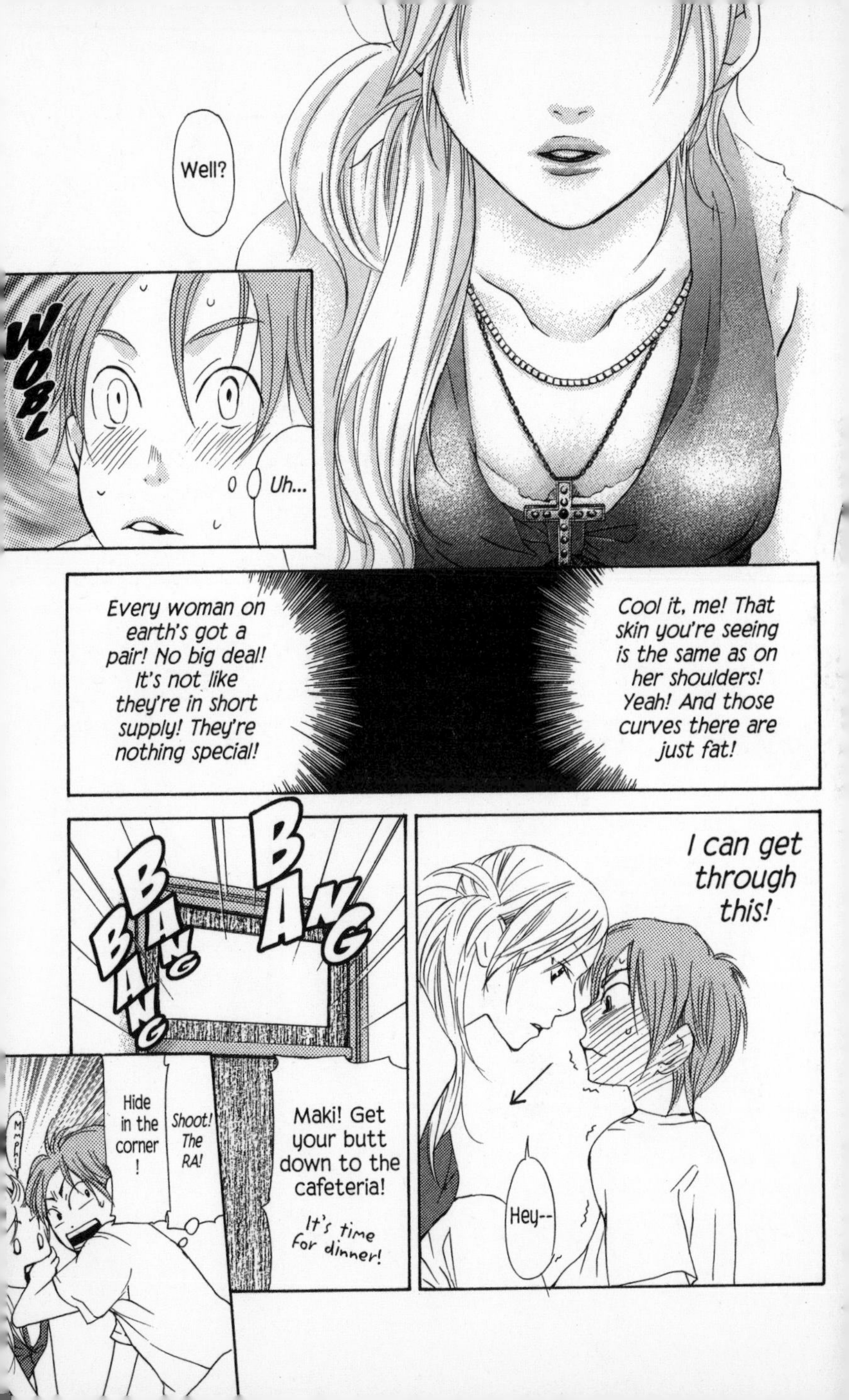
Well?
WOBL
Uh...
Cool it, me! That skin you're seeing is the same as on her shoulders! Yeah! And those curves there are just fat!
Every woman on earth's got a pair! No big deal! It's not like they're in short supply! They're nothing special!
I can get through this!
Hey--
BANG
BANG
BANG
Maki! Get your butt down to the cafeteria!
It's time for dinner!
Shoot! The RA!
Hide in the corner!

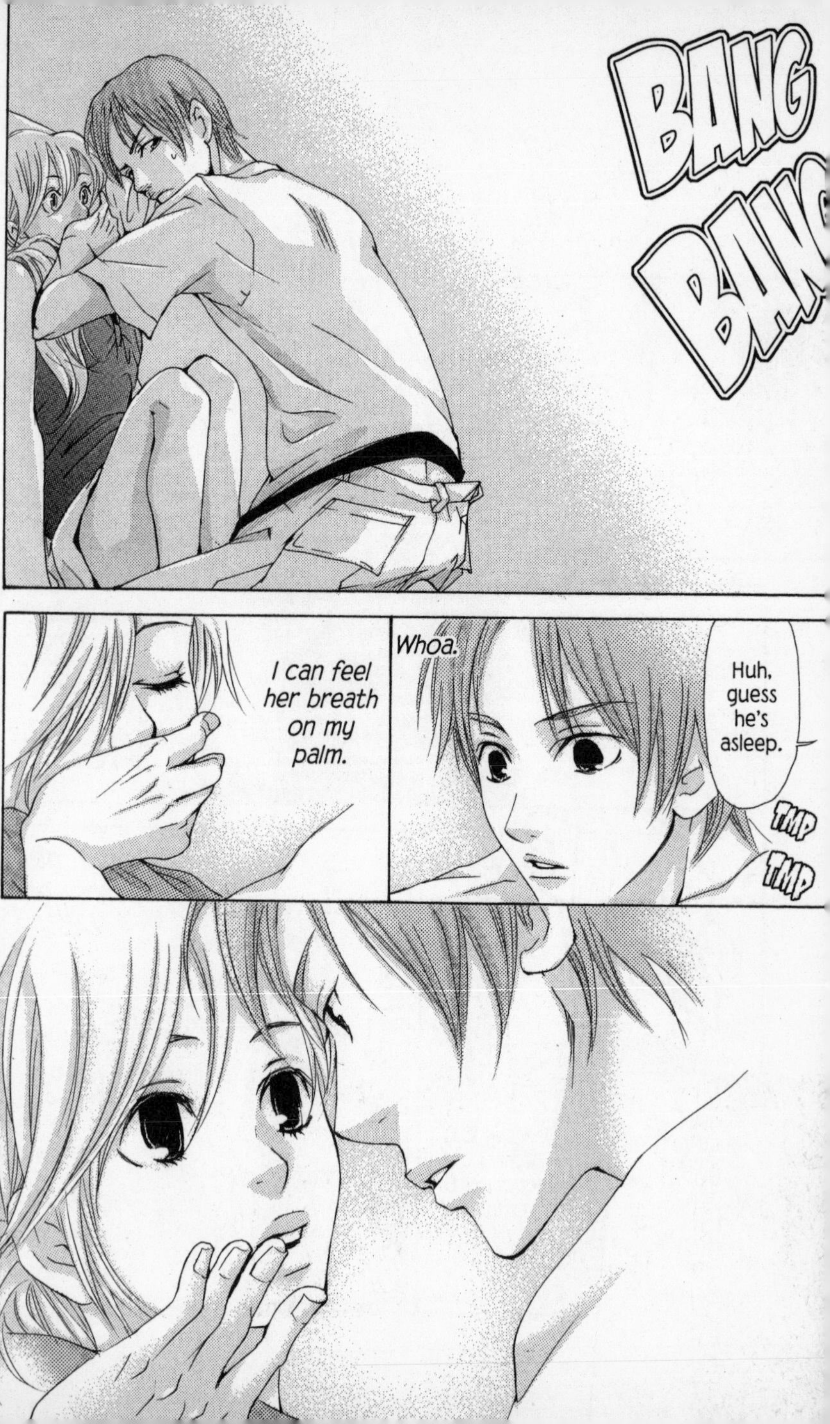
BANG
BANG
Huh, guess he's asleep.
TMP
TMP
Whoa.
I can feel her breath on my palm.

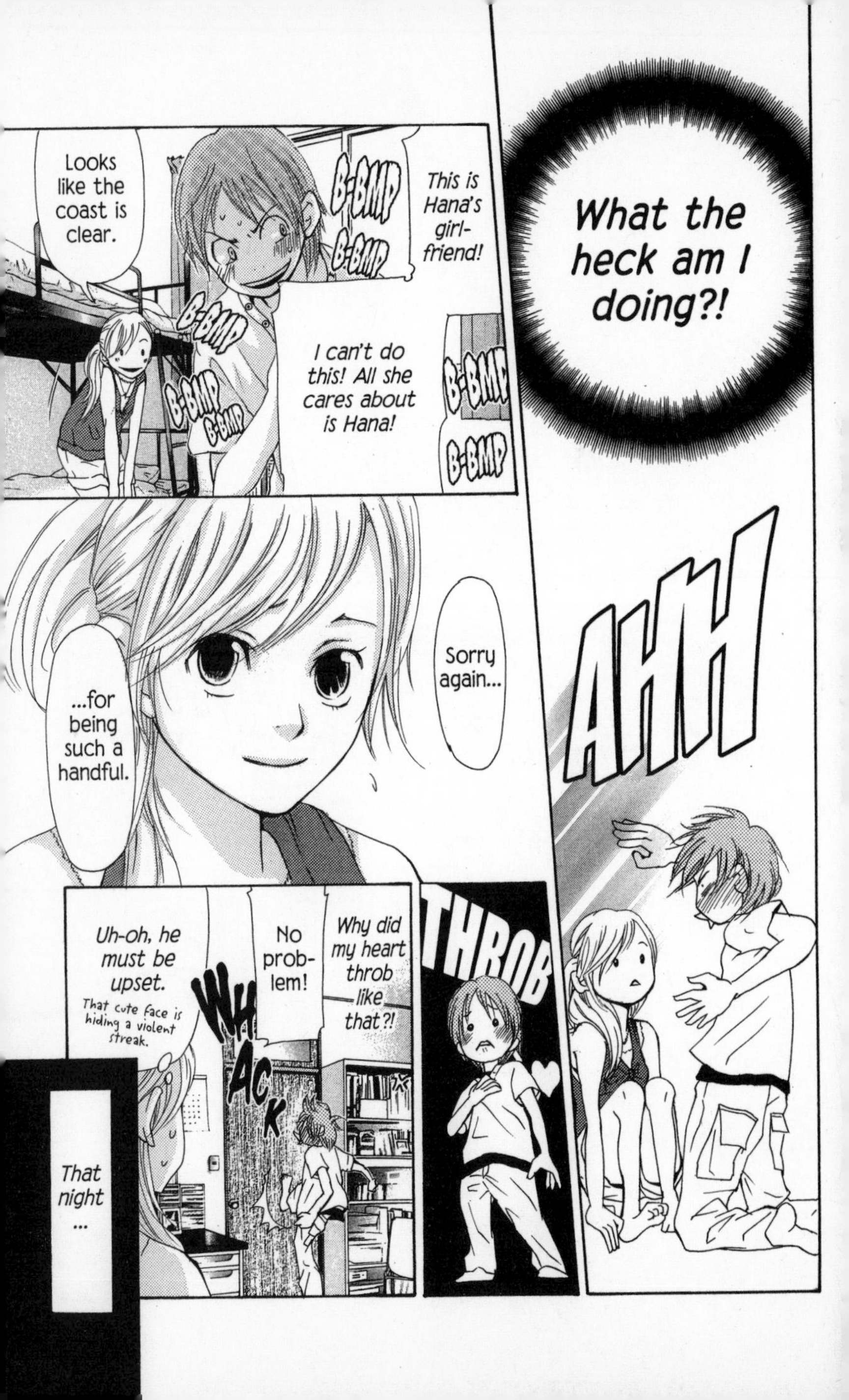
What the heck am I doing?!
AHH
B-BMP
B-BMP
This is Hana's girl-friend!
B-BMP
B-BMP
I can't do this! All she cares about is Hana!
B-BMP
B-BMP
B-BMP
Looks like the coast is clear.
Sorry again...
...for being such a handful.
THROB
Why did my heart throb like that?!
No problem!
WHACK
Uh-oh, he must be upset.
That cute face is hiding a violent streak.
That night ...

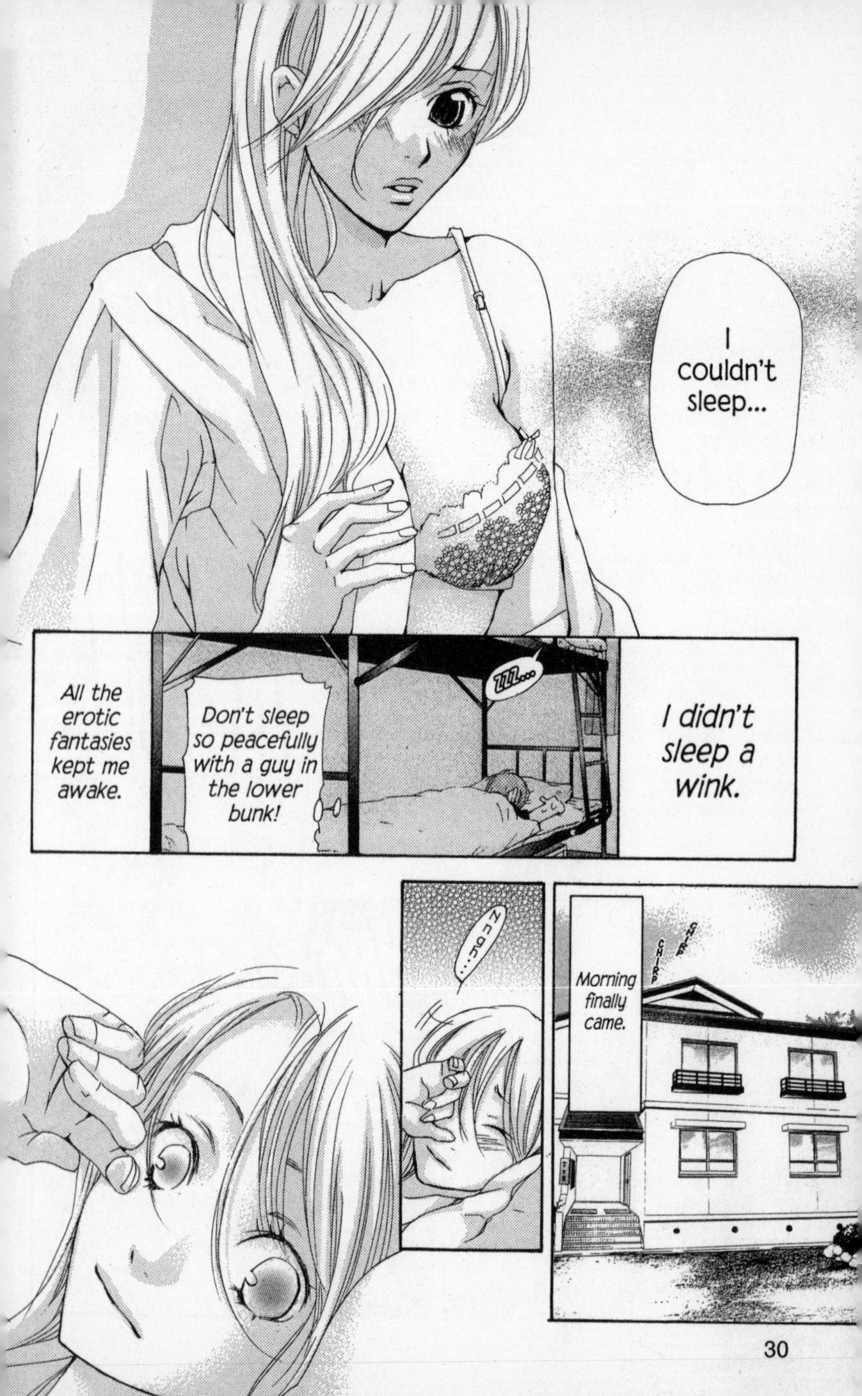
I couldn't sleep...
I didn't sleep a wink.
ZZZ...
Don't sleep so peacefully with a guy in the lower bunk!
All the erotic fantasies kept me awake.
CHIRP
CHIRP
Morning finally came.
Nngh...

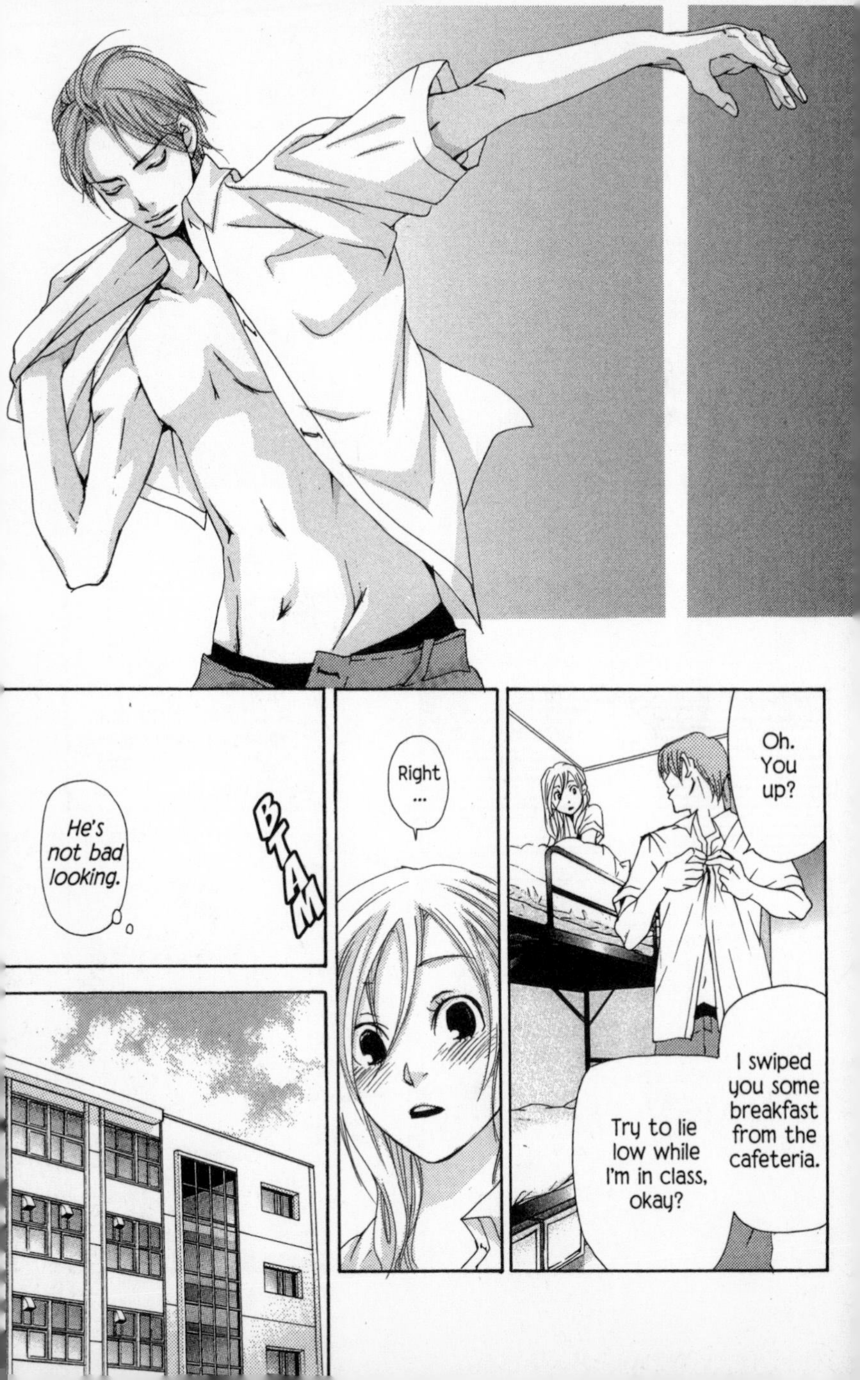
Oh. You up?
I swiped you some breakfast from the cafeteria.
Try to lie low while I'm in class, okay?
Right ...
BTAM
He's not bad looking.

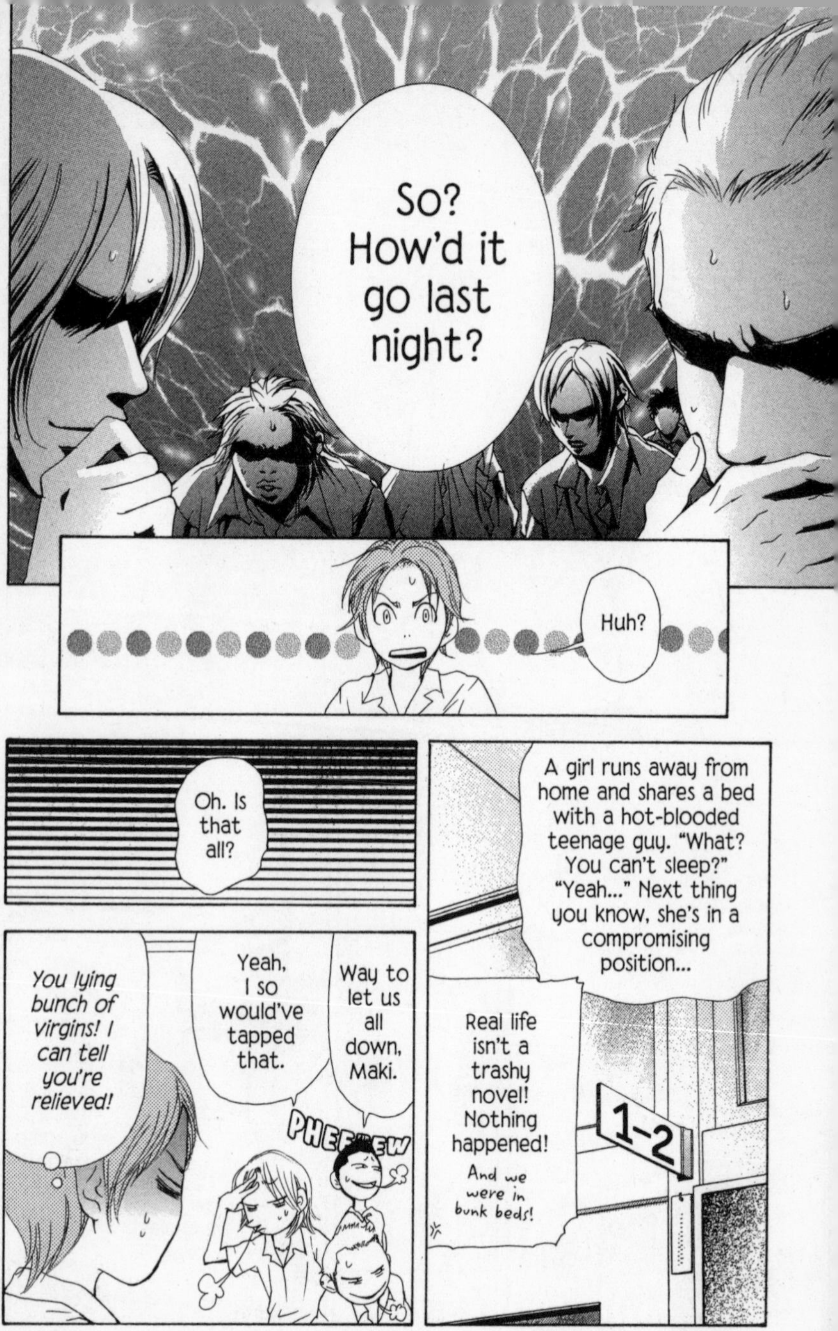
So? How'd it go last night?
Huh?
A girl runs away from home and shares a bed with a hot-blooded teenage guy. "What? You can't sleep?" "Yeah..." Next thing you know, she's in a compromising position...
Real life isn't a trashy novel! Nothing happened!
And we were in bunk beds!
1-2
Oh. Is that all?
Way to let us all down, Maki.
Yeah, I so would've tapped that.
You lying bunch of virgins! I can tell you're relieved!

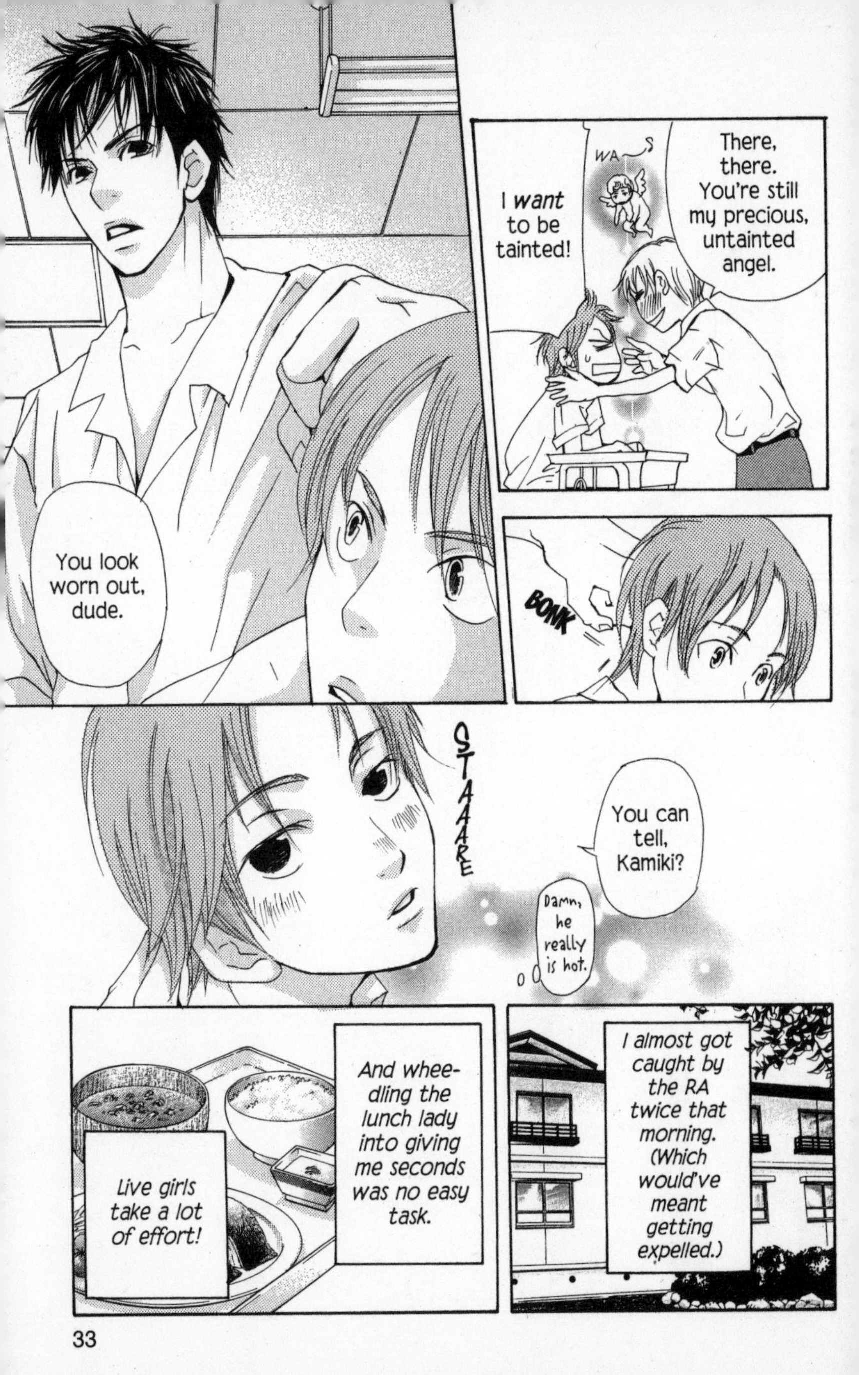
There, there. You're still my precious, untainted angel.
I *want* to be tainted!
BONK
You look worn out, dude.
STAAAARE
You can tell, Kamiki?
Damn, he really is hot.
I almost got caught by the RA twice that morning. (Which would've meant getting expelled.)
And wheedling the lunch lady into giving me seconds was no easy task.
Live girls take a lot of effort!

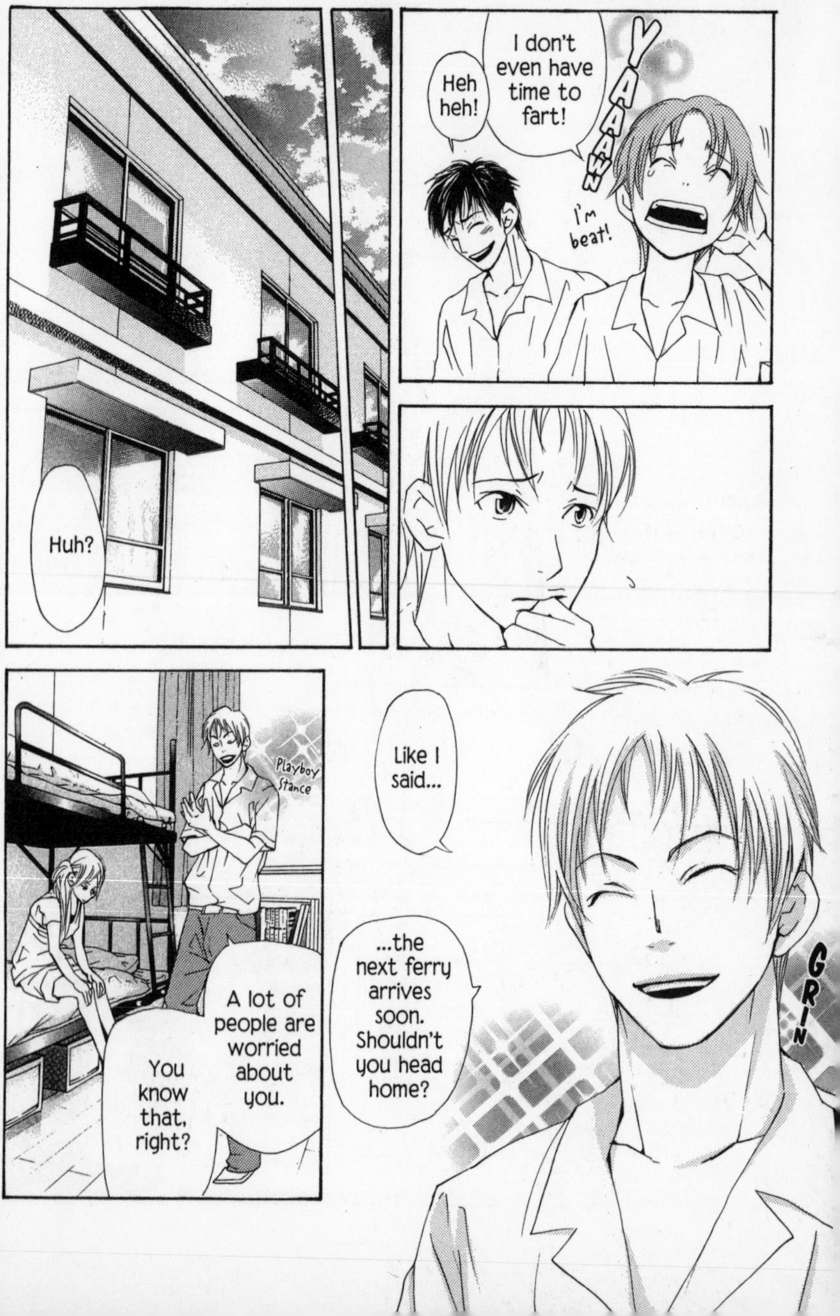
YAAAAWN
I don't even have time to fart!
Heh heh!
I'm beat!
Huh?
Like I said...
...the next ferry arrives soon. Shouldn't you head home?
GRIN
Playboy Stance
A lot of people are worried about you.
You know that, right?

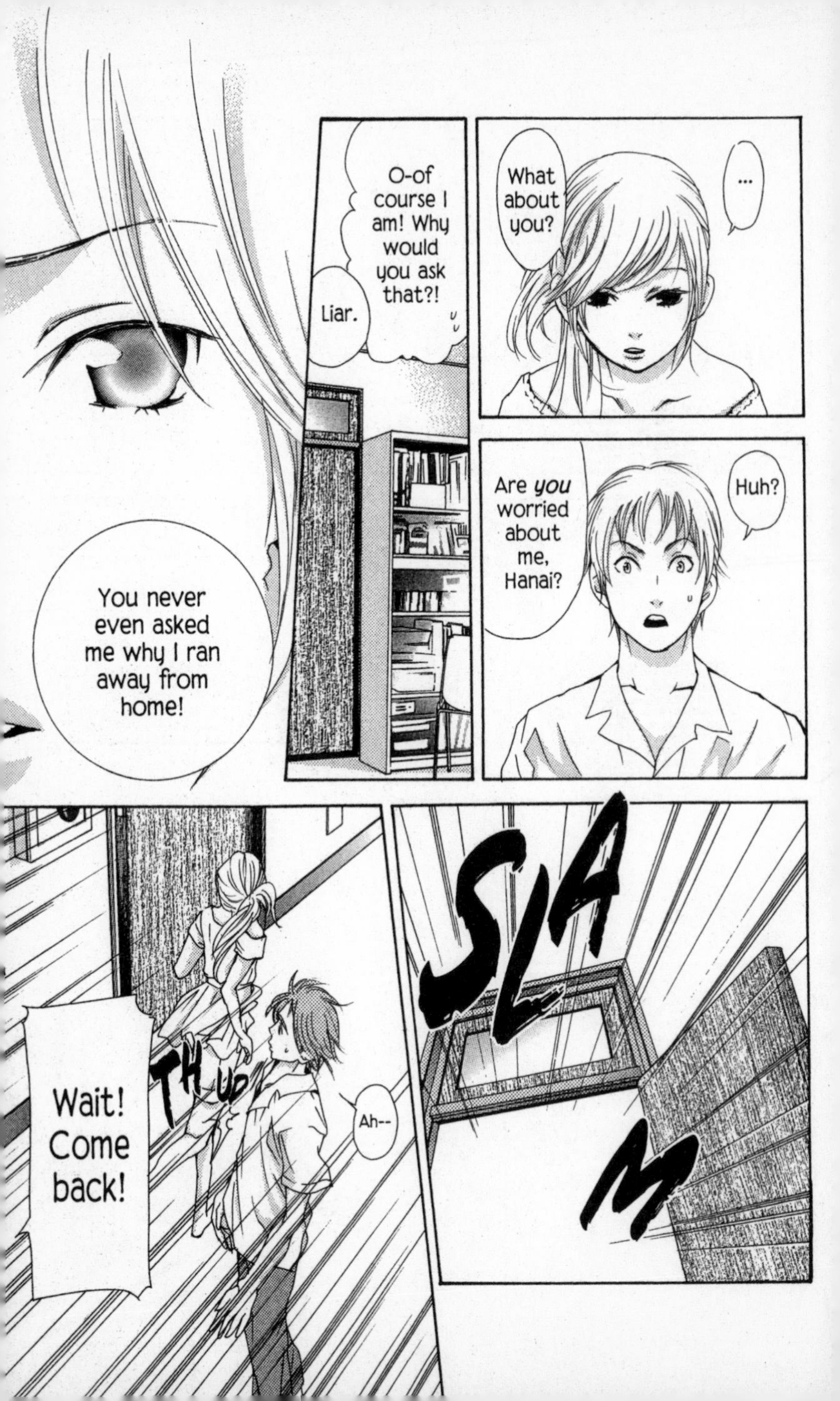
...
What about you?
Huh?
Are *you* worried about me, Hanai?
O-of course I am! Why would you ask that?!
Liar.
You never even asked me why I ran away from home!
SLAM
Ah--
THUD
Wait! Come back!

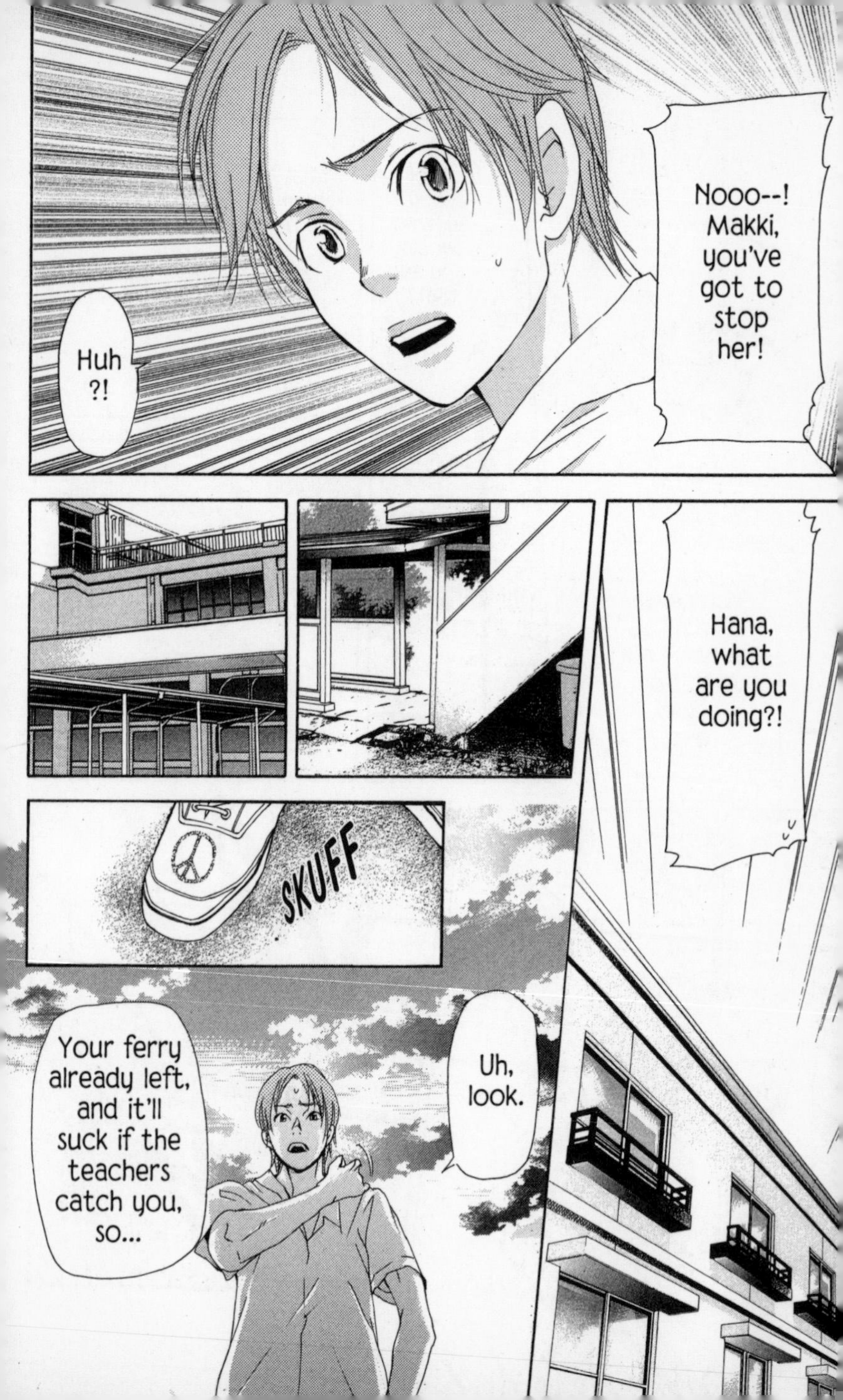
Nooo--! Makki, you've got to stop her!
Huh ?!
Hana, what are you doing?!
SKUFF
Uh, look.
Your ferry already left, and it'll suck if the teachers catch you, so...

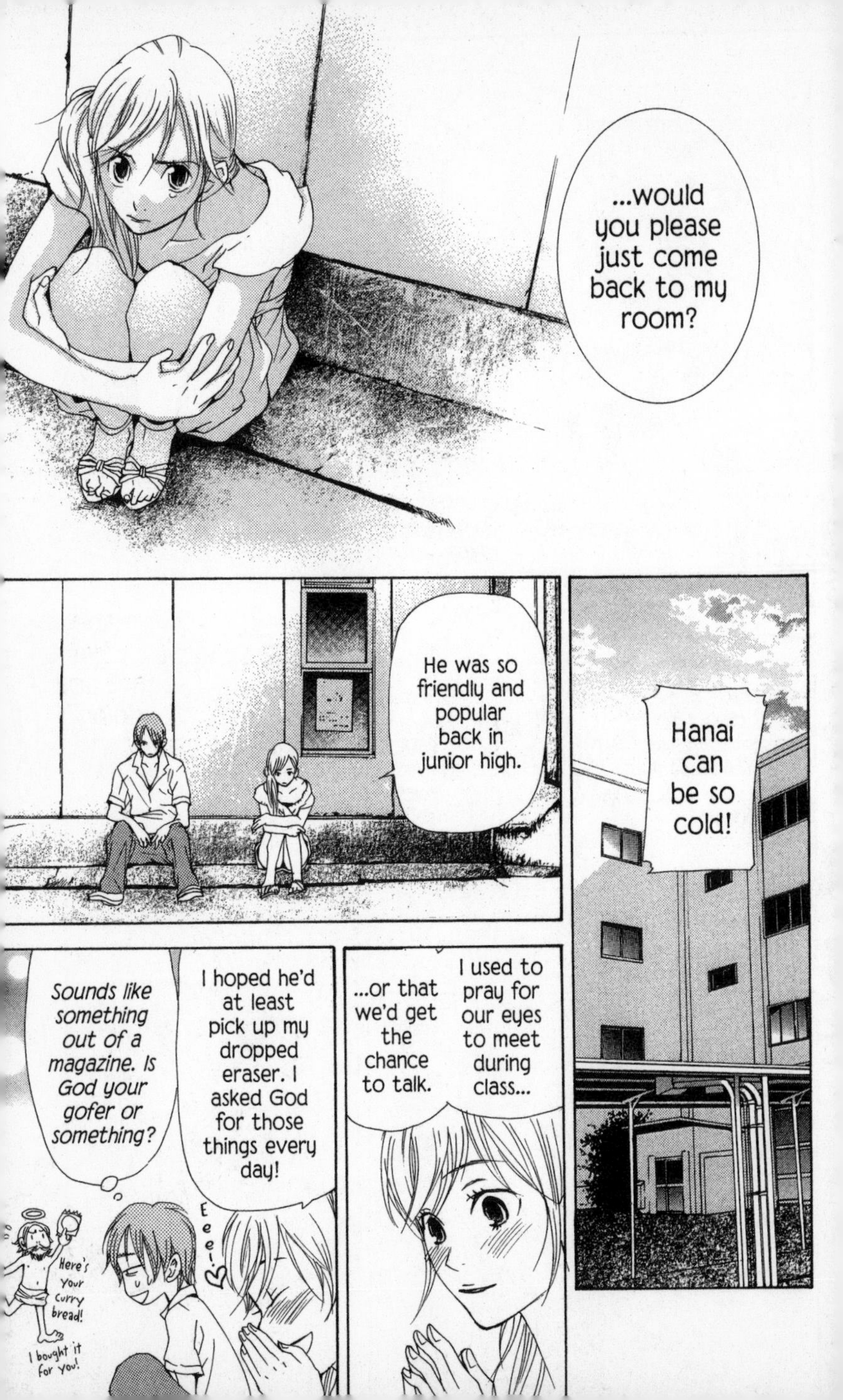
...would you please just come back to my room?
Hanai can be so cold!
He was so friendly and popular back in junior high.
I used to pray for our eyes to meet during class...
...or that we'd get the chance to talk.
I hoped he'd at least pick up my dropped eraser. I asked God for those things every day!
Eeee!
Sounds like something out of a magazine. Is God your gofer or something?
Here's your curry bread!
I bought it for you!

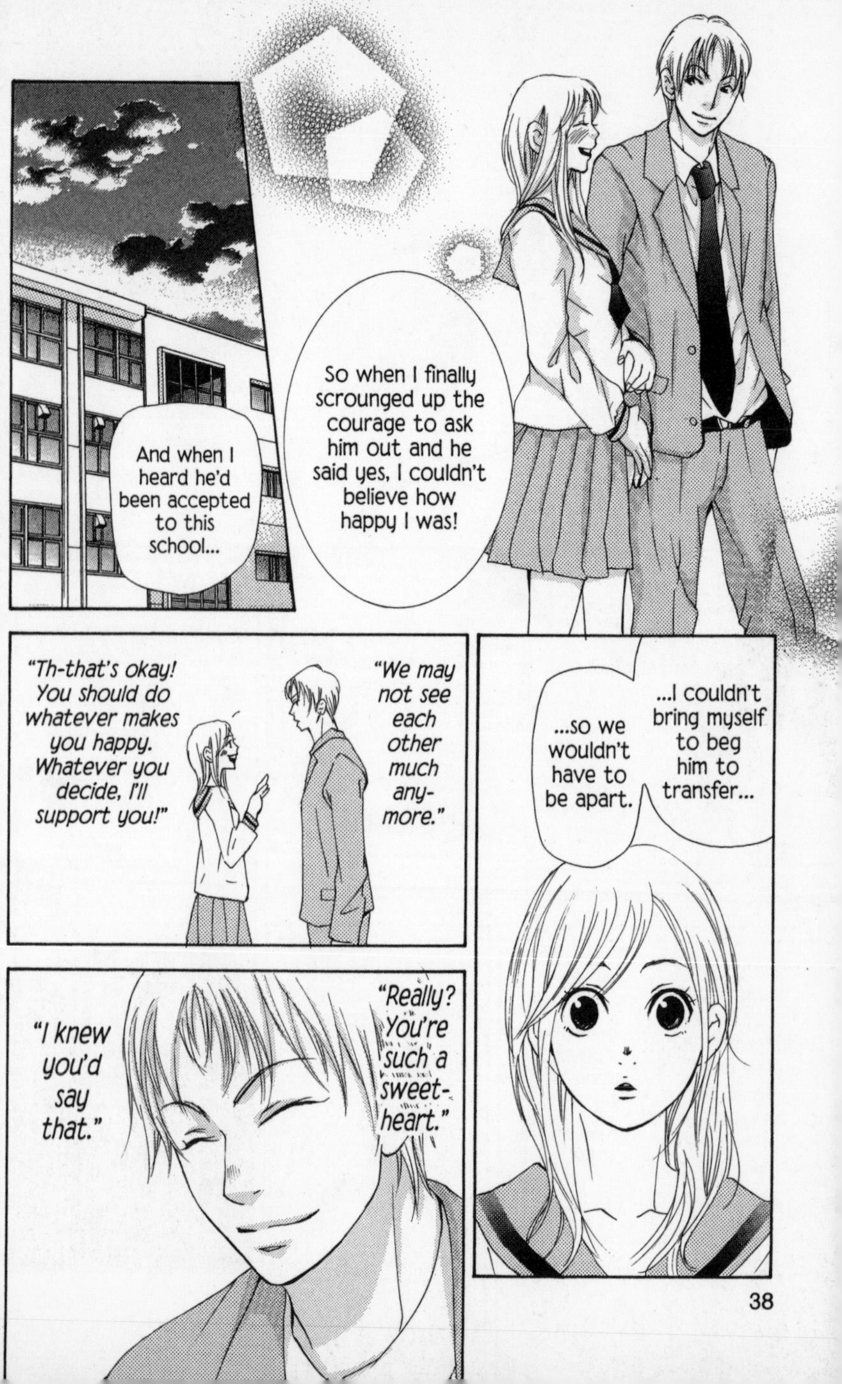

So when I finally scrounged up the courage to ask him out and he said yes, I couldn't believe how happy I was!
And when I heard he'd been accepted to this school...
...I couldn't bring myself to beg him to transfer...
...so we wouldn't have to be apart.
"We may not see each other much anymore."
"Th-that's okay! You should do whatever makes you happy. Whatever you decide, I'll support you!"
"Really? You're such a sweet-heart."
"I knew you'd say that."

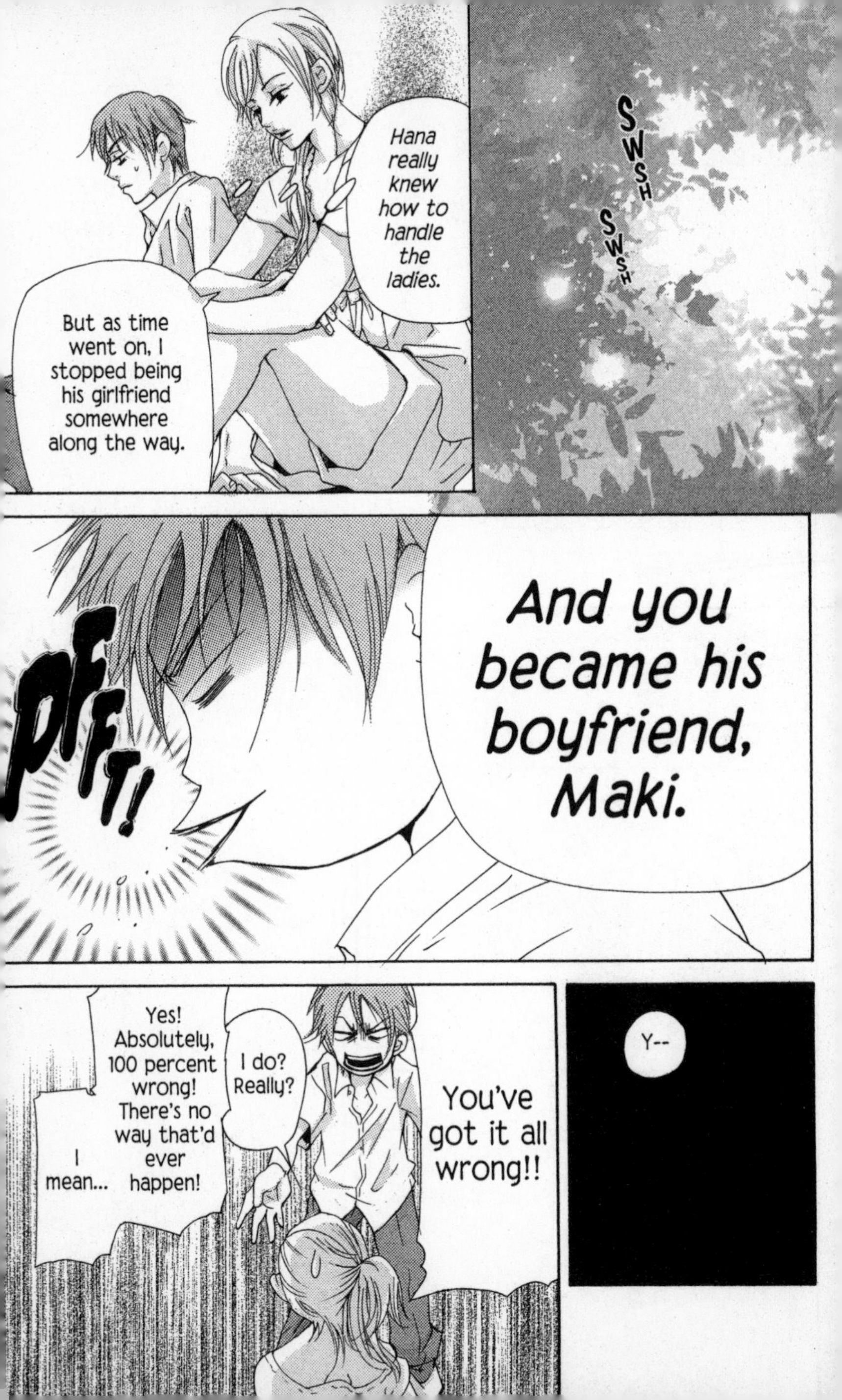
SWSH SWSH
Hana really knew how to handle the ladies.
But as time went on, I stopped being his girlfriend somewhere along the way.
And you became his boyfriend, Maki.
PFFT!
Y--
You've got it all wrong!!
I do? Really?
Yes! Absolutely, 100 percent wrong! There's no way that'd ever happen!
I mean...

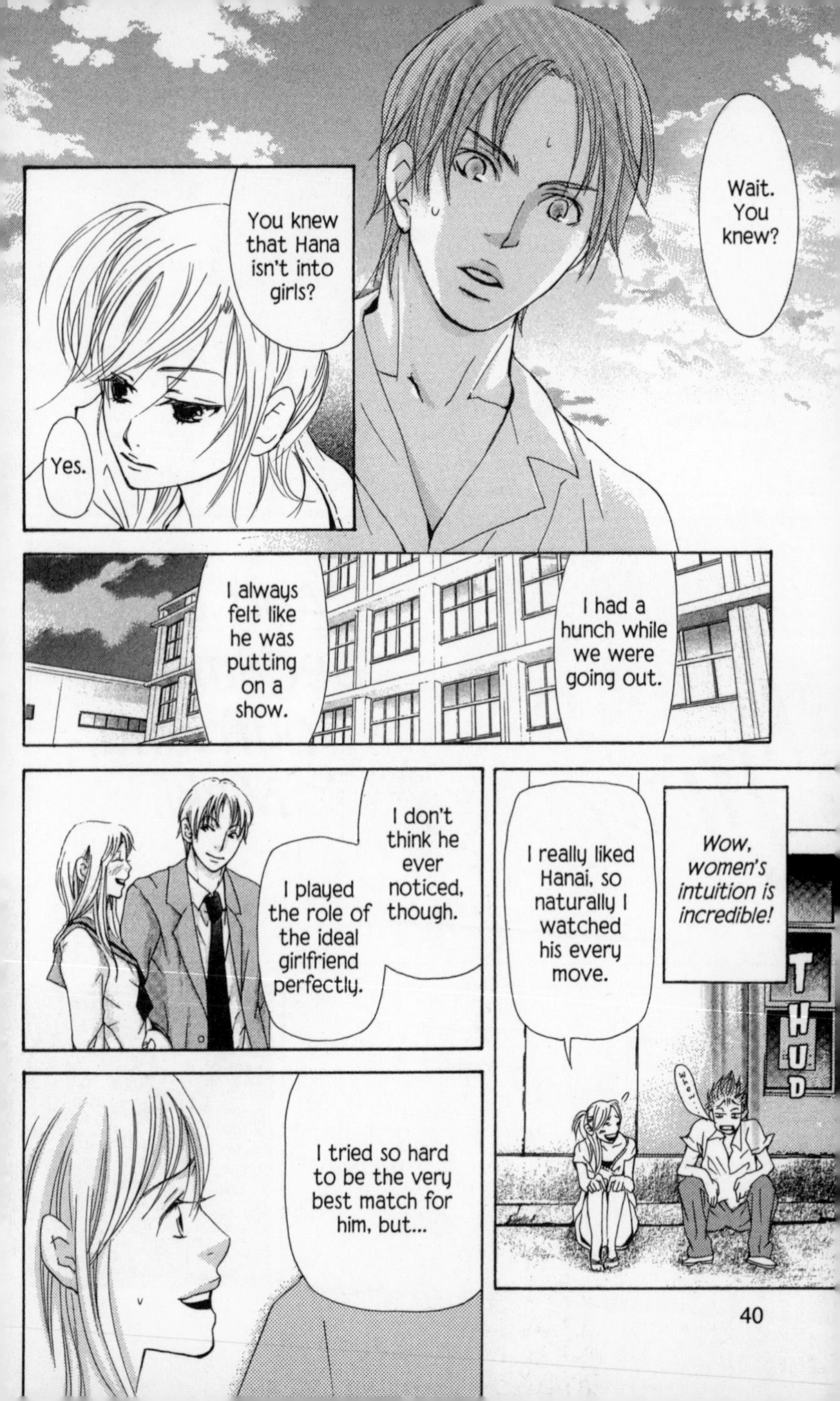

Wait. You knew?
You knew that Hana isn't into girls?
Yes.
I had a hunch while we were going out.
I always felt like he was putting on a show.
Wow, women's intuition is incredible!
THUD
I really liked Hanai, so naturally I watched his every move.
I don't think he ever noticed, though.
I played the role of the ideal girlfriend perfectly.
I tried so hard to be the very best match for him, but...

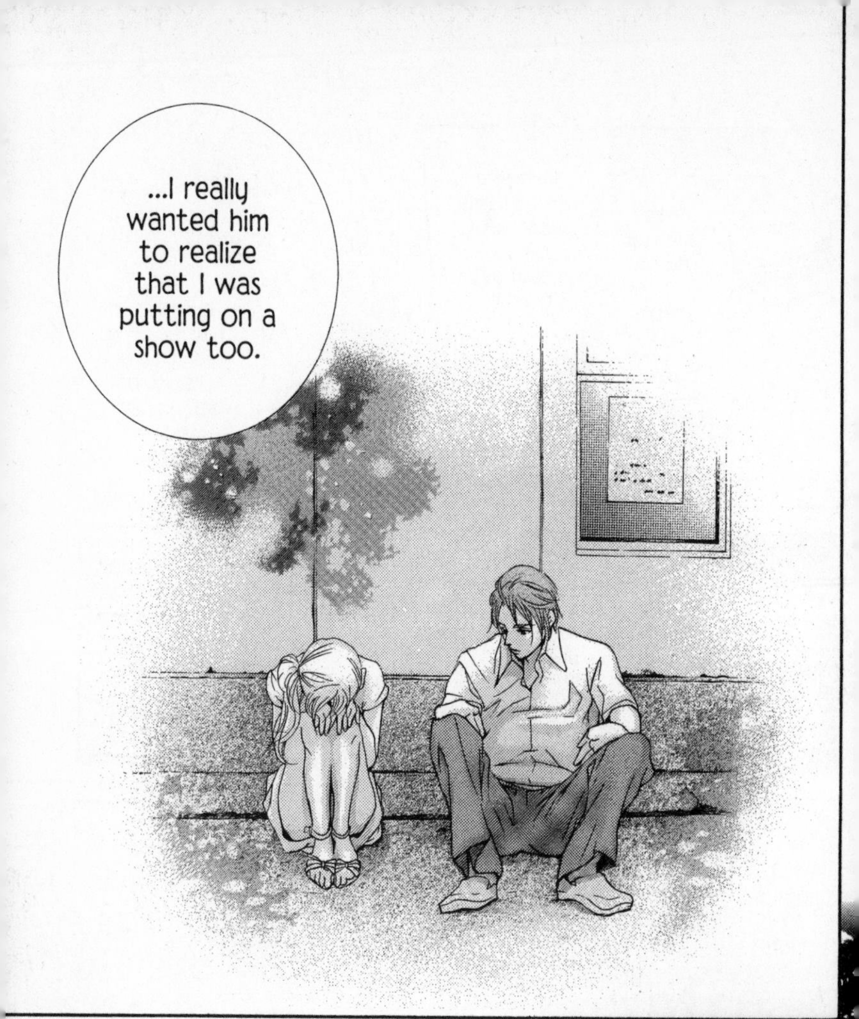
...I really wanted him to realize that I was putting on a show too.
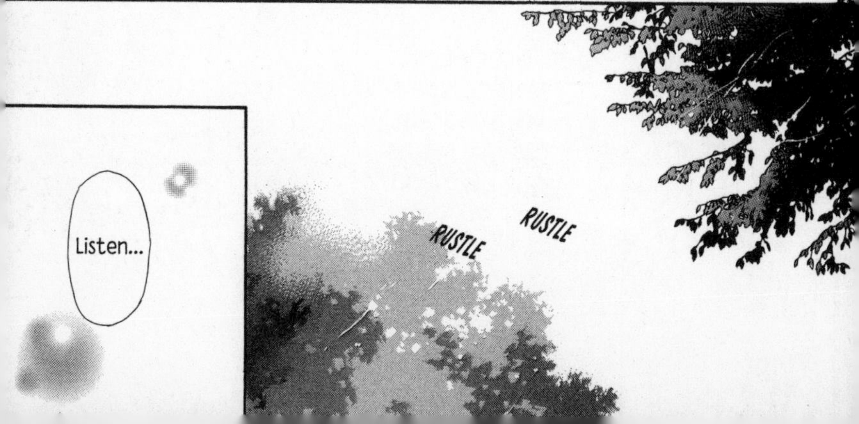
RUSTLE
RUSTLE
Listen...

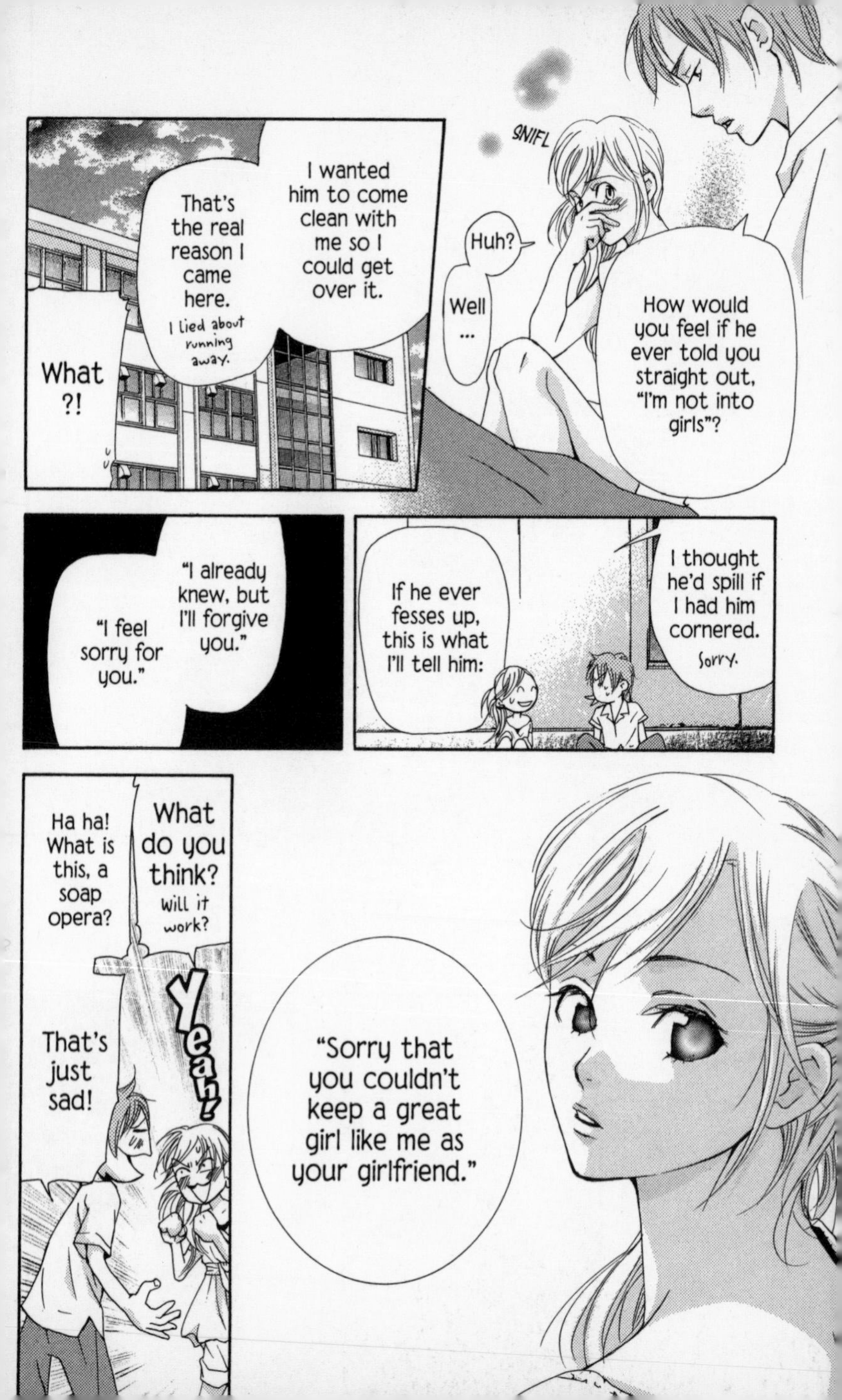
SNIFL
How would you feel if he ever told you straight out, "I'm not into girls"?
Huh?
Well ...
I wanted him to come clean with me so I could get over it.
That's the real reason I came here.
I lied about running away.
What ?!
I thought he'd spill if I had him cornered.
Sorry.
If he ever fesses up, this is what I'll tell him:
"I already knew, but I'll forgive you."
"I feel sorry for you."
"Sorry that you couldn't keep a great girl like me as your girlfriend."
What do you think?
Will it work?
Ha ha! What is this, a soap opera?
Yeah!
That's just sad!

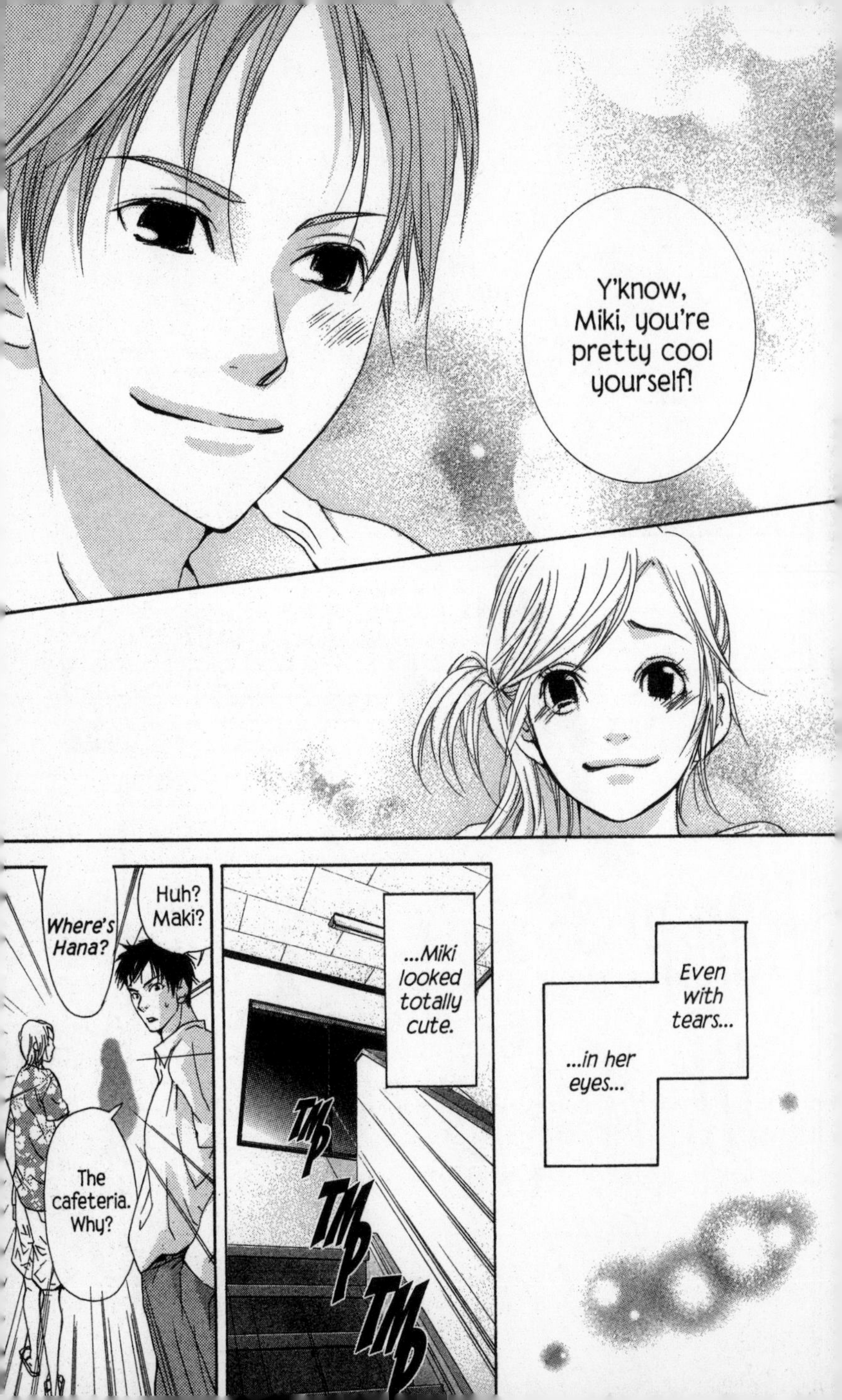
Y'know, Miki, you're pretty cool yourself!
Even with tears...
...in her eyes...
...Miki looked totally cute.
TMP
TMP
TMP
Huh? Maki?
Where's Hana?
The cafeteria. Why?

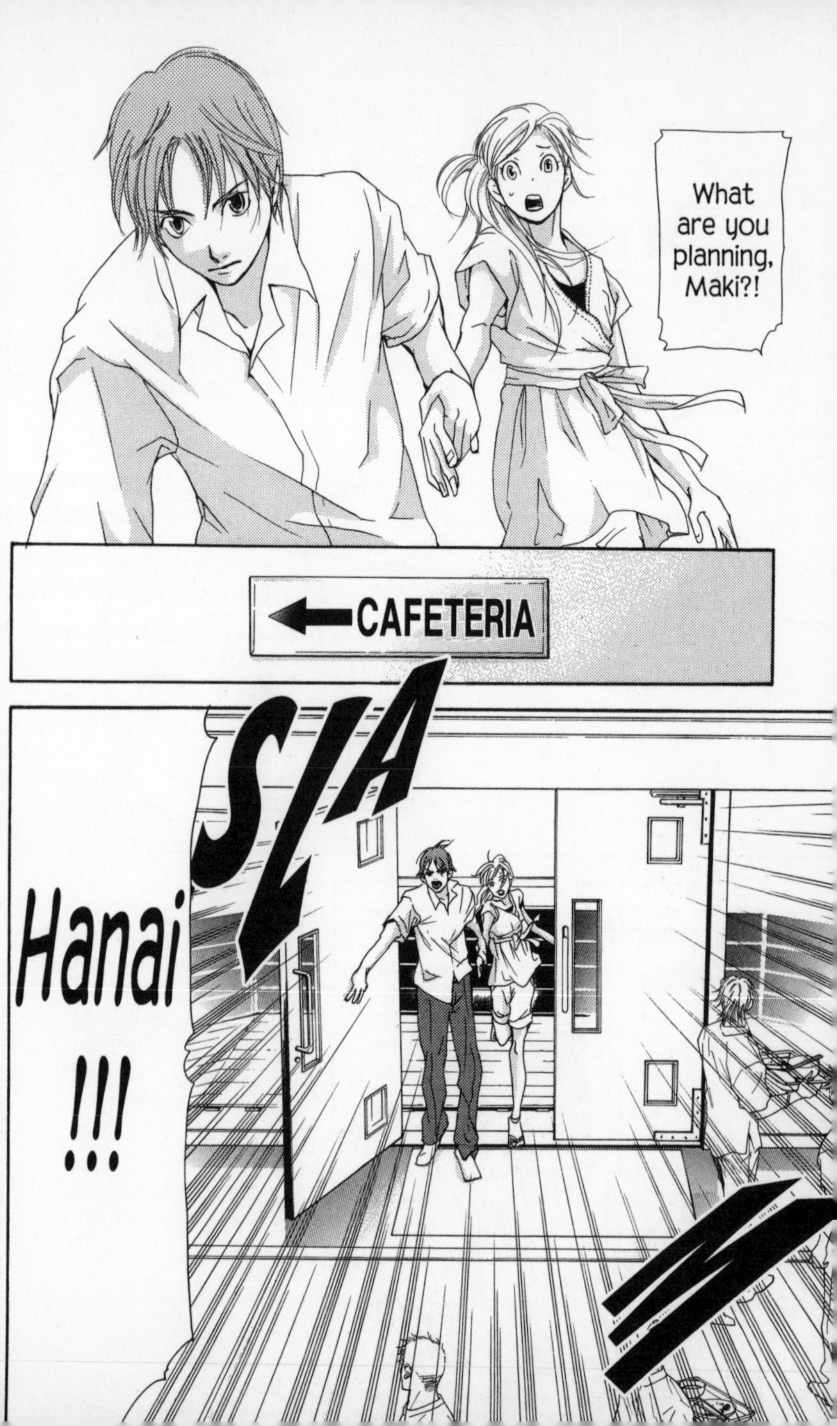

What are you planning, Maki?!
CAFETERIA
SLAM
Hanai!!!

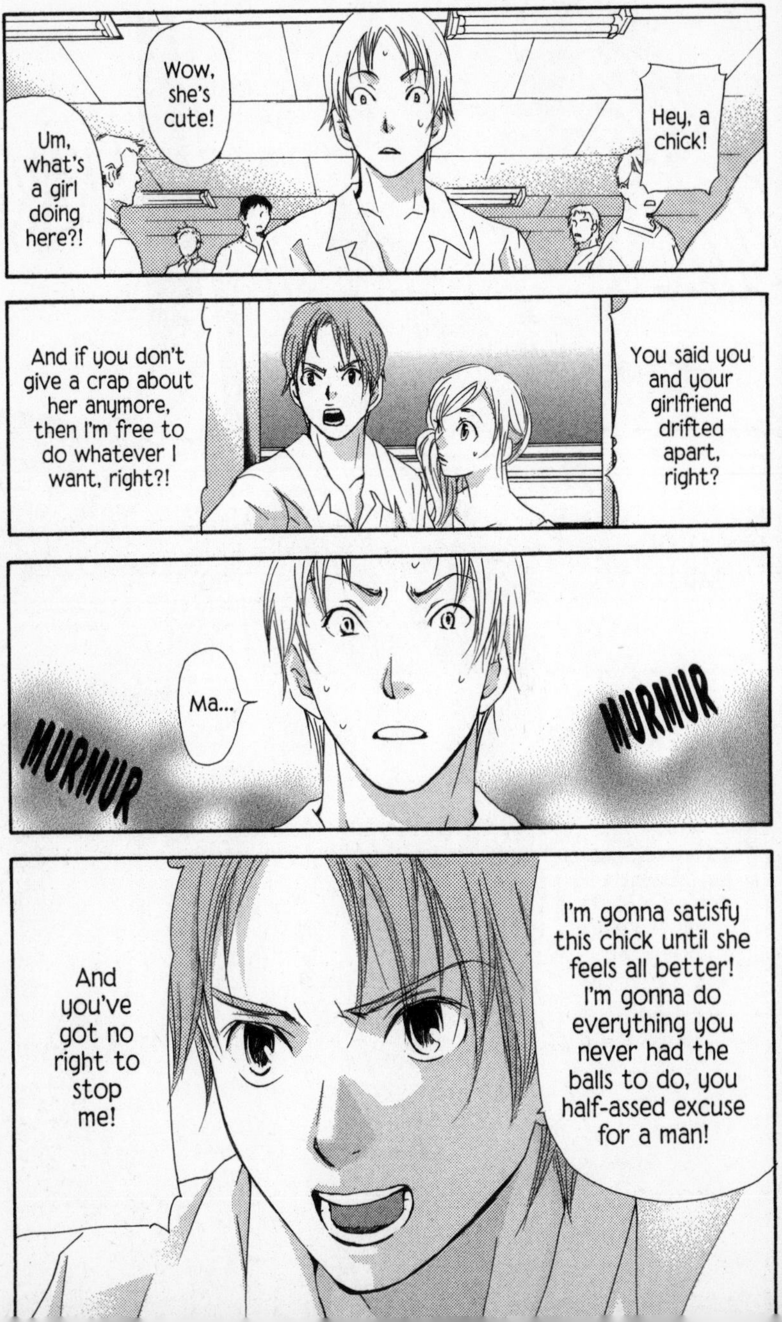
Hey, a chick!
Wow, she's cute!
Um, what's a girl doing here?!
You said you and your girlfriend drifted apart, right?
And if you don't give a crap about her anymore, then I'm free to do whatever I want, right?!
MURMUR
Ma...
MURMUR
I'm gonna satisfy this chick until she feels all better! I'm gonna do everything you never had the balls to do, you half-assed excuse for a man!
And you've got no right to stop me!

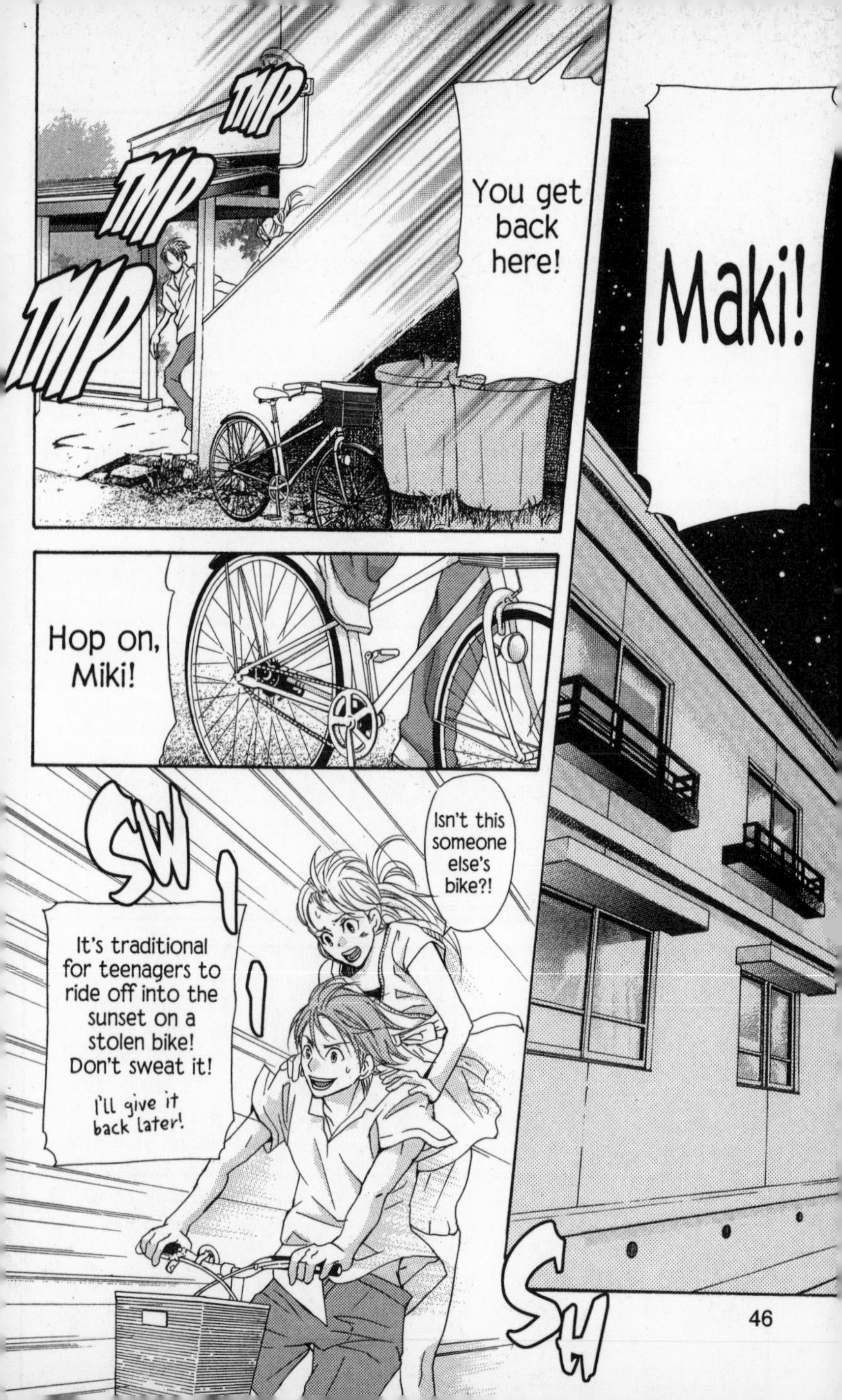

Maki!
You get back here!
TMP
TMP
TMP
Hop on, Miki!
Isn't this someone else's bike?!
SW
It's traditional for teenagers to ride off into the sunset on a stolen bike! Don't sweat it!
I'll give it back later!
SH

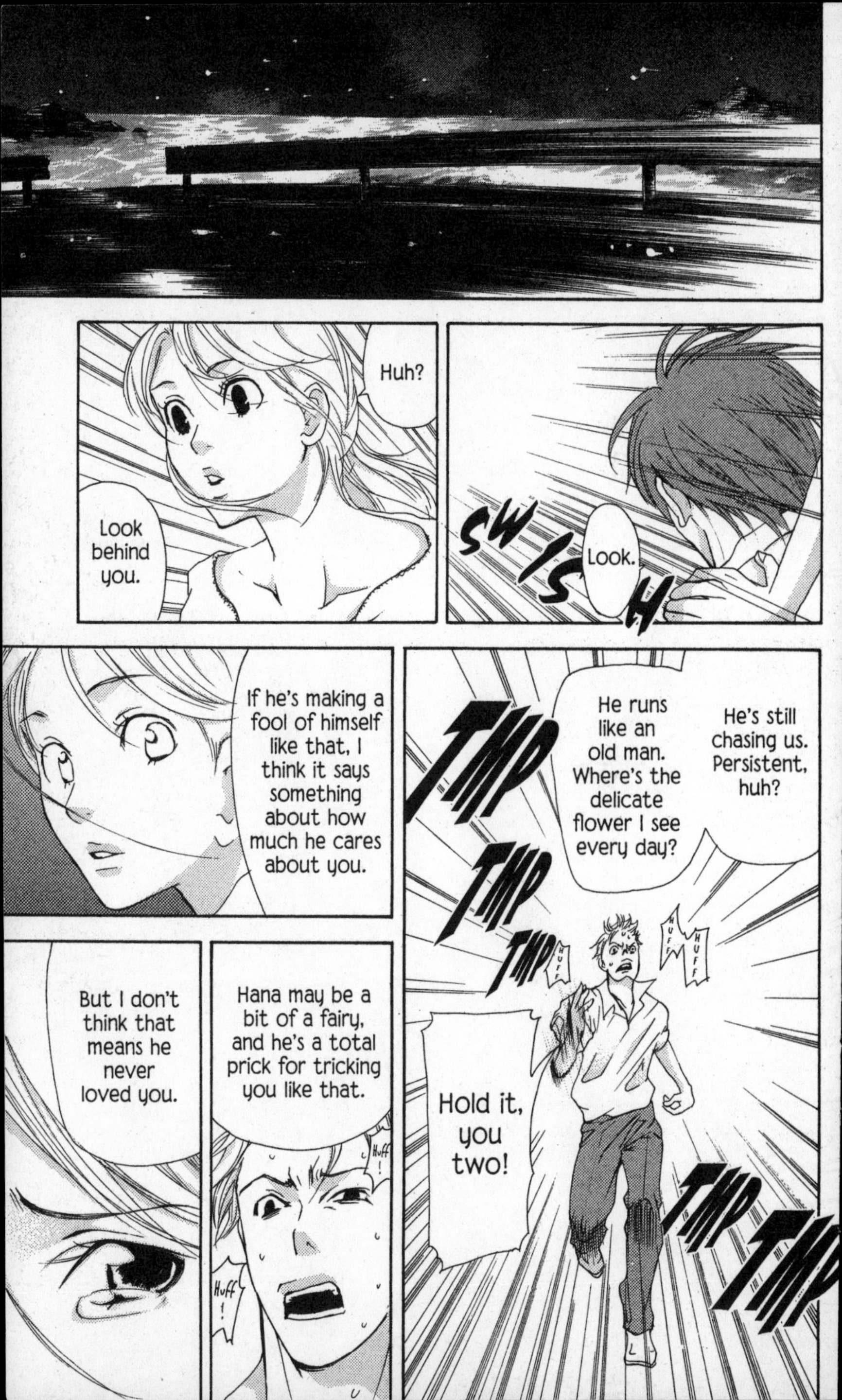
SWISH
Look.
Huh?
Look behind you.
He's still chasing us. Persistent, huh?
He runs like an old man. Where's the delicate flower I see every day?
TMP
TMP
TMP
HUFF
HUFF
HUFF
Hold it, you two!
TMP
TMP
If he's making a fool of himself like that, I think it says something about how much he cares about you.
Hana may be a bit of a fairy, and he's a total prick for tricking you like that.
Huff!
Huff!
But I don't think that means he never loved you.

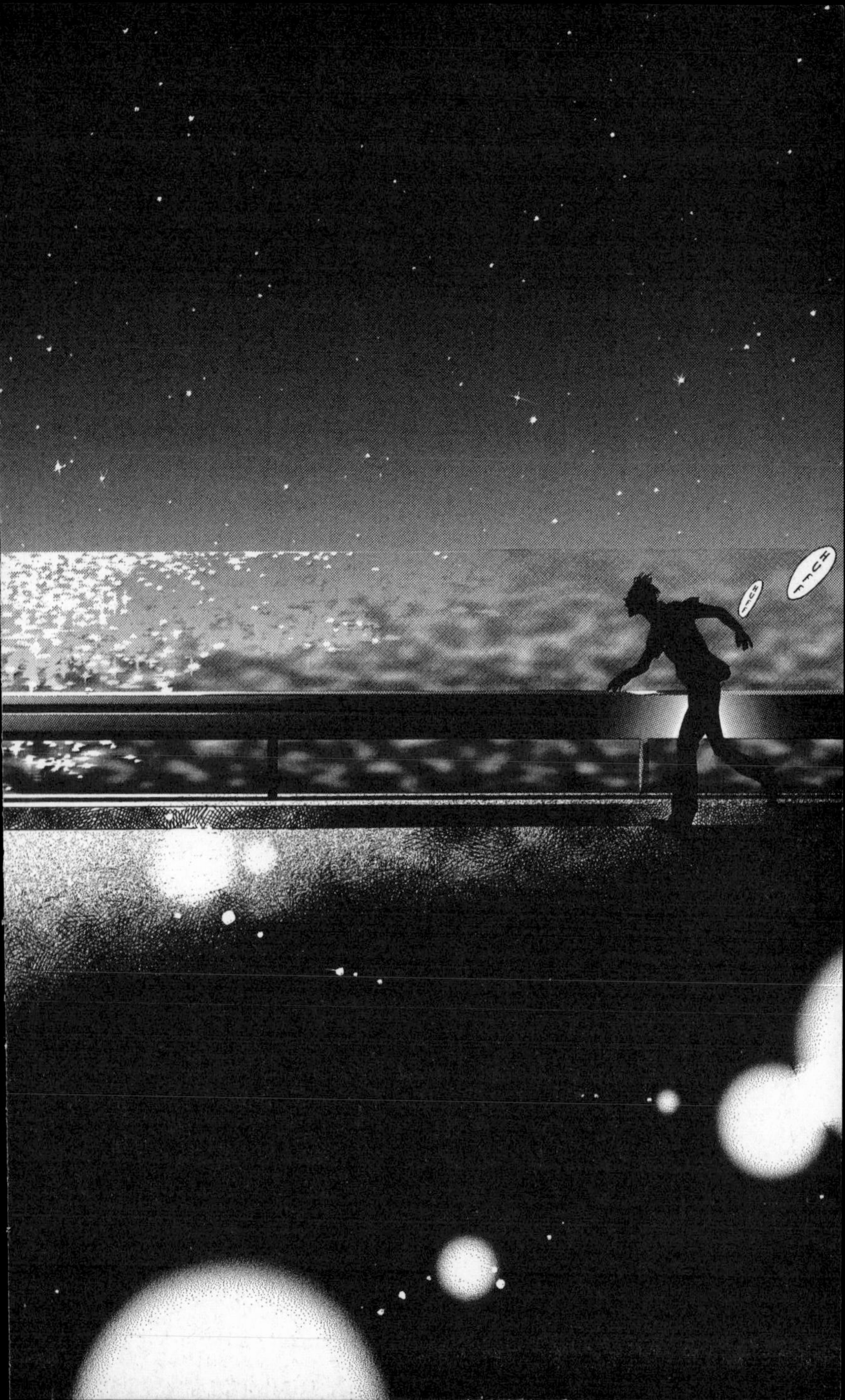
HUFF
HUFF

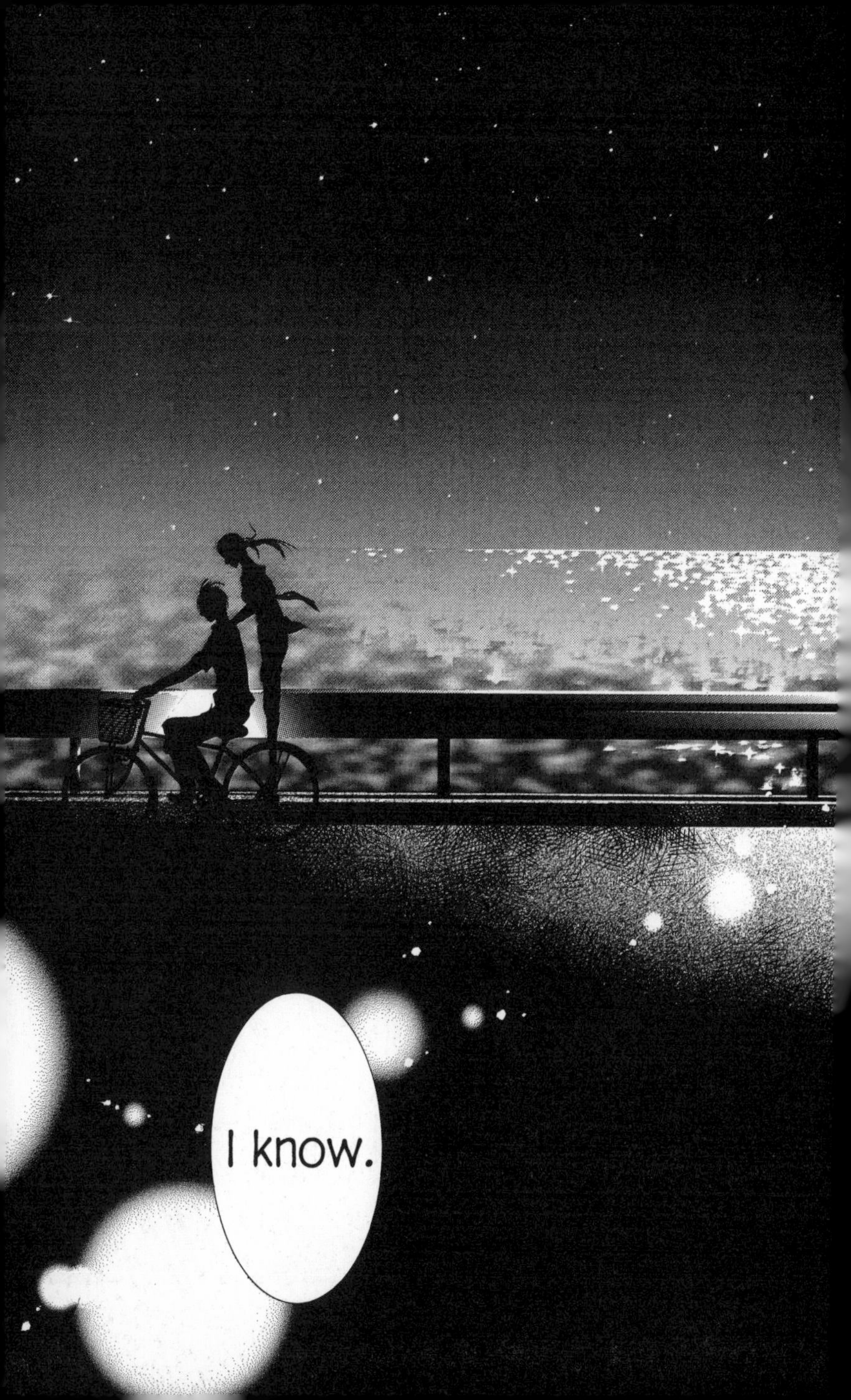
I know.

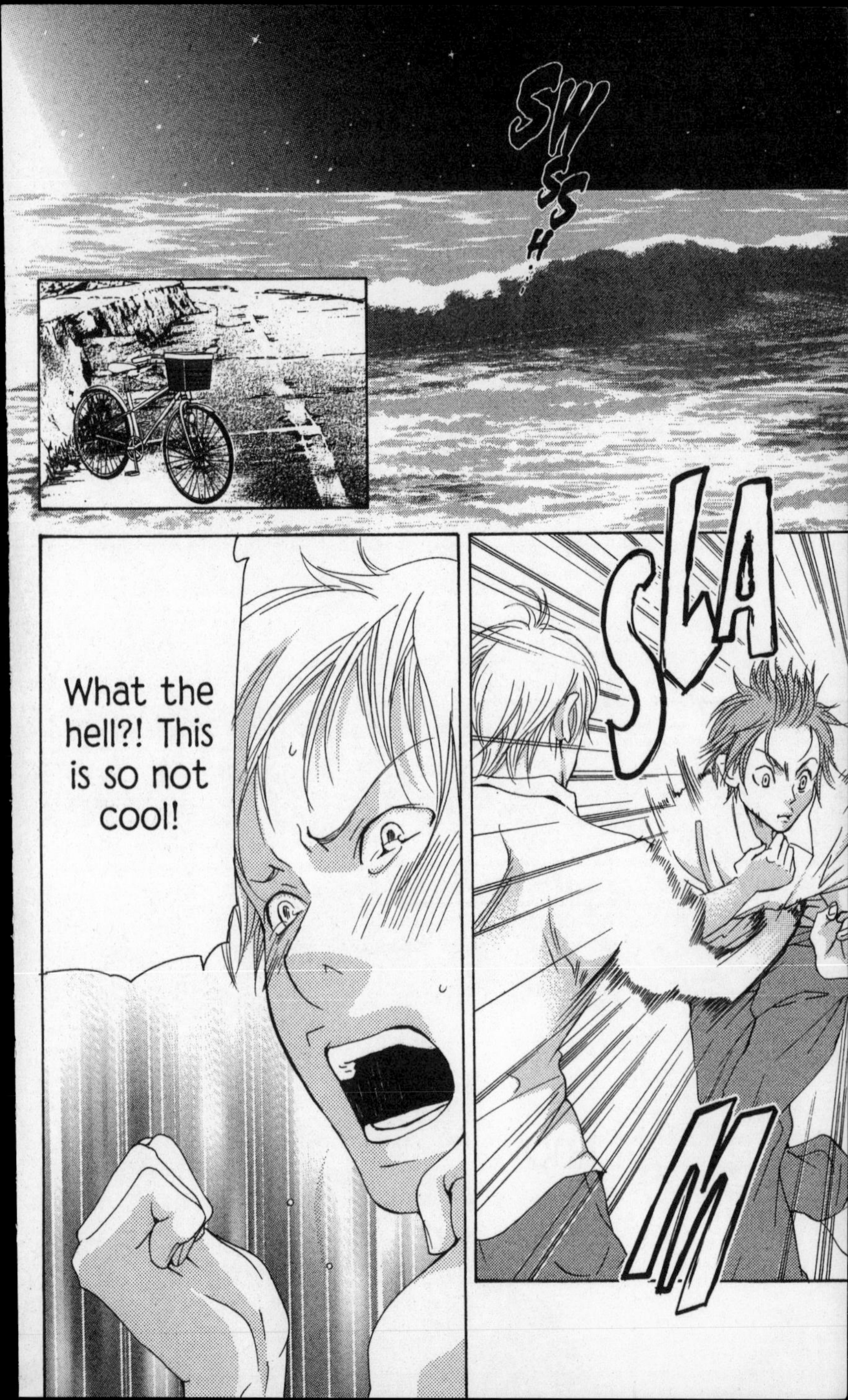
SWSSH...
SLAM
What the hell?! This is so not cool!

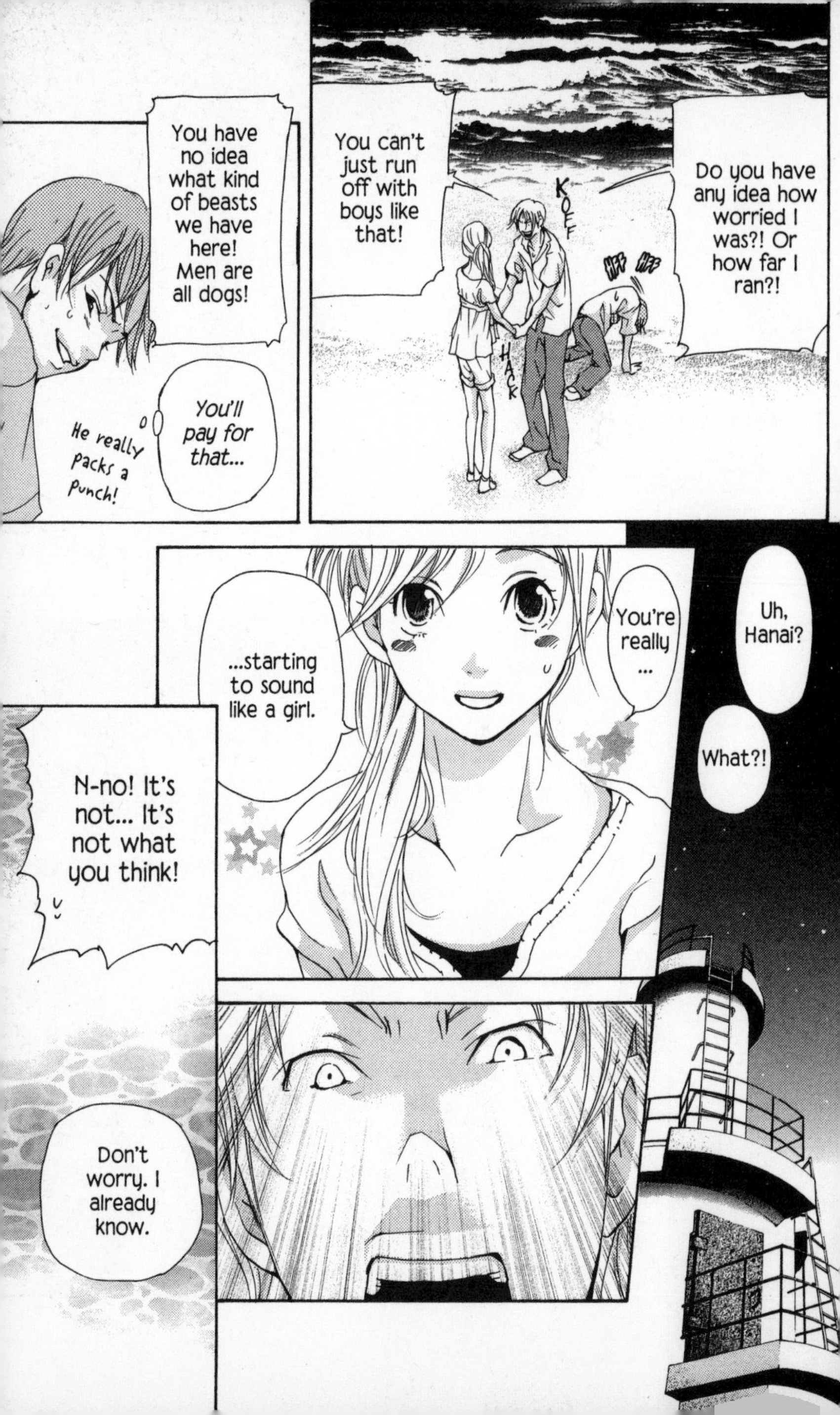
Do you have any idea how worried I was?! Or how far I ran?!
You can't just run off with boys like that!
KOFF
HFF HFF
HACK
You have no idea what kind of beasts we have here! Men are all dogs!
You'll pay for that...
He really packs a punch!
Uh, Hanai?
What?!
You're really ...
...starting to sound like a girl.
N-no! It's not... It's not what you think!
Don't worry. I already know.

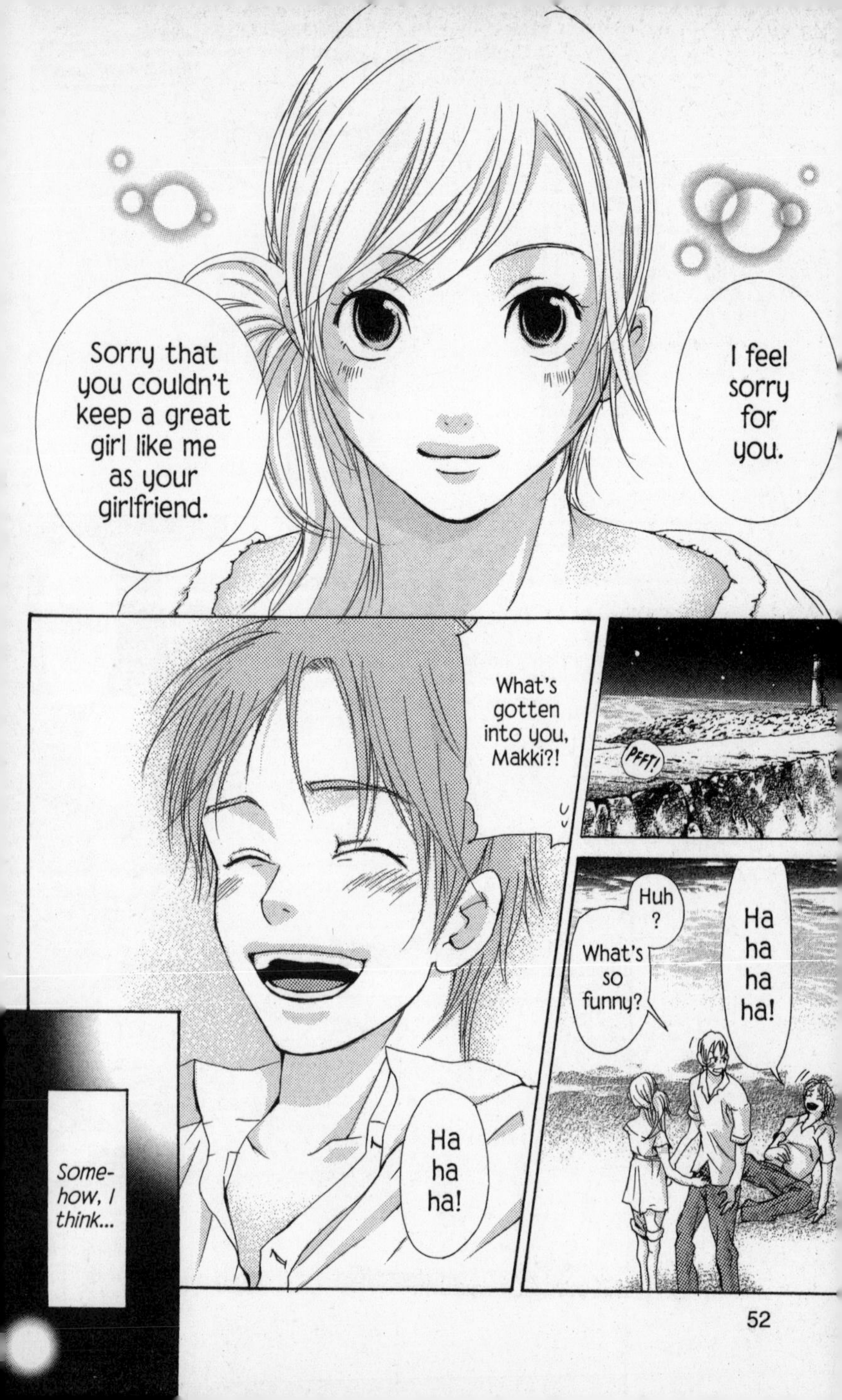
I feel sorry for you.
Sorry that you couldn't keep a great girl like me as your girlfriend.
PFFT!
Ha ha ha ha!
Huh? What's so funny?
What's gotten into you, Makki?!
Ha ha ha!
Some-how, I think...

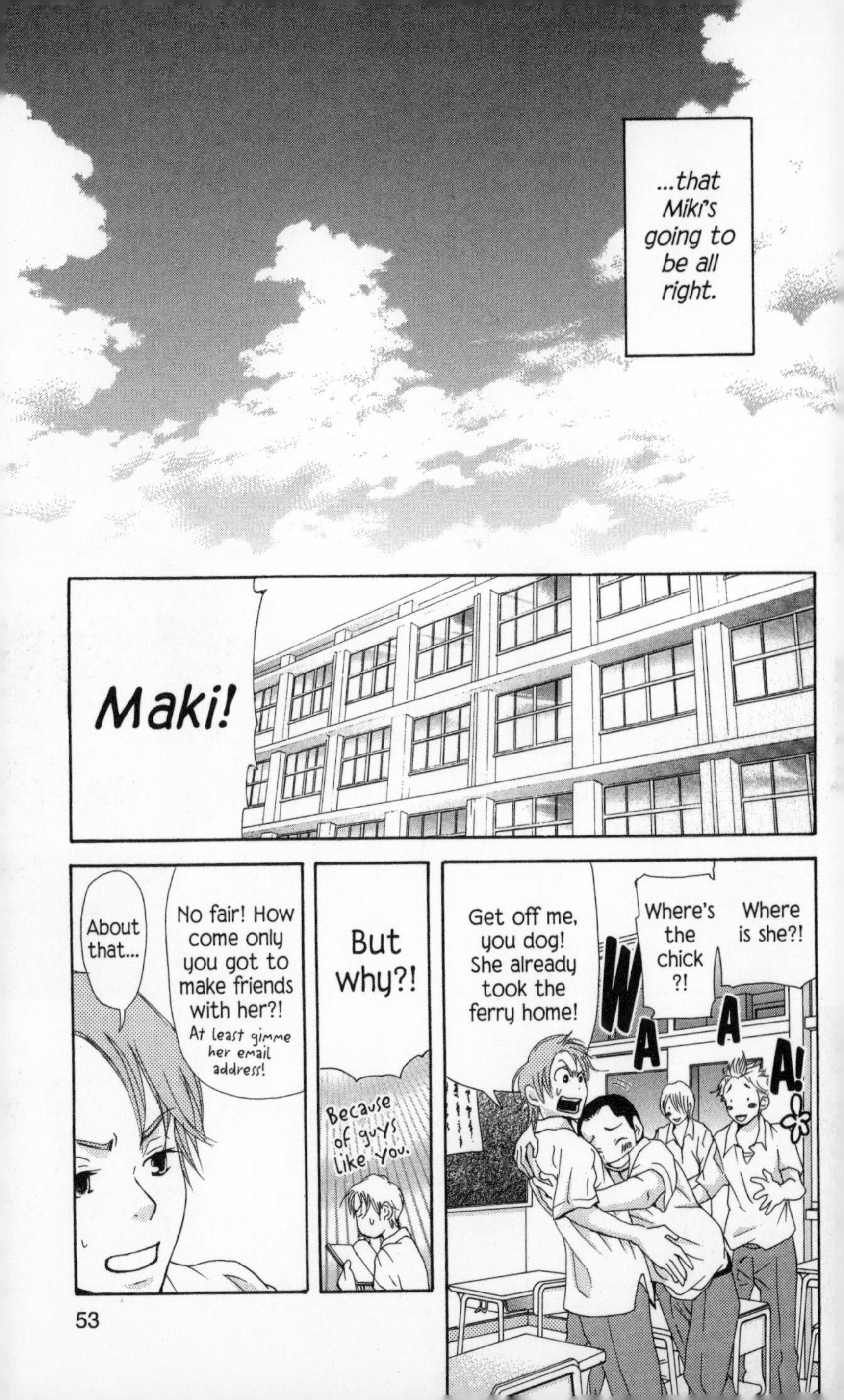
...that Miki's going to be all right.
Maki!
Where is she?!
Where's the chick?!
Get off me, you dog! She already took the ferry home!
WAAA!
But why?!
Because of guys like you.
No fair! How come only you got to make friends with her?!
At least gimme her email address!
About that...

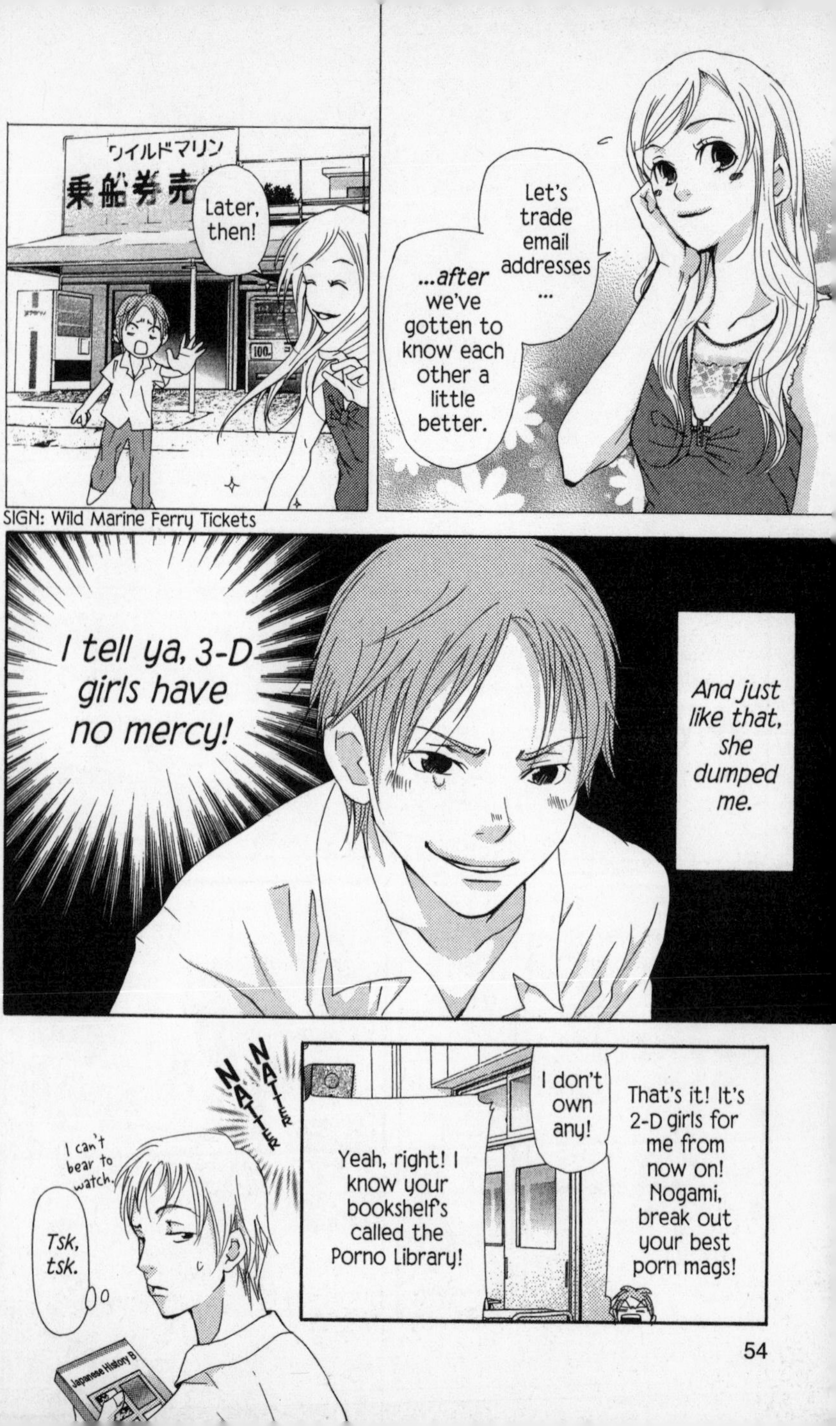
Let's trade email addresses ...
...after we've gotten to know each other a little better.
ワイルドマリン 乗船券売
Later, then!
SIGN: Wild Marine Ferry Tickets
And just like that, she dumped me.
I tell ya, 3-D girls have no mercy!
That's it! It's 2-D girls for me from now on! Nogami, break out your best porn mags!
I don't own any!
Yeah, right! I know your bookshelf's called the Porno Library!
NATTER NATTER
I can't bear to watch.
Tsk, tsk.
Japanese History B

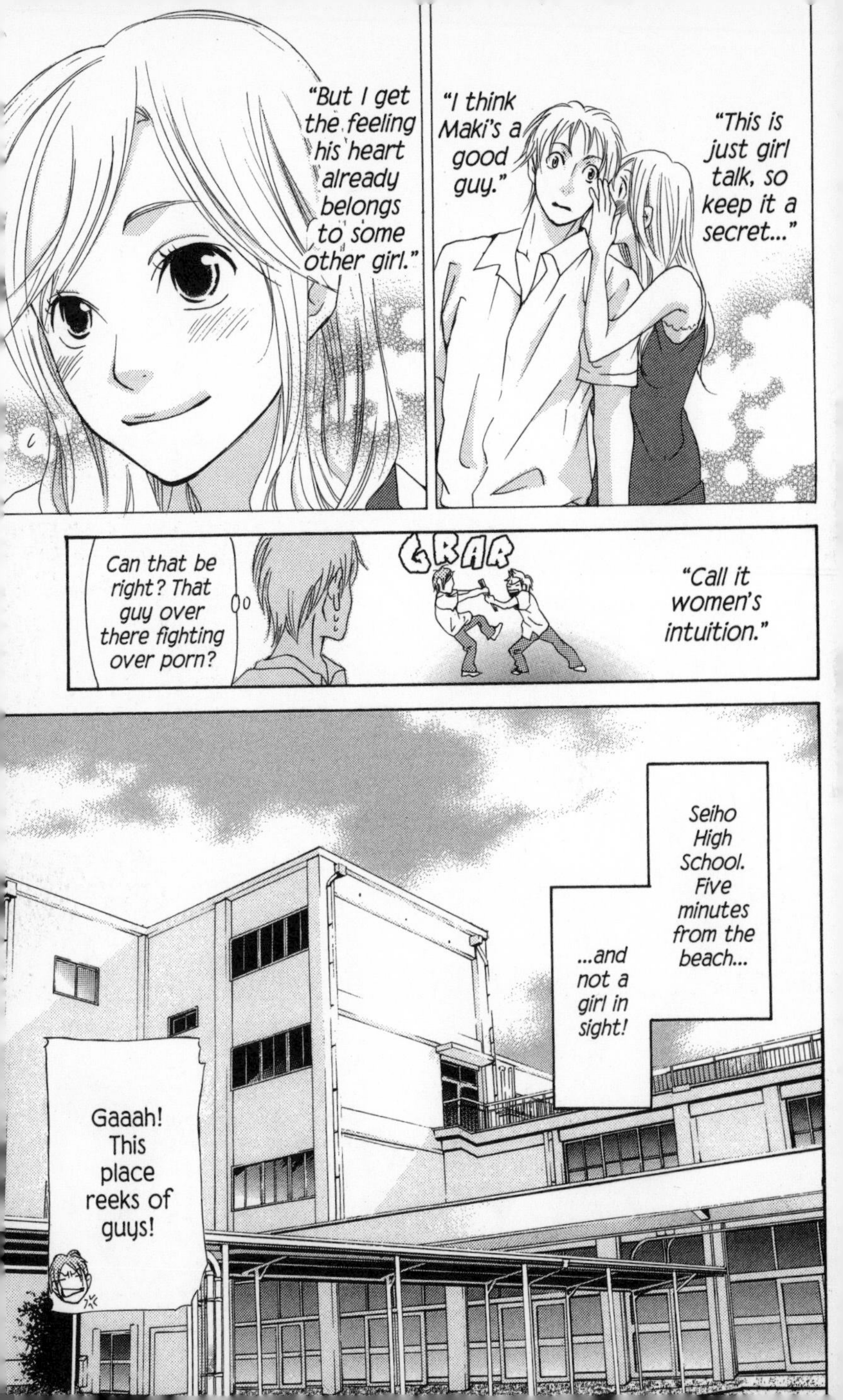
"This is just girl talk, so keep it a secret..."
"I think Maki's a good guy."
"But I get the feeling his heart already belongs to some other girl."
"Call it women's intuition."
GRAR
Can that be right? That guy over there fighting over porn?
Seiho High School. Five minutes from the beach...
...and not a girl in sight!
Gaaah! This place reeks of guys!

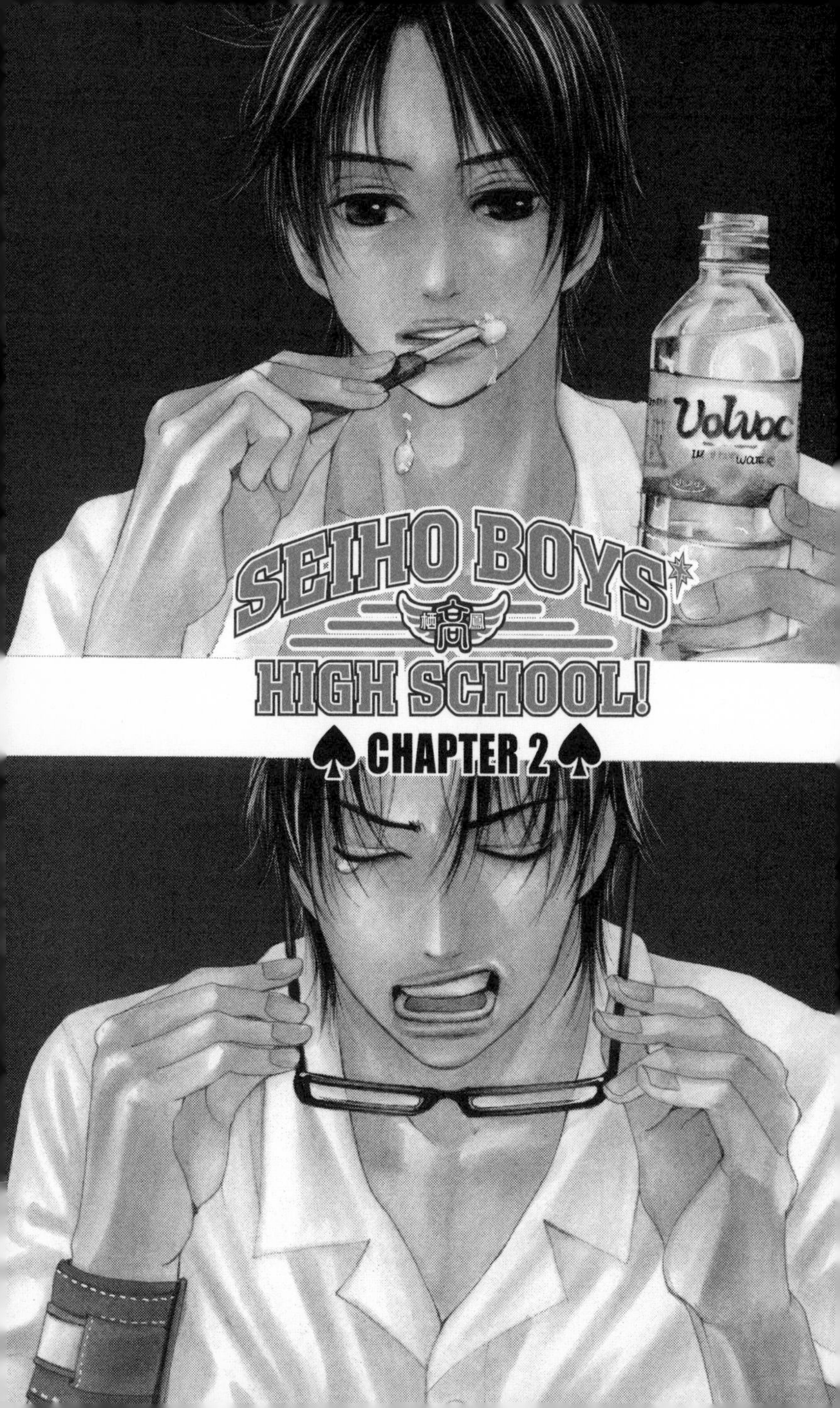
SEIHO BOYS' HIGH SCHOOL!
CHAPTER 2
Volvoc

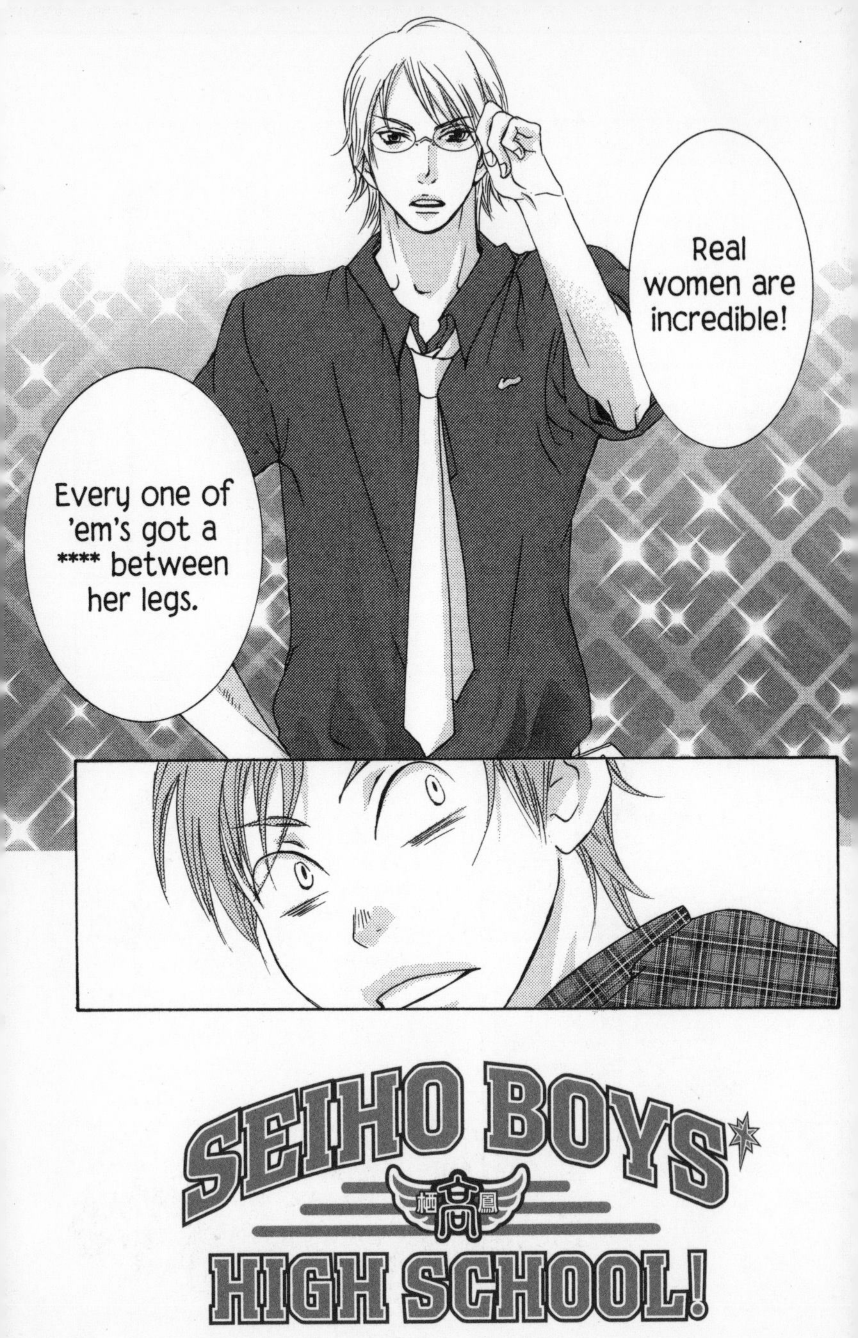
Real women are incredible!
Every one of 'em's got a **** between her legs.

SEIHO BOYS HIGH SCHOOL!

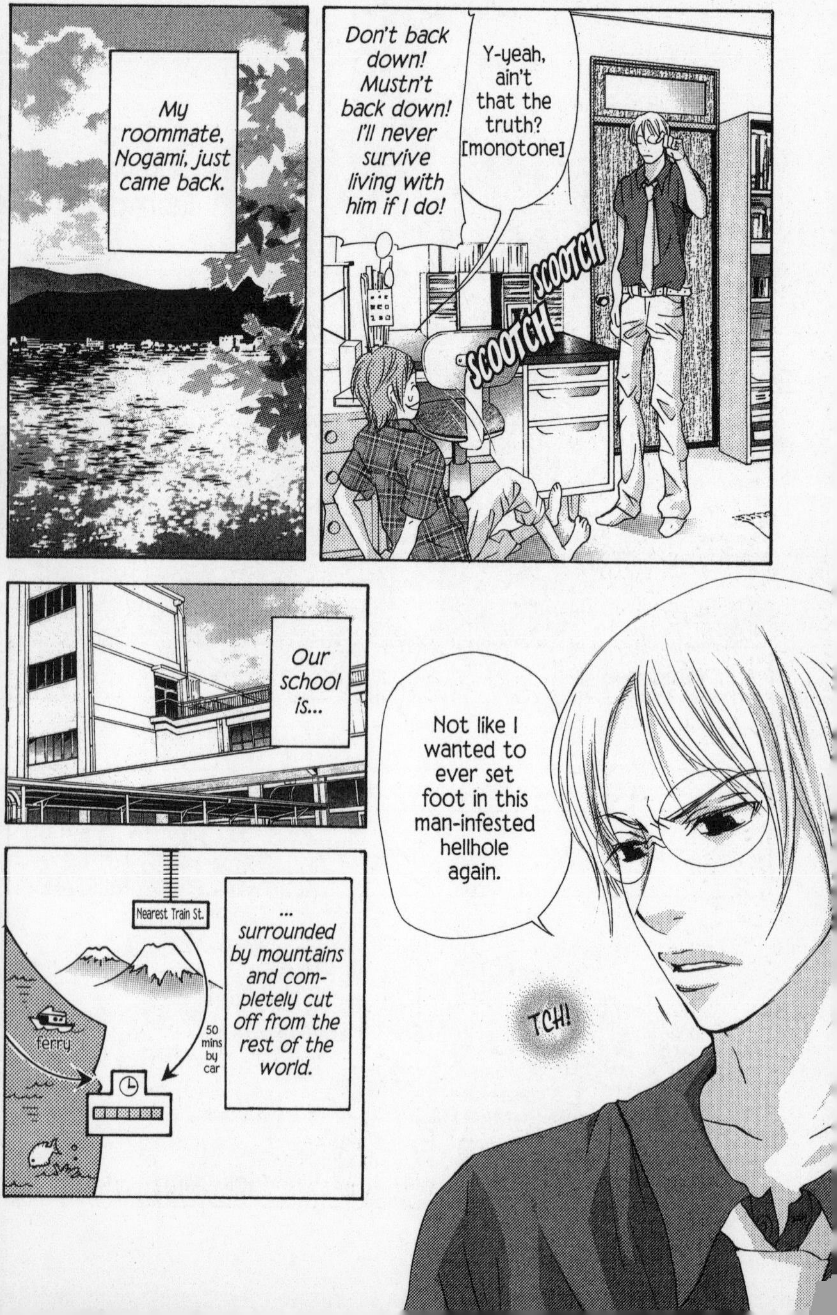

Y-yeah, ain't that the truth? [monotone]
Don't back down! Mustn't back down! I'll never survive living with him if I do!
SCOOTCH
SCOOTCH
My roommate, Nogami, just came back.
Not like I wanted to ever set foot in this man-infested hellhole again.
TCH!
Our school is...
... surrounded by mountains and completely cut off from the rest of the world.
Nearest Train St.
50 mins by car
ferry

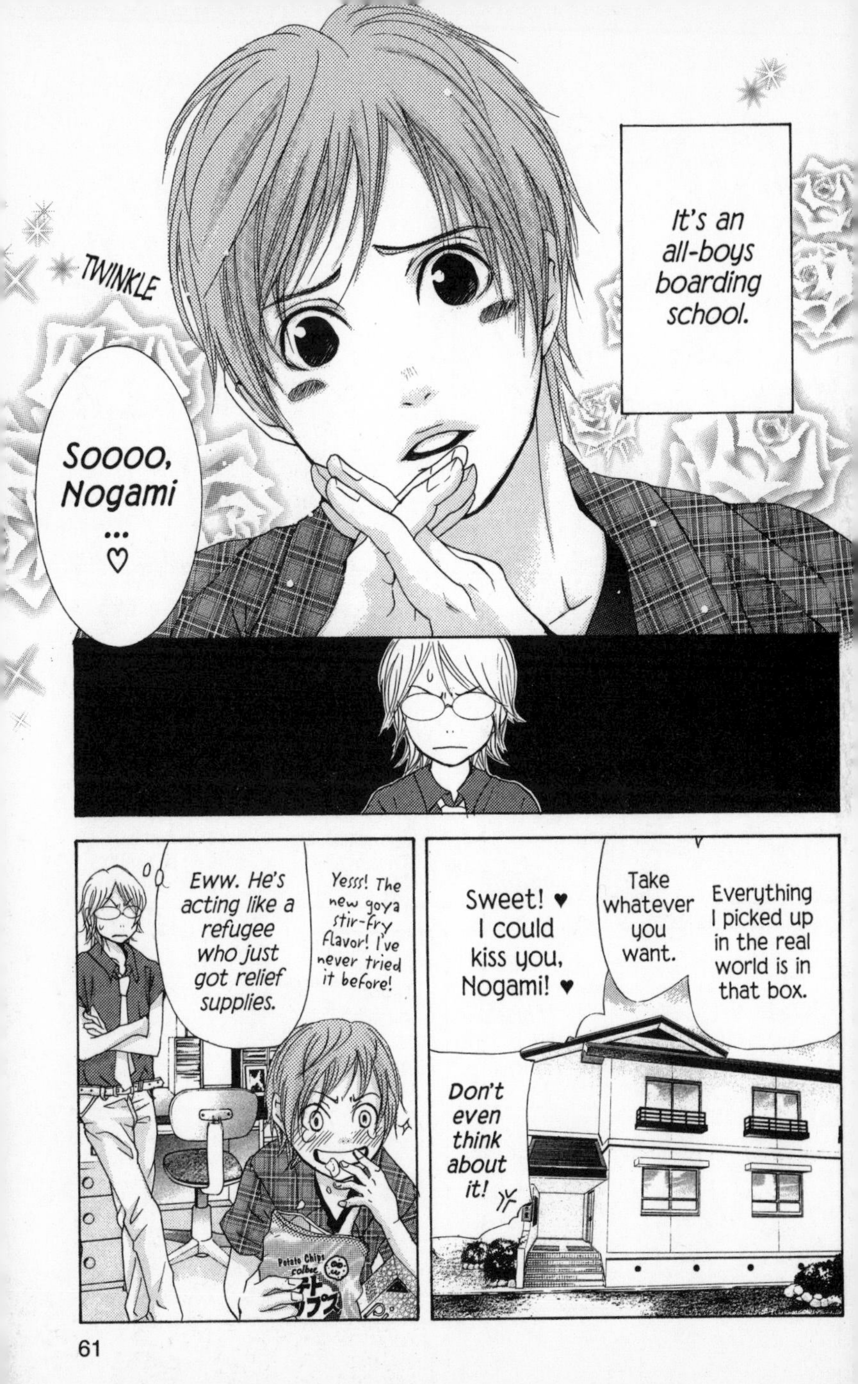
It's an all-boys boarding school.
TWINKLE
Soooo, Nogami ... ♡
Everything I picked up in the real world is in that box.
Take whatever you want.
Sweet! ♥ I could kiss you, Nogami! ♥
Don't even think about it!
Yesss! The new goya stir-fry flavor! I've never tried it before!
Eww. He's acting like a refugee who just got relief supplies.

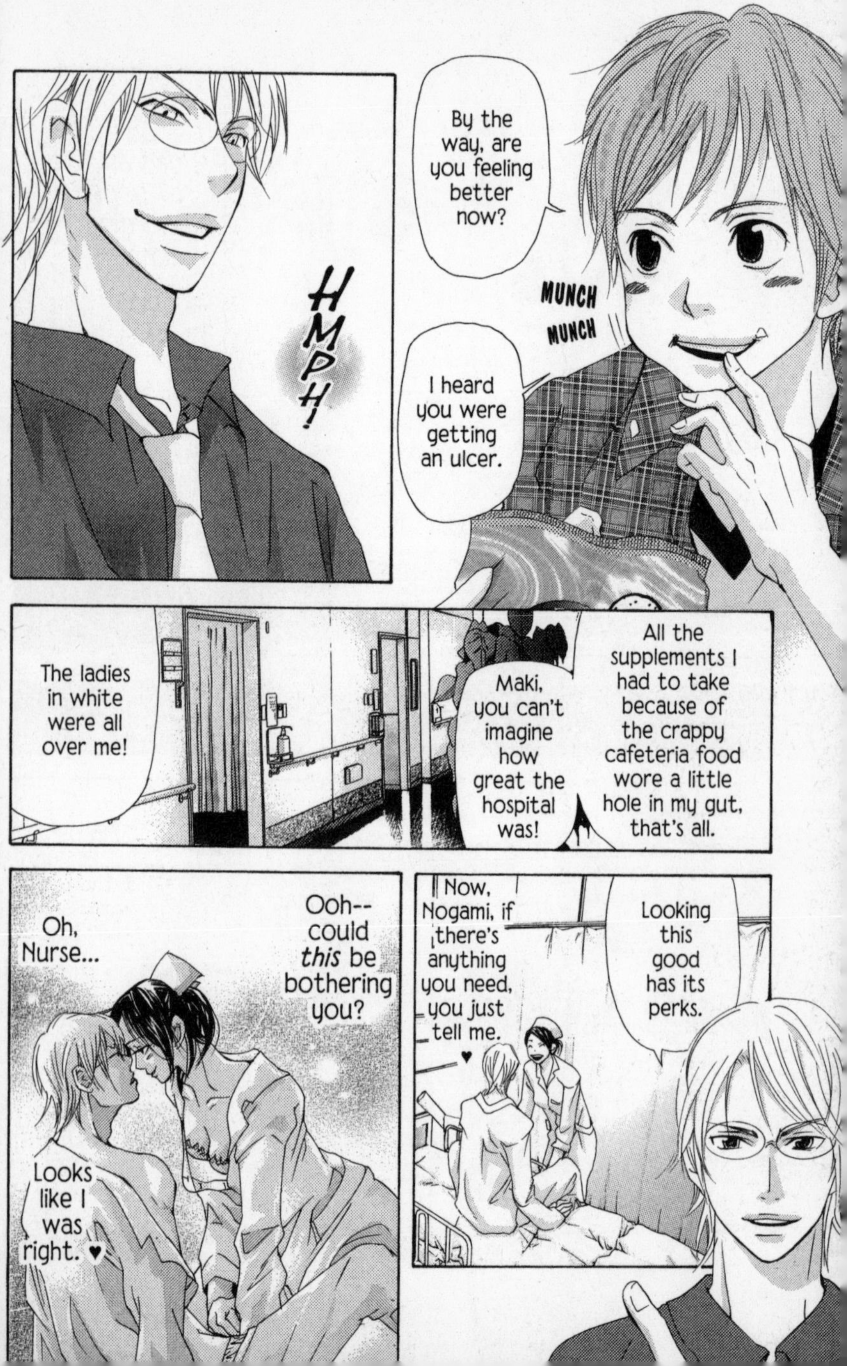
By the way, are you feeling better now?
MUNCH
MUNCH
I heard you were getting an ulcer.
HMPH!
All the supplements I had to take because of the crappy cafeteria food wore a little hole in my gut, that's all.
Maki, you can't imagine how great the hospital was!
The ladies in white were all over me!
Looking this good has its perks.
Now, Nogami, if there's anything you need, you just tell me. ♥
Ooh-- could *this* be bothering you?
Oh, Nurse...
Looks like I was right. ♥

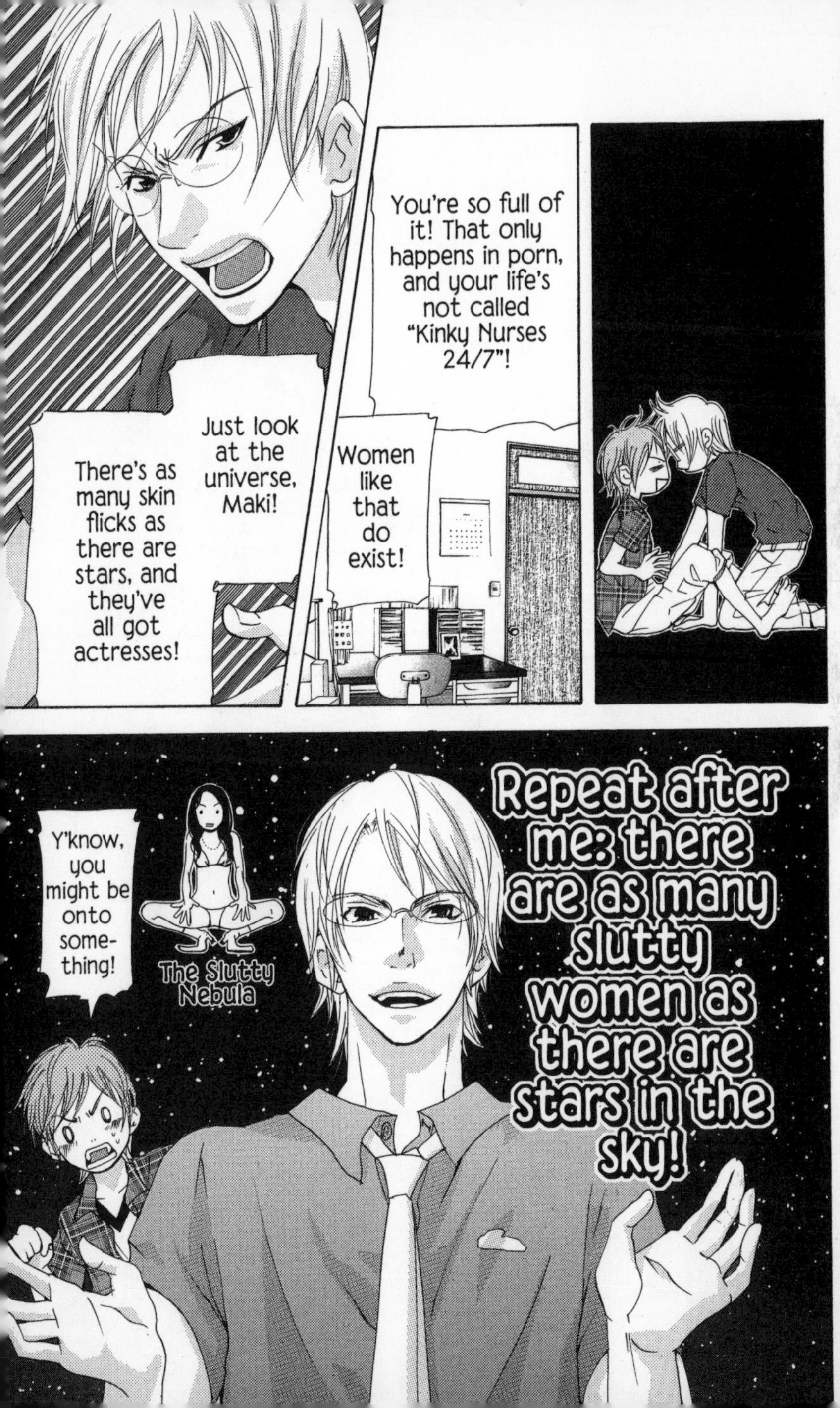
You're so full of it! That only happens in porn, and your life's not called "Kinky Nurses 24/7"!
Women like that do exist!
Just look at the universe, Maki!
There's as many skin flicks as there are stars, and they've all got actresses!
Repeat after me: there are as many slutty women as there are stars in the sky!
The Slutty Nebula
Y'know, you might be onto some-thing!

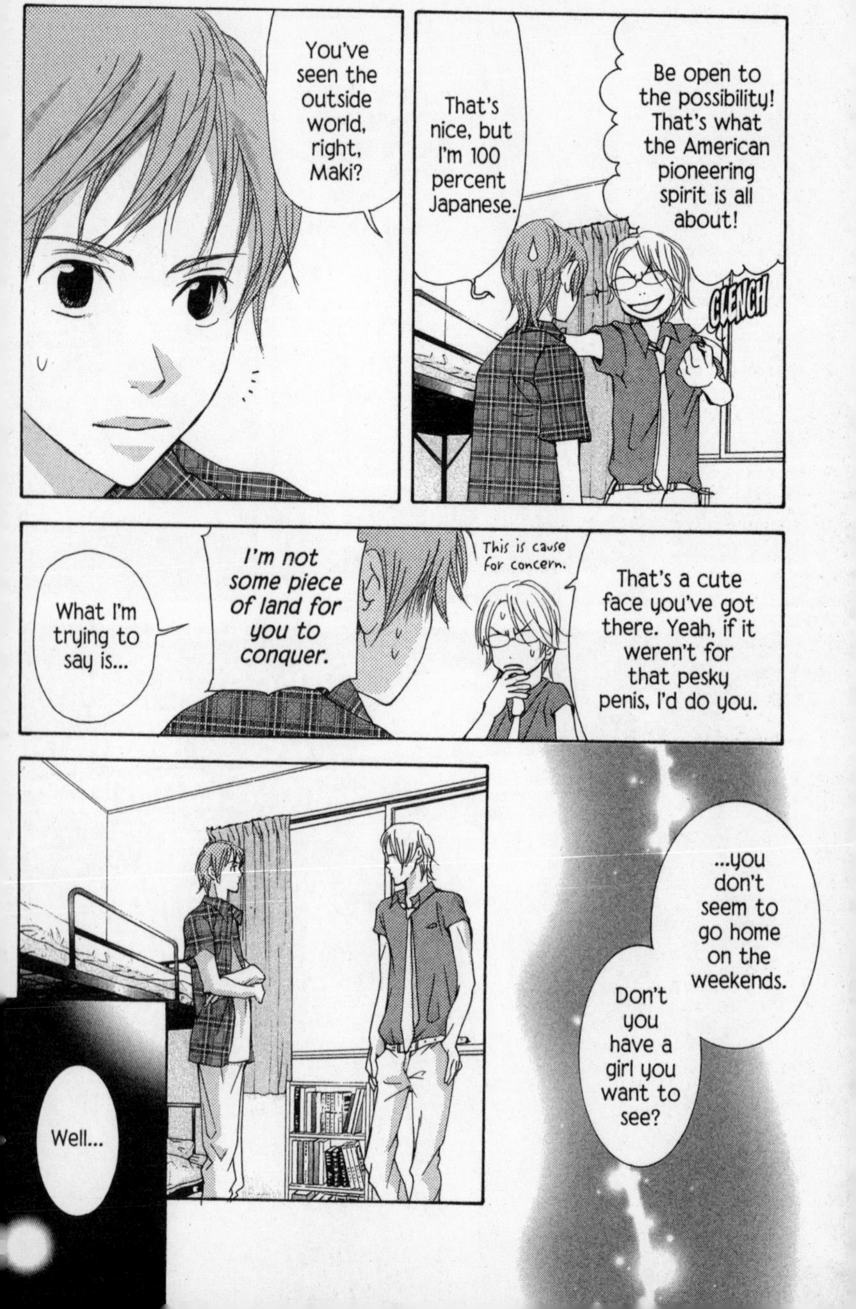
Be open to the possibility! That's what the American pioneering spirit is all about!
That's nice, but I'm 100 percent Japanese.
CLENCH
You've seen the outside world, right, Maki?
That's a cute face you've got there. Yeah, if it weren't for that pesky penis, I'd do you.
This is cause for concern.
I'm not some piece of land for you to conquer.
What I'm trying to say is...
...you don't seem to go home on the weekends.
Don't you have a girl you want to see?
Well...

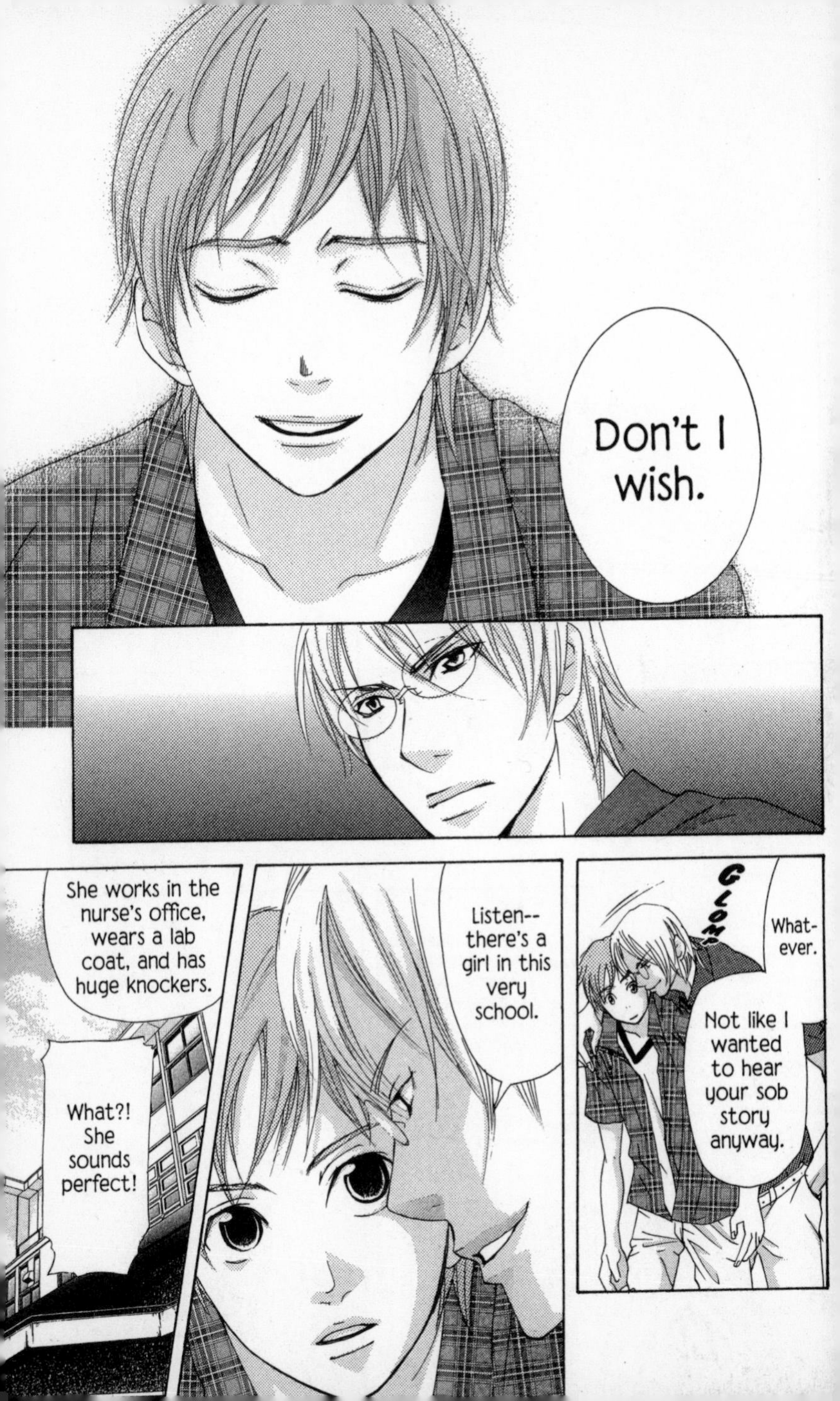
Don't I wish.
GLOMP
Whatever.
Not like I wanted to hear your sob story anyway.
Listen-- there's a girl in this very school.
She works in the nurse's office, wears a lab coat, and has huge knockers.
What?! She sounds perfect!

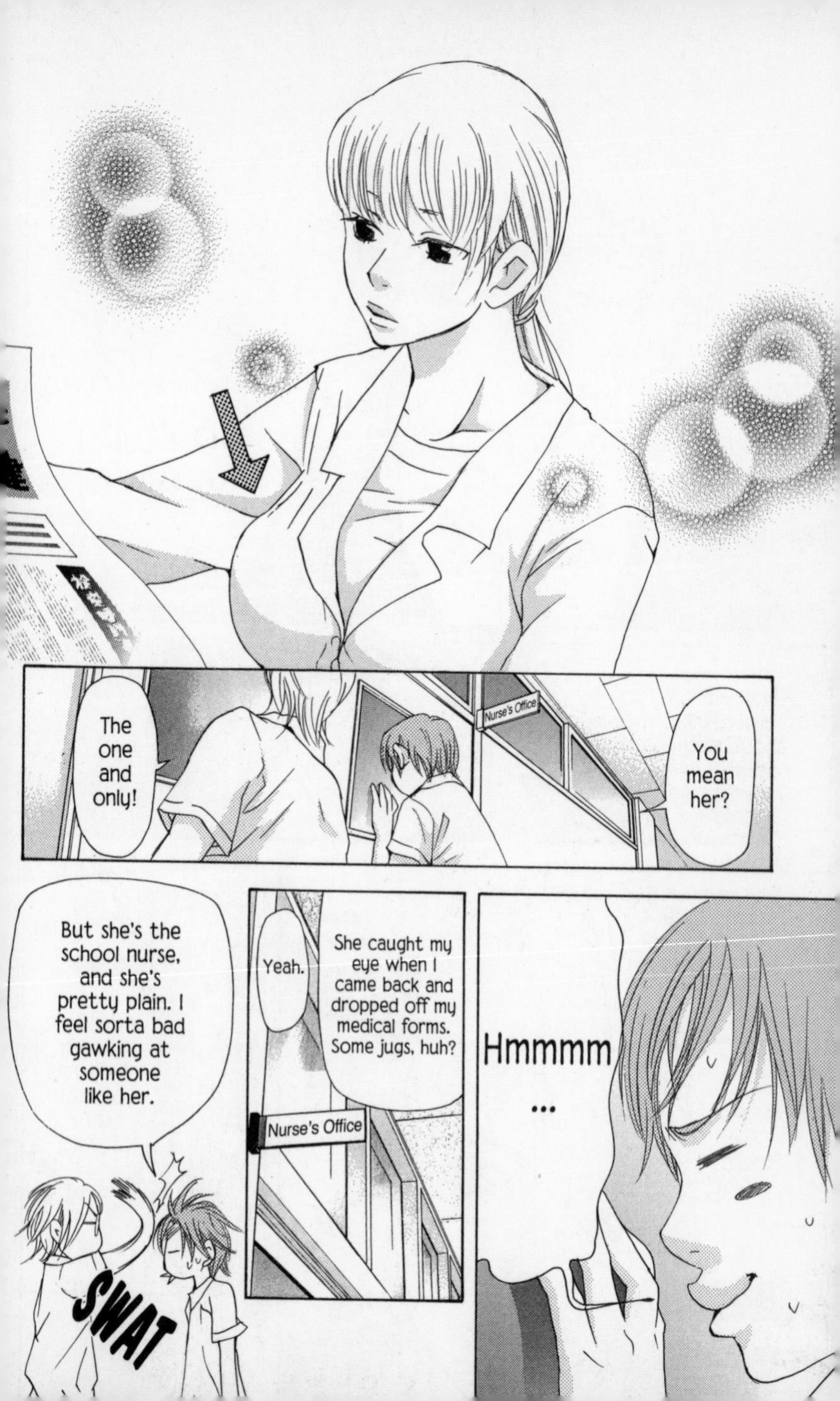
You mean her?
Nurse's Office
The one and only!
Hmmmm ...
She caught my eye when I came back and dropped off my medical forms. Some jugs, huh?
Yeah.
Nurse's Office
But she's the school nurse, and she's pretty plain. I feel sorta bad gawking at someone like her.
SWAT

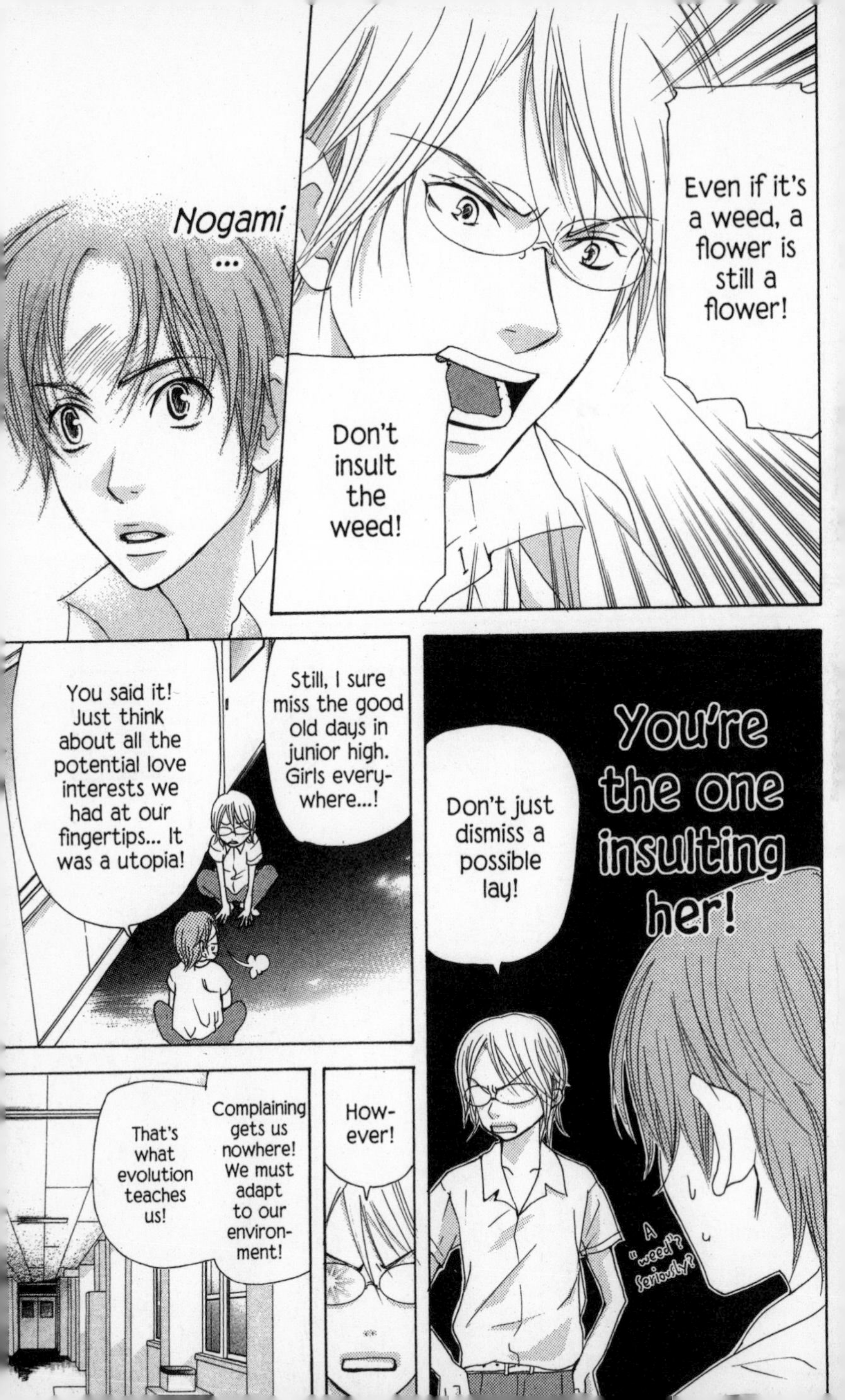
Even if it's a weed, a flower is still a flower!
Don't insult the weed!
Nogami ...
You're the one insulting her!
Don't just dismiss a possible lay!
A "weed"? Seriously?
Still, I sure miss the good old days in junior high. Girls everywhere...!
You said it! Just think about all the potential love interests we had at our fingertips... It was a utopia!
How-ever!
Complaining gets us nowhere! We must adapt to our environment!
That's what evolution teaches us!

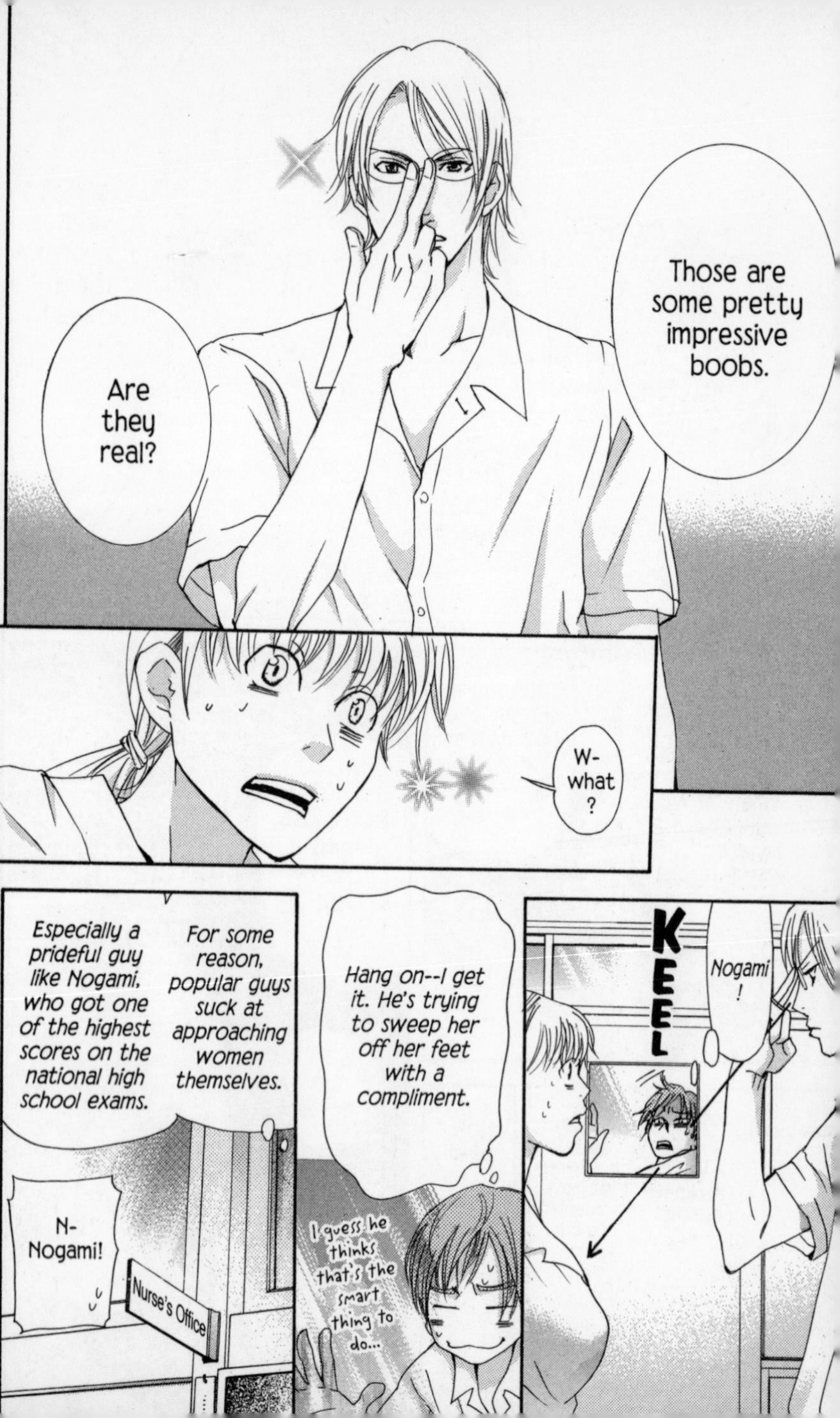

Those are some pretty impressive boobs.
Are they real?
W-what?
KEEL
Nogami!
Hang on--I get it. He's trying to sweep her off her feet with a compliment.
I guess he thinks that's the smart thing to do...
For some reason, popular guys suck at approaching women themselves.
Especially a prideful guy like Nogami, who got one of the highest scores on the national high school exams.
N-Nogami!
Nurse's Office

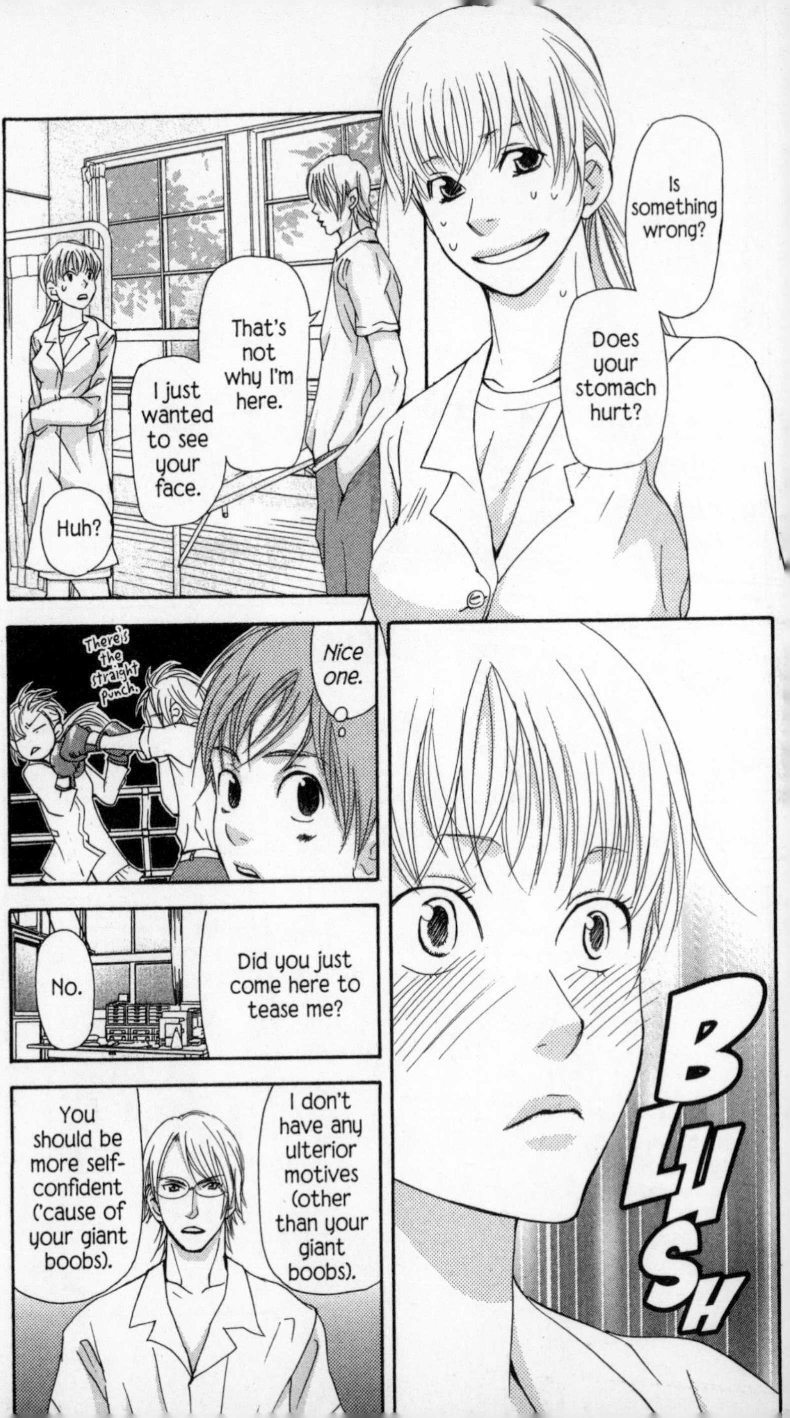

Is something wrong?
Does your stomach hurt?
That's not why I'm here.
I just wanted to see your face.
Huh?
BLUSH
Nice one.
There's the straight punch.
Did you just come here to tease me?
No.
I don't have any ulterior motives (other than your giant boobs).
You should be more self-confident ('cause of your giant boobs).

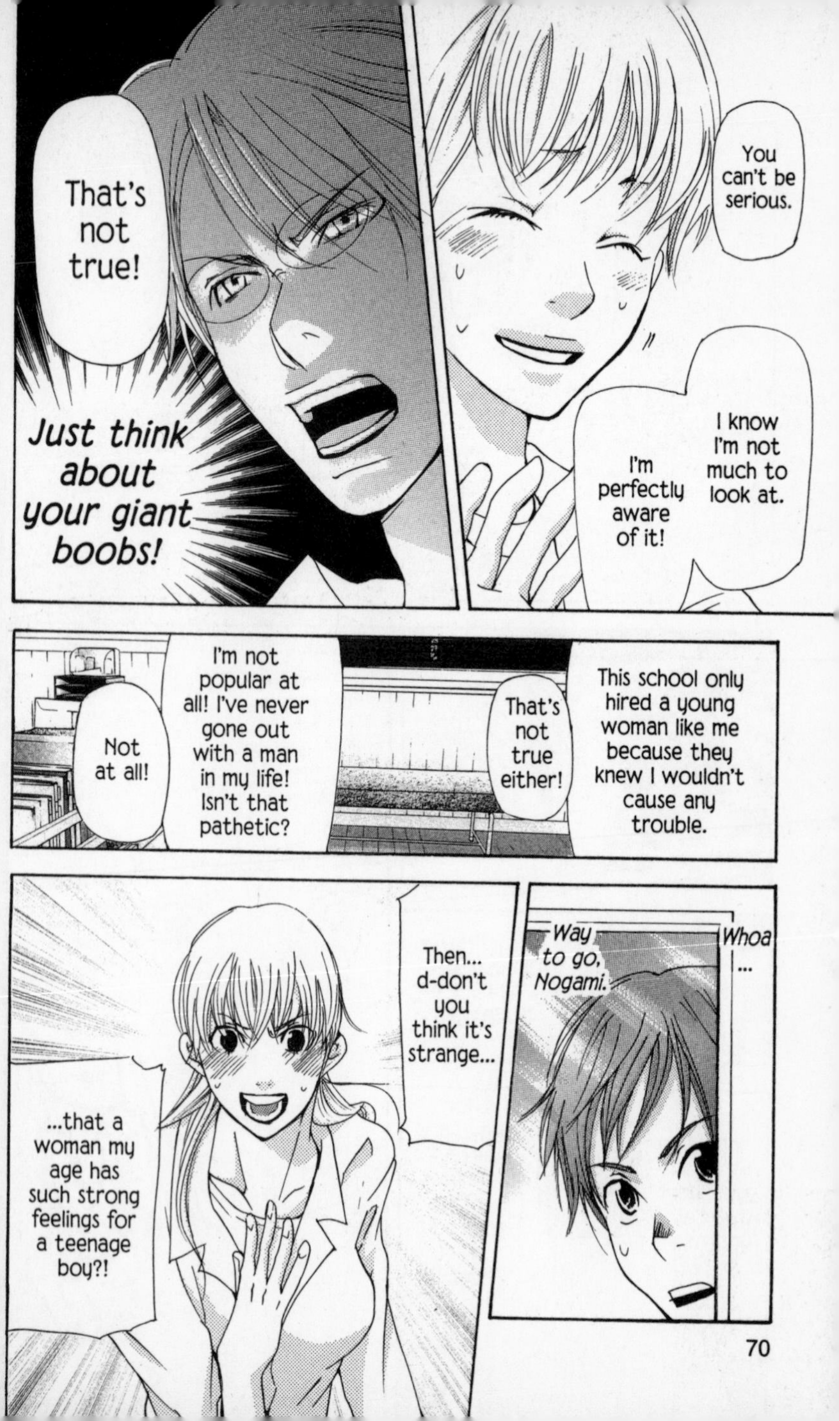

You can't be serious.
I know I'm not much to look at.
I'm perfectly aware of it!
That's not true!
Just think about your giant boobs!
This school only hired a young woman like me because they knew I wouldn't cause any trouble.
That's not true either!
I'm not popular at all! I've never gone out with a man in my life! Isn't that pathetic?
Not at all!
Whoa...
Way to go, Nogami.
Then... d-don't you think it's strange...
...that a woman my age has such strong feelings for a teenage boy?!

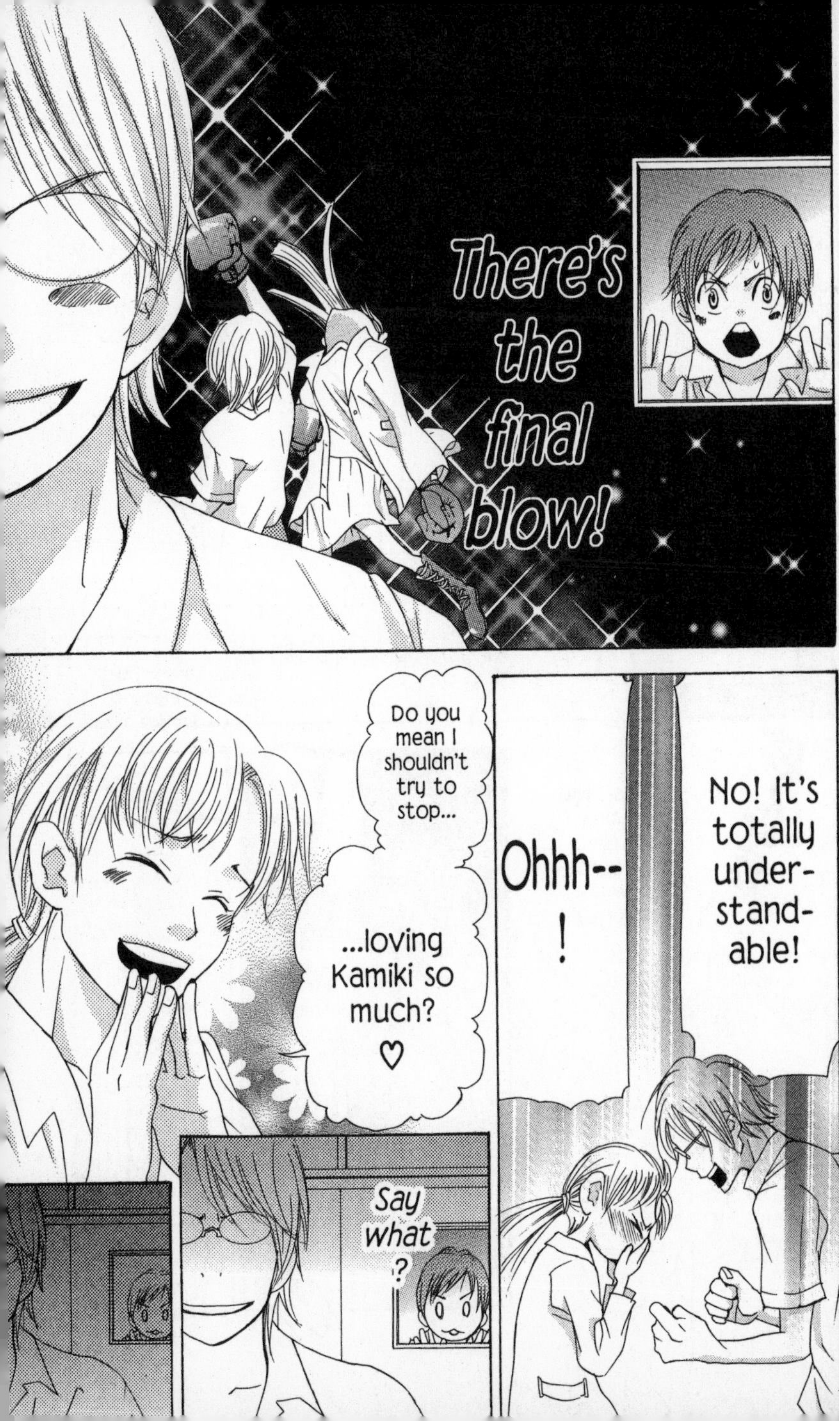
There's the final blow!
No! It's totally under-standable!
Ohhh--!
Do you mean I shouldn't try to stop...
...loving Kamiki so much? ♡
Say what?

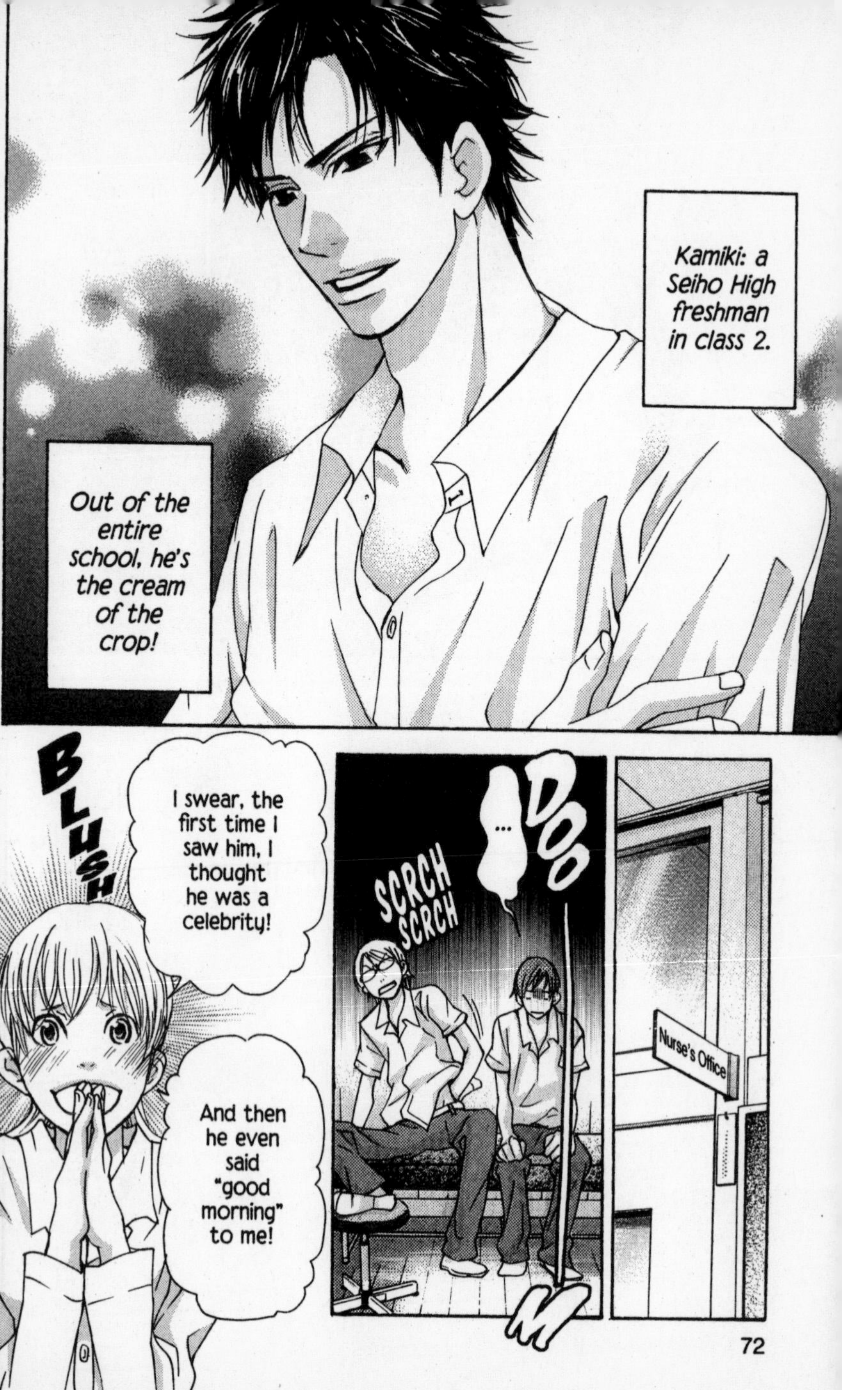
Kamiki: a Seiho High freshman in class 2.
Out of the entire school, he's the cream of the crop!
Nurse's Office
DOOM
...
SCRCH SCRCH
BLUSH
I swear, the first time I saw him, I thought he was a celebrity!
And then he even said "good morning" to me!

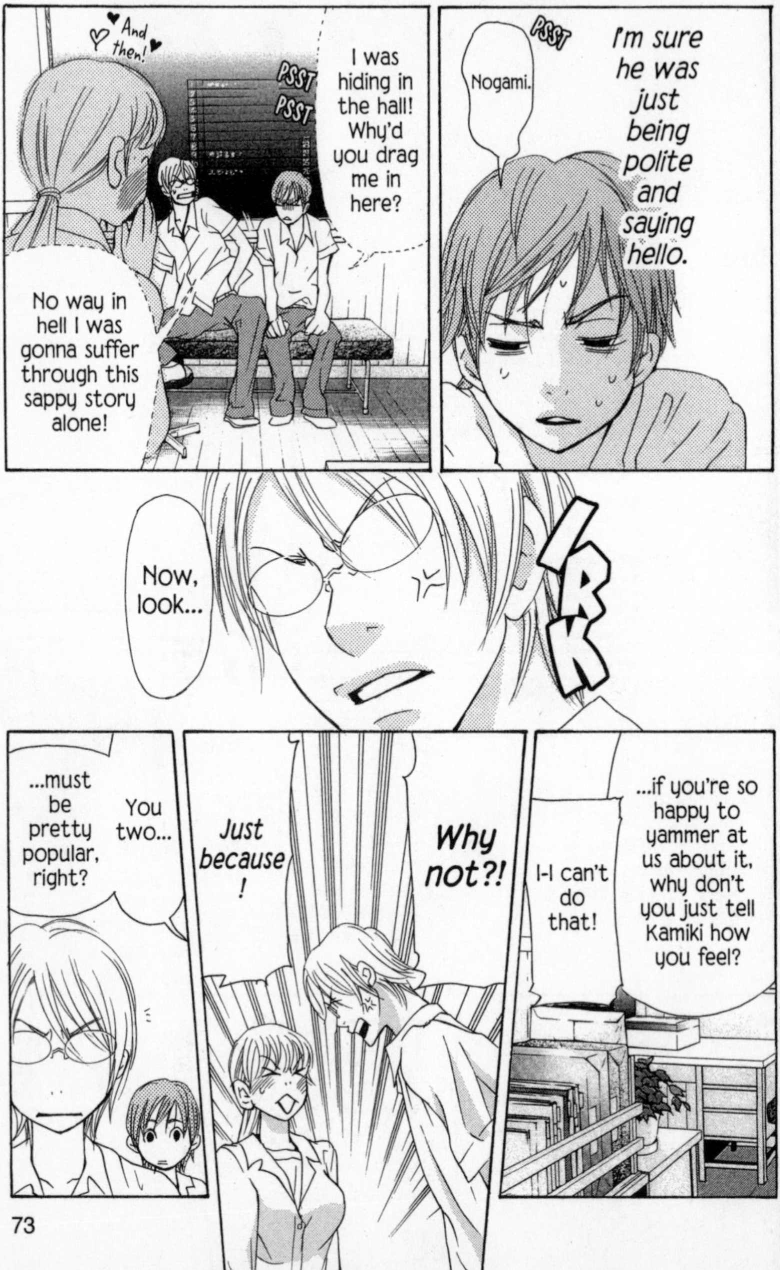
PSST
I'm sure he was just being polite and saying hello.
Nogami.
PSST
PSST
I was hiding in the hall! Why'd you drag me in here?
And then!
No way in hell I was gonna suffer through this sappy story alone!
IRK
Now, look...
...if you're so happy to yammer at us about it, why don't you just tell Kamiki how you feel?
I-I can't do that!
Why not?!
Just because!
You two...
...must be pretty popular, right?

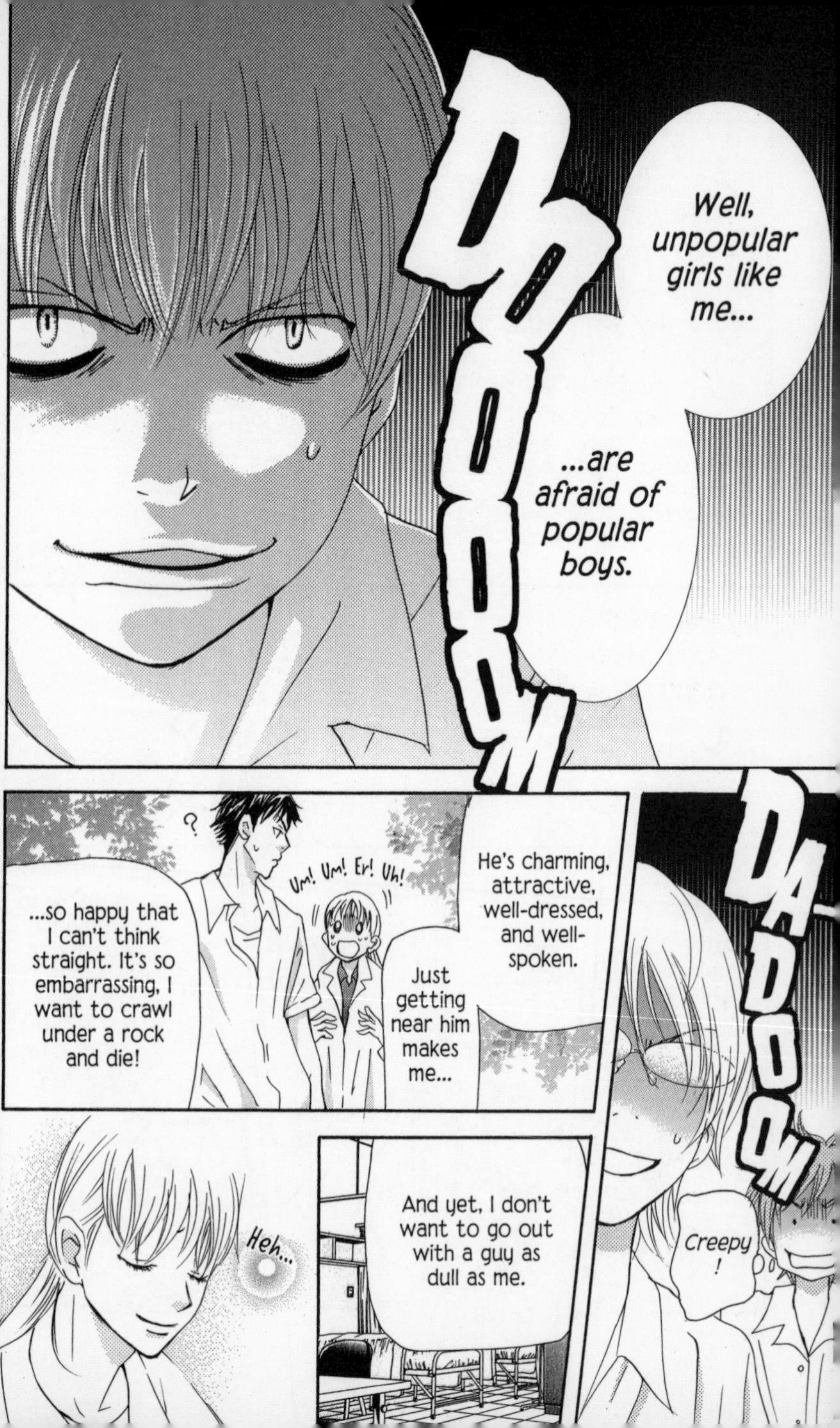
Well, unpopular girls like me...
DOOOOOM
...are afraid of popular boys.
DA-DOOM
Creepy!
He's charming, attractive, well-dressed, and well-spoken.
Just getting near him makes me...
Um! Um! Er! Uh!
?
...so happy that I can't think straight. It's so embarrassing, I want to crawl under a rock and die!
And yet, I don't want to go out with a guy as dull as me.
Heh...

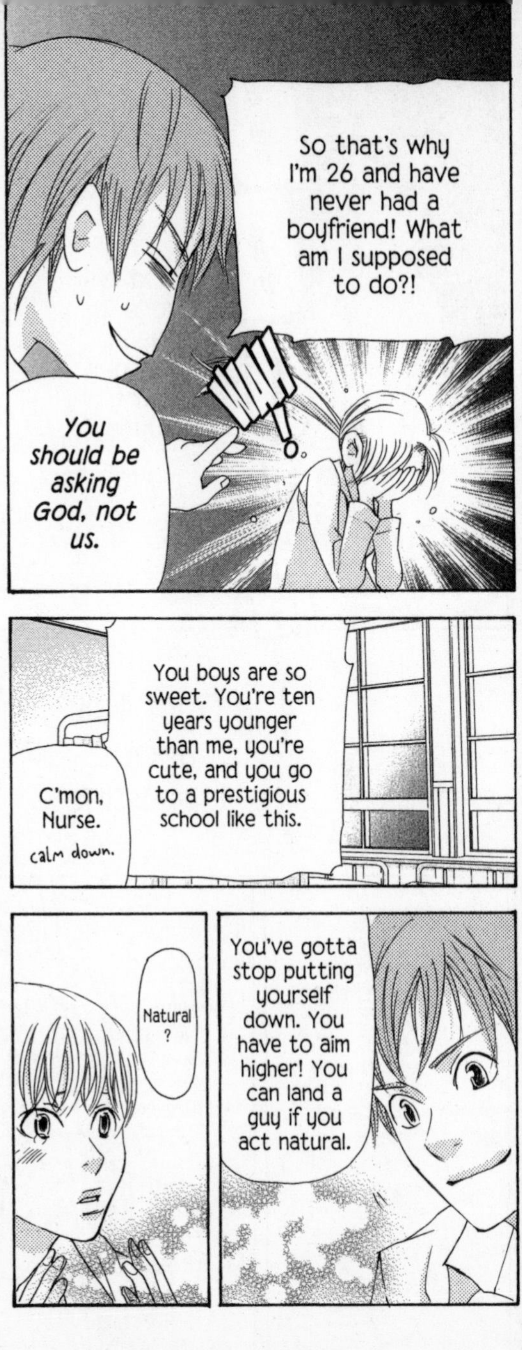

So that's why I'm 26 and have never had a boyfriend! What am I supposed to do?!
WAH!
You should be asking God, not us.
You boys are so sweet. You're ten years younger than me, you're cute, and you go to a prestigious school like this.
C'mon, Nurse.
calm down.
You've gotta stop putting yourself down. You have to aim higher! You can land a guy if you act natural.
Natural?

1/3
Half-Assed Space Filler

Introducing gifts I don't appreciate!

#2
From: Unknown
Frog Postcards

There's only one thing I want to say!

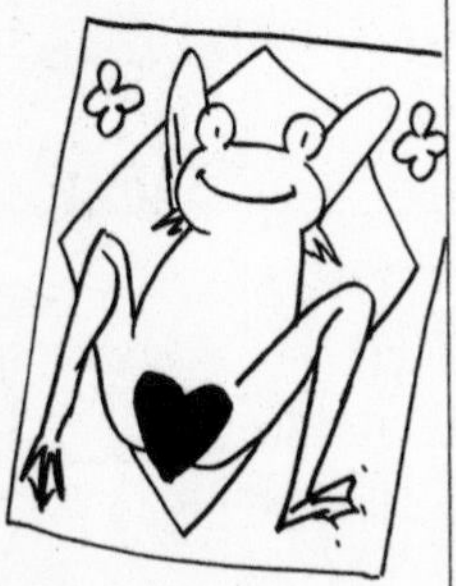

Do something about the heart on its crotch!

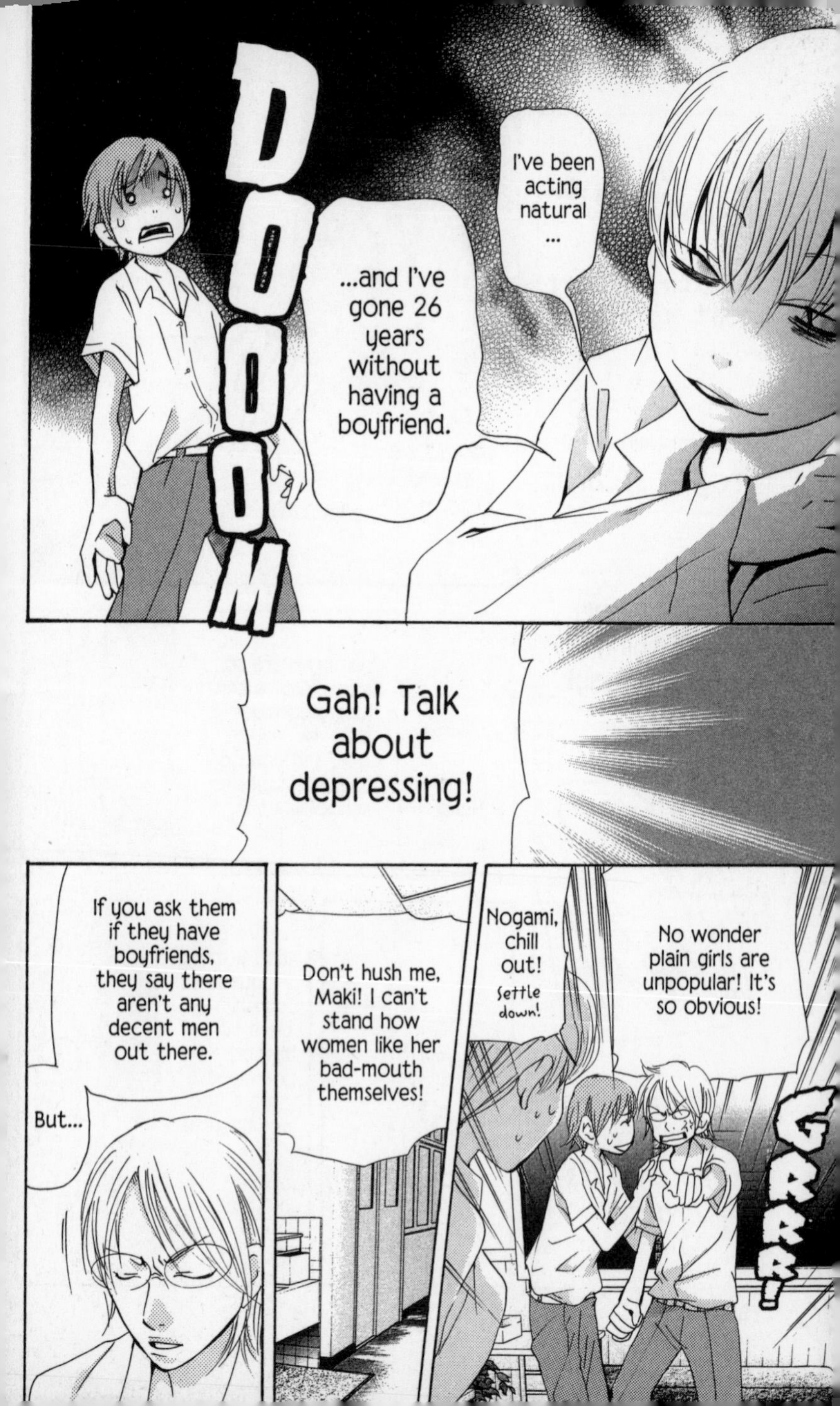
I've been acting natural ...
...and I've gone 26 years without having a boyfriend.
DOOOOM
Gah! Talk about depressing!
No wonder plain girls are unpopular! It's so obvious!
GRRR!
Nogami, chill out!
Settle down!
Don't hush me, Maki! I can't stand how women like her bad-mouth themselves!
If you ask them if they have boyfriends, they say there aren't any decent men out there.
But...

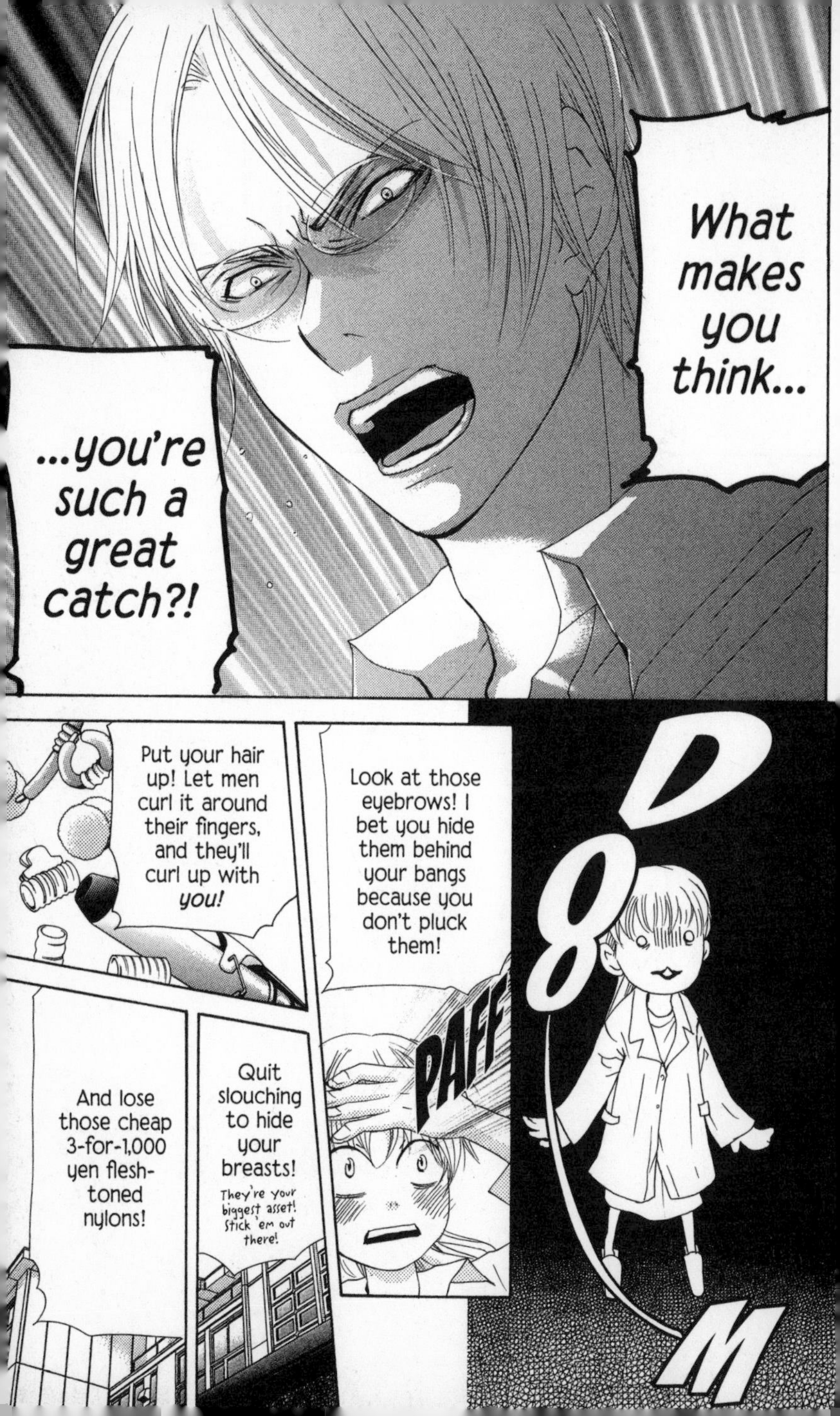

What makes you think...
...you're such a great catch?!
DOOM
Look at those eyebrows! I bet you hide them behind your bangs because you don't pluck them!
PAFF
Put your hair up! Let men curl it around their fingers, and they'll curl up with *you!*
Quit slouching to hide your breasts!
They're your biggest asset! Stick 'em out there!
And lose those cheap 3-for-1,000 yen flesh-toned nylons!

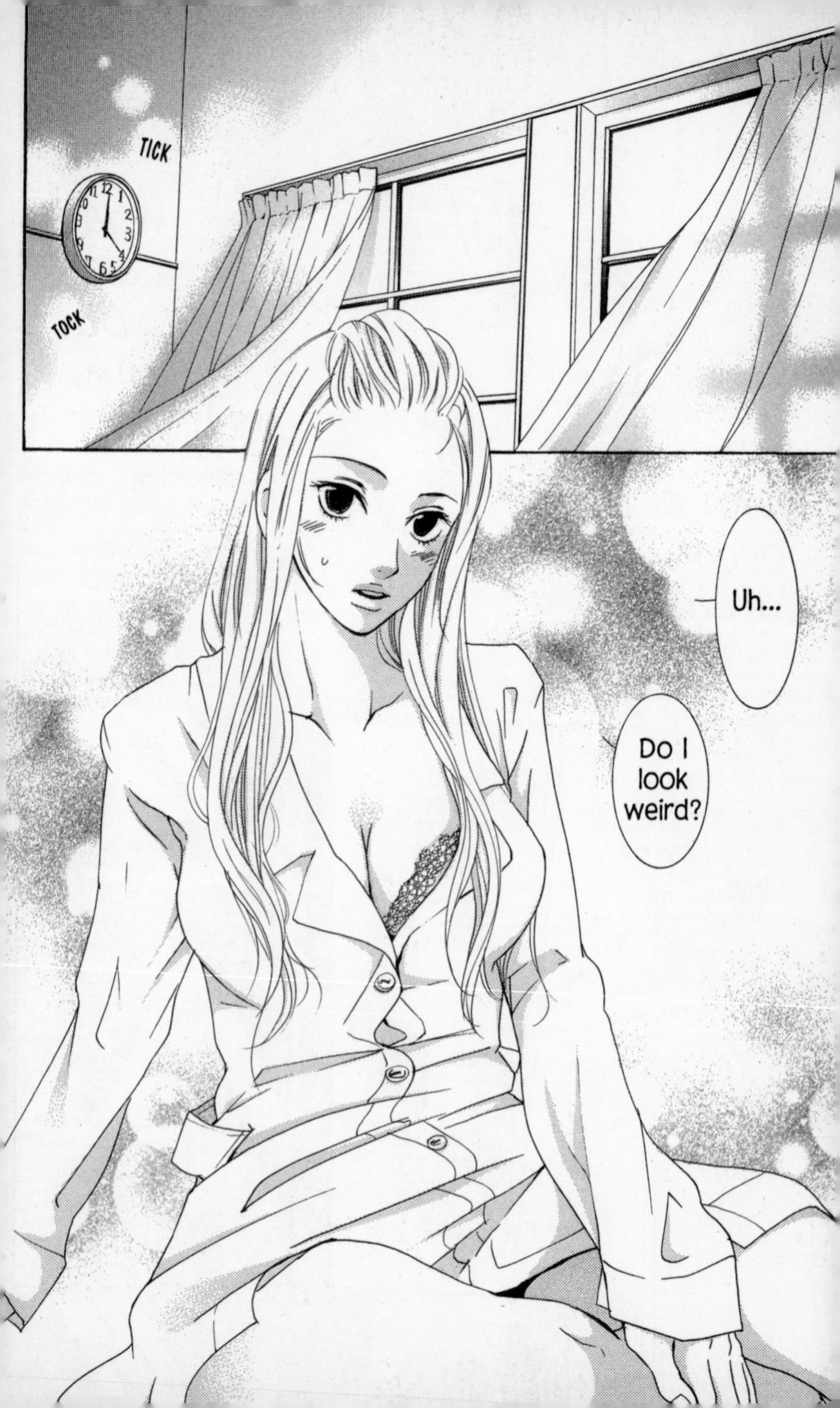
TICK
TOCK
Uh...
Do I look weird?

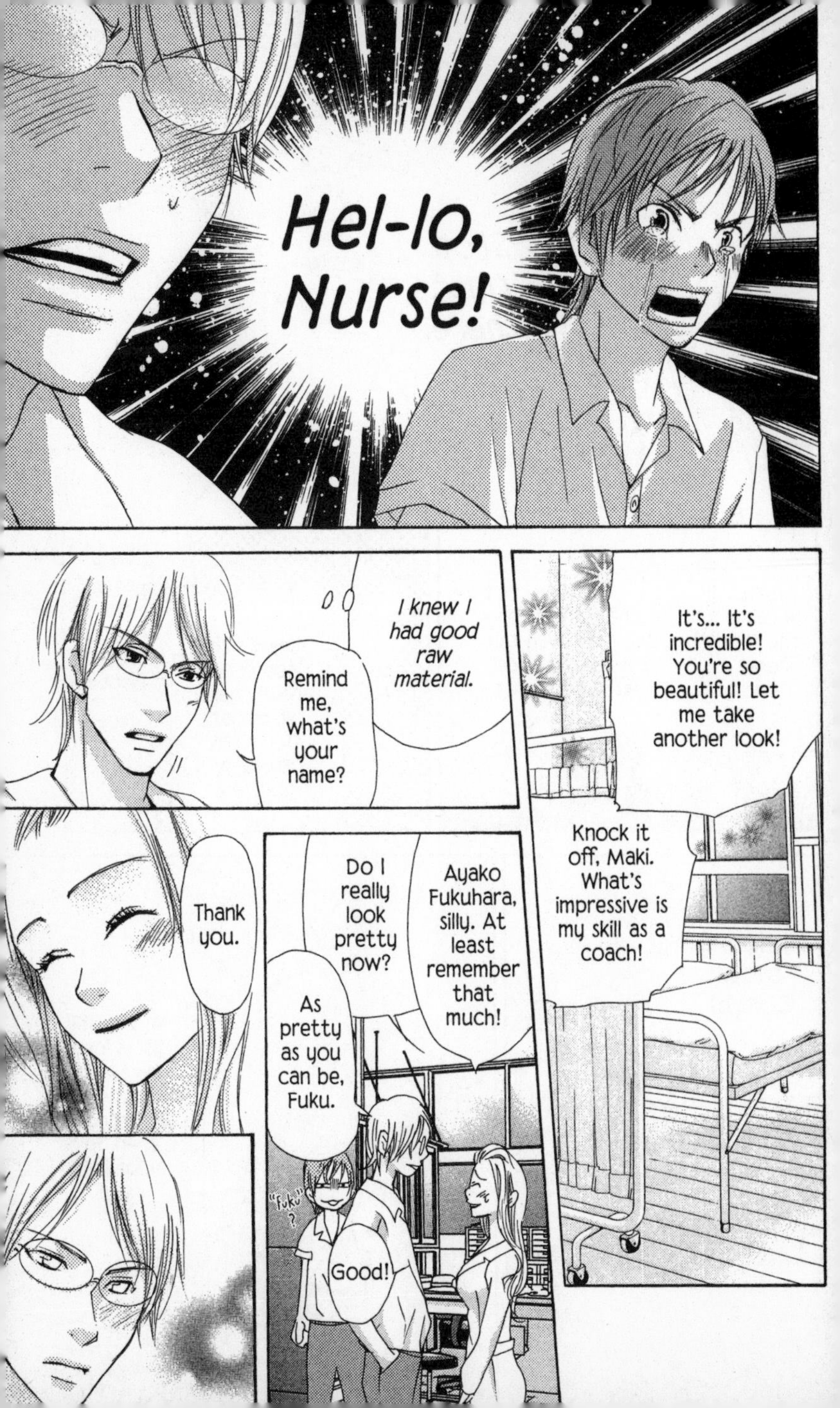
Hel-lo, Nurse!
It's... It's incredible! You're so beautiful! Let me take another look!
Knock it off, Maki. What's impressive is my skill as a coach!
I knew I had good raw material.
Remind me, what's your name?
Ayako Fukuhara, silly. At least remember that much!
Do I really look pretty now?
As pretty as you can be, Fuku.
"Fuku"?
Good!
Thank you.

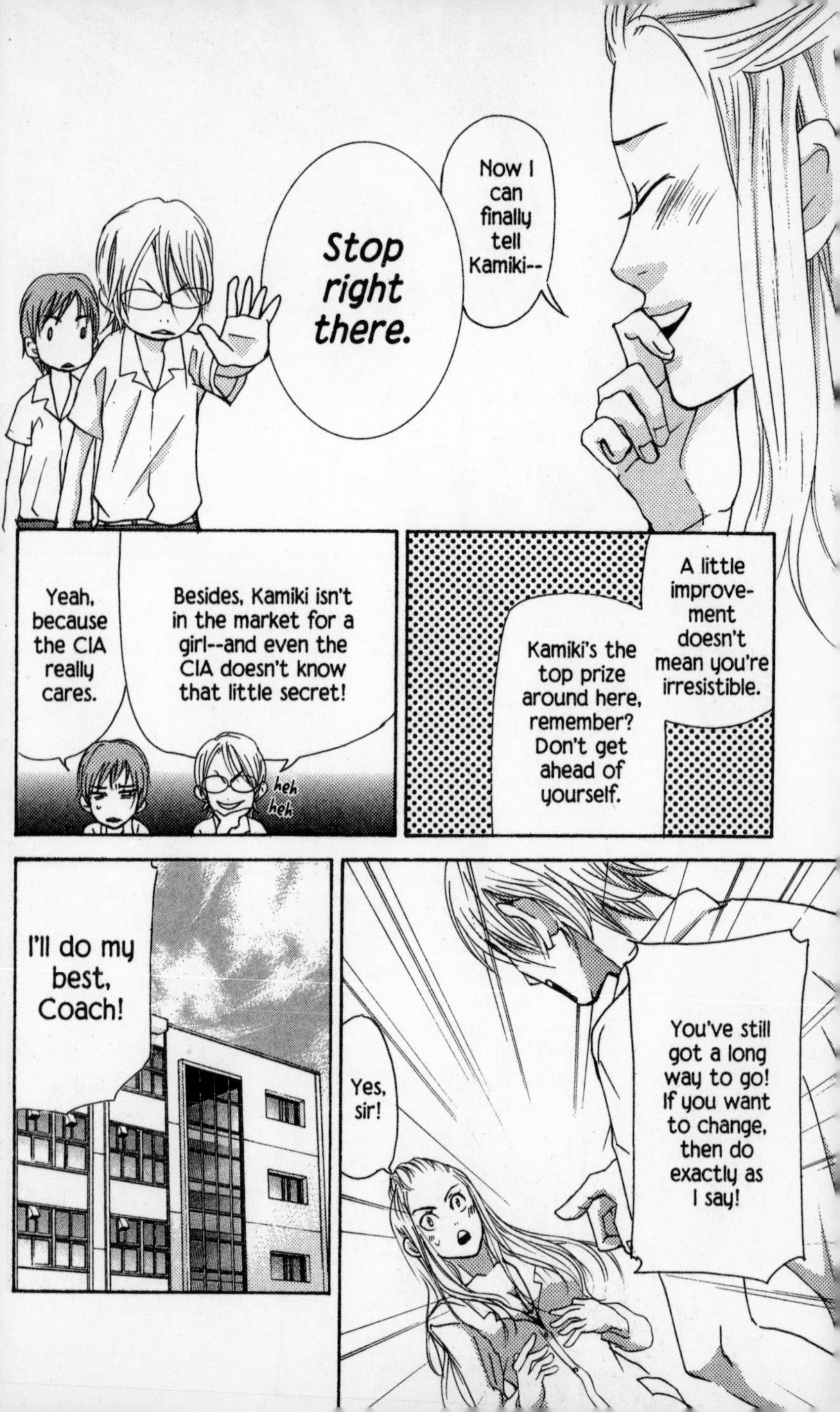
Now I can finally tell Kamiki--
Stop right there.
A little improvement doesn't mean you're irresistible.
Kamiki's the top prize around here, remember? Don't get ahead of yourself.
Besides, Kamiki isn't in the market for a girl--and even the CIA doesn't know that little secret!
Yeah, because the CIA really cares.
heh heh
You've still got a long way to go! If you want to change, then do exactly as I say!
Yes, sir!
I'll do my best, Coach!

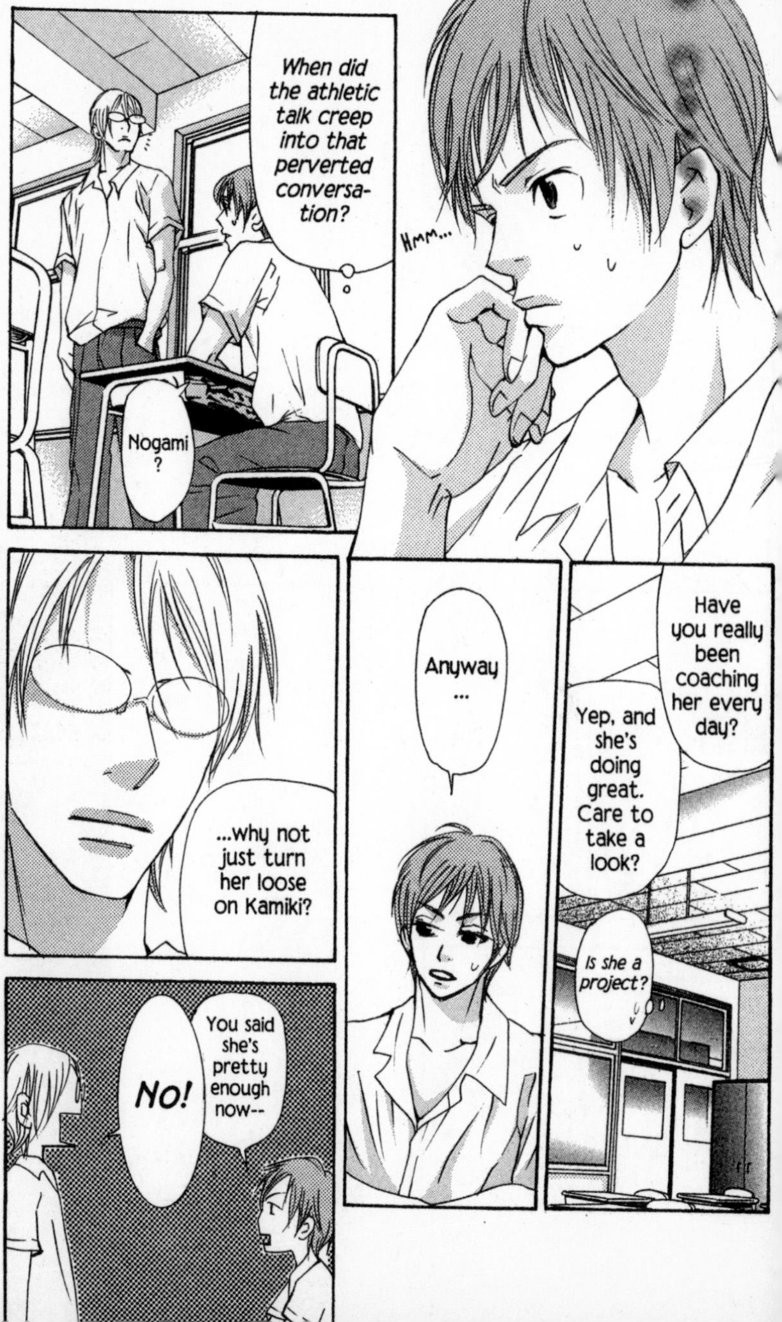
Hmm...
When did the athletic talk creep into that perverted conversation?
Nogami?
Have you really been coaching her every day?
Yep, and she's doing great. Care to take a look?
Is she a project?
Anyway...
...why not just turn her loose on Kamiki?
You said she's pretty enough now--
No!

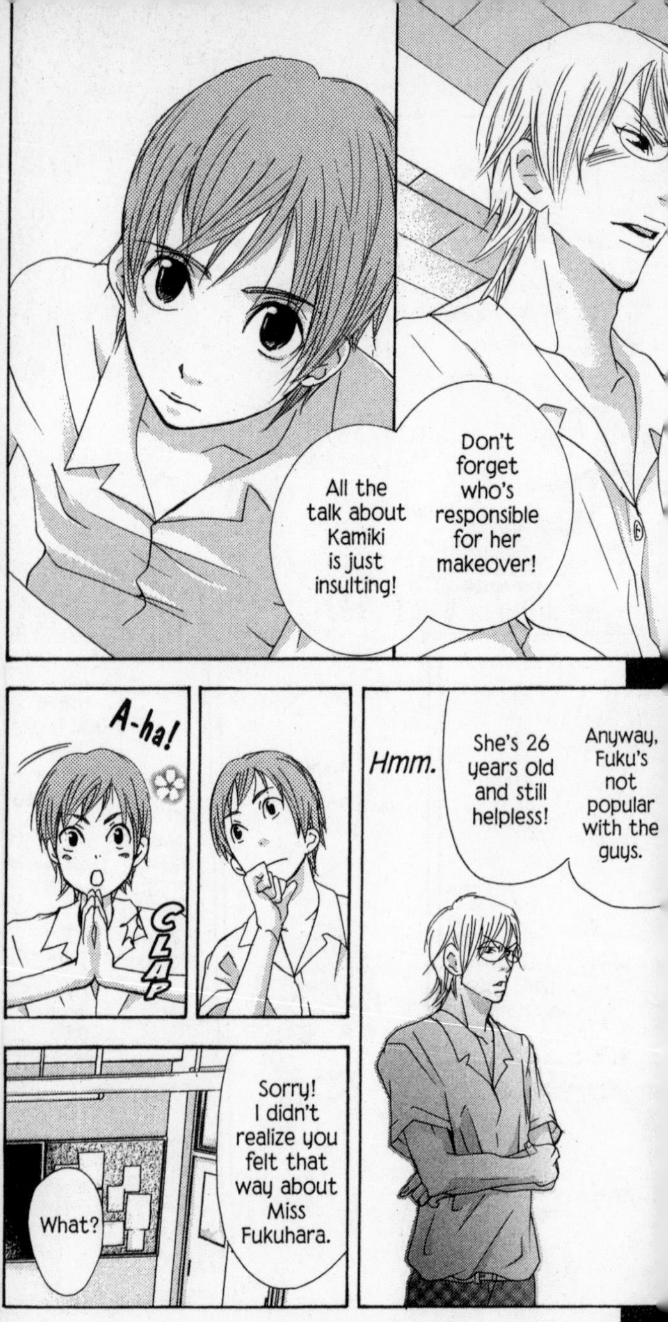
Don't forget who's responsible for her makeover!
All the talk about Kamiki is just insulting!
Anyway, Fuku's not popular with the guys.
She's 26 years old and still helpless!
Hmm.
A-ha!
CLAP
Sorry! I didn't realize you felt that way about Miss Fukuhara.
What?

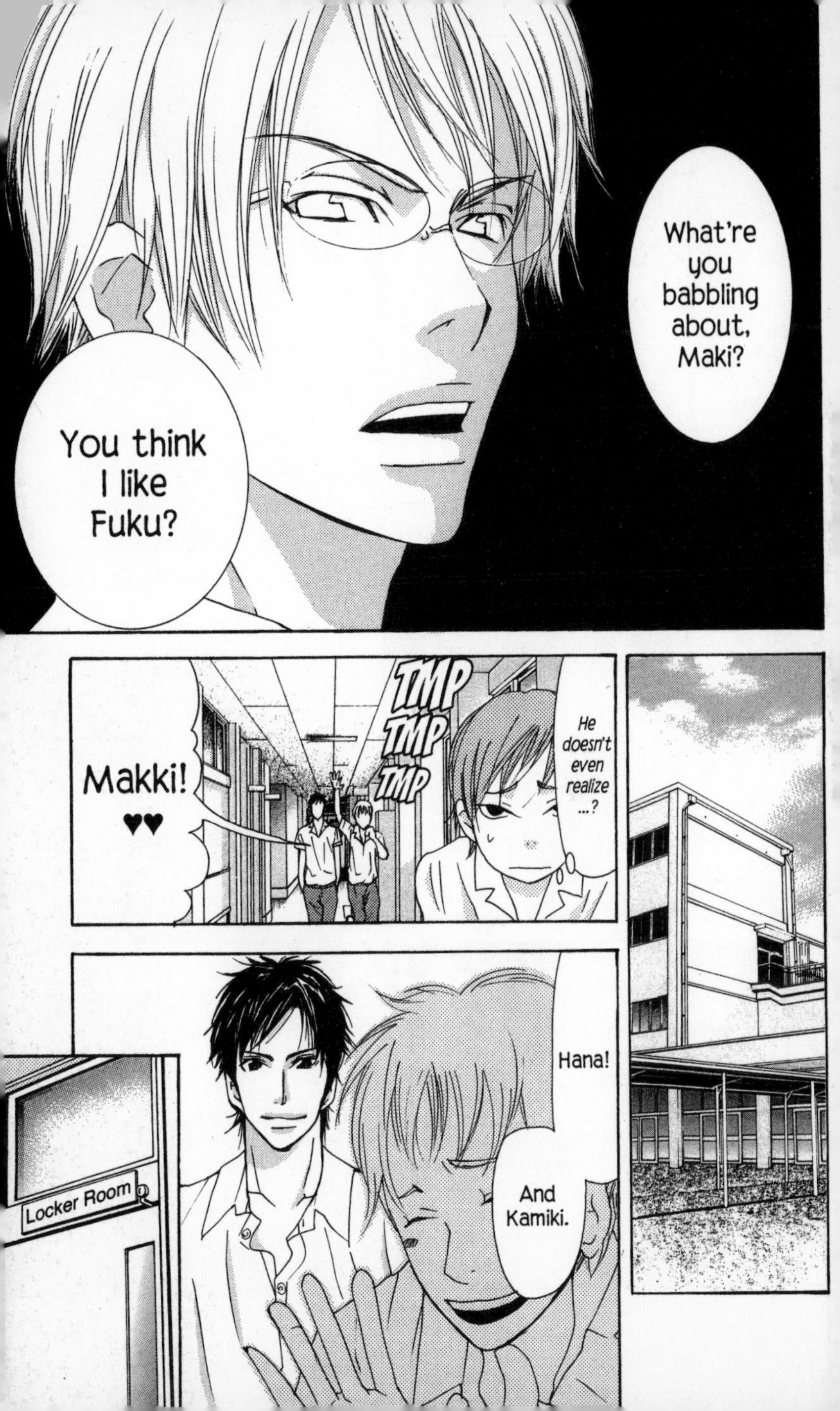
What're you babbling about, Maki?
You think I like Fuku?
He doesn't even realize ...?
TMP TMP TMP
Makki! ♥♥
Hana!
And Kamiki.
Locker Room

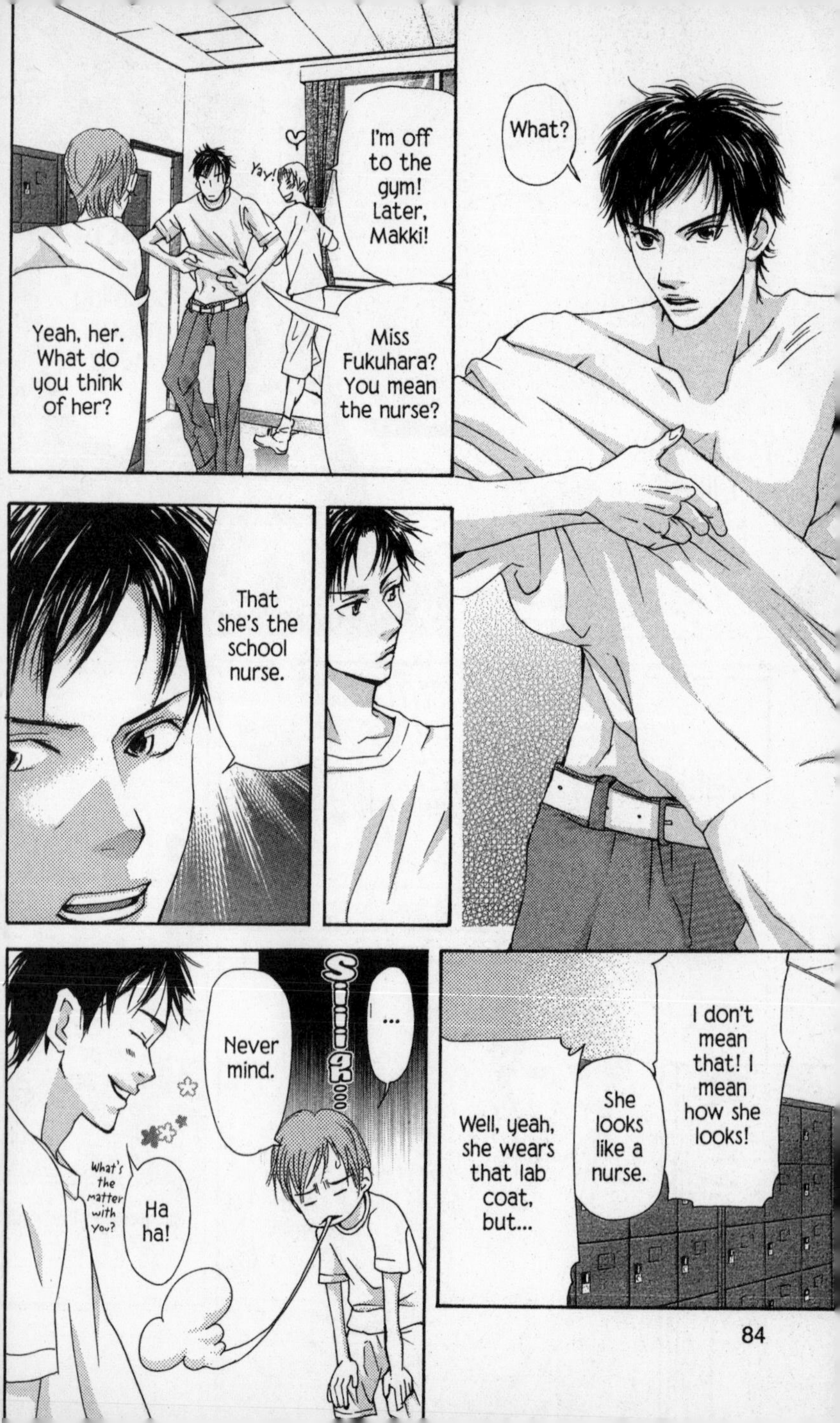
I'm off to the gym! Later, Makki!
Yay!
Miss Fukuhara? You mean the nurse?
Yeah, her. What do you think of her?
What?
That she's the school nurse.
I don't mean that! I mean how she looks!
She looks like a nurse.
Well, yeah, she wears that lab coat, but...
...
Never mind.
Siiiigh...
Ha ha!
What's the matter with you?

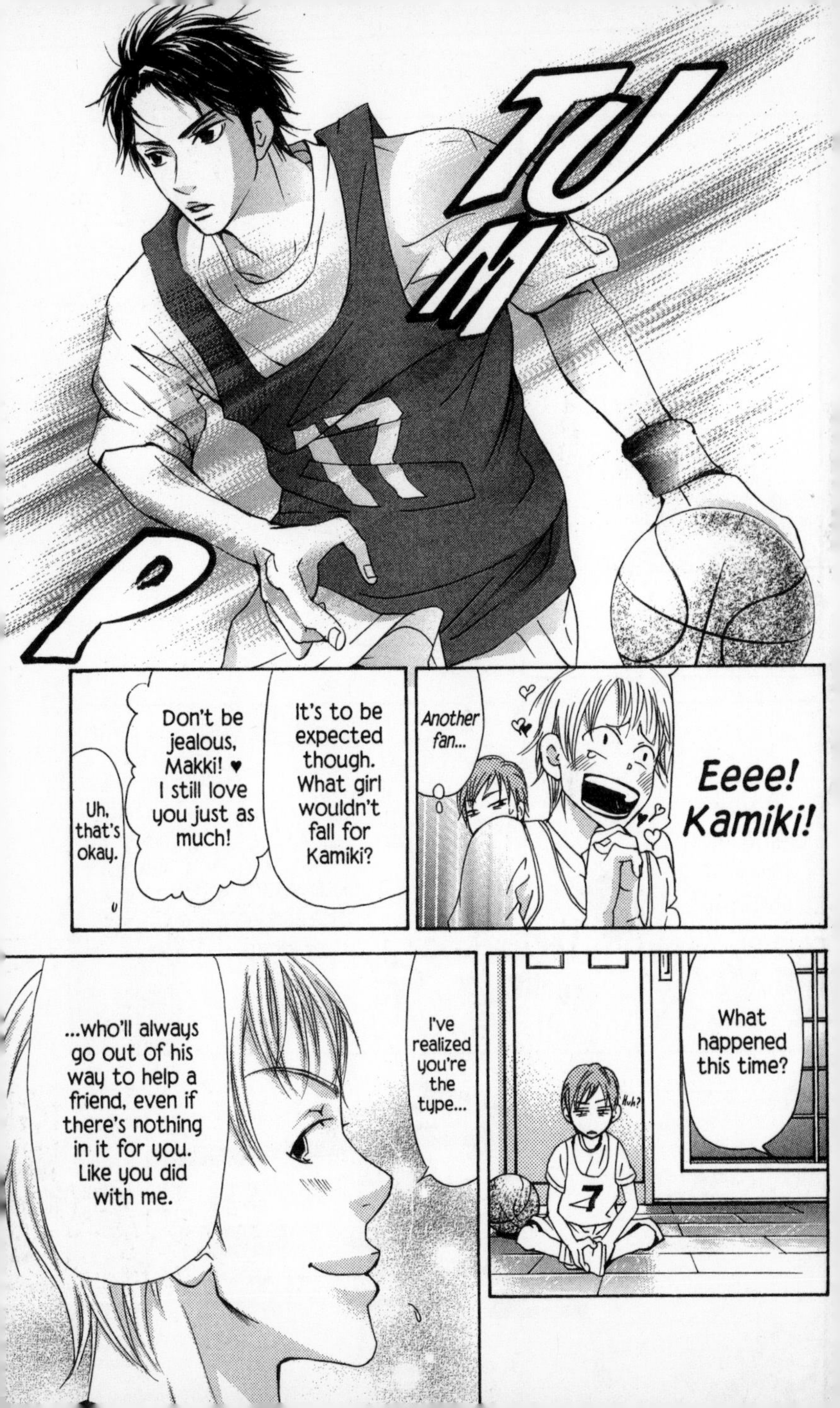
Eeee! Kamiki!
Another fan...
It's to be expected though. What girl wouldn't fall for Kamiki?
Don't be jealous, Makki! ♥ I still love you just as much!
Uh, that's okay.
What happened this time?
Huh?
I've realized you're the type...
...who'll always go out of his way to help a friend, even if there's nothing in it for you. Like you did with me.

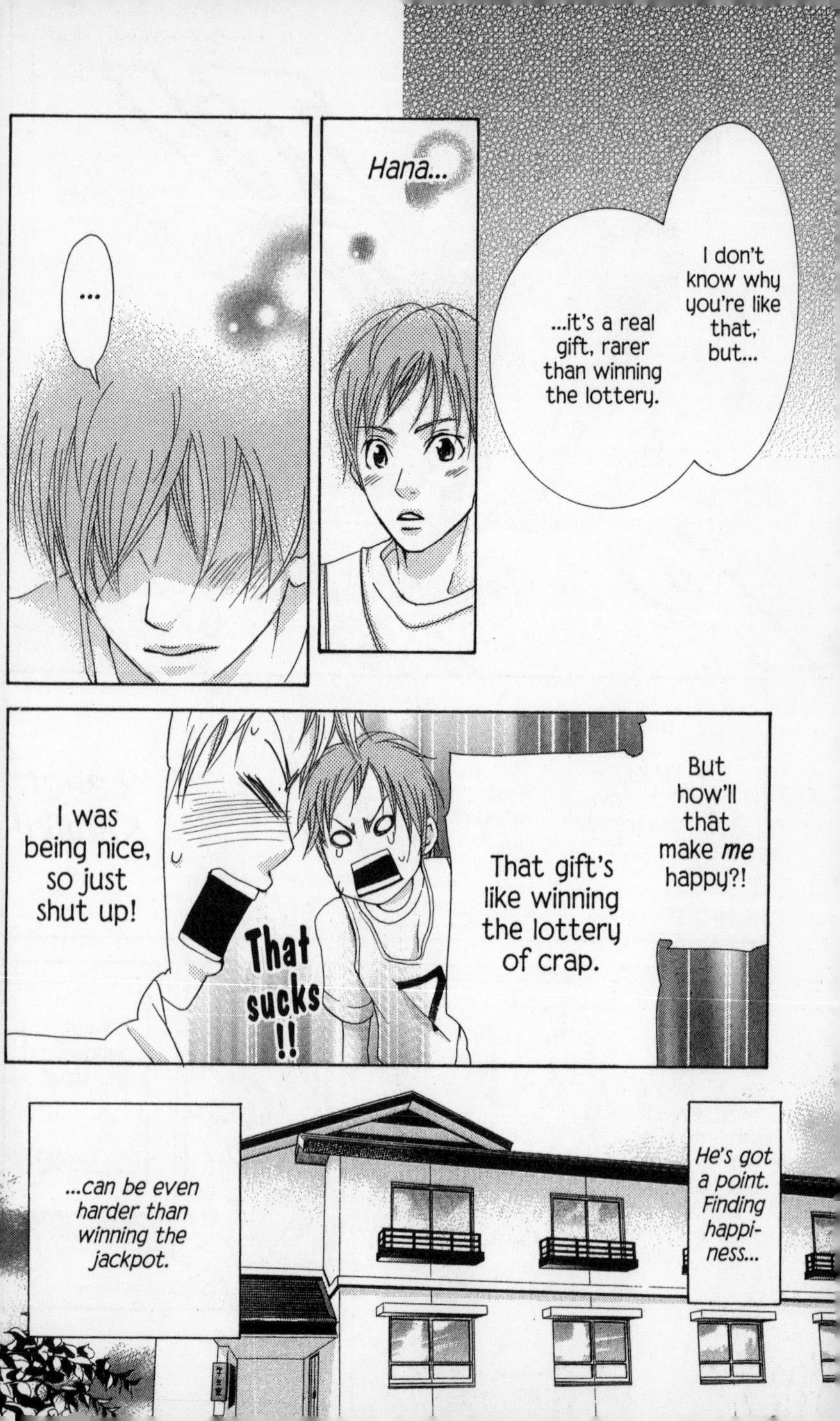
I don't know why you're like that, but...
...it's a real gift, rarer than winning the lottery.
Hana...
...
But how'll that make *me* happy?!
That gift's like winning the lottery of crap.
That sucks!!
I was being nice, so just shut up!
He's got a point. Finding happi-ness...
...can be even harder than winning the jackpot.

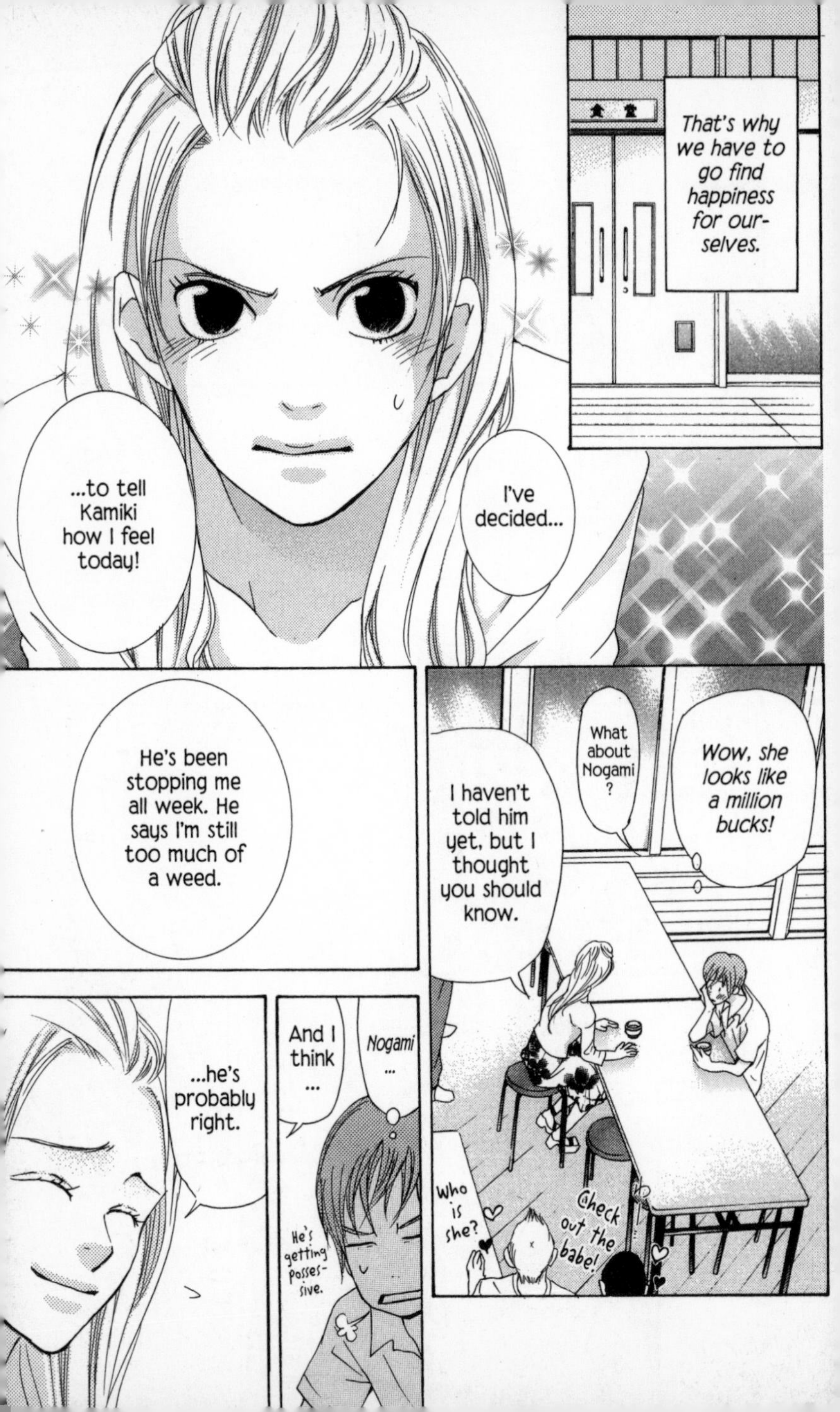
食堂
That's why we have to go find happiness for our-selves.
I've decided...
...to tell Kamiki how I feel today!
Wow, she looks like a million bucks!
What about Nogami?
I haven't told him yet, but I thought you should know.
Check out the babe!
Who is she?
He's been stopping me all week. He says I'm still too much of a weed.
Nogami...
And I think...
He's getting posses-sive.
...he's probably right.

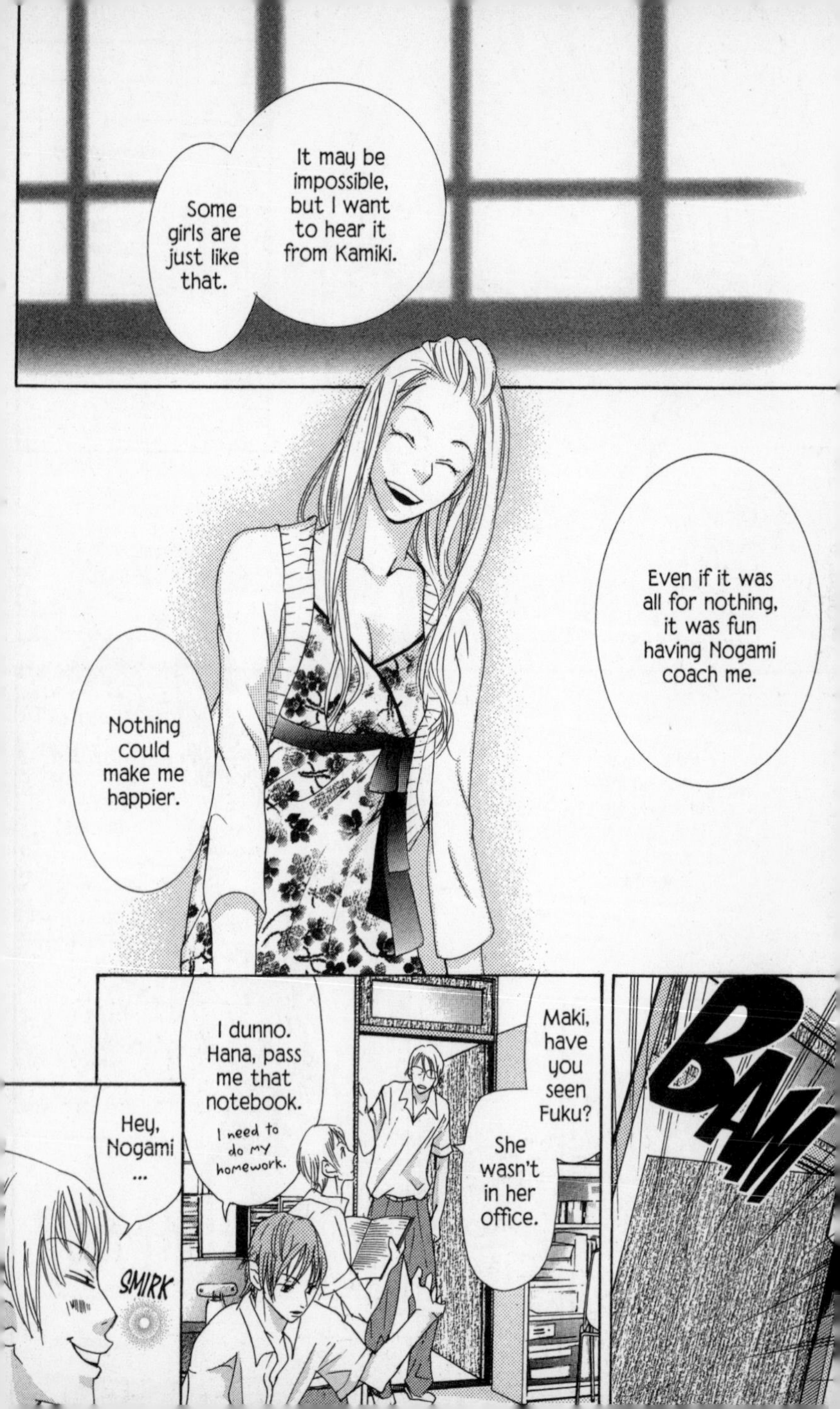
It may be impossible, but I want to hear it from Kamiki.
Some girls are just like that.
Even if it was all for nothing, it was fun having Nogami coach me.
Nothing could make me happier.
BAM
Maki, have you seen Fuku?
She wasn't in her office.
I dunno. Hana, pass me that notebook.
I need to do my homework.
Hey, Nogami ...
SMIRK

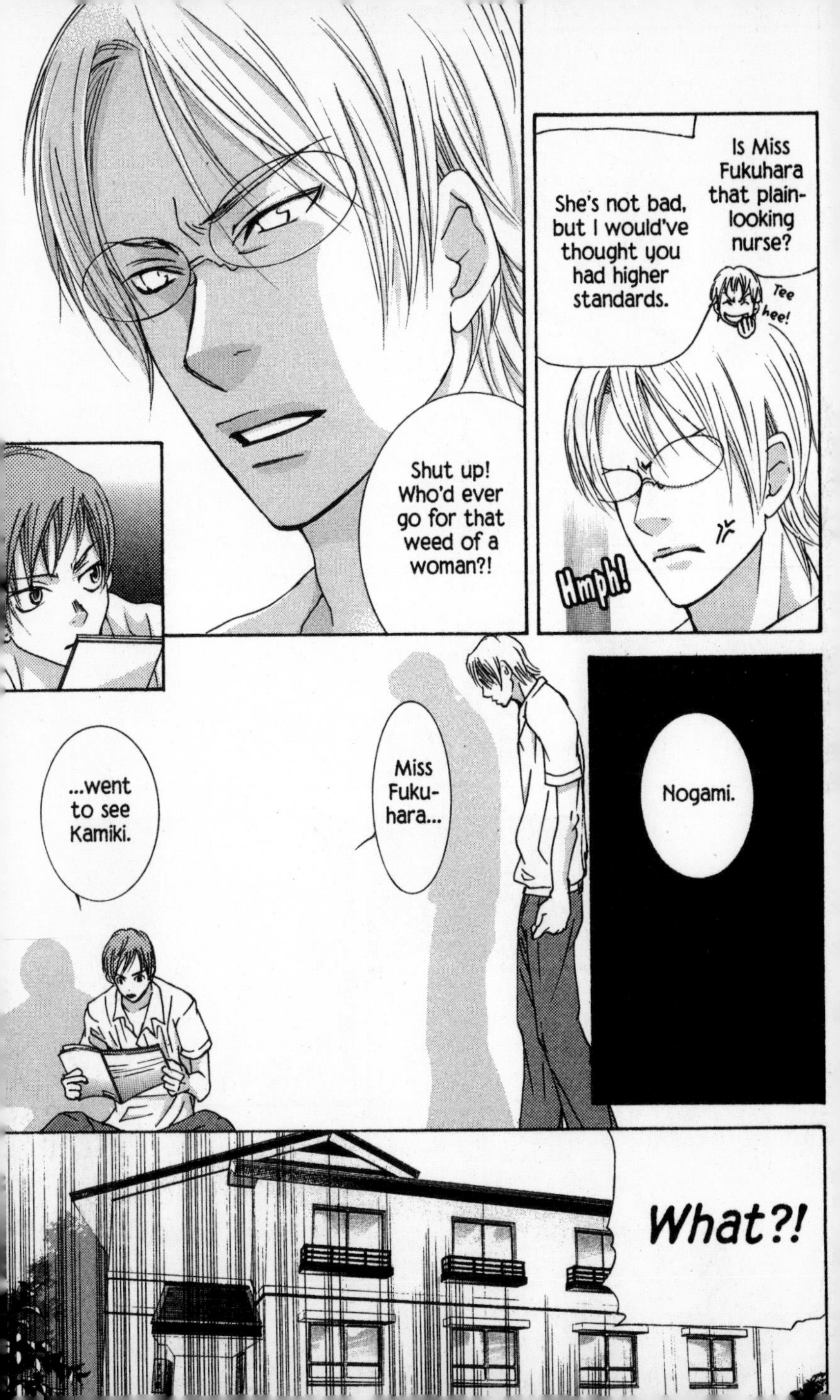
Is Miss Fukuhara that plain-looking nurse?
She's not bad, but I would've thought you had higher standards.
Tee hee!
Hmph!
Shut up! Who'd ever go for that weed of a woman?!
Nogami.
Miss Fuku-hara...
...went to see Kamiki.
What?!

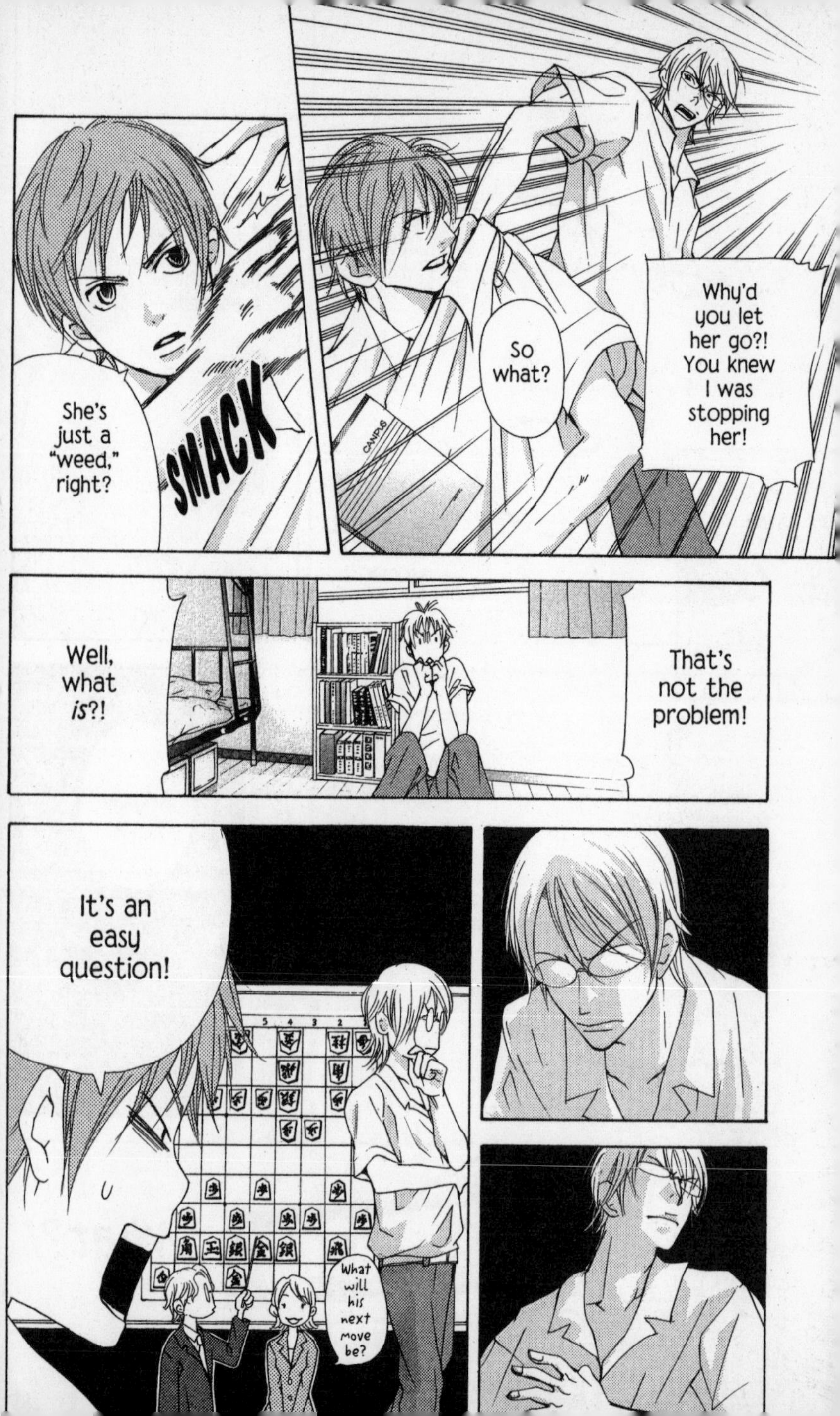
Why'd you let her go?! You knew I was stopping her!
So what?
She's just a "weed," right?
SMACK
That's not the problem!
Well, what is?!
It's an easy question!
What will his next move be?

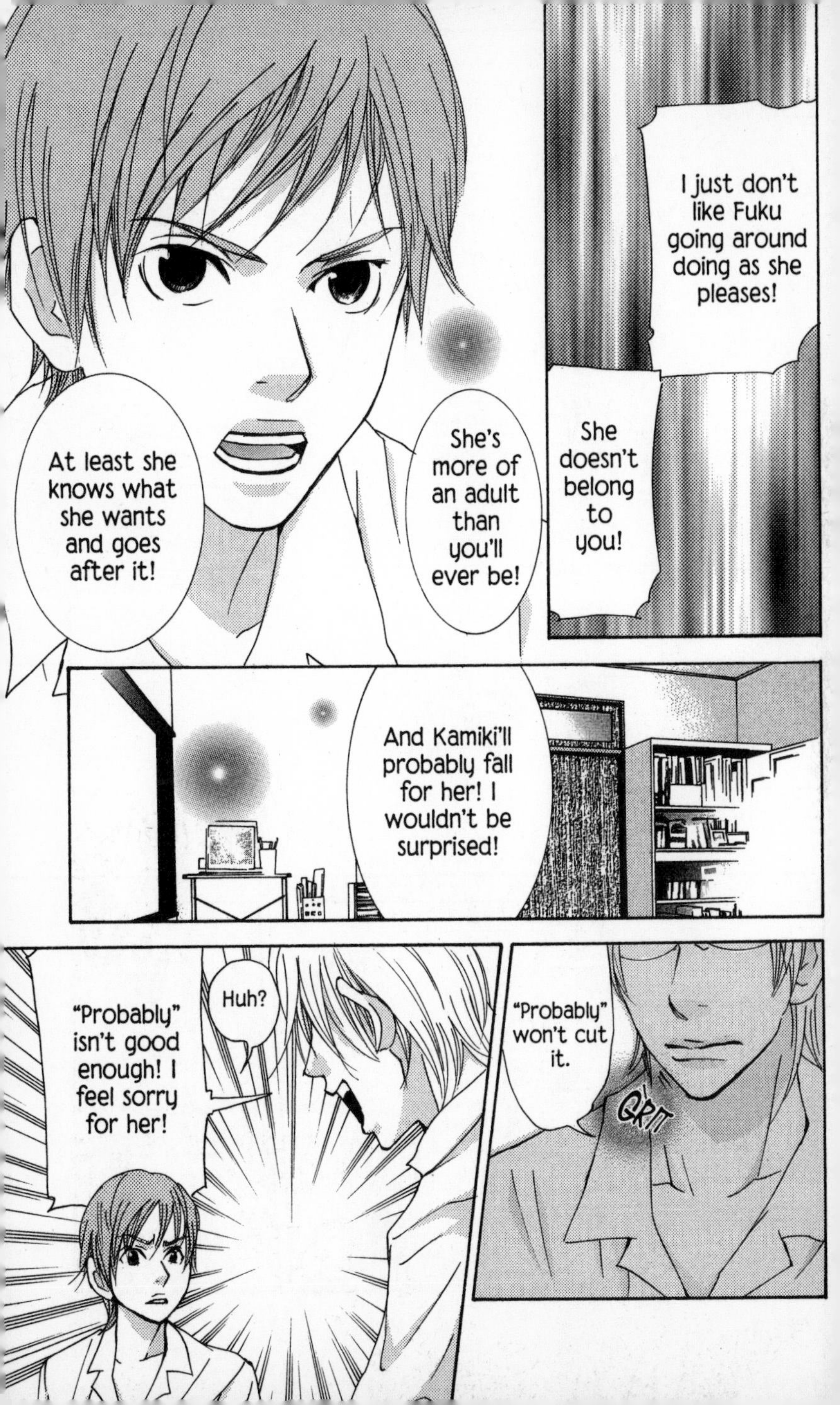
I just don't like Fuku going around doing as she pleases!
She doesn't belong to you!
She's more of an adult than you'll ever be!
At least she knows what she wants and goes after it!
And Kamiki'll probably fall for her! I wouldn't be surprised!
"Probably" won't cut it.
GRIT
Huh?
"Probably" isn't good enough! I feel sorry for her!

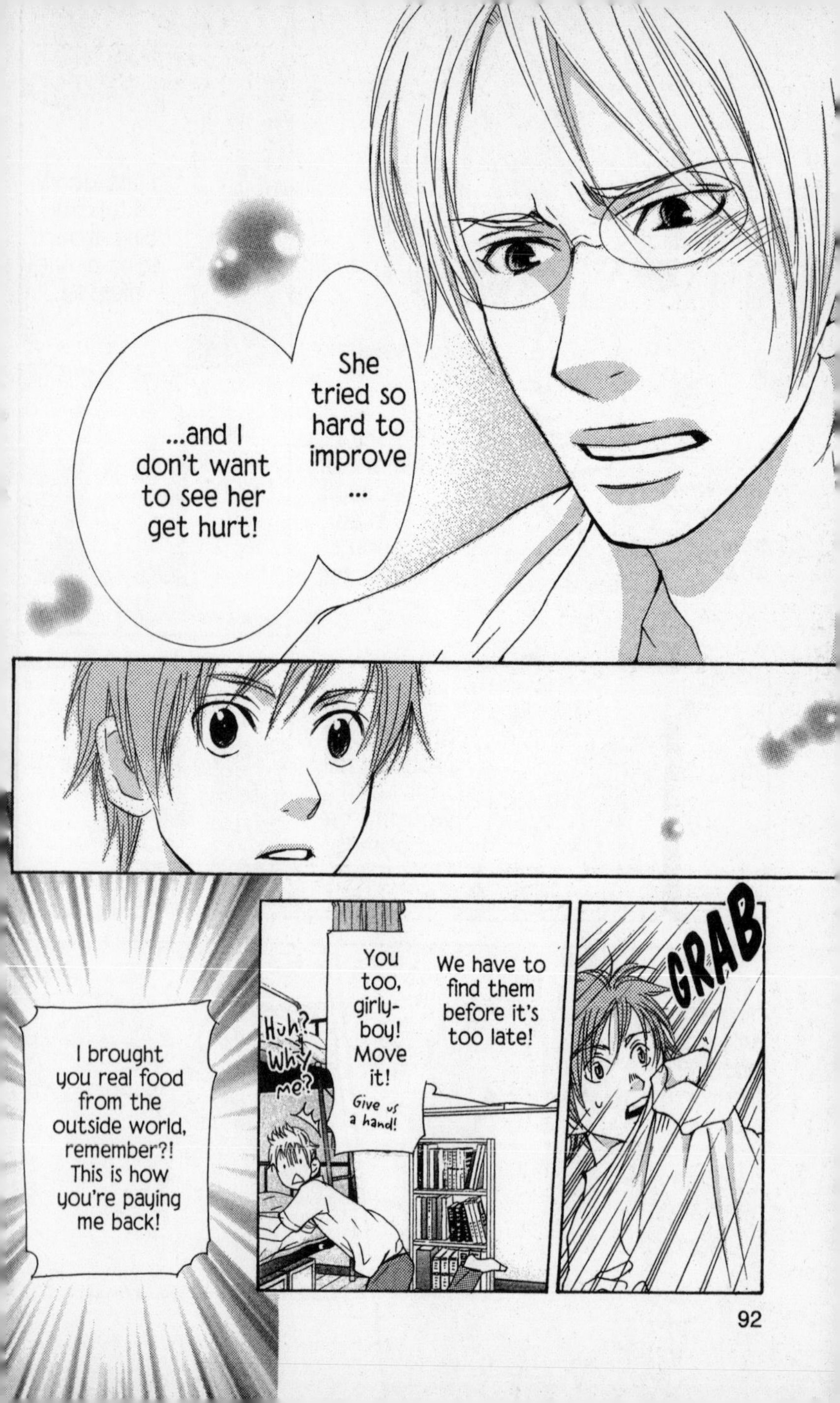
She tried so hard to improve...
...and I don't want to see her get hurt!
GRAB
We have to find them before it's too late!
You too, girly-boy! Move it!
Give us a hand!
Huh?! Why me?
I brought you real food from the outside world, remember?! This is how you're paying me back!

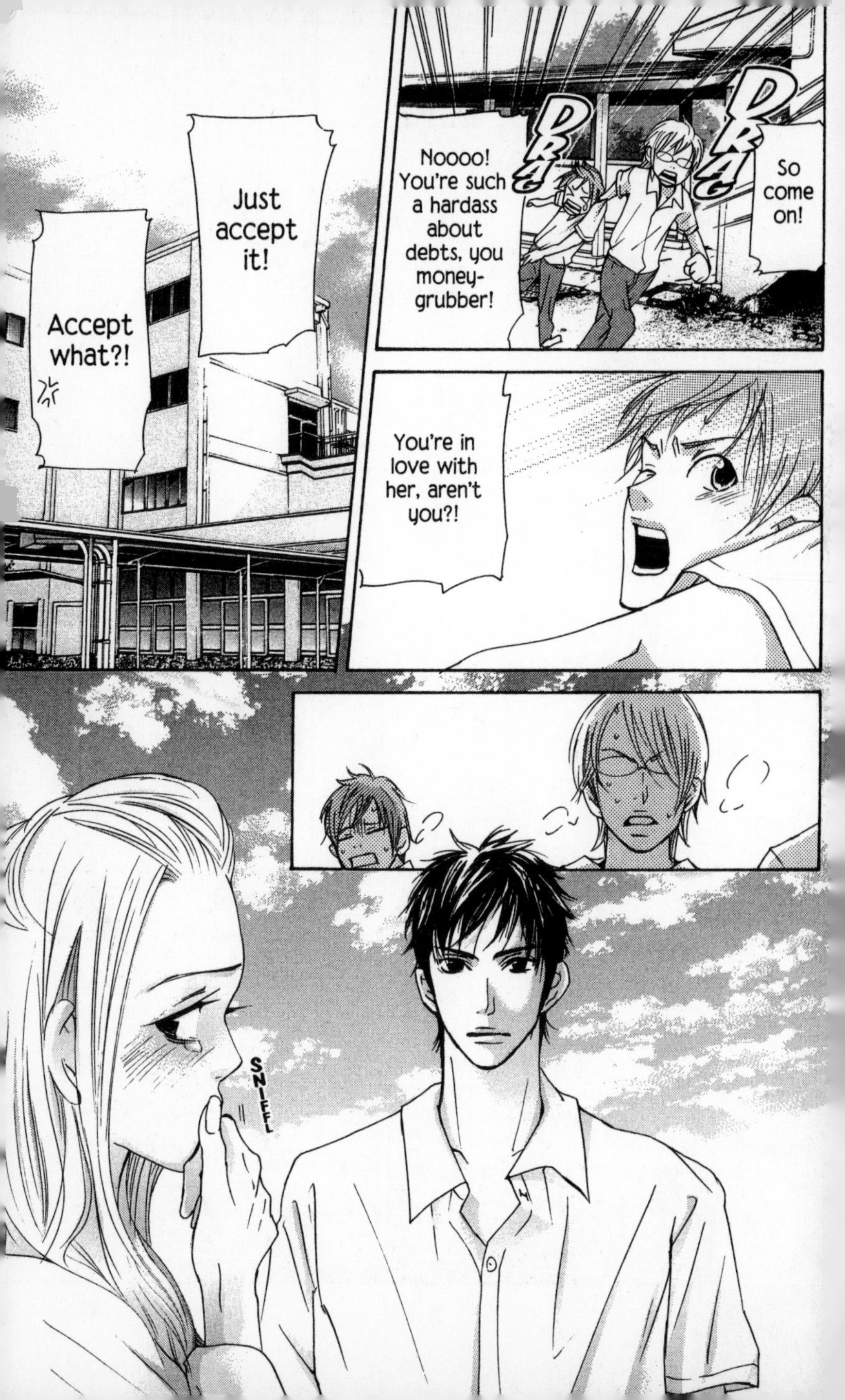
DRAG
DRAG
So come on!
Noooo! You're such a hardass about debts, you money-grubber!
You're in love with her, aren't you?!
Just accept it!
Accept what?!
SNIFF

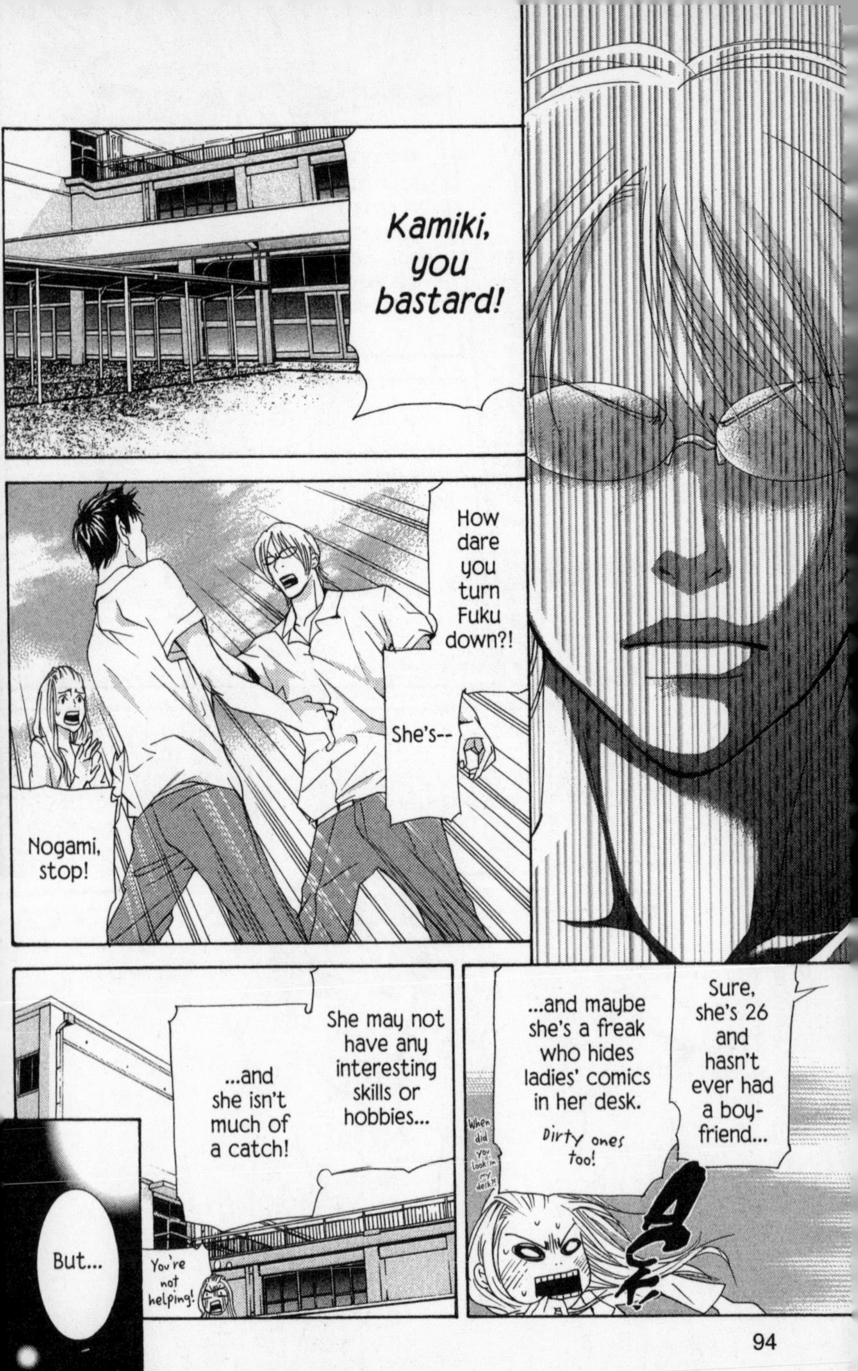

Kamiki, you bastard!
How dare you turn Fuku down?!
She's--
Nogami, stop!
Sure, she's 26 and hasn't ever had a boy-friend...
...and maybe she's a freak who hides ladies' comics in her desk.
Dirty ones too!
When did you look in my desk?!
ACK!
She may not have any interesting skills or hobbies...
...and she isn't much of a catch!
You're not helping!
But...

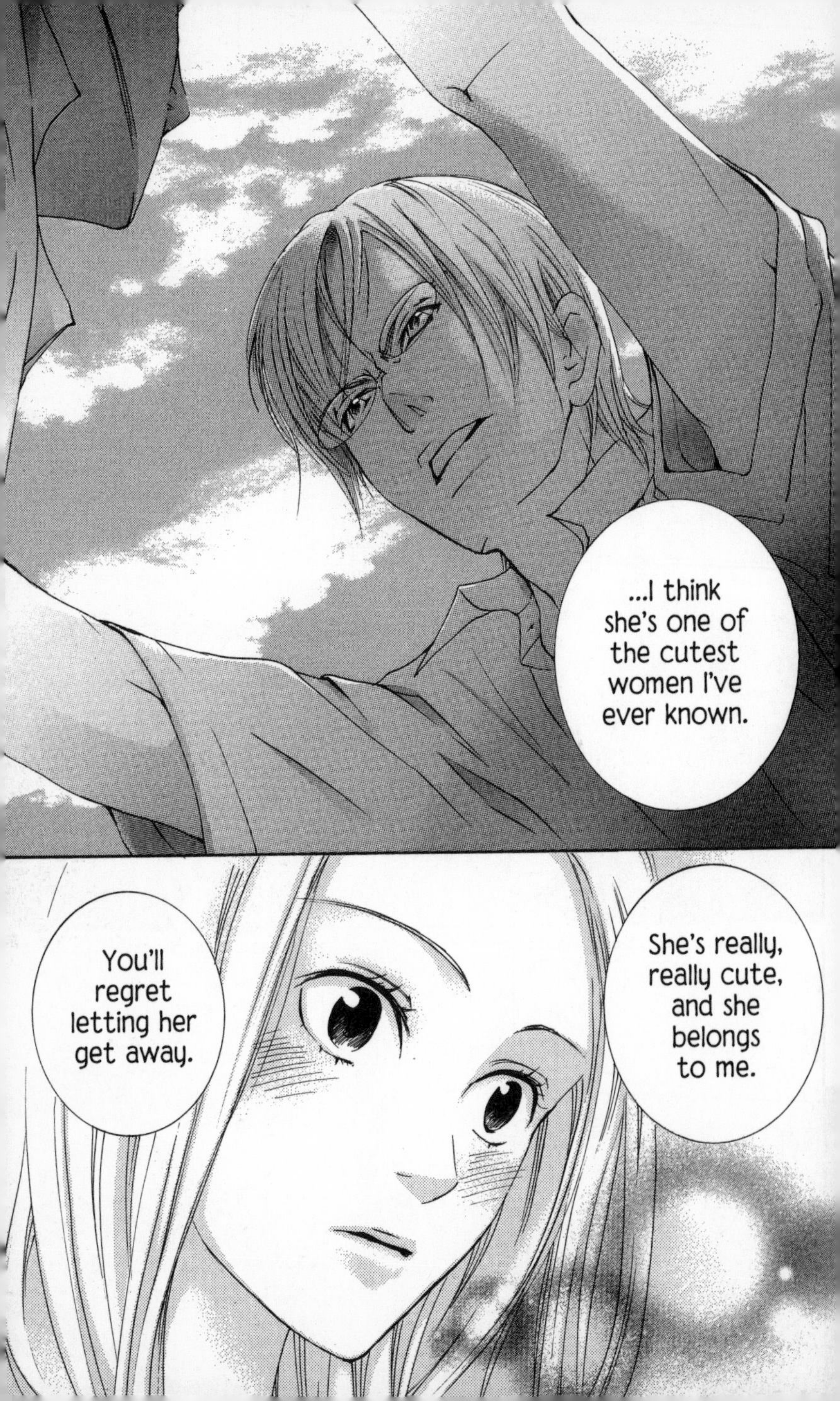
...I think she's one of the cutest women I've ever known.
She's really, really cute, and she belongs to me.
You'll regret letting her get away.

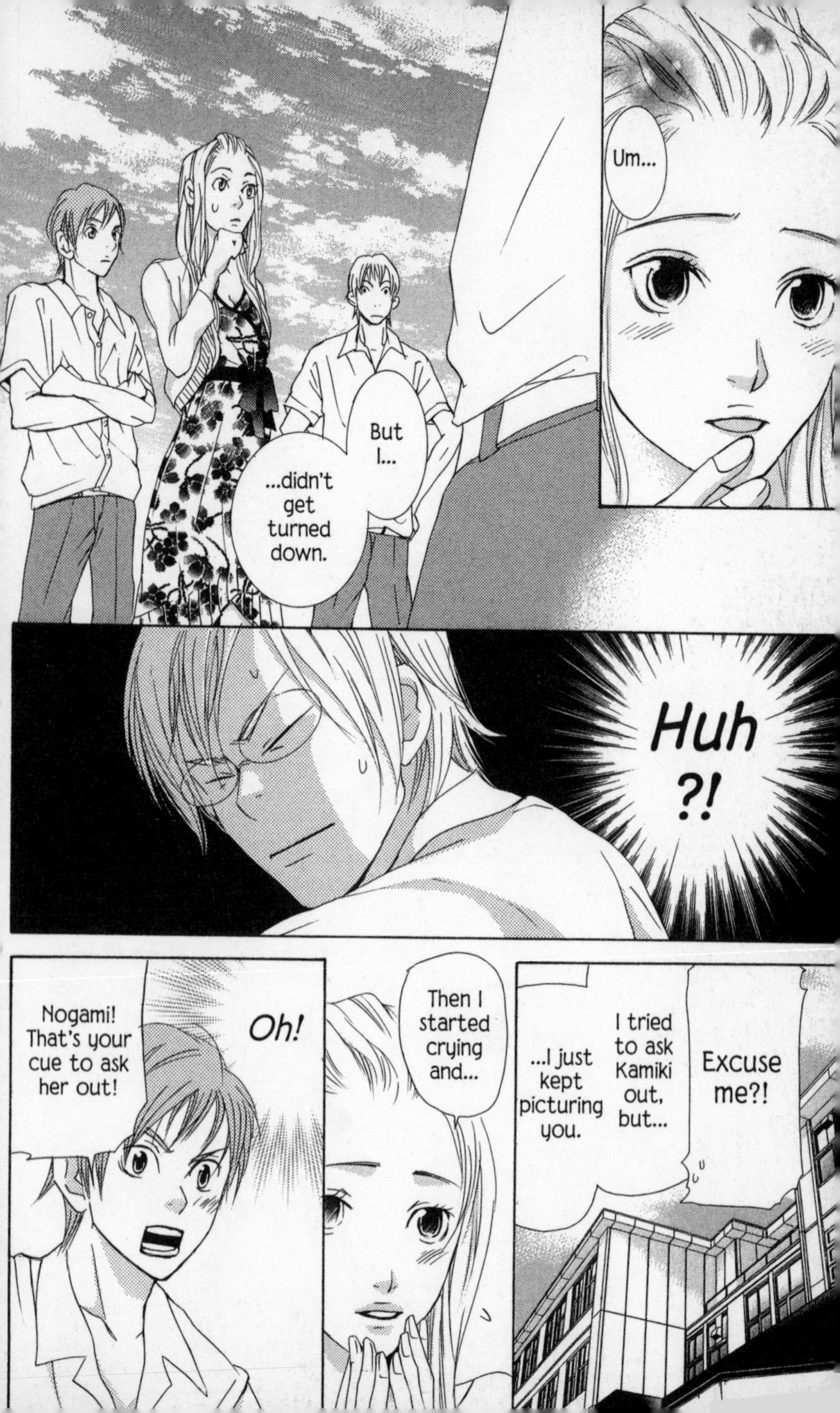
Um...
But I...
...didn't get turned down.
Huh ?!
Excuse me?!
I tried to ask Kamiki out, but...
...I just kept picturing you.
Then I started crying and...
Oh!
Nogami! That's your cue to ask her out!

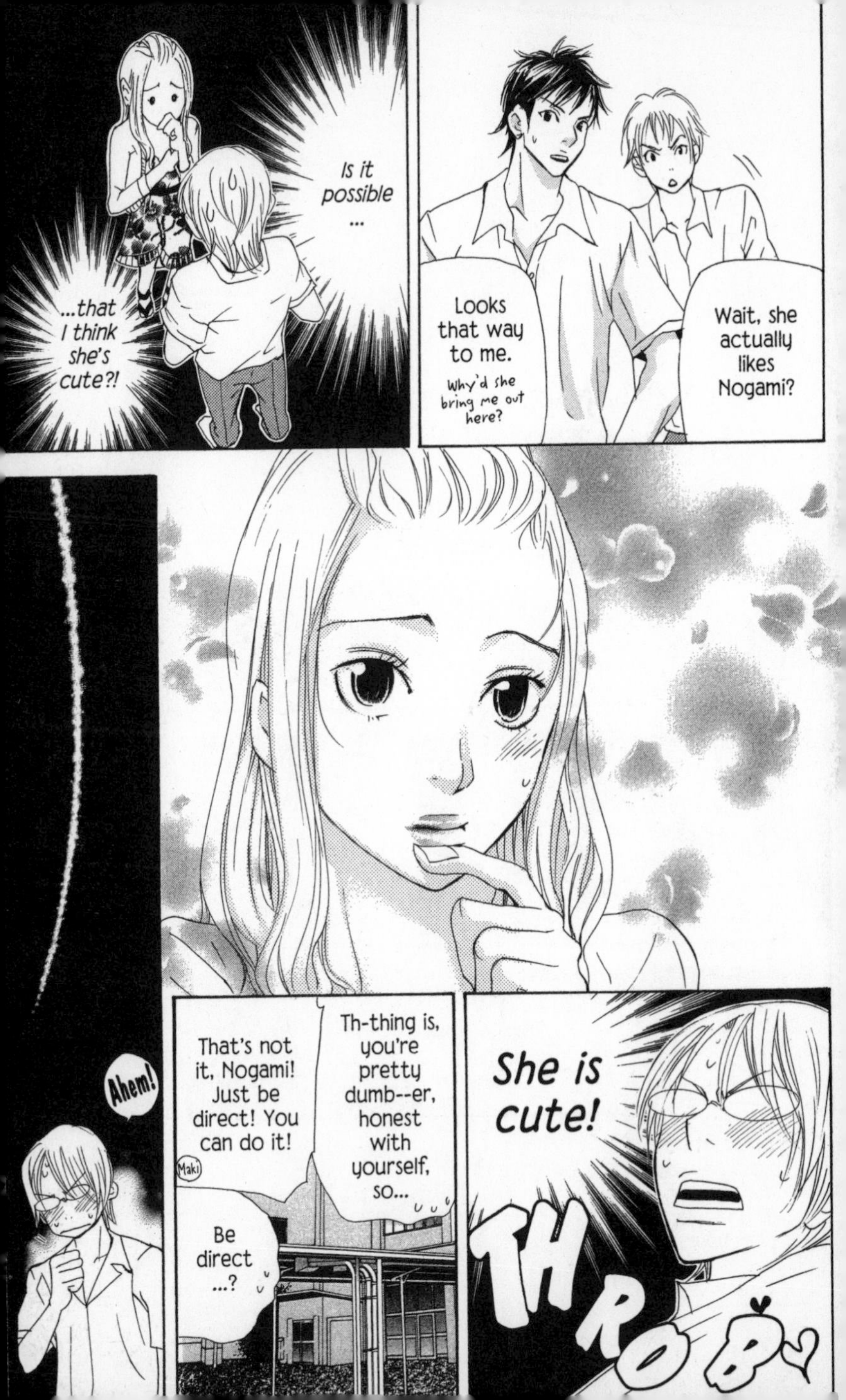
Wait, she actually likes Nogami?
Looks that way to me.
Why'd she bring me out here?
Is it possible ...
...that I think she's cute?!
She is cute!
THROB
Th-thing is, you're pretty dumb--er, honest with yourself, so...
That's not it, Nogami! Just be direct! You can do it!
Maki
Be direct ...?
Ahem!

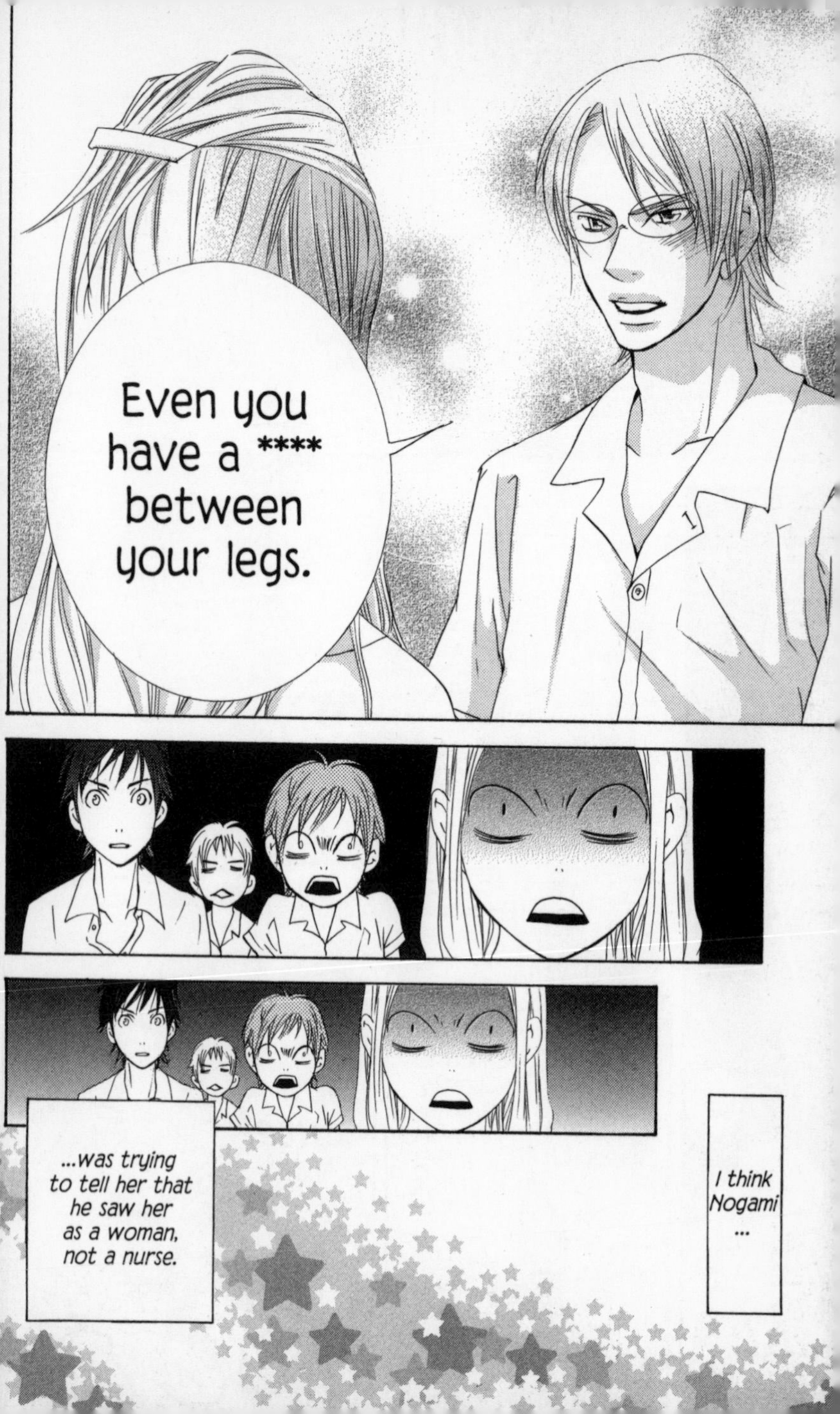
Even you have a **** between your legs.
I think Nogami ...
...was trying to tell her that he saw her as a woman, not a nurse.

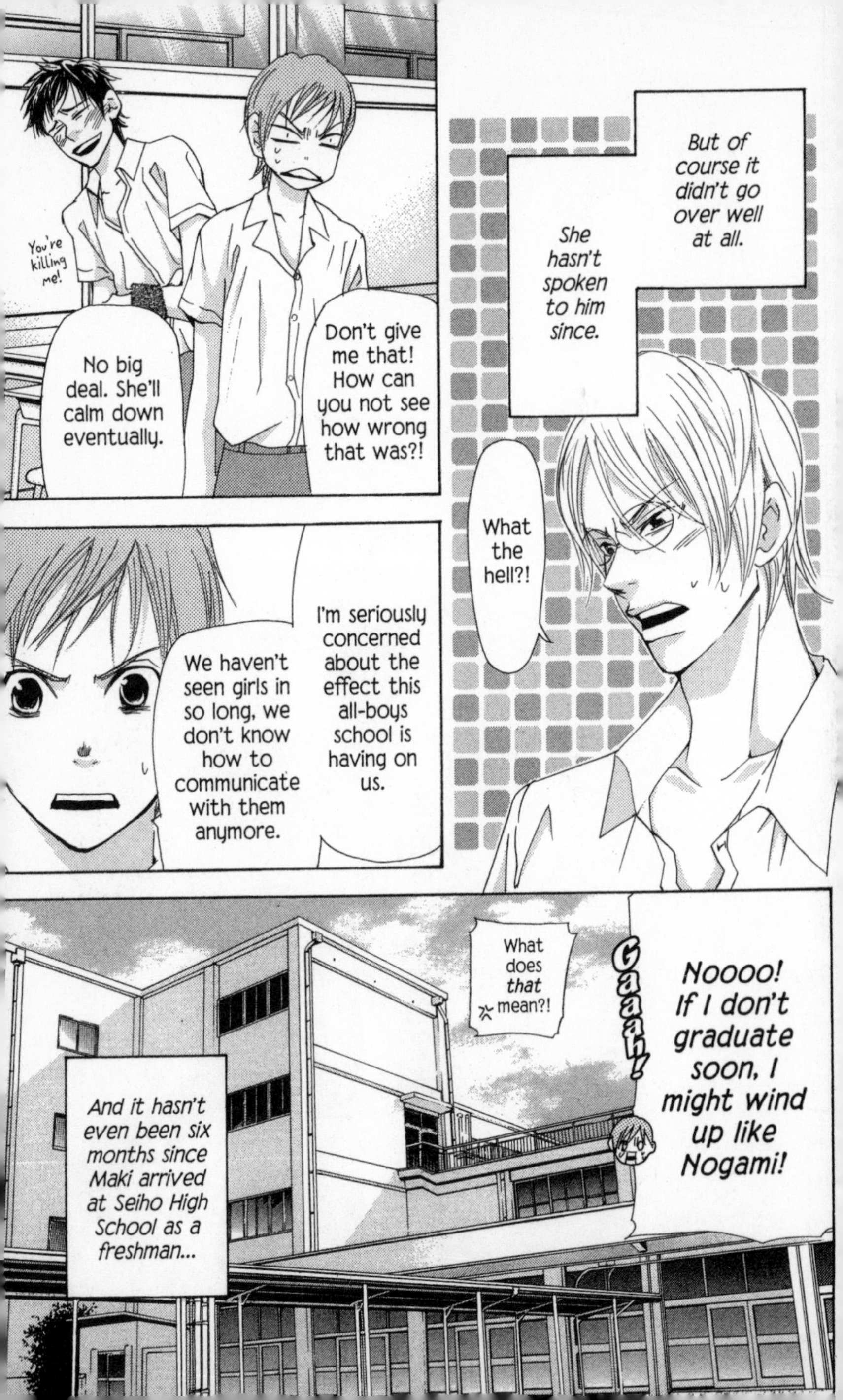

But of course it didn't go over well at all.
She hasn't spoken to him since.
What the hell?!
Don't give me that! How can you not see how wrong that was?!
You're killing me!
No big deal. She'll calm down eventually.
I'm seriously concerned about the effect this all-boys school is having on us.
We haven't seen girls in so long, we don't know how to communicate with them anymore.
Noooo! If I don't graduate soon, I might wind up like Nogami!
Gaaah!
What does *that* mean?!
And it hasn't even been six months since Maki arrived at Seiho High School as a freshman...

SEIHO BOYS' HIGH SCHOOL!

♠ CHAPTER 3 ♠

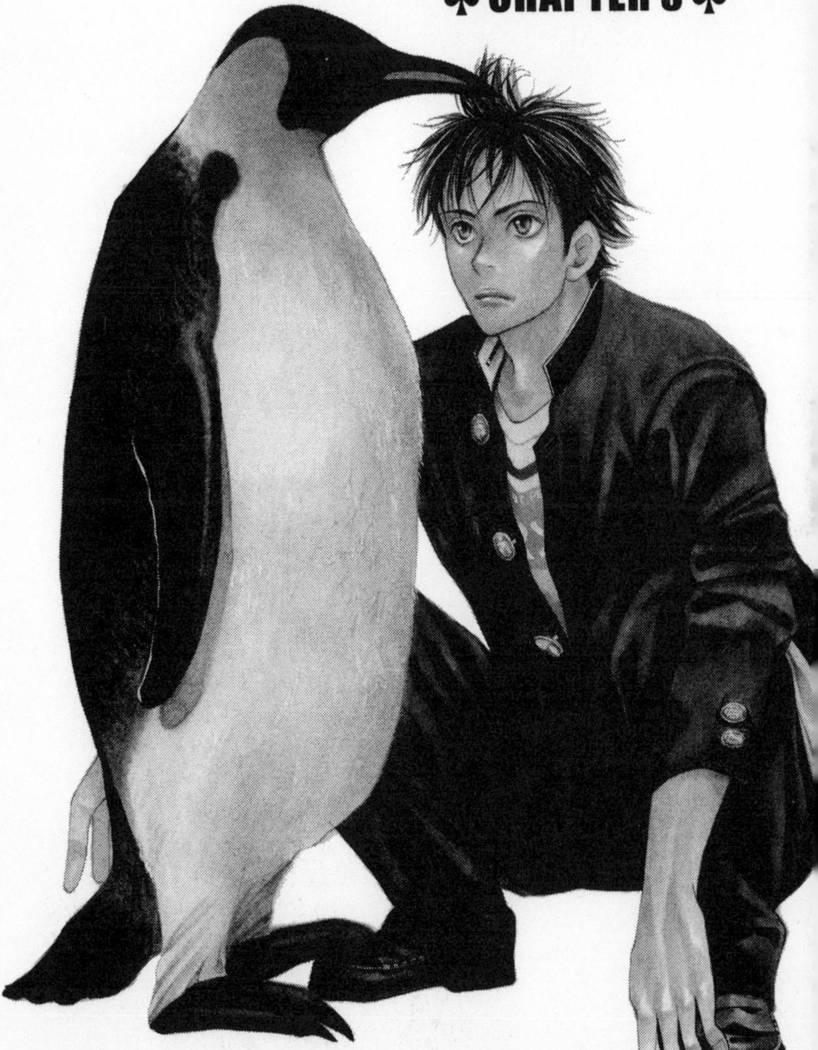

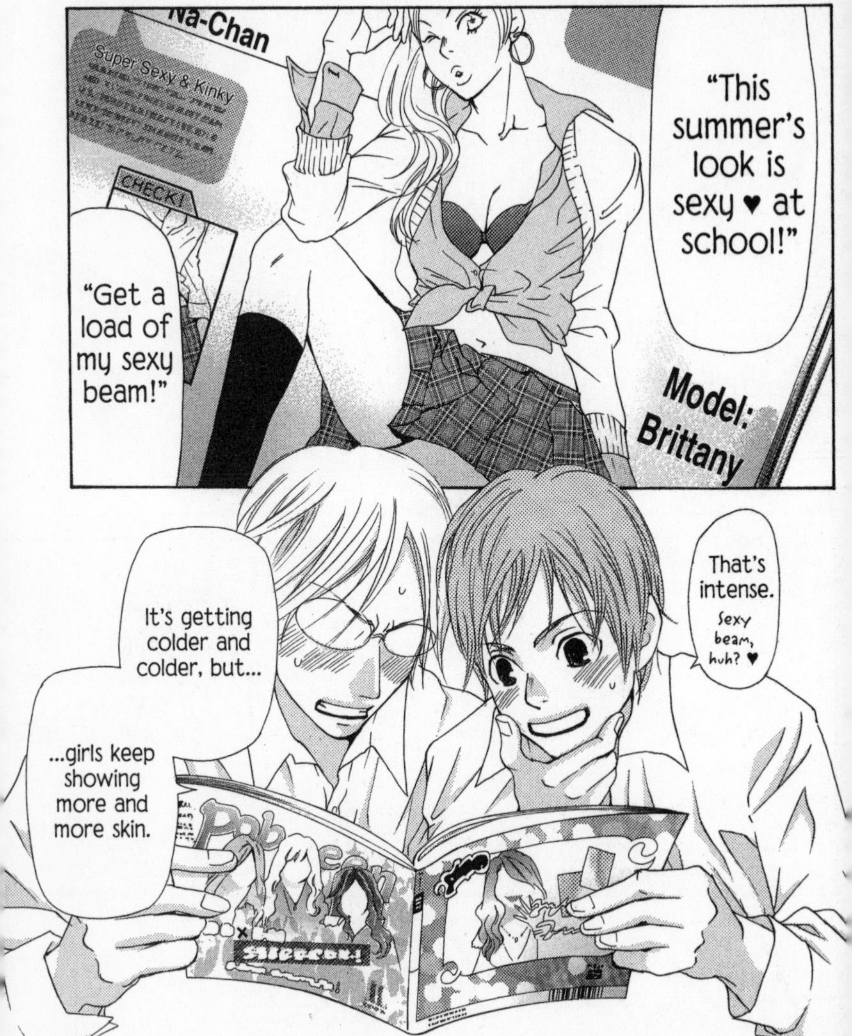
"This summer's look is sexy ♥ at school!"
Model: Brittany
Na-Chan
Super Sexy & Kinky
CHECK!
"Get a load of my sexy beam!"
That's intense.
Sexy beam, huh? ♥
It's getting colder and colder, but...
...girls keep showing more and more skin.

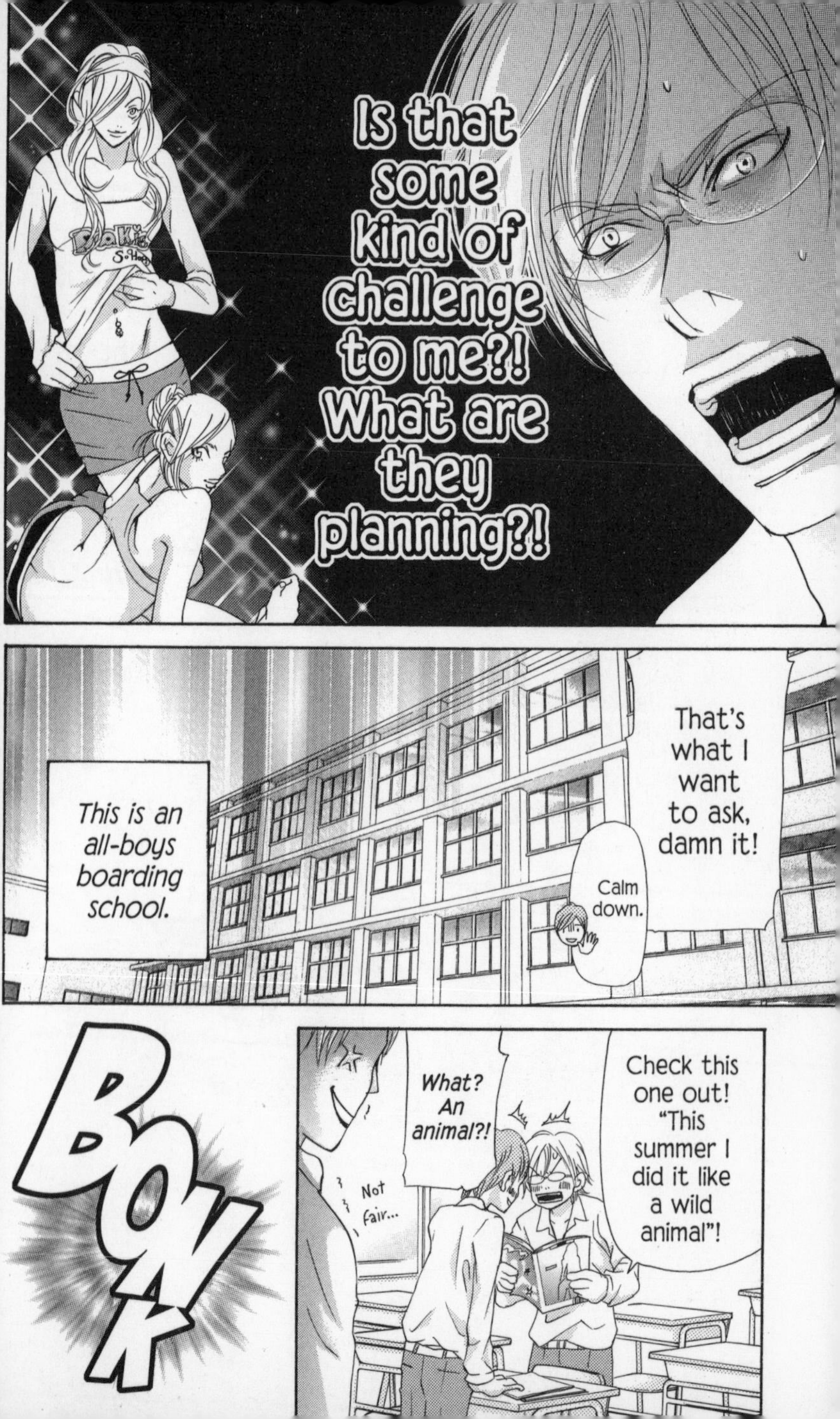
Is that some kind of challenge to me?! What are they planning?!
That's what I want to ask, damn it!
Calm down.
This is an all-boys boarding school.
Check this one out! "This summer I did it like a wild animal"!
What? An animal?!
Not fair...
BONK

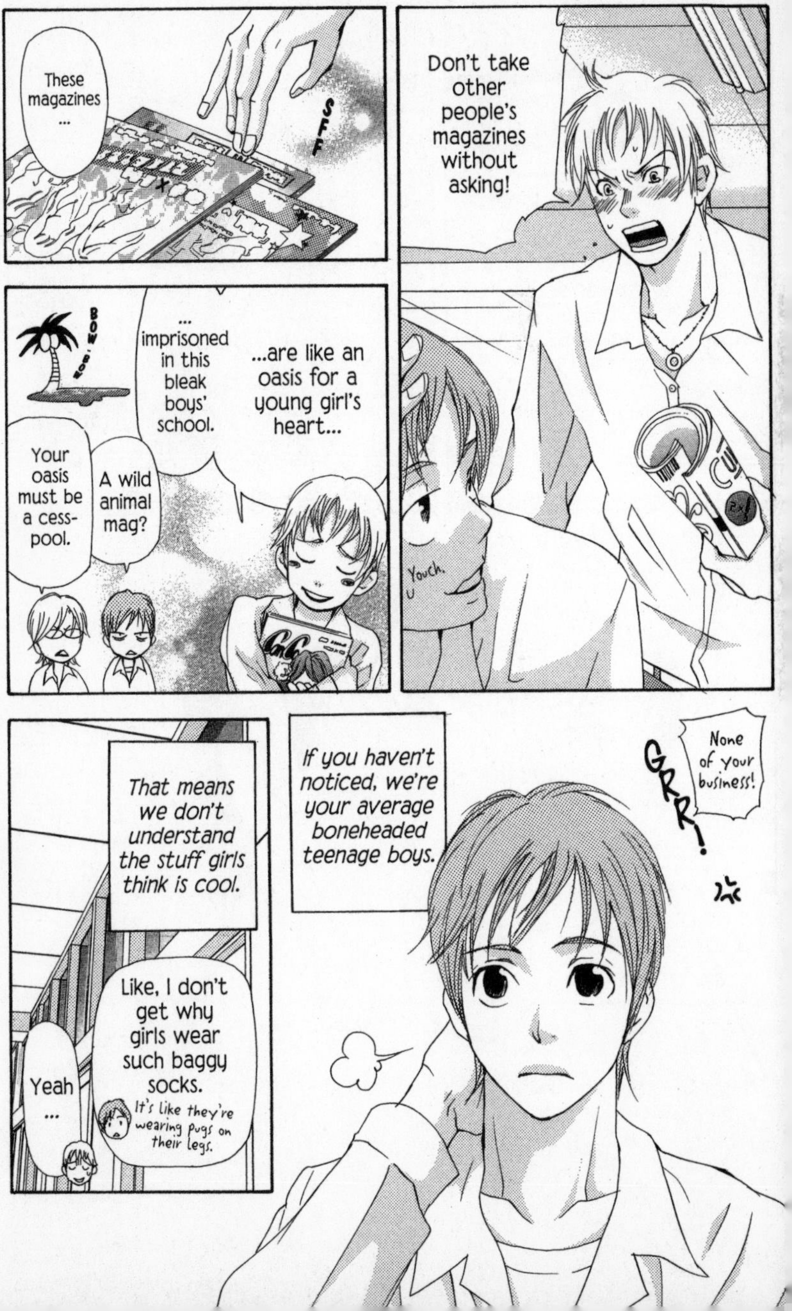
Don't take other people's magazines without asking!
Youch.
These magazines...
SFF
...are like an oasis for a young girl's heart...
... imprisoned in this bleak boys' school.
BOW-BOW
A wild animal mag?
Your oasis must be a cess-pool.
None of your business!
GRRR!
If you haven't noticed, we're your average boneheaded teenage boys.
That means we don't understand the stuff girls think is cool.
Like, I don't get why girls wear such baggy socks.
It's like they're wearing pugs on their legs.
Yeah...

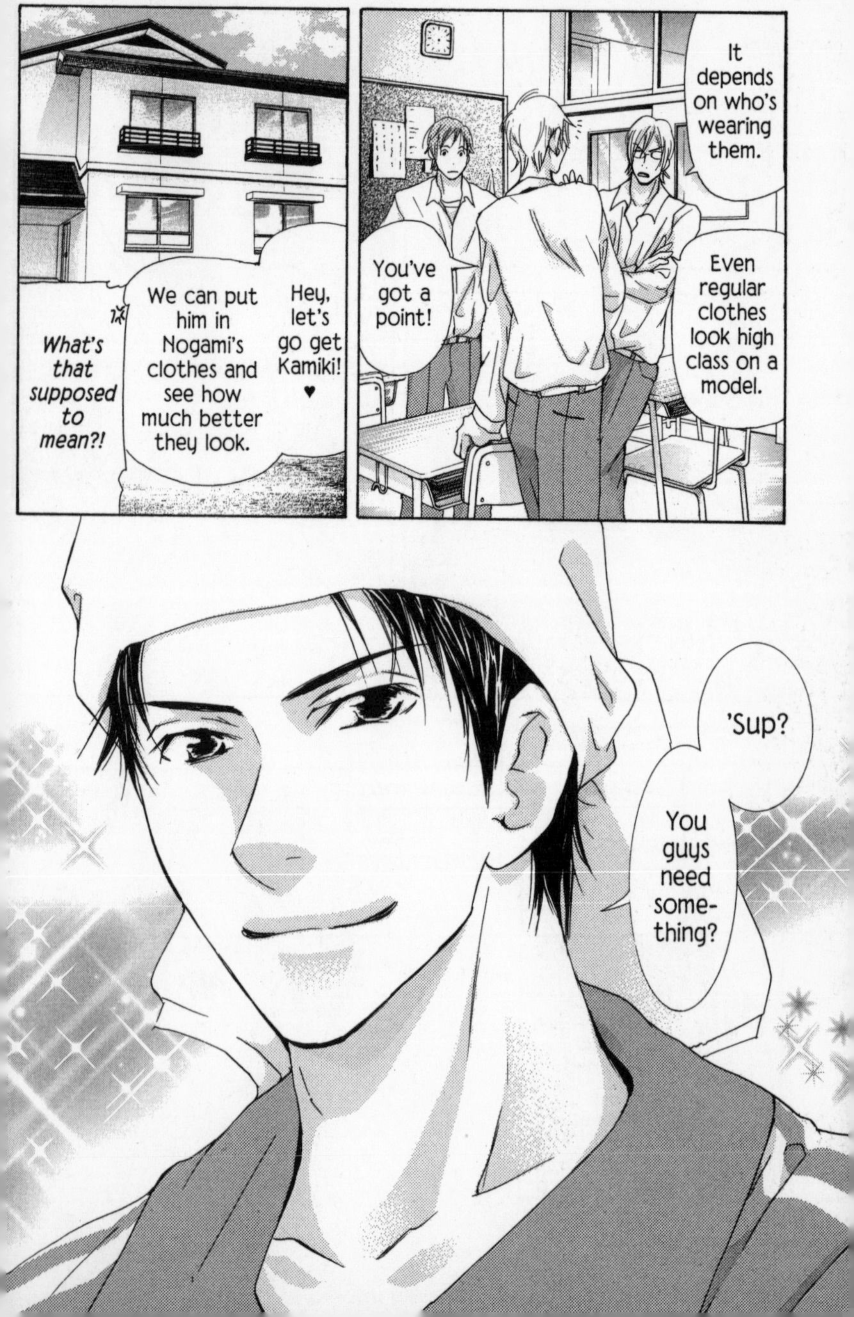
It depends on who's wearing them.
Even regular clothes look high class on a model.
You've got a point!
Hey, let's go get Kamiki! ♥
We can put him in Nogami's clothes and see how much better they look.
What's that supposed to mean?!
'Sup?
You guys need something?

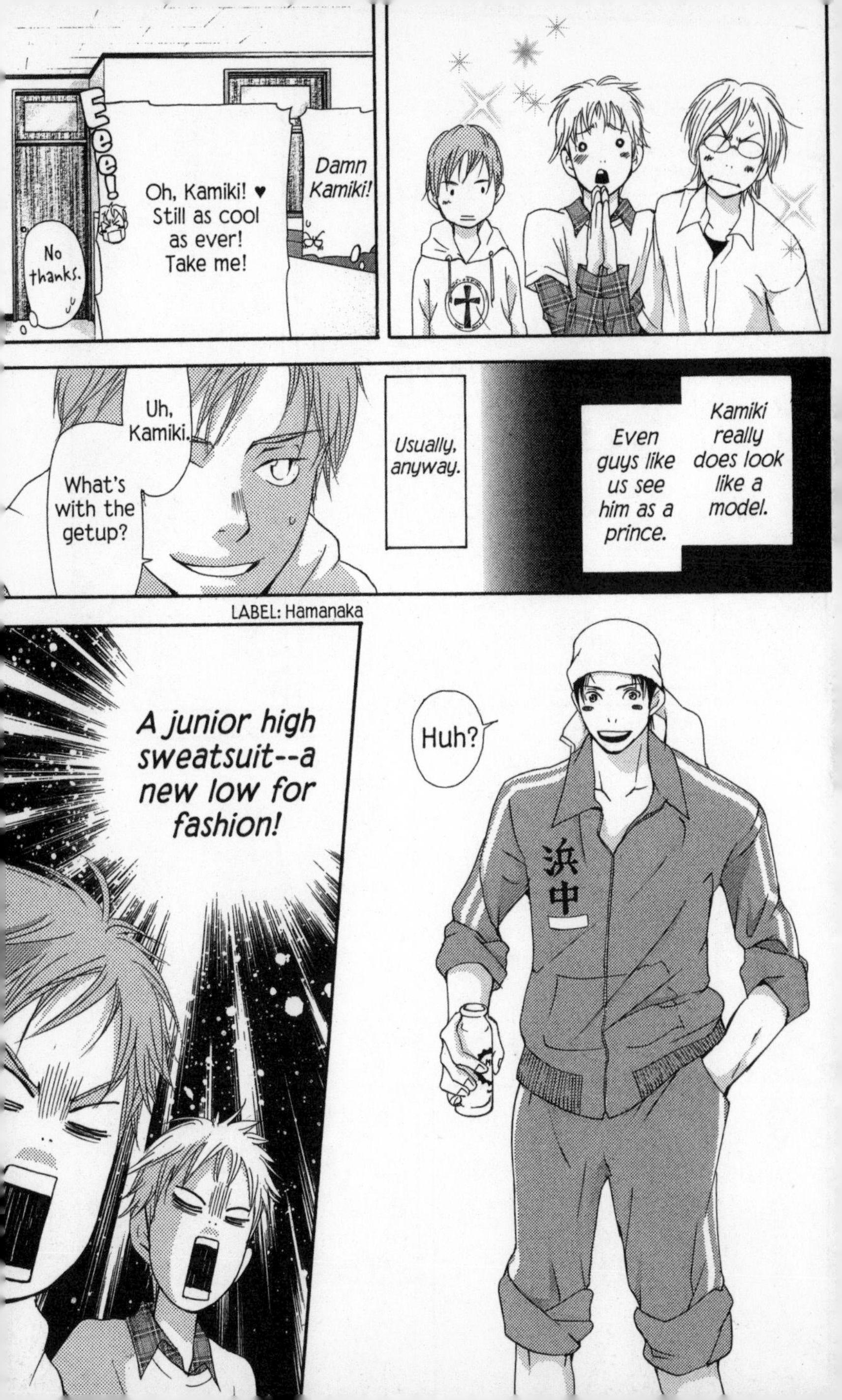
Damn Kamiki!
Oh, Kamiki! ♥ Still as cool as ever! Take me!
Eee!
No thanks.
Kamiki really does look like a model.
Even guys like us see him as a prince.
Usually, anyway.
Uh, Kamiki.
What's with the getup?
LABEL: Hamanaka
Huh?
浜中
A junior high sweatsuit--a new low for fashion!

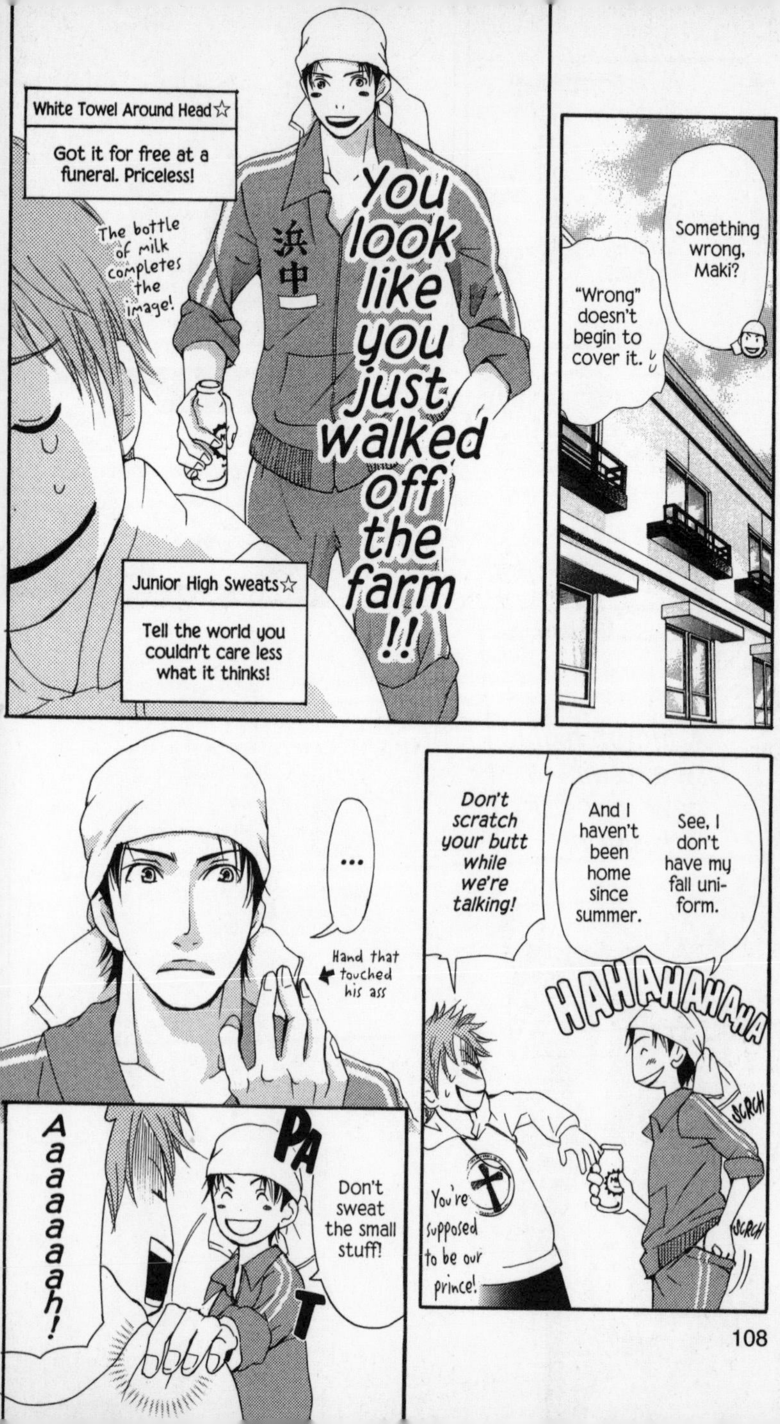
Something wrong, Maki?
"Wrong" doesn't begin to cover it.
White Towel Around Head☆
Got it for free at a funeral. Priceless!
You look like you just walked off the farm!!
浜中
The bottle of milk completes the image!
Junior High Sweats☆
Tell the world you couldn't care less what it thinks!
See, I don't have my fall uniform.
And I haven't been home since summer.
Don't scratch your butt while we're talking!
HAHAHAHAHAHA
SCRCH
SCRCH
You're supposed to be our prince!
...
Hand that touched his ass
PAT
Don't sweat the small stuff!
Aaaaaaaah!

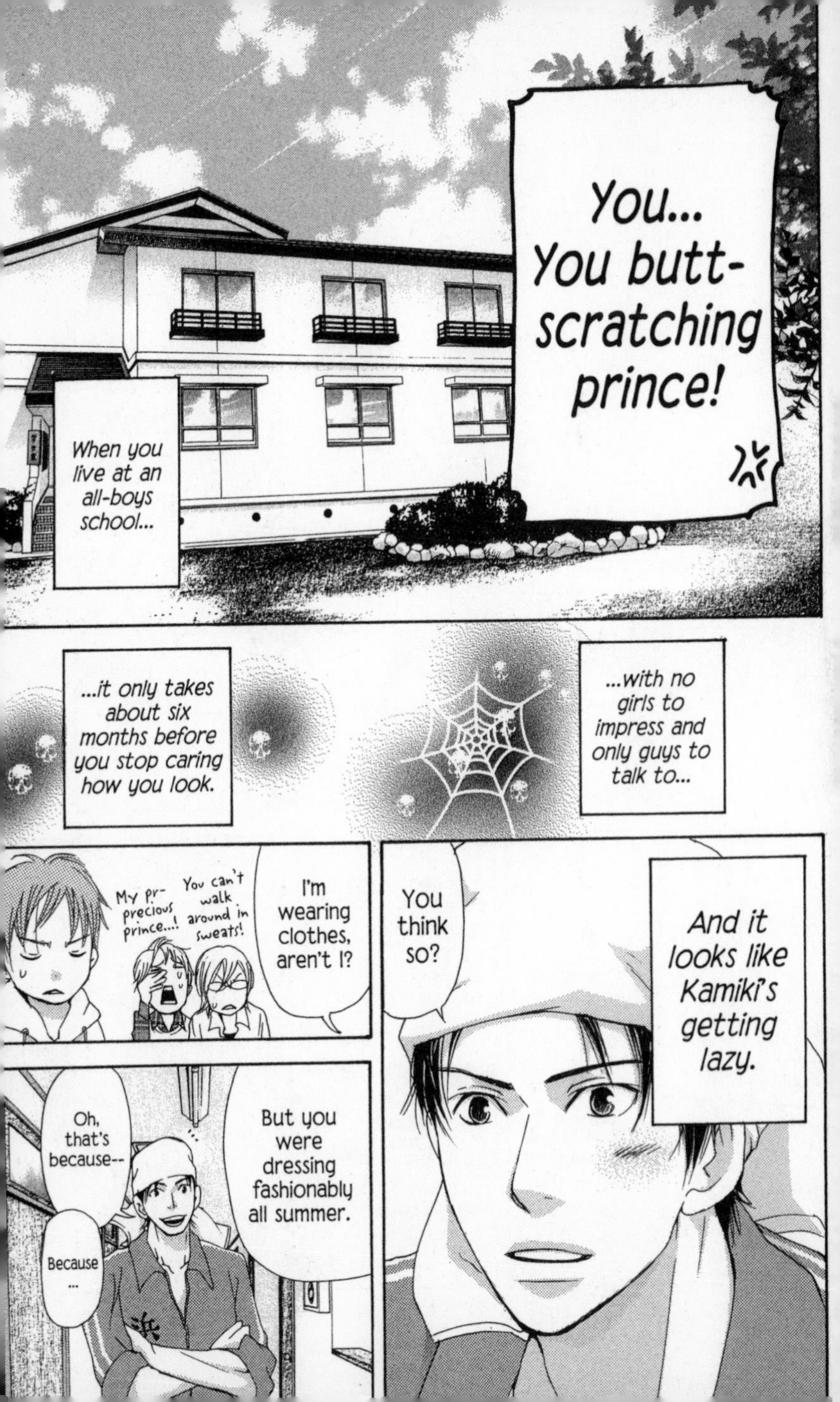
You...
You butt-scratching prince!
When you live at an all-boys school...
...with no girls to impress and only guys to talk to...
...it only takes about six months before you stop caring how you look.
And it looks like Kamiki's getting lazy.
You think so?
I'm wearing clothes, aren't I?
You can't walk around in sweats!
My pr- precious prince...!
But you were dressing fashionably all summer.
Oh, that's because--
Because ...

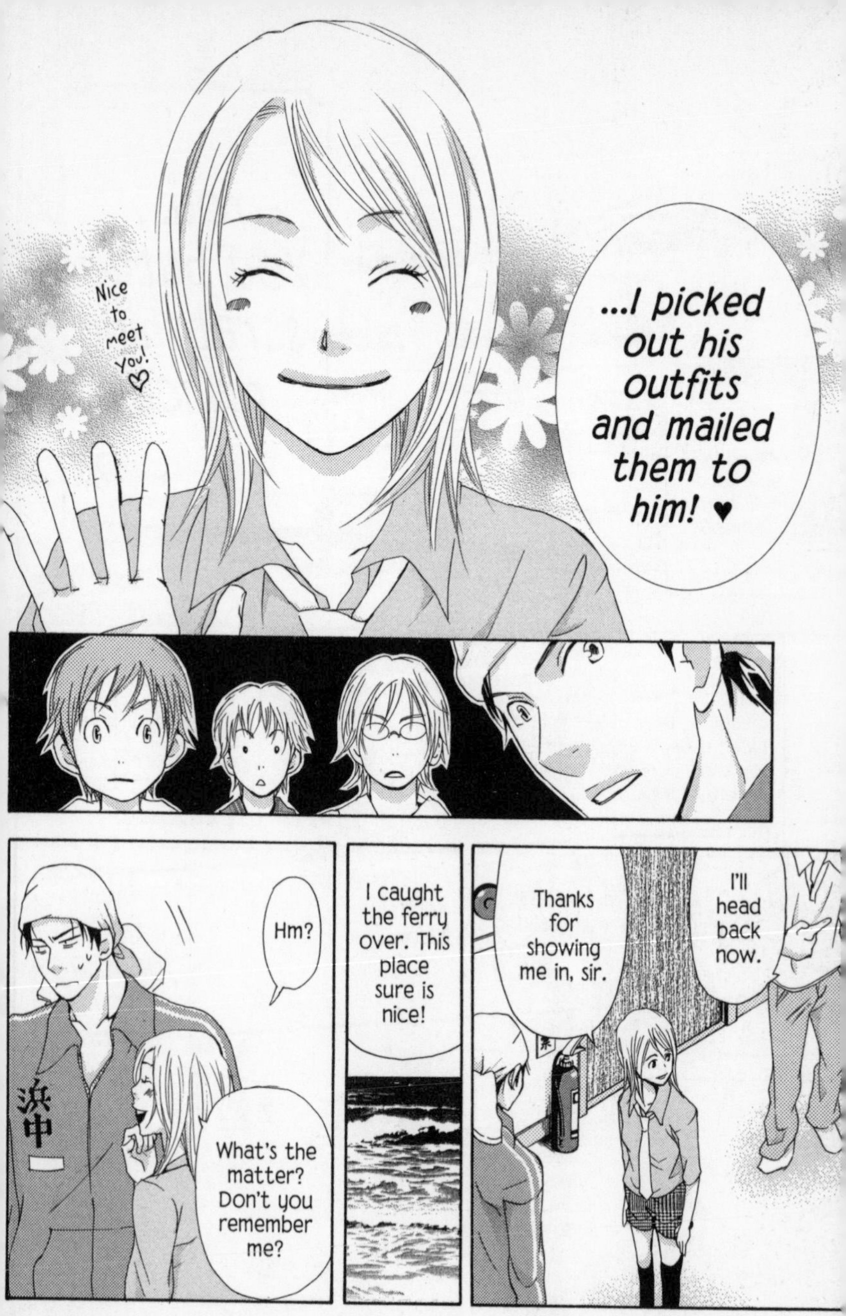
...I picked out his outfits and mailed them to him! ♥
Nice to meet you! ♡
I'll head back now.
Thanks for showing me in, sir.
I caught the ferry over. This place sure is nice!
Hm?
What's the matter? Don't you remember me?
浜中

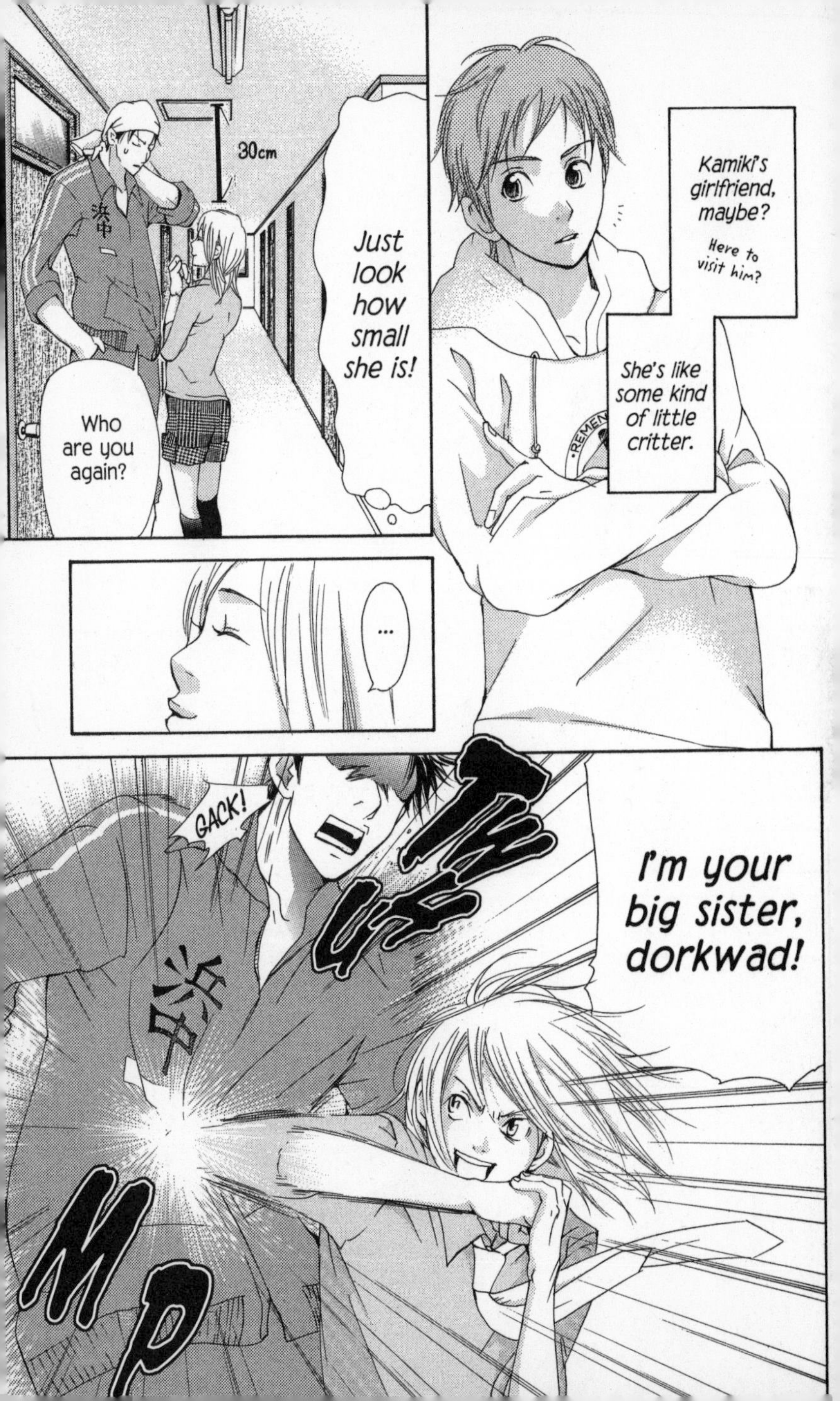
Kamiki's girlfriend, maybe?
Here to visit him?
She's like some kind of little critter.
Just look how small she is!
30cm
Who are you again?
...
I'm your big sister, dorkwad!
GACK!
THWUMP

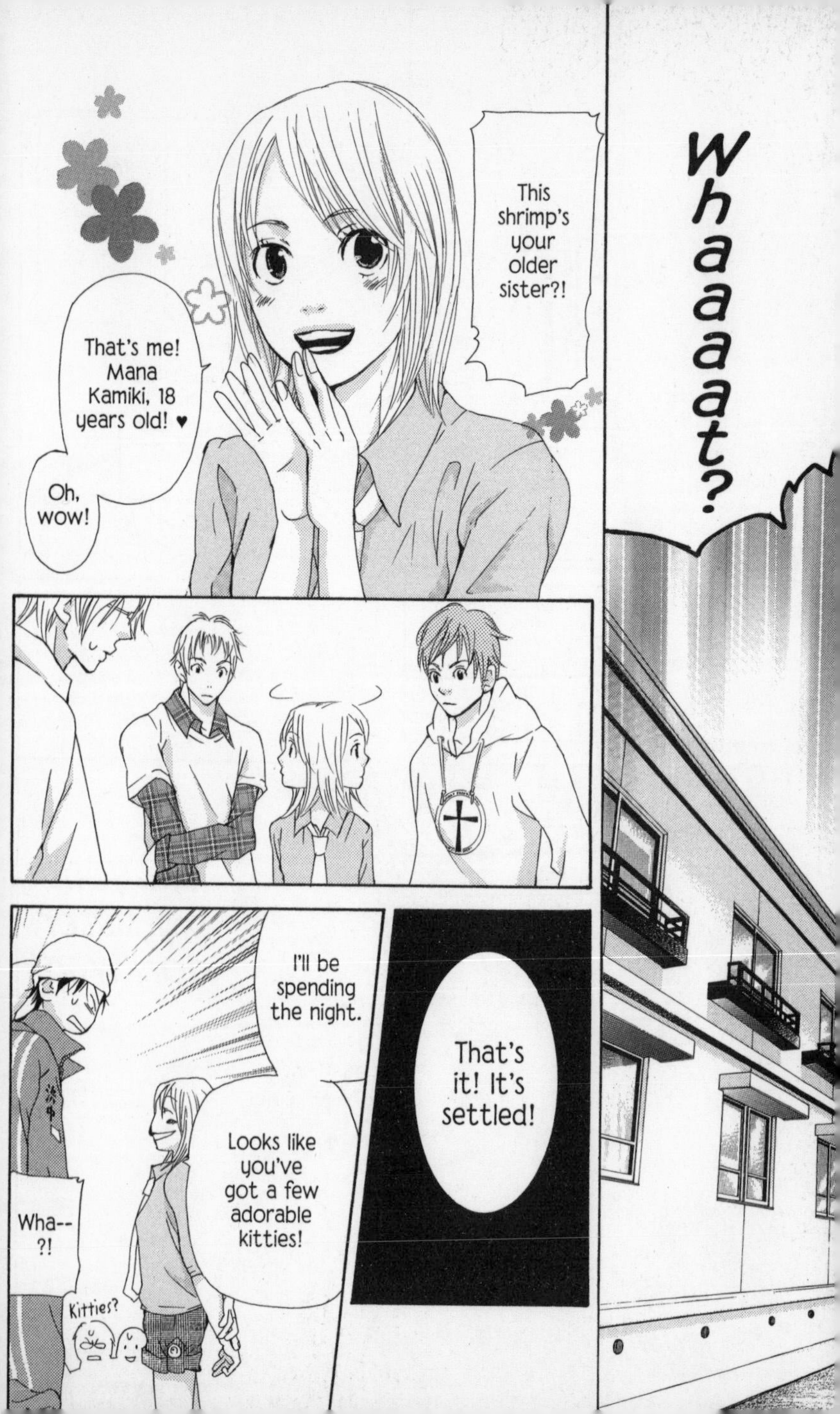
Whaaaaat?
This shrimp's your older sister?!
That's me! Mana Kamiki, 18 years old! ♥
Oh, wow!
That's it! It's settled!
I'll be spending the night.
Looks like you've got a few adorable kitties!
Wha-- ?!
Kitties?

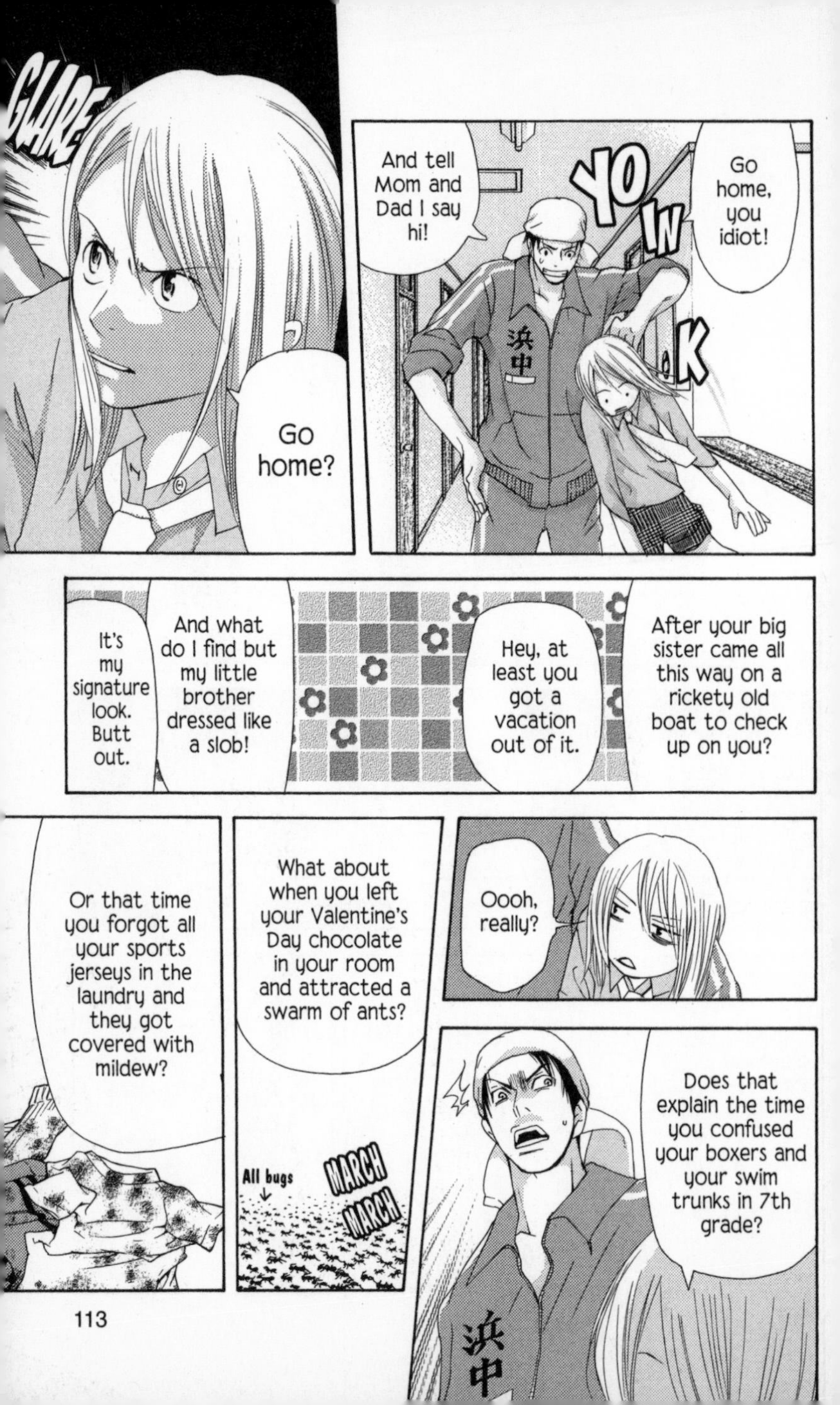

Go home, you idiot!
YOINK
And tell Mom and Dad I say hi!
GLARE
Go home?
After your big sister came all this way on a rickety old boat to check up on you?
Hey, at least you got a vacation out of it.
And what do I find but my little brother dressed like a slob!
It's my signature look. Butt out.
Oooh, really?
Does that explain the time you confused your boxers and your swim trunks in 7th grade?
What about when you left your Valentine's Day chocolate in your room and attracted a swarm of ants?
All bugs
MARCH MARCH
Or that time you forgot all your sports jerseys in the laundry and they got covered with mildew?
浜中

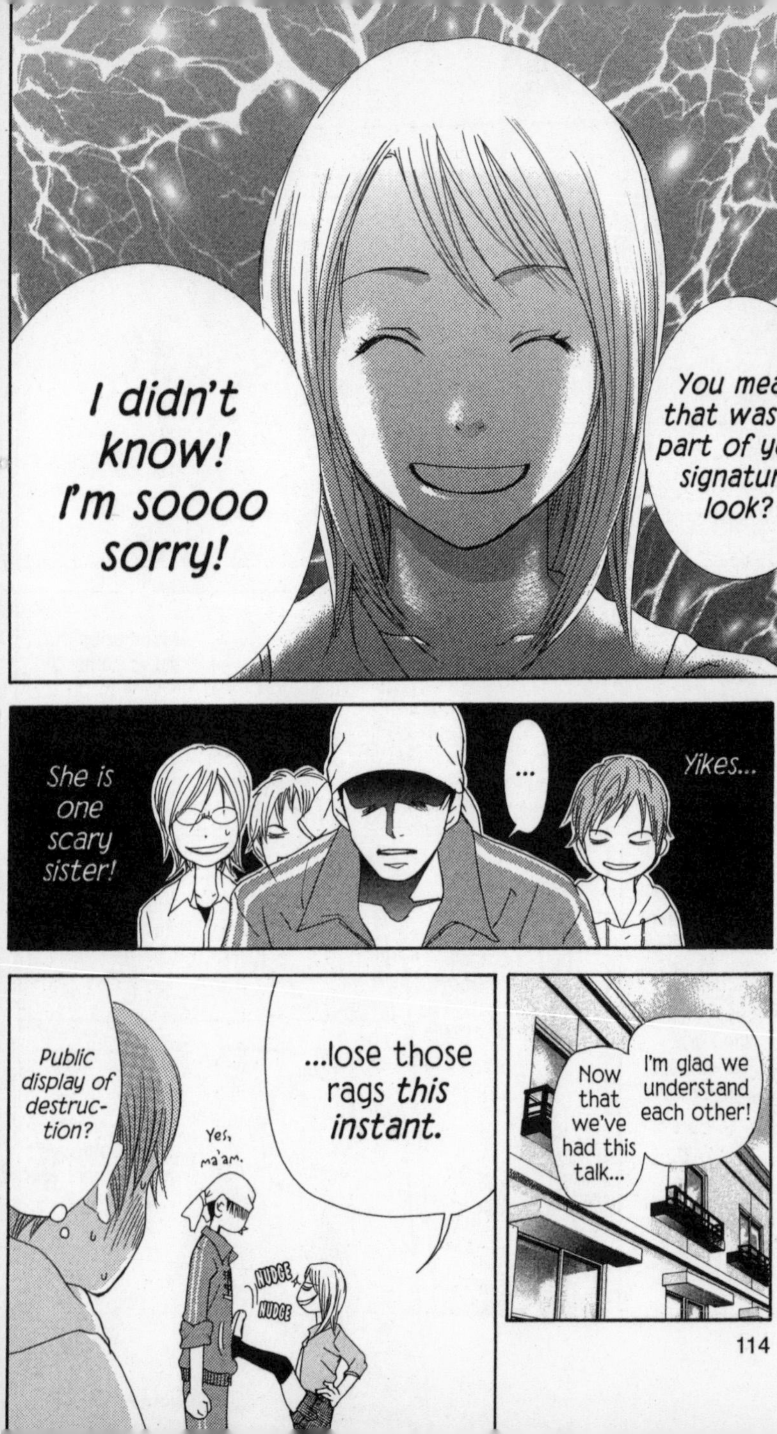
You mean that was all part of your signature look?
I didn't know! I'm soooo sorry!
Yikes...
...
She is one scary sister!
I'm glad we understand each other!
Now that we've had this talk...
...lose those rags *this instant.*
Yes, ma'am.
NUDGE NUDGE
Public display of destruction?

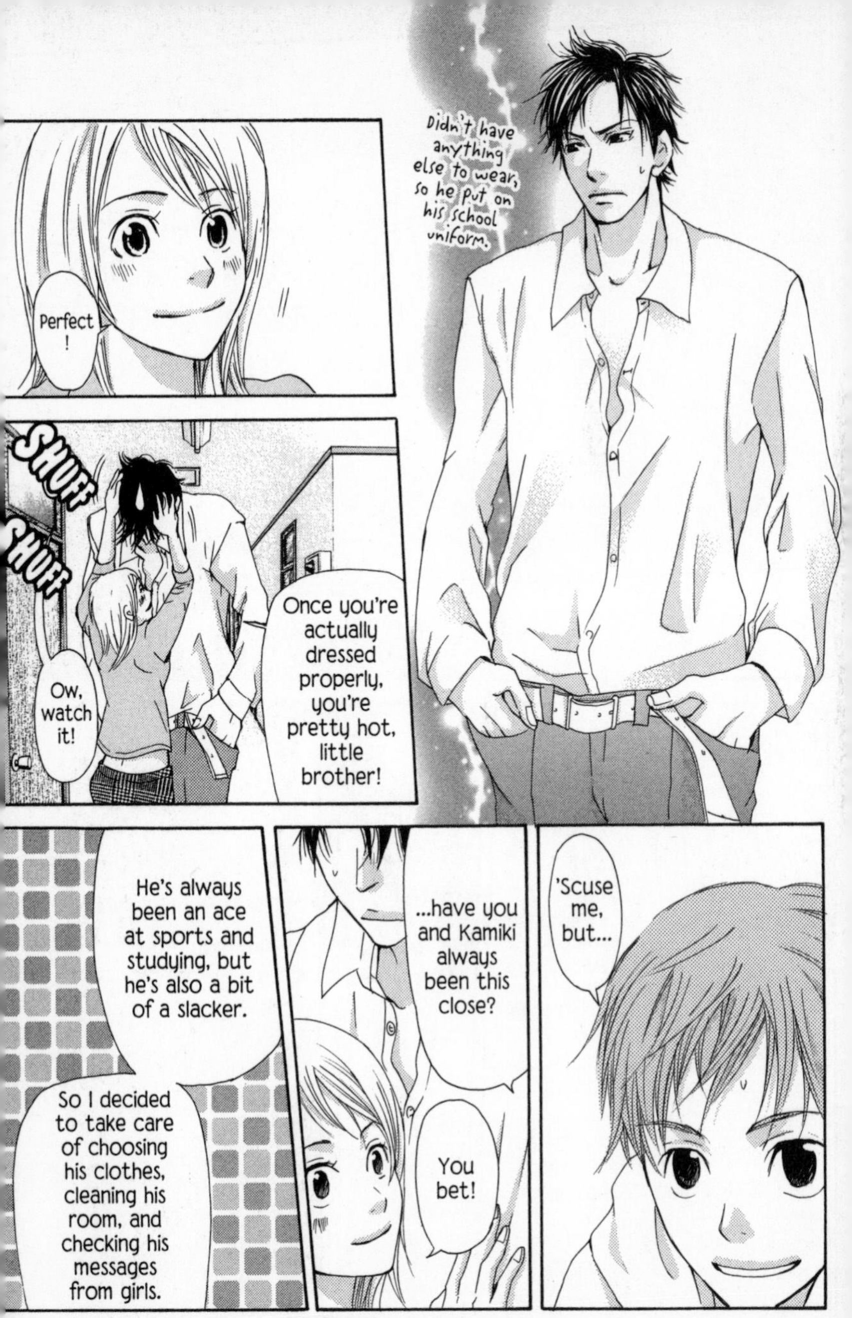
Didn't have anything else to wear, so he put on his school uniform.
Perfect!
SHUFF SHUFF
Once you're actually dressed properly, you're pretty hot, little brother!
Ow, watch it!
'Scuse me, but...
...have you and Kamiki always been this close?
You bet!
He's always been an ace at sports and studying, but he's also a bit of a slacker.
So I decided to take care of choosing his clothes, cleaning his room, and checking his messages from girls.

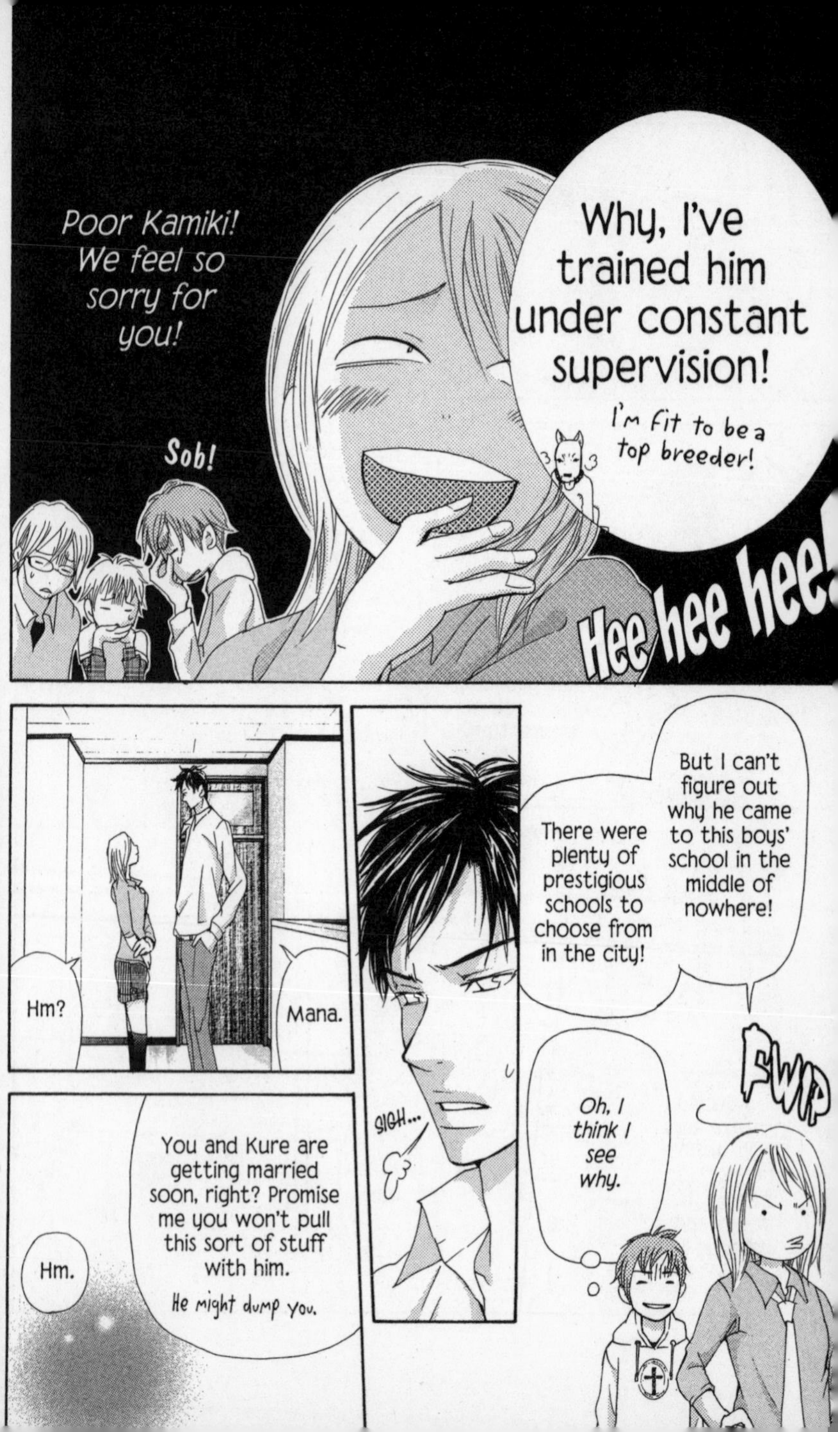
Why, I've trained him under constant supervision!
I'm fit to be a top breeder!
Poor Kamiki! We feel so sorry for you!
Sob!
Hee hee hee!
But I can't figure out why he came to this boys' school in the middle of nowhere!
There were plenty of prestigious schools to choose from in the city!
SIGH...
FWIP
Oh, I think I see why.
Mana.
Hm?
You and Kure are getting married soon, right? Promise me you won't pull this sort of stuff with him.
He might dump you.
Hm.

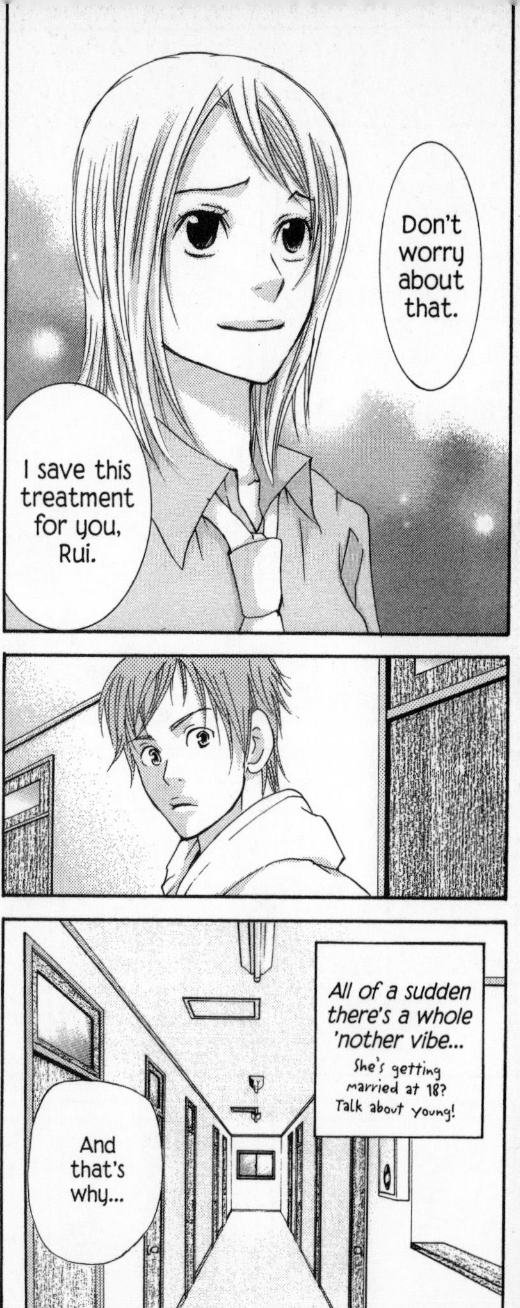
Don't worry about that.
I save this treatment for you, Rui.
All of a sudden there's a whole 'nother vibe...
She's getting married at 18? Talk about young!
And that's why...

1/3 Half-Assed Space Filler

Introducing gifts I don't appreciate!

#3
From: Vietnam(?)
Wooden Cat Statue

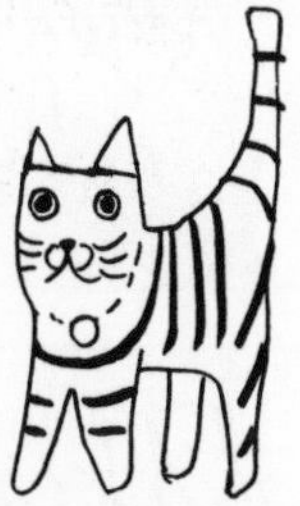

The thing that bothers me is that I received another one identical to this, except it was supposedly from **Bali!** Plus...

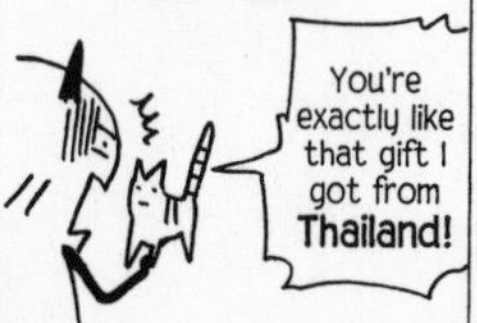
You're exactly like that gift I got from Thailand!

It's almost like that cat's **multiplying!**

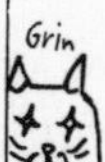
Grin

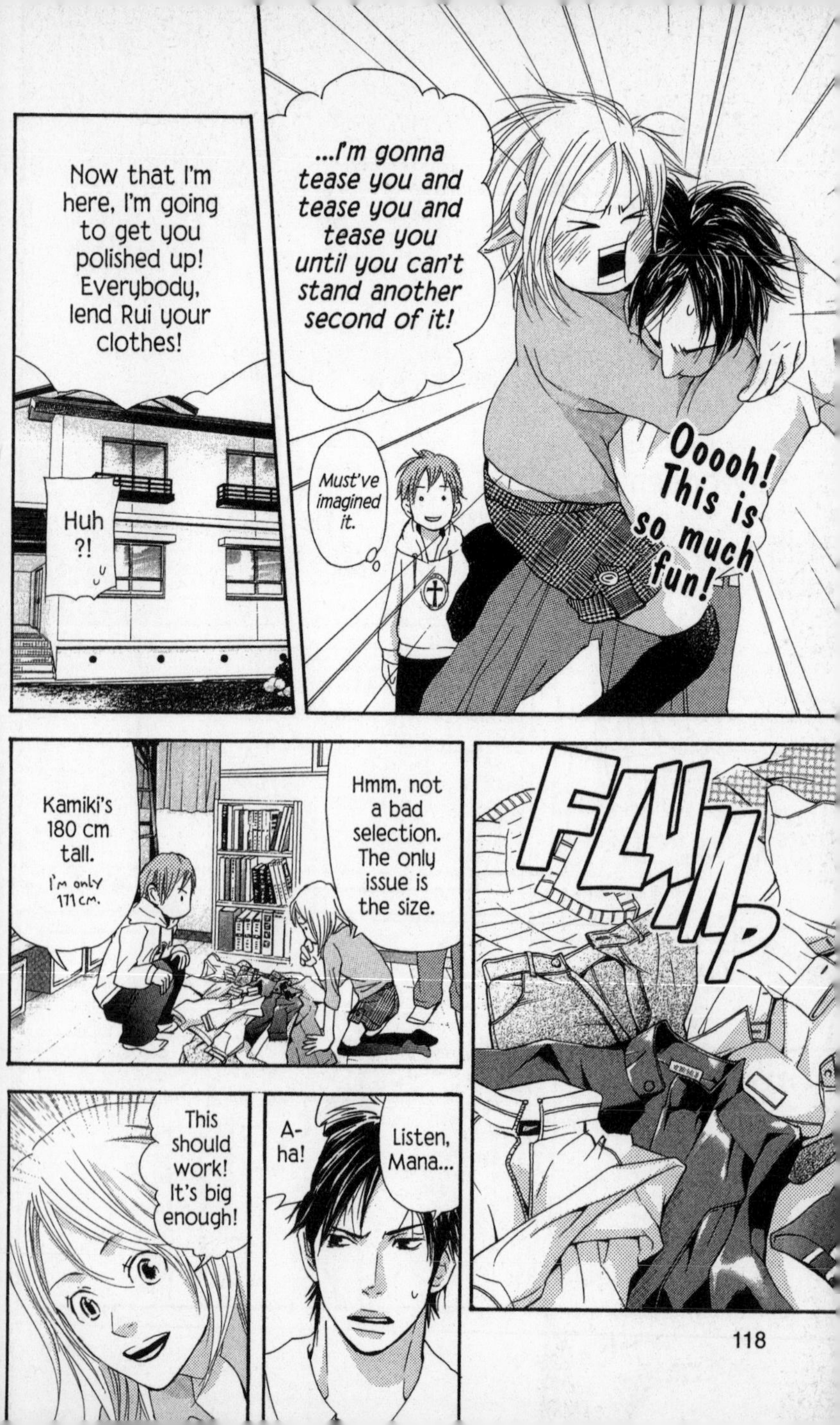

...I'm gonna tease you and tease you and tease you until you can't stand another second of it!
Ooooh! This is so much fun!
Must've imagined it.
Now that I'm here, I'm going to get you polished up! Everybody, lend Rui your clothes!
Huh?!
FLUMP
Hmm, not a bad selection. The only issue is the size.
Kamiki's 180 cm tall.
I'm only 171 cm.
Listen, Mana...
A-ha!
This should work! It's big enough!

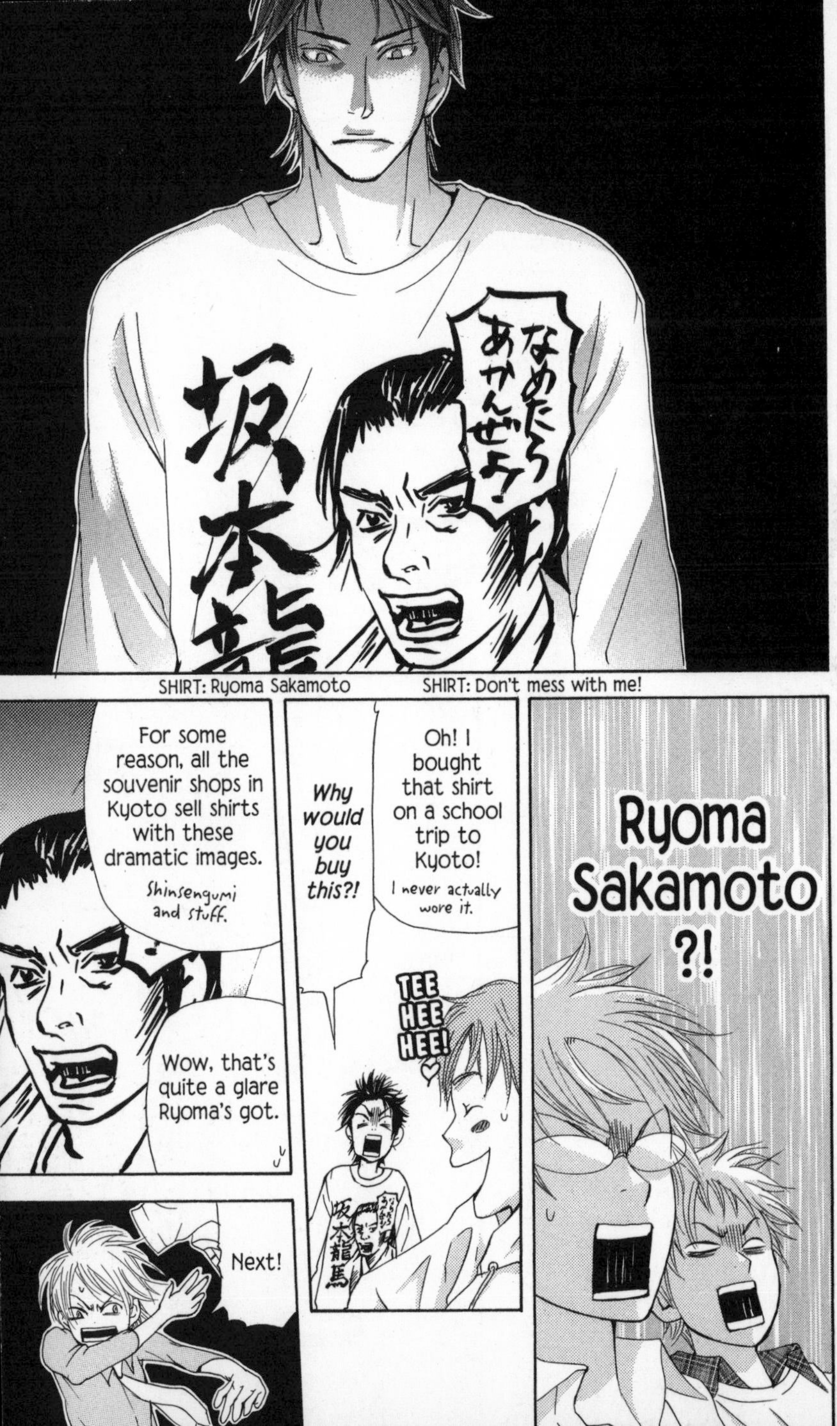
なめたらあかんぜよ!
SHIRT: Ryoma Sakamoto
SHIRT: Don't mess with me!
Ryoma Sakamoto ?!
Oh! I bought that shirt on a school trip to Kyoto!
I never actually wore it.
Why would you buy this?!
TEE HEE HEE!
For some reason, all the souvenir shops in Kyoto sell shirts with these dramatic images.
Shinsengumi and stuff.
Wow, that's quite a glare Ryoma's got.
Next!

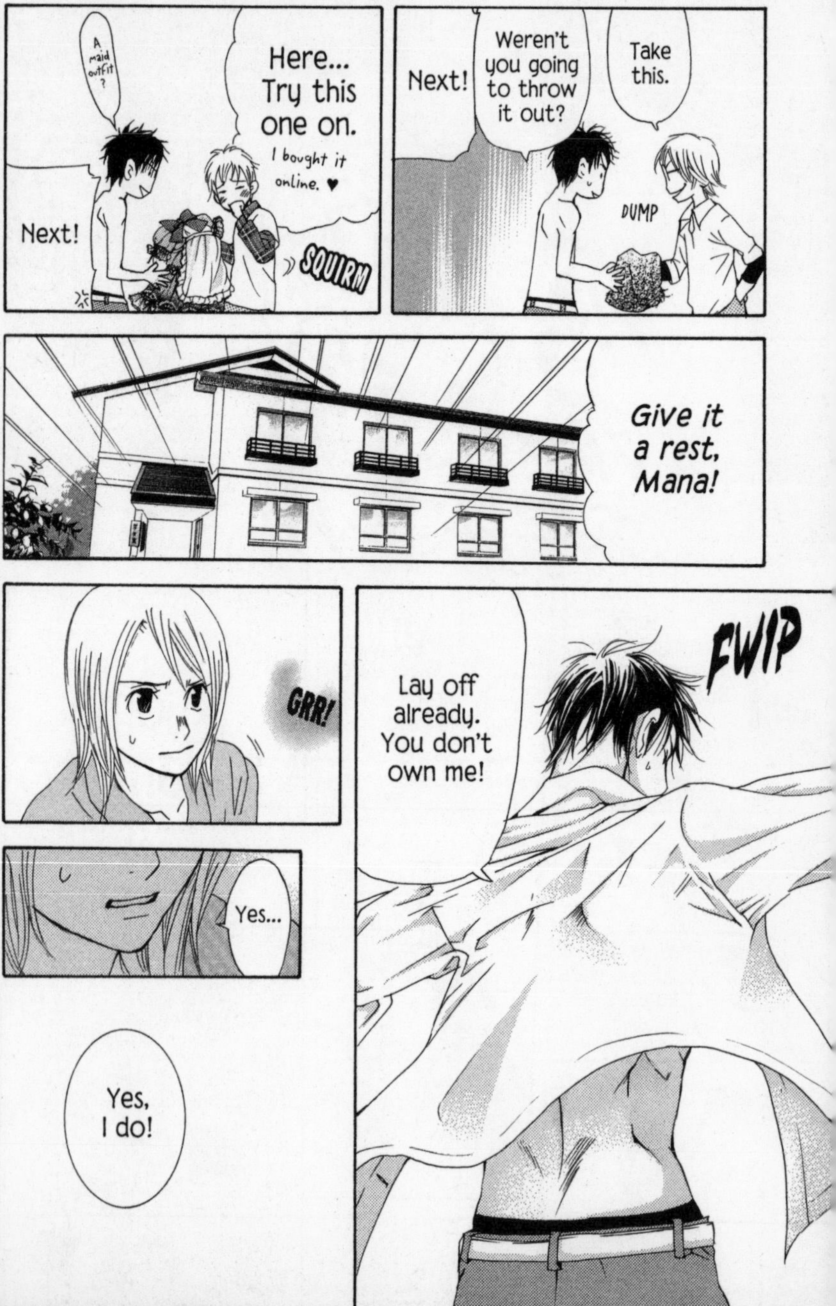
Take this.
Weren't you going to throw it out?
Next!
DUMP
Here... Try this one on.
I bought it online. ♥
A maid outfit?
Next!
SQUIRM
Give it a rest, Mana!
FWIP
Lay off already. You don't own me!
GRR!
Yes...
Yes, I do!

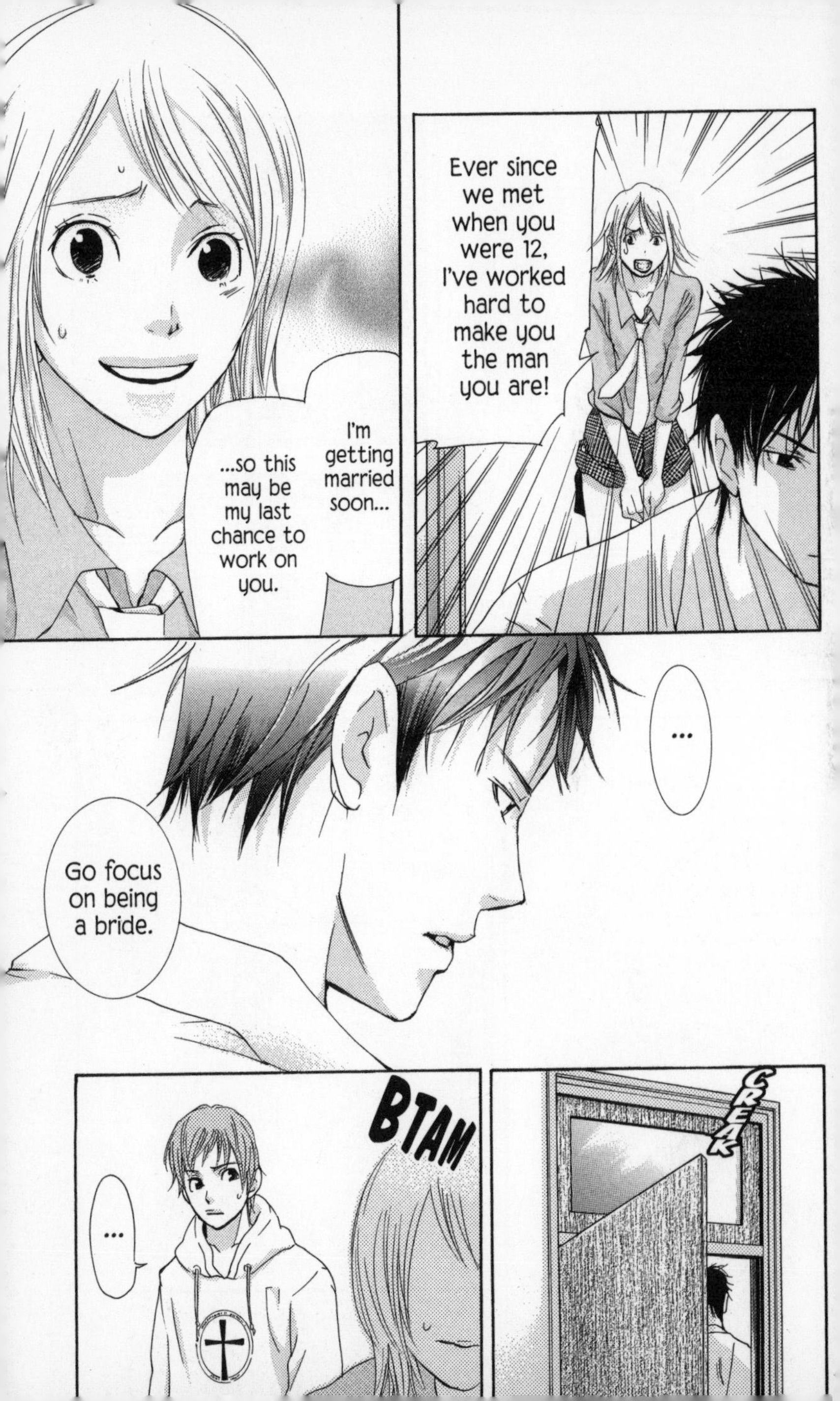
Ever since we met when you were 12, I've worked hard to make you the man you are!
I'm getting married soon...
...so this may be my last chance to work on you.
...
Go focus on being a bride.
CREAK
BTAM
...

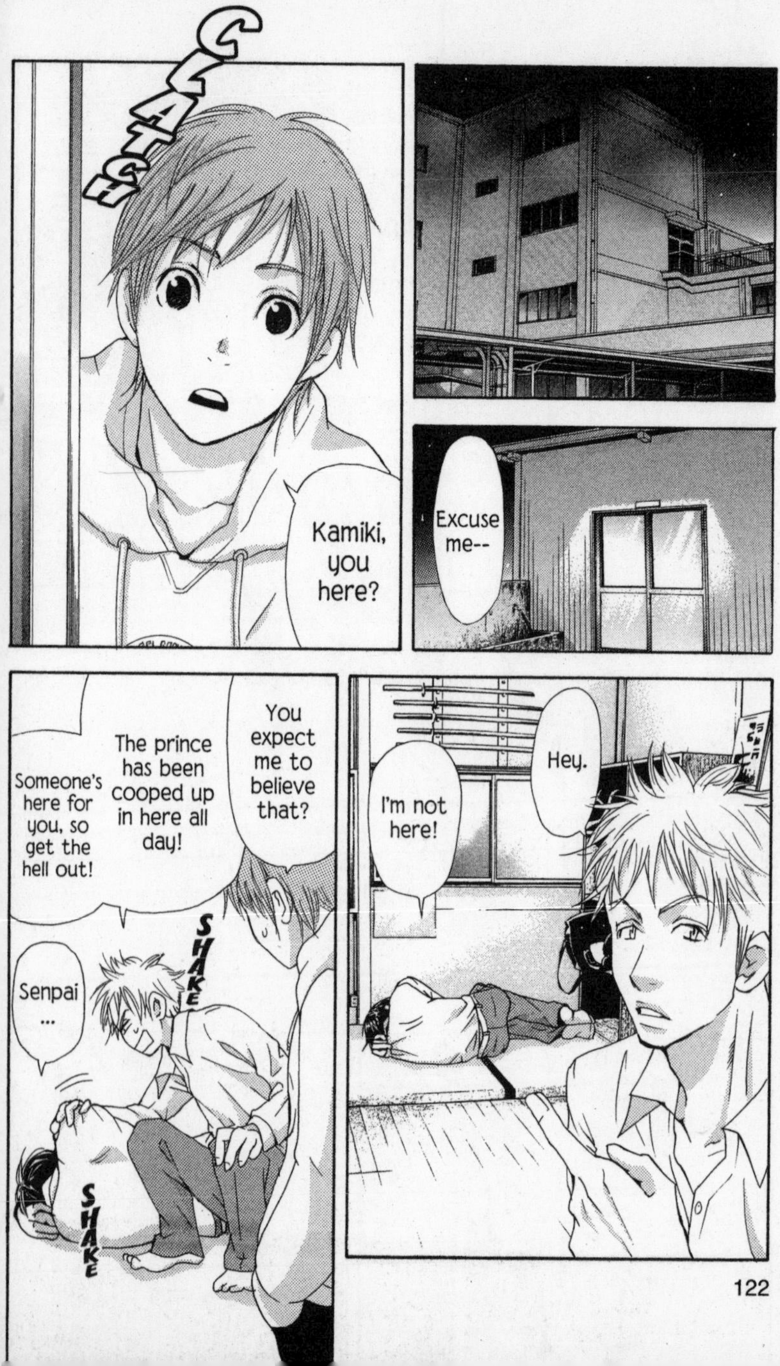

Excuse me--
CLATCH
Kamiki, you here?
Hey.
I'm not here!
You expect me to believe that?
The prince has been cooped up in here all day!
Someone's here for you, so get the hell out!
SHAKE
Senpai ...
SHAKE

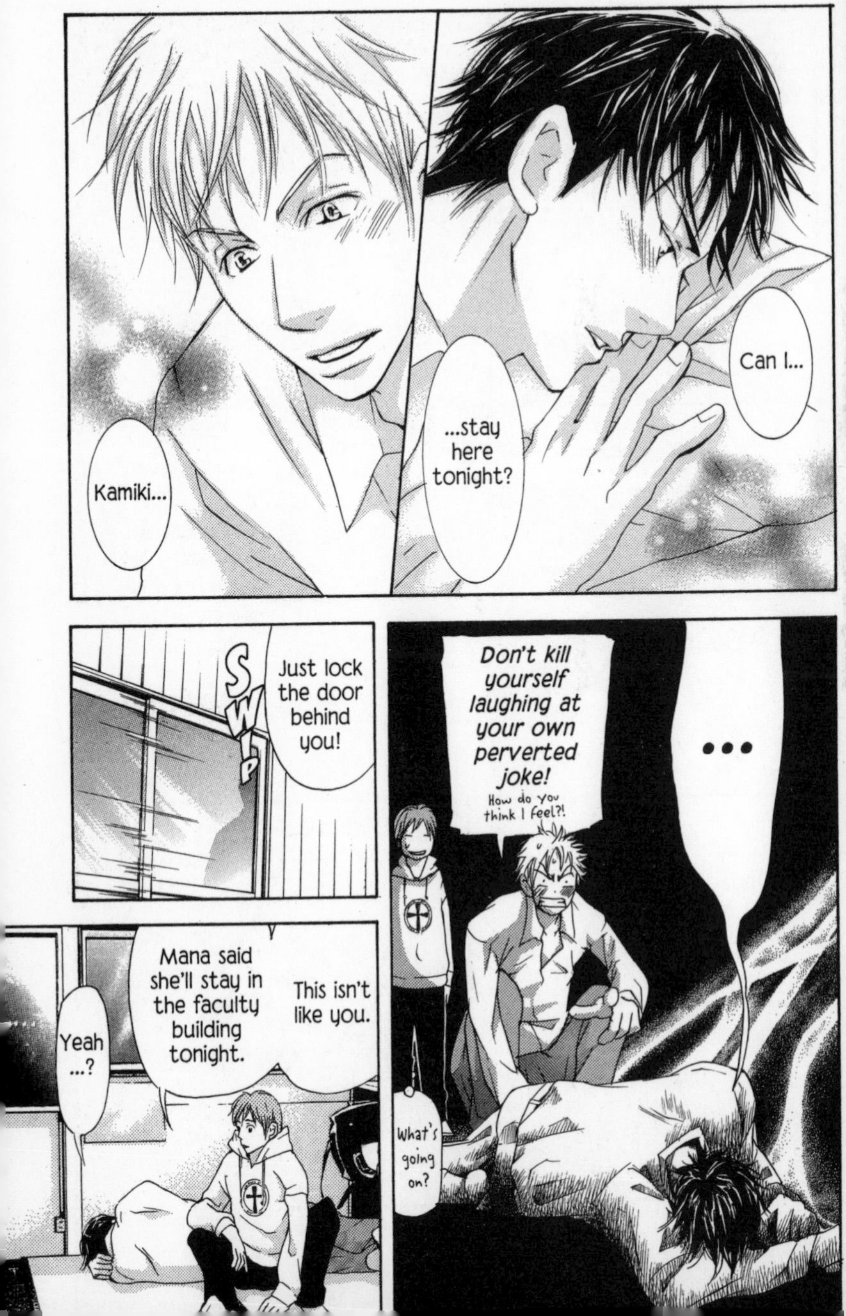
Can I...
...stay here tonight?
Kamiki...
•••
Don't kill yourself laughing at your own perverted joke!
How do you think I feel?!
What's going on?
SWIP
Just lock the door behind you!
This isn't like you.
Mana said she'll stay in the faculty building tonight.
Yeah ...?

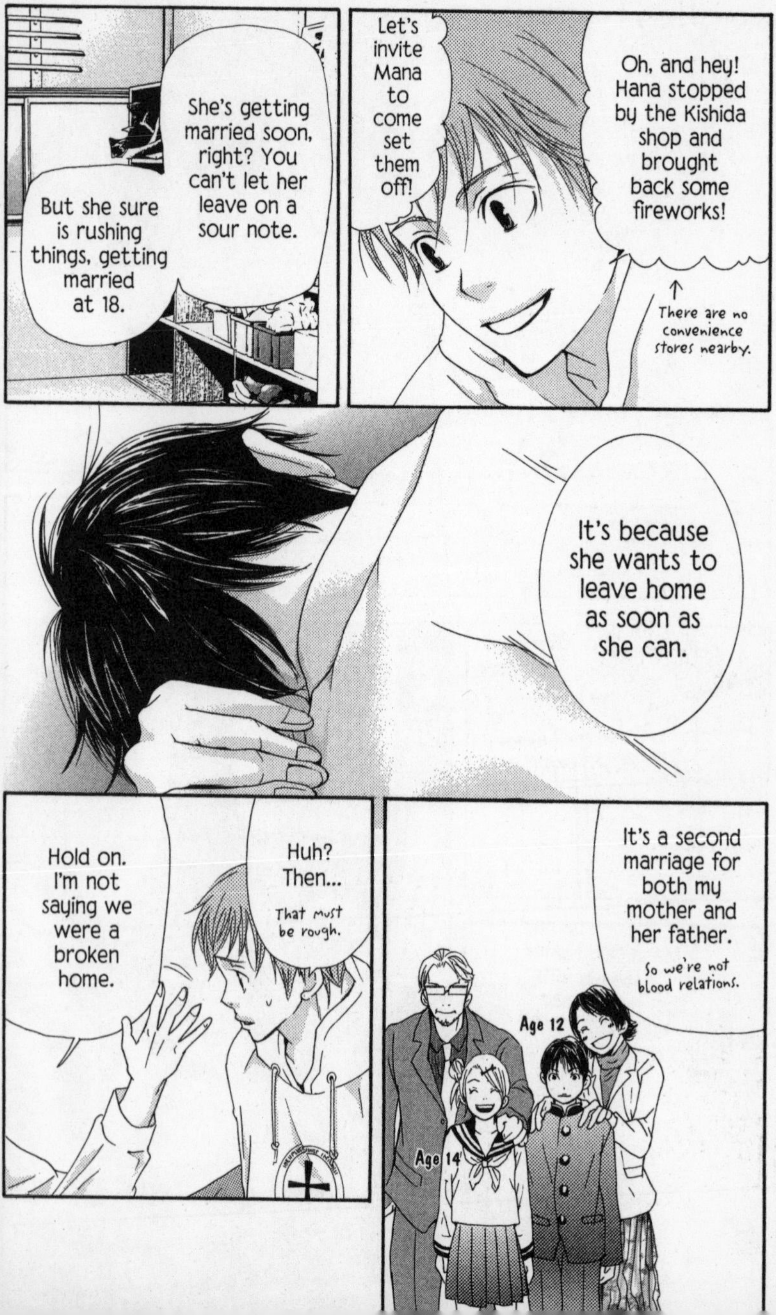
Oh, and hey! Hana stopped by the Kishida shop and brought back some fireworks!
Let's invite Mana to come set them off!
There are no convenience stores nearby.
She's getting married soon, right? You can't let her leave on a sour note.
But she sure is rushing things, getting married at 18.
It's because she wants to leave home as soon as she can.
It's a second marriage for both my mother and her father.
So we're not blood relations.
Age 12
Age 14
Huh? Then...
That must be rough.
Hold on. I'm not saying we were a broken home.

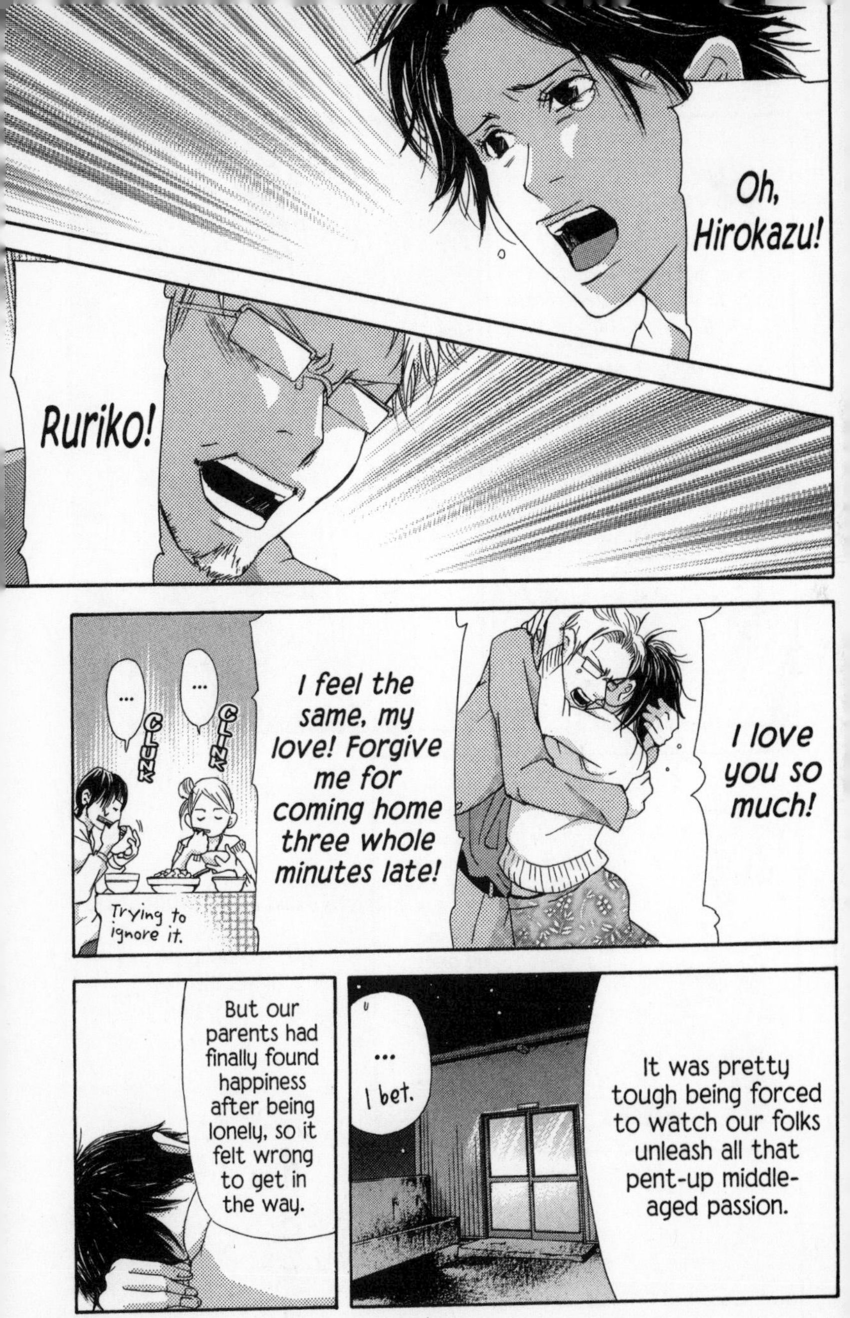
Oh, Hirokazu!
Ruriko!
I love you so much!
I feel the same, my love! Forgive me for coming home three whole minutes late!
...
CLINK
...
CLUNK
Trying to ignore it.
It was pretty tough being forced to watch our folks unleash all that pent-up middle-aged passion.
... I bet.
But our parents had finally found happiness after being lonely, so it felt wrong to get in the way.

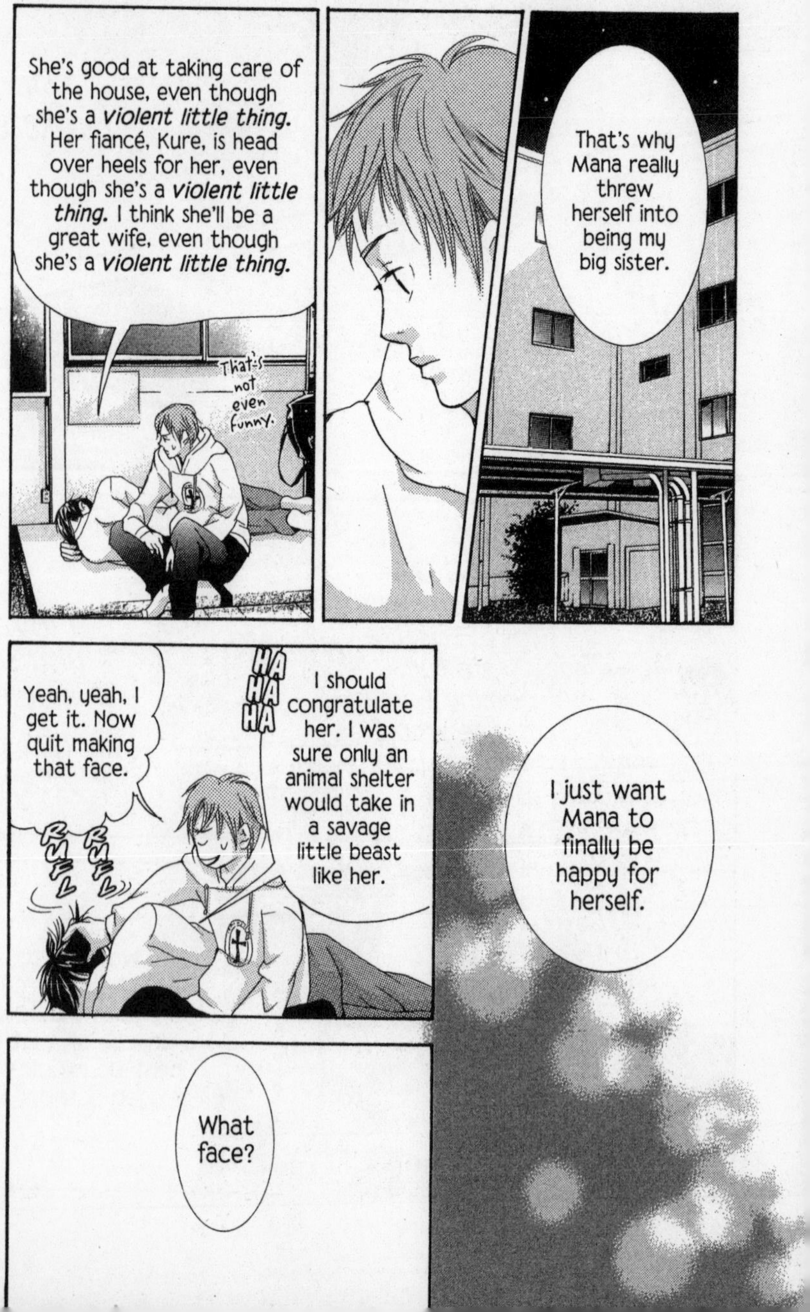
That's why Mana really threw herself into being my big sister.
She's good at taking care of the house, even though she's a *violent little thing.* Her fiancé, Kure, is head over heels for her, even though she's a *violent little thing.* I think she'll be a great wife, even though she's a *violent little thing.*
That's not even funny.
I just want Mana to finally be happy for herself.
HA HA HA
I should congratulate her. I was sure only an animal shelter would take in a savage little beast like her.
Yeah, yeah, I get it. Now quit making that face.
RUFF RUFF
What face?

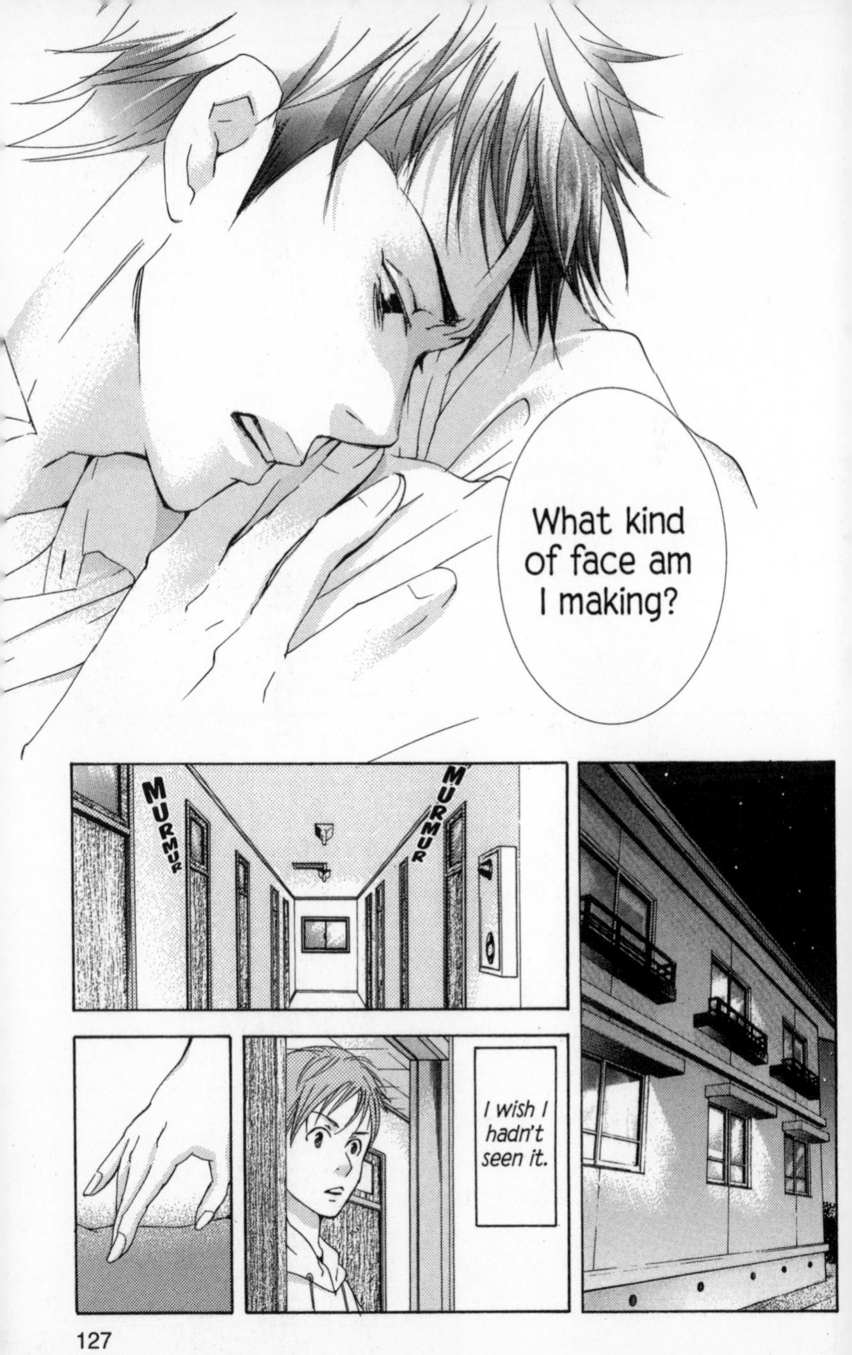
What kind of face am I making?
MURMUR
MURMUR
I wish I hadn't seen it.

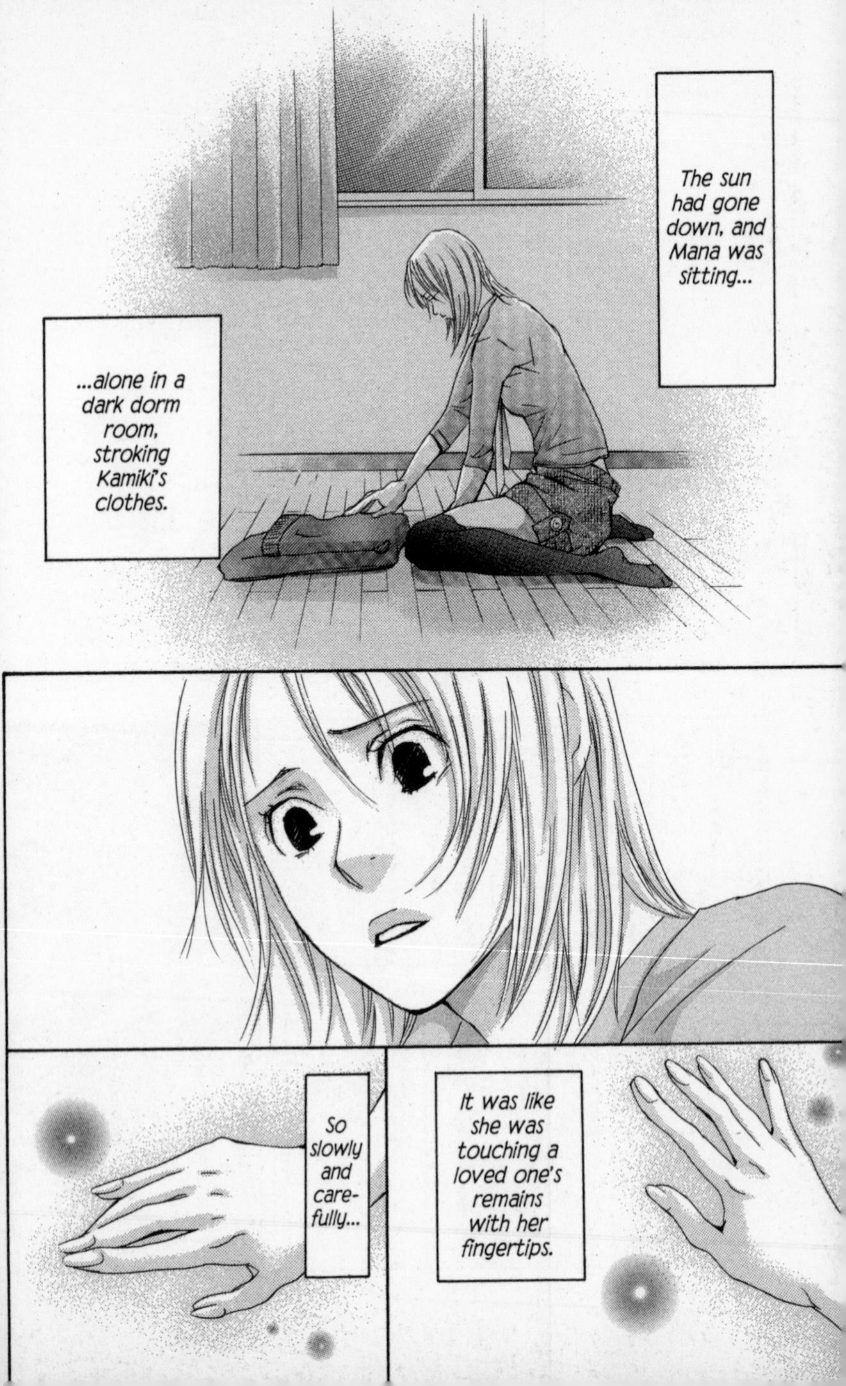
The sun had gone down, and Mana was sitting...
...alone in a dark dorm room, stroking Kamiki's clothes.
It was like she was touching a loved one's remains with her fingertips.
So slowly and care-fully...

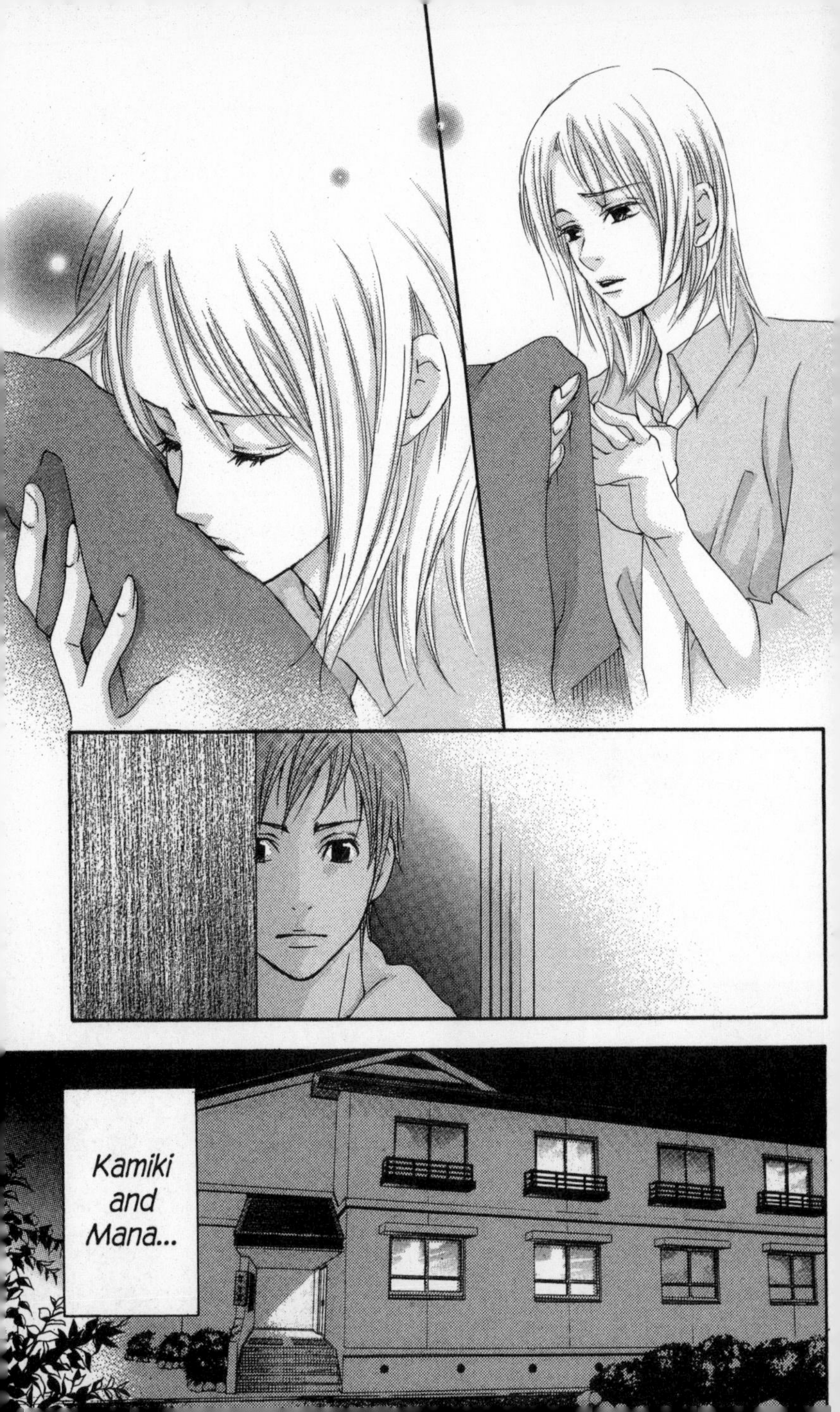
Kamiki and Mana...

...must really love each other.

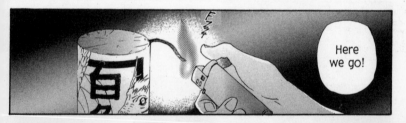

Here we go!

GULP

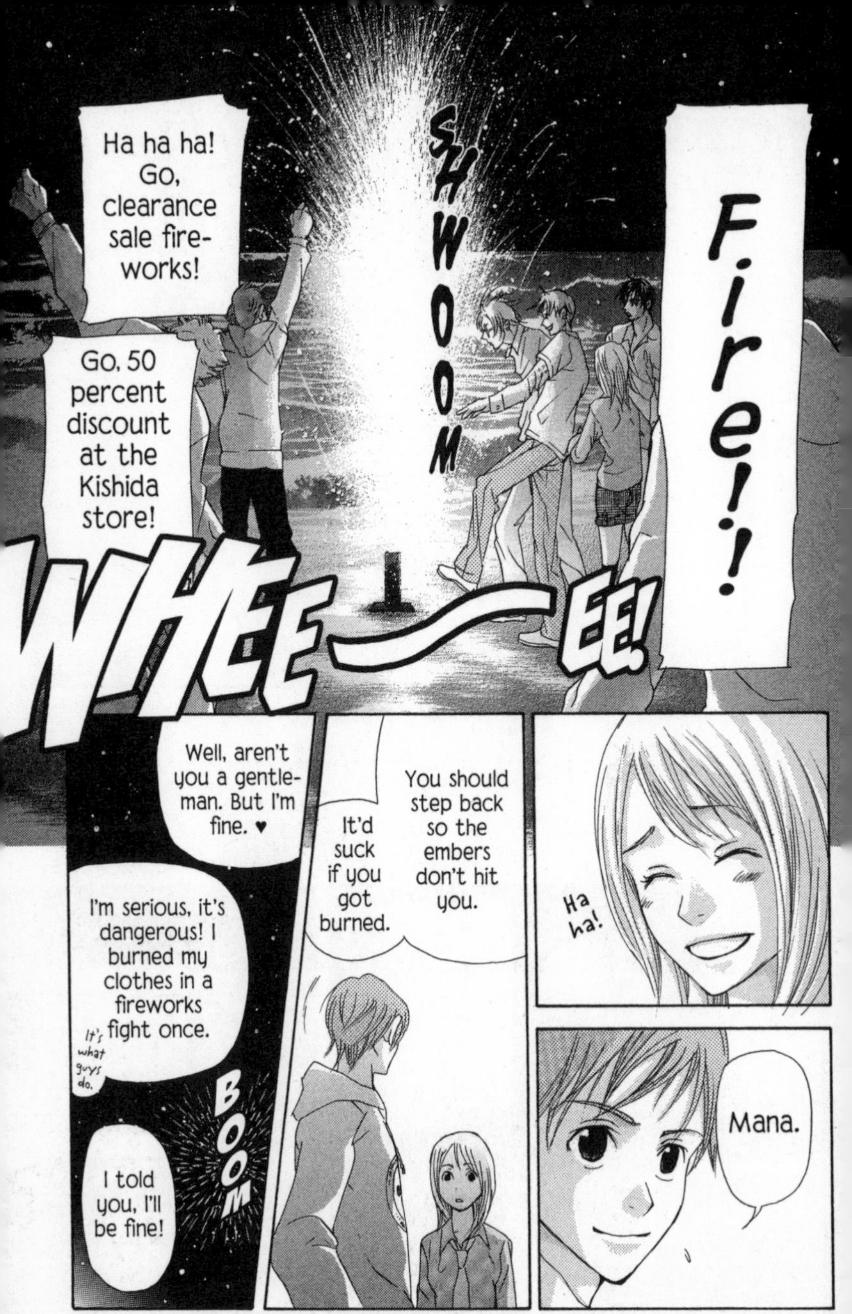
Fire!!
SHWOOM
Ha ha ha! Go, clearance sale fire-works!
Go, 50 percent discount at the Kishida store!
WHEE—EE!
Ha ha!
Mana.
You should step back so the embers don't hit you.
It'd suck if you got burned.
Well, aren't you a gentle-man. But I'm fine. ♥
I'm serious, it's dangerous! I burned my clothes in a fireworks fight once.
It's what guys do.
BOOM
I told you, I'll be fine!

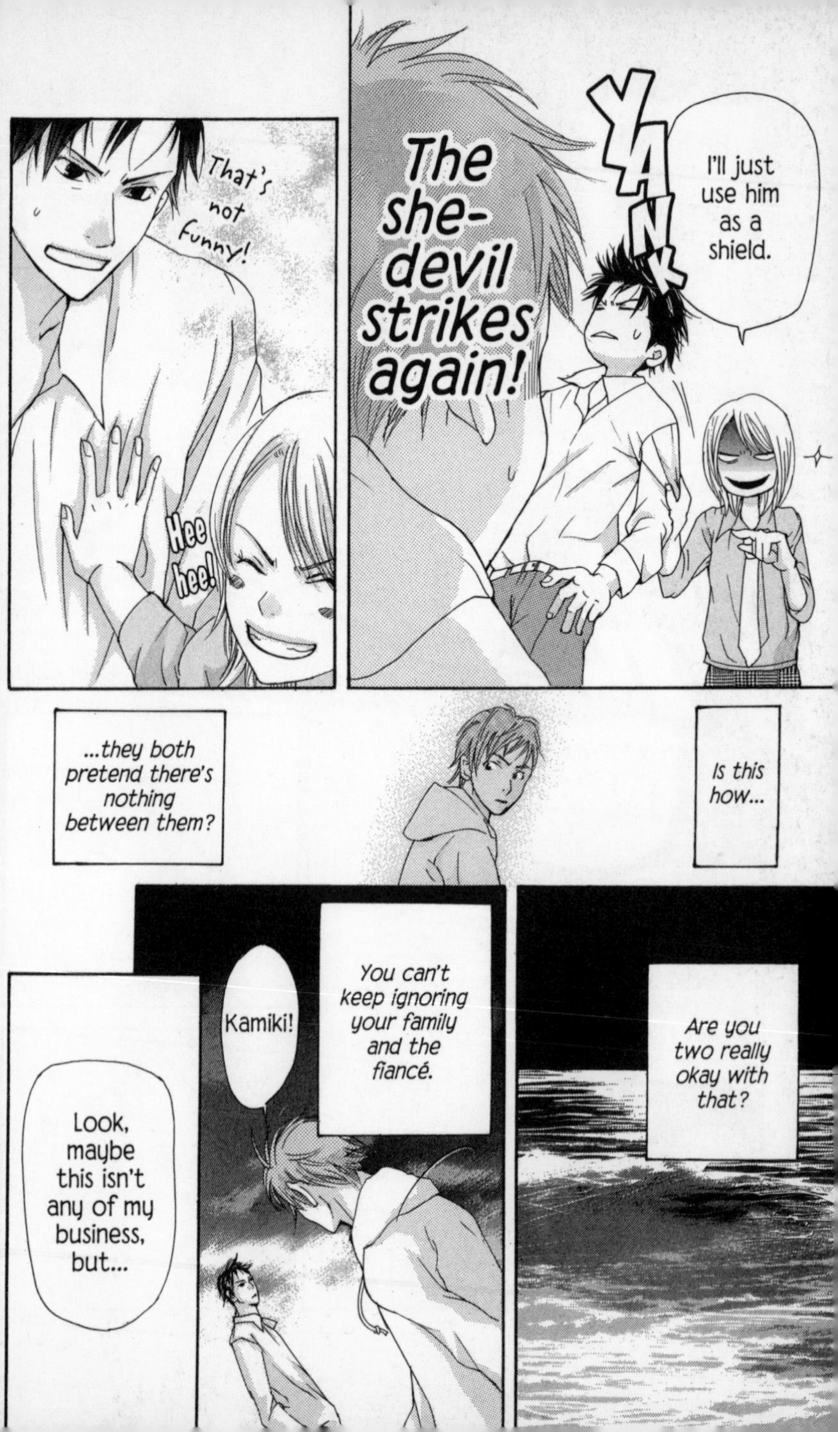
YANK
I'll just use him as a shield.
The she-devil strikes again!
That's not funny!
Hee hee!
Is this how...
...they both pretend there's nothing between them?
Are you two really okay with that?
You can't keep ignoring your family and the fiancé.
Kamiki!
Look, maybe this isn't any of my business, but...

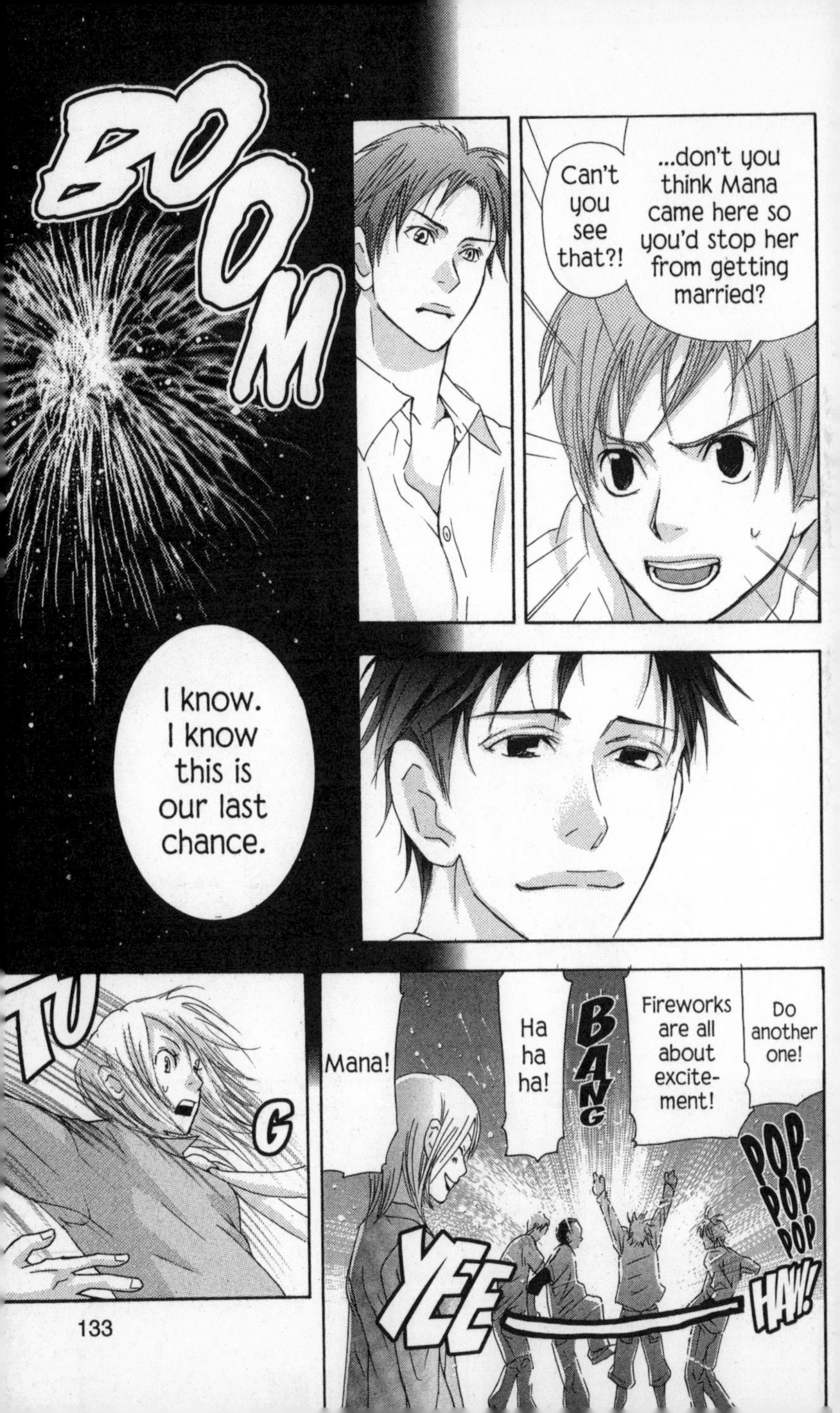
...don't you think Mana came here so you'd stop her from getting married?
Can't you see that?!
BOOM
I know. I know this is our last chance.
Do another one!
Fireworks are all about excitement!
BANG
Ha ha ha!
Mana!
POP POP POP
YEE HAW!
TUG

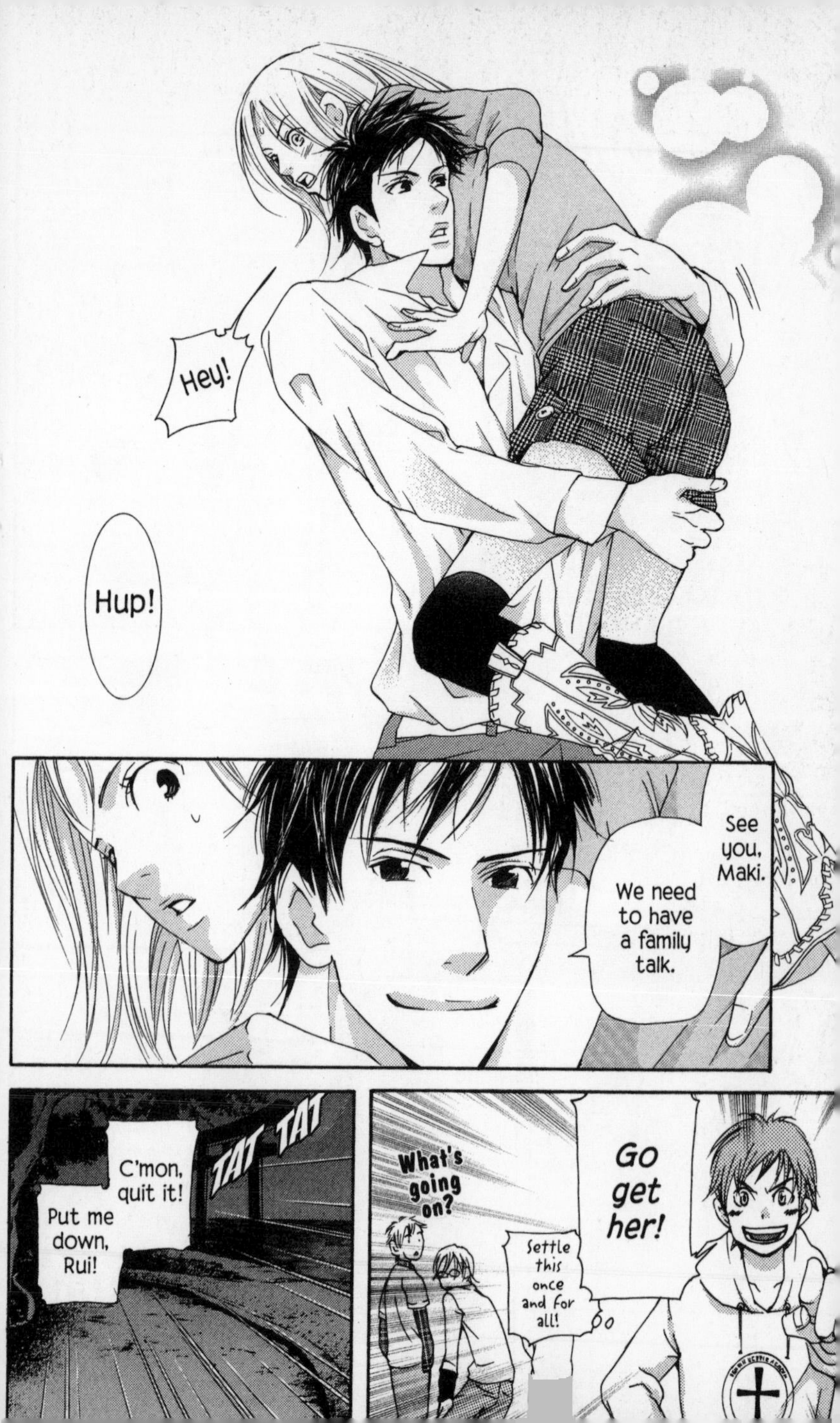
Hey!
Hup!
See you, Maki.
We need to have a family talk.
Go get her!
Settle this once and for all!
What's going on?
TAT TAT
C'mon, quit it!
Put me down, Rui!

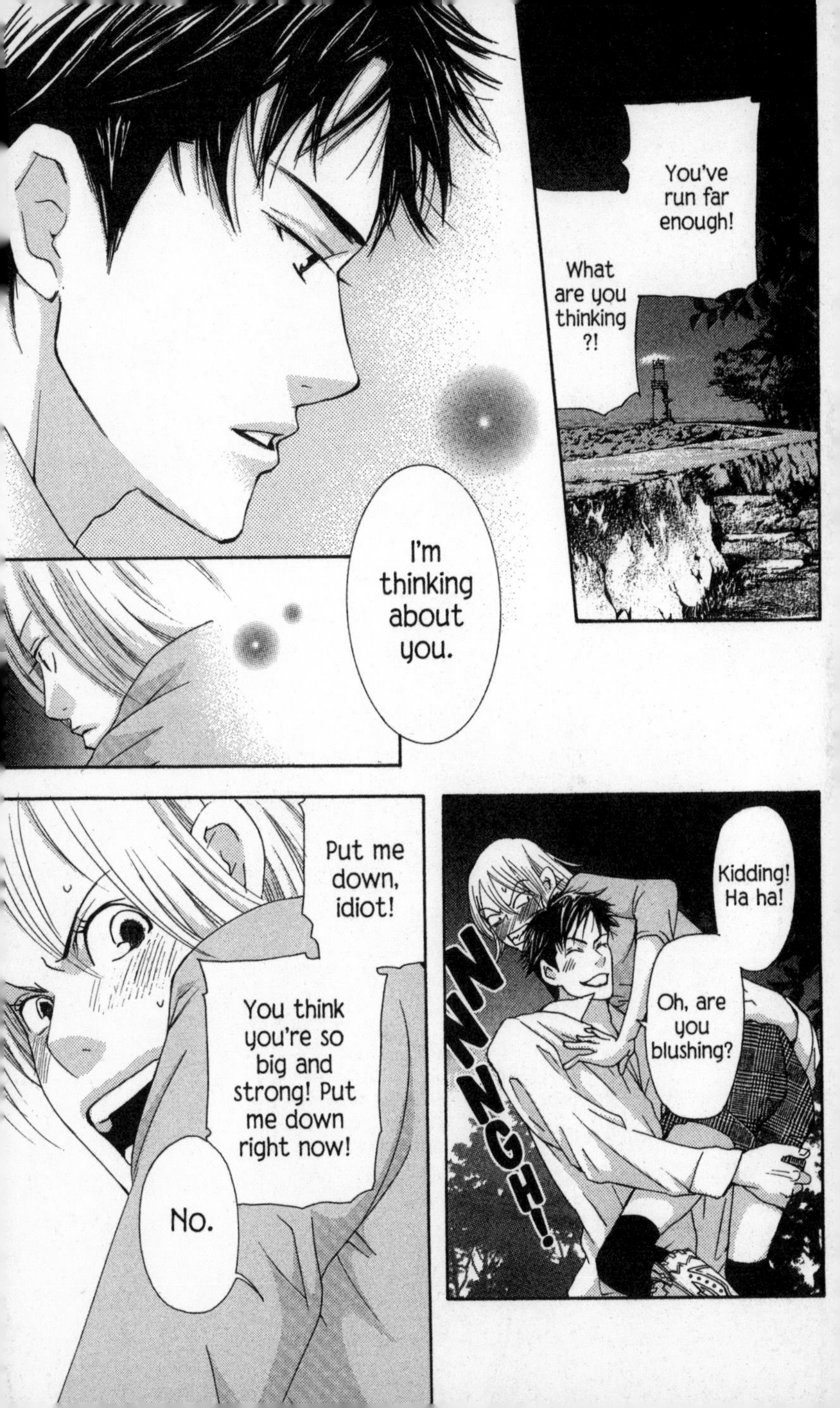
You've run far enough!
What are you thinking?!
I'm thinking about you.
Kidding! Ha ha!
Oh, are you blushing?
NNNGH!!
Put me down, idiot!
You think you're so big and strong! Put me down right now!
No.

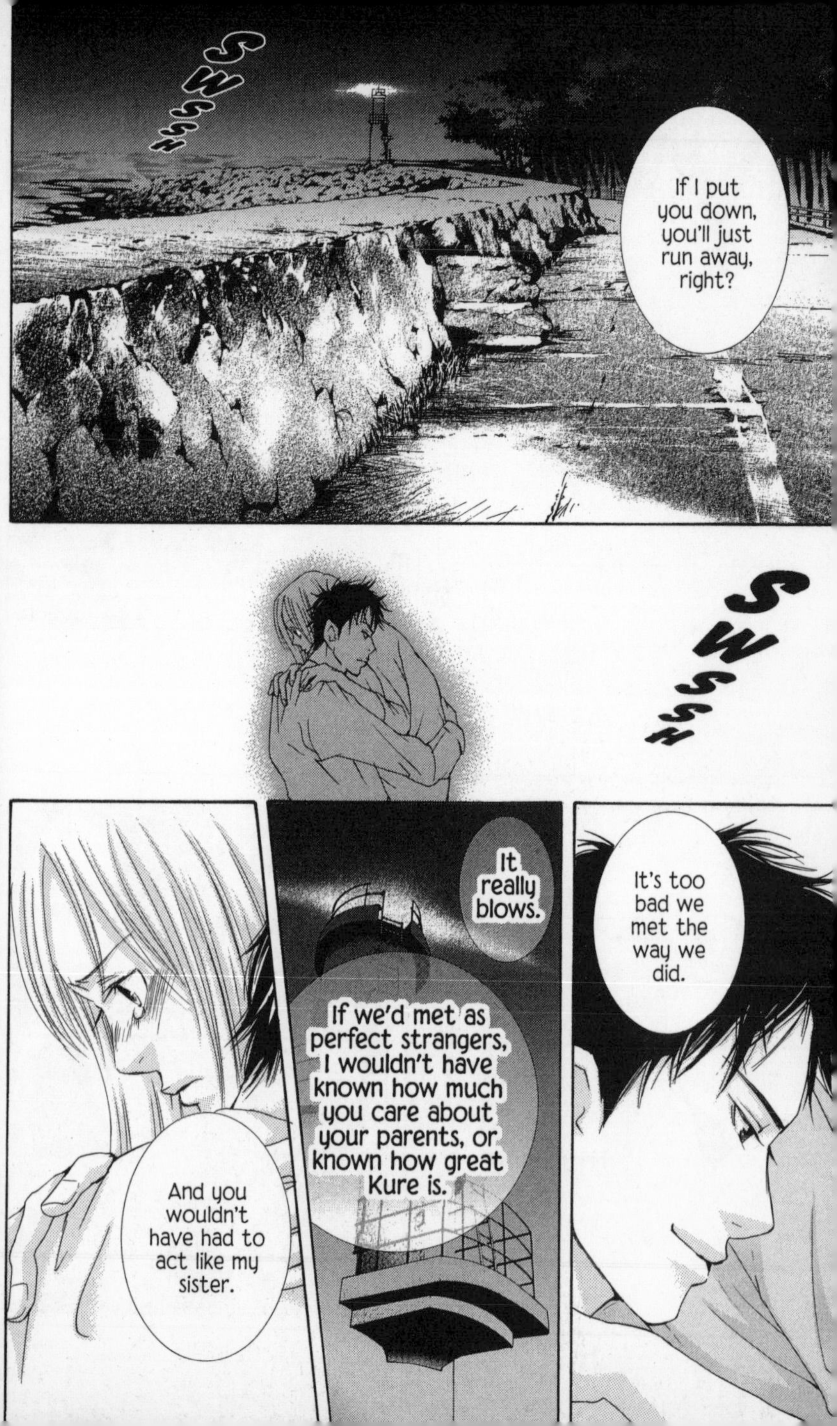
SWSSH
If I put you down, you'll just run away, right?
SWSSH
It's too bad we met the way we did.
It really blows.
If we'd met as perfect strangers, I wouldn't have known how much you care about your parents, or known how great Kure is.
And you wouldn't have had to act like my sister.

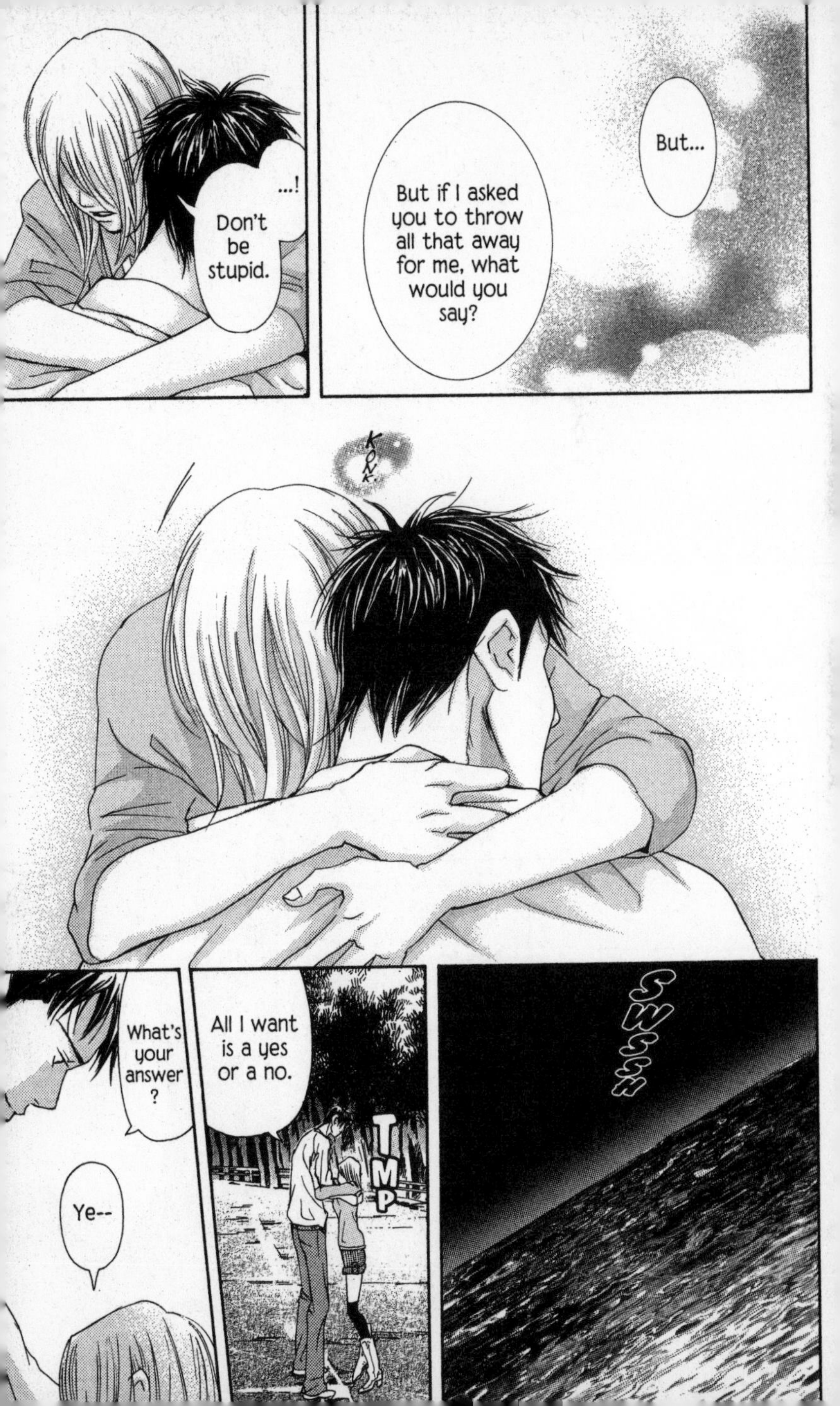
But...
But if I asked you to throw all that away for me, what would you say?
...!
Don't be stupid.
KONK
SWSSH
All I want is a yes or a no.
TMP
What's your answer?
Ye--

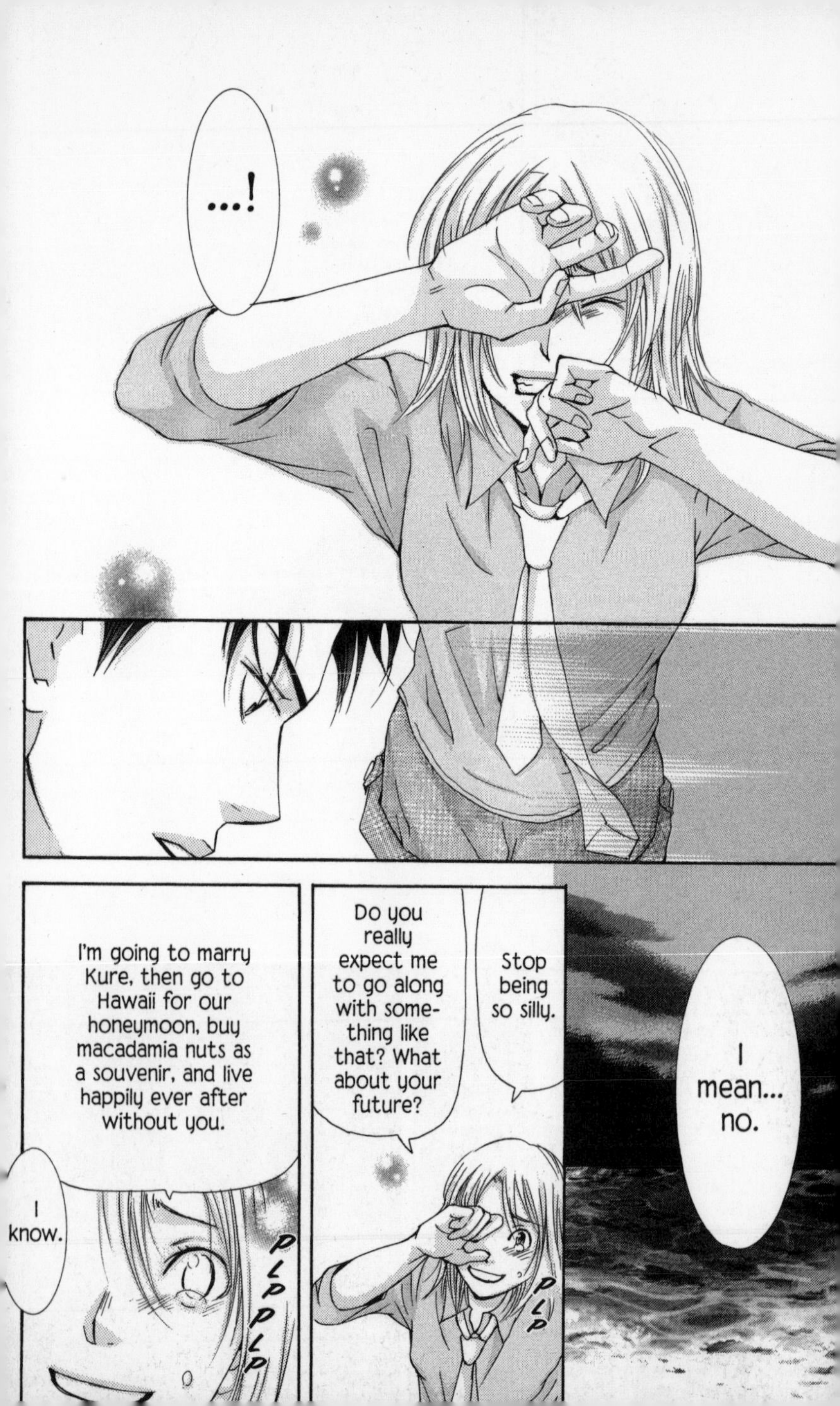
...!
I mean... no.
Stop being so silly.
Do you really expect me to go along with something like that? What about your future?
PLP
I'm going to marry Kure, then go to Hawaii for our honeymoon, buy macadamia nuts as a souvenir, and live happily ever after without you.
PLP PLP
I know.

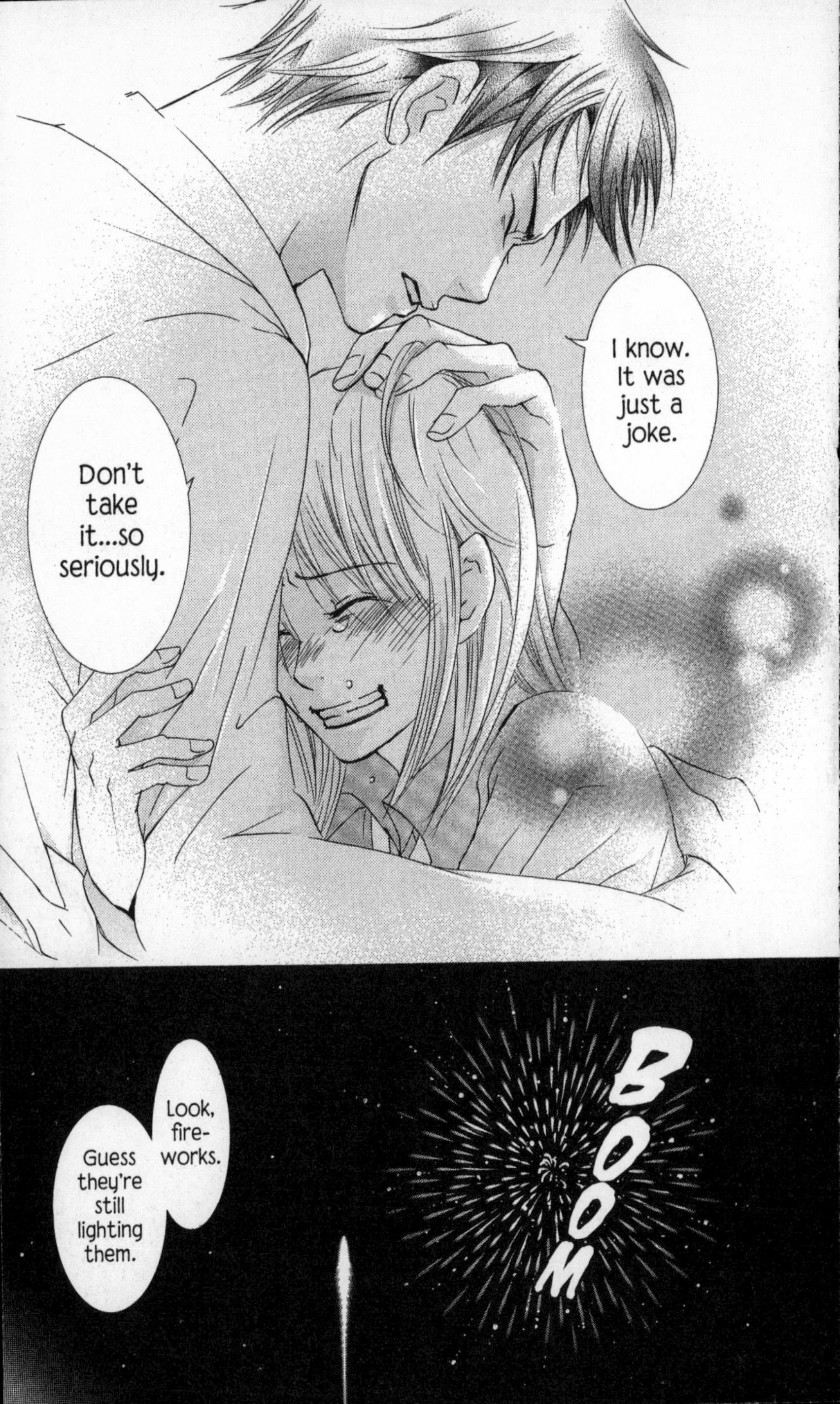
I know. It was just a joke.
Don't take it...so seriously.
BOOM
Look, fire-works.
Guess they're still lighting them.

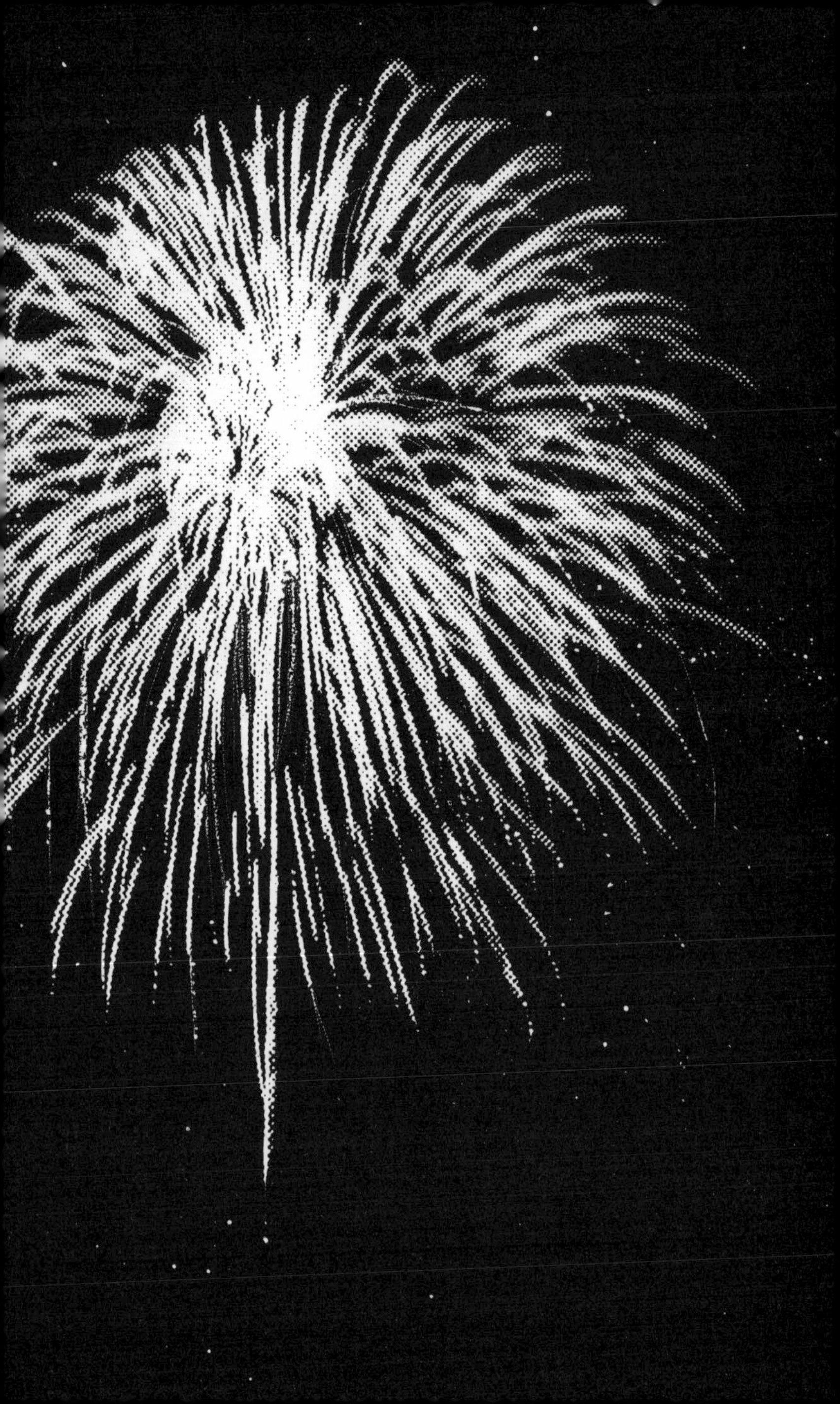

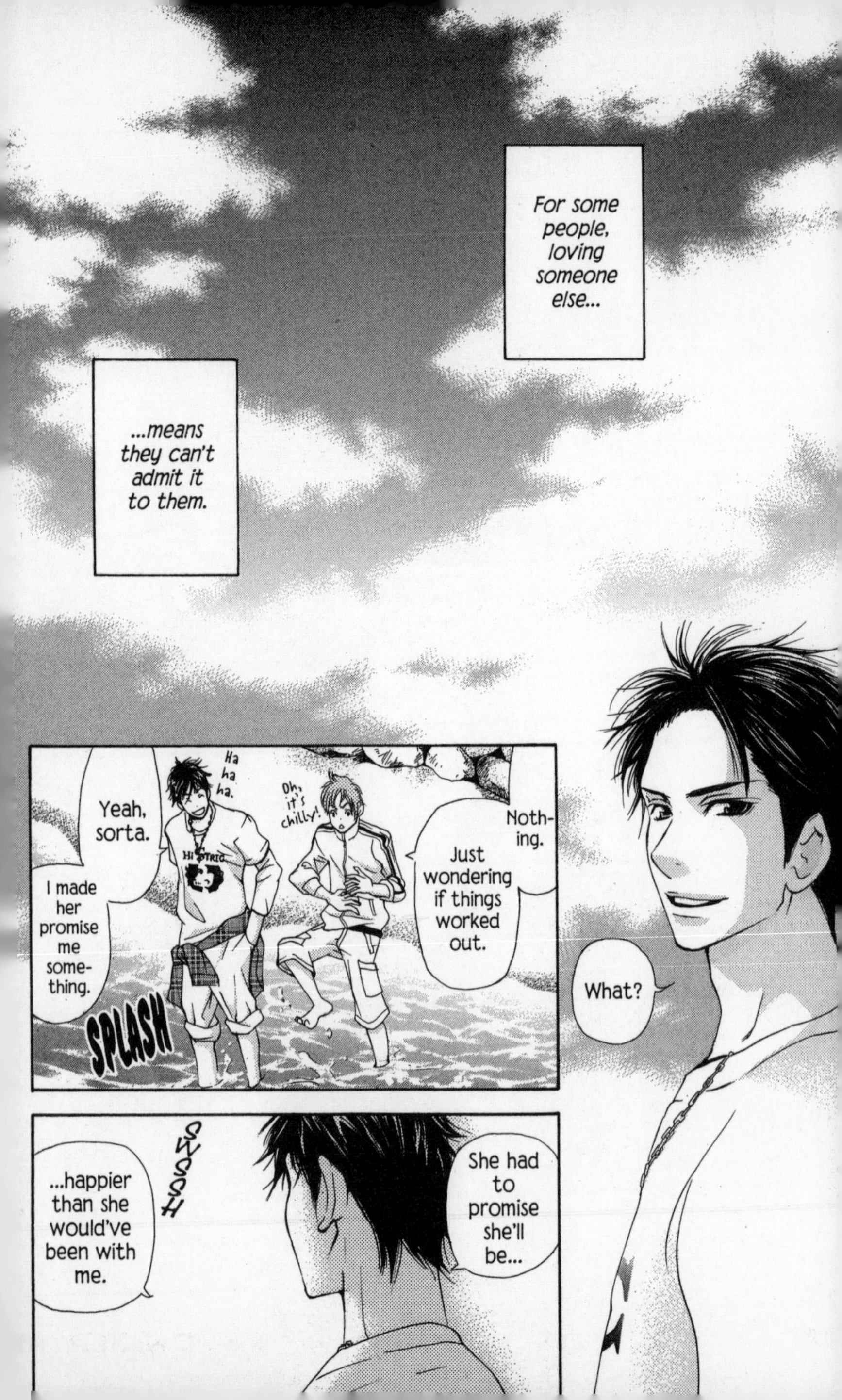
For some people, loving someone else...
...means they can't admit it to them.
What?
Noth-ing.
Just wondering if things worked out.
Oh, it's chilly!
Ha ha ha.
Yeah, sorta.
I made her promise me something.
SPLASH
She had to promise she'll be...
SWSCH
...happier than she would've been with me.

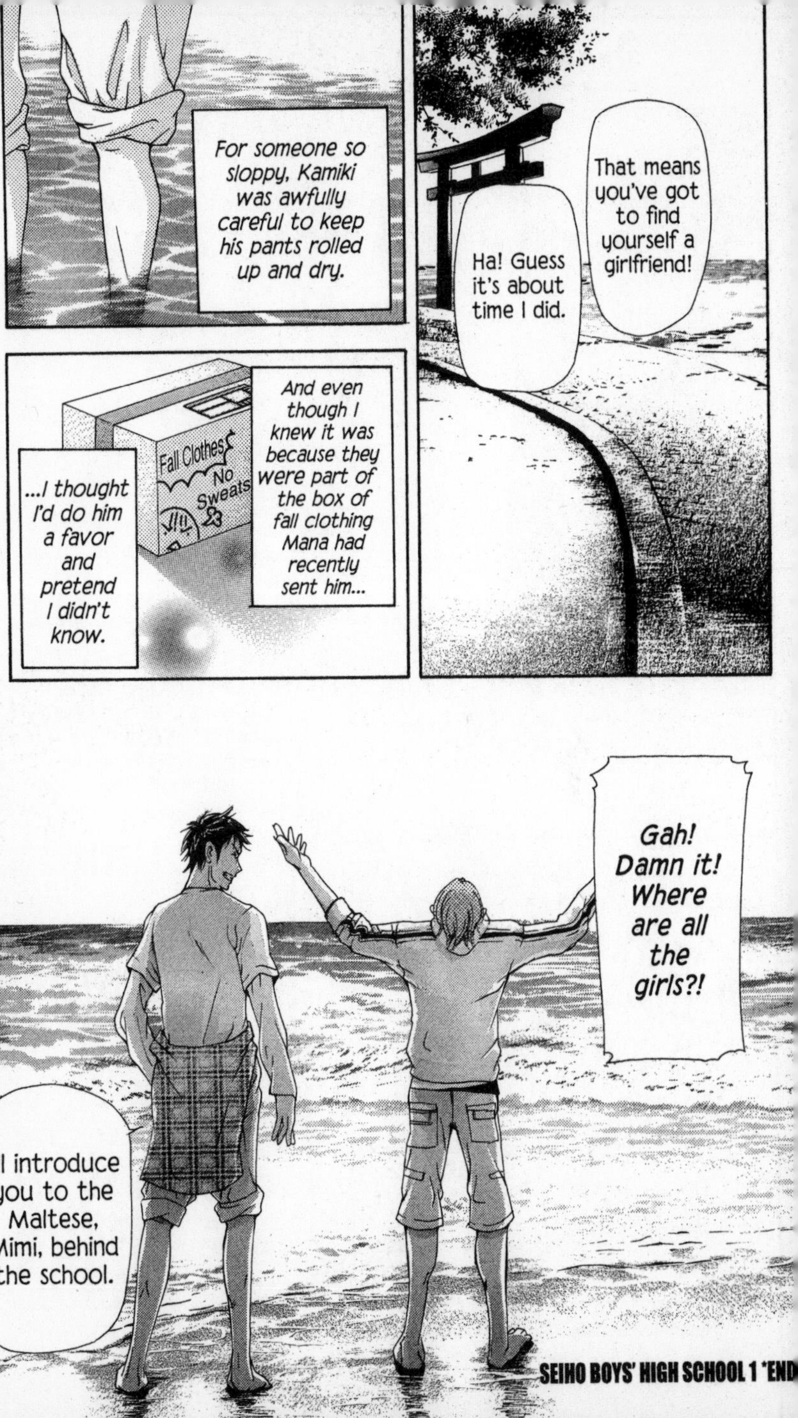
That means you've got to find yourself a girlfriend!
Ha! Guess it's about time I did.
For someone so sloppy, Kamiki was awfully careful to keep his pants rolled up and dry.
And even though I knew it was because they were part of the box of fall clothing Mana had recently sent him...
Fall Clothes
No Sweats
...I thought I'd do him a favor and pretend I didn't know.
Gah! Damn it! Where are all the girls?!
I'll introduce you to the Maltese, Mimi, behind the school.

SEIHO BOYS' HIGH SCHOOL 1 *END

Preview for the Next Volume!

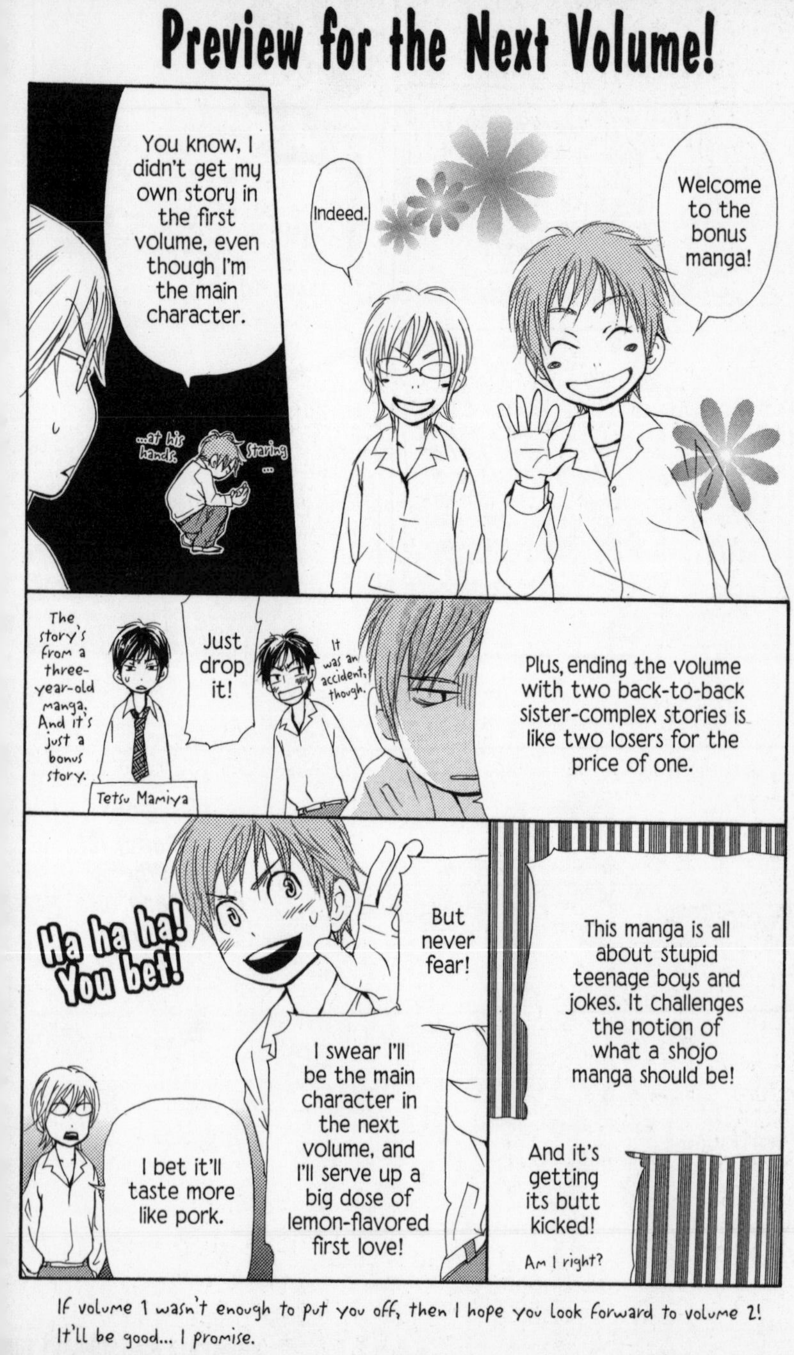
Welcome to the bonus manga!
Indeed.
You know, I didn't get my own story in the first volume, even though I'm the main character.
Staring...
...at his hands.
Plus, ending the volume with two back-to-back sister-complex stories is like two losers for the price of one.
It was an accident, though.
Just drop it!
The story's from a three-year-old manga. And it's just a bonus story.
Tetsu Mamiya
This manga is all about stupid teenage boys and jokes. It challenges the notion of what a shojo manga should be!
And it's getting its butt kicked!
Am I right?
But never fear!
Ha ha ha! You bet!
I swear I'll be the main character in the next volume, and I'll serve up a big dose of lemon-flavored first love!
I bet it'll taste more like pork.

If volume 1 wasn't enough to put you off, then I hope you look forward to volume 2! It'll be good... I promise.

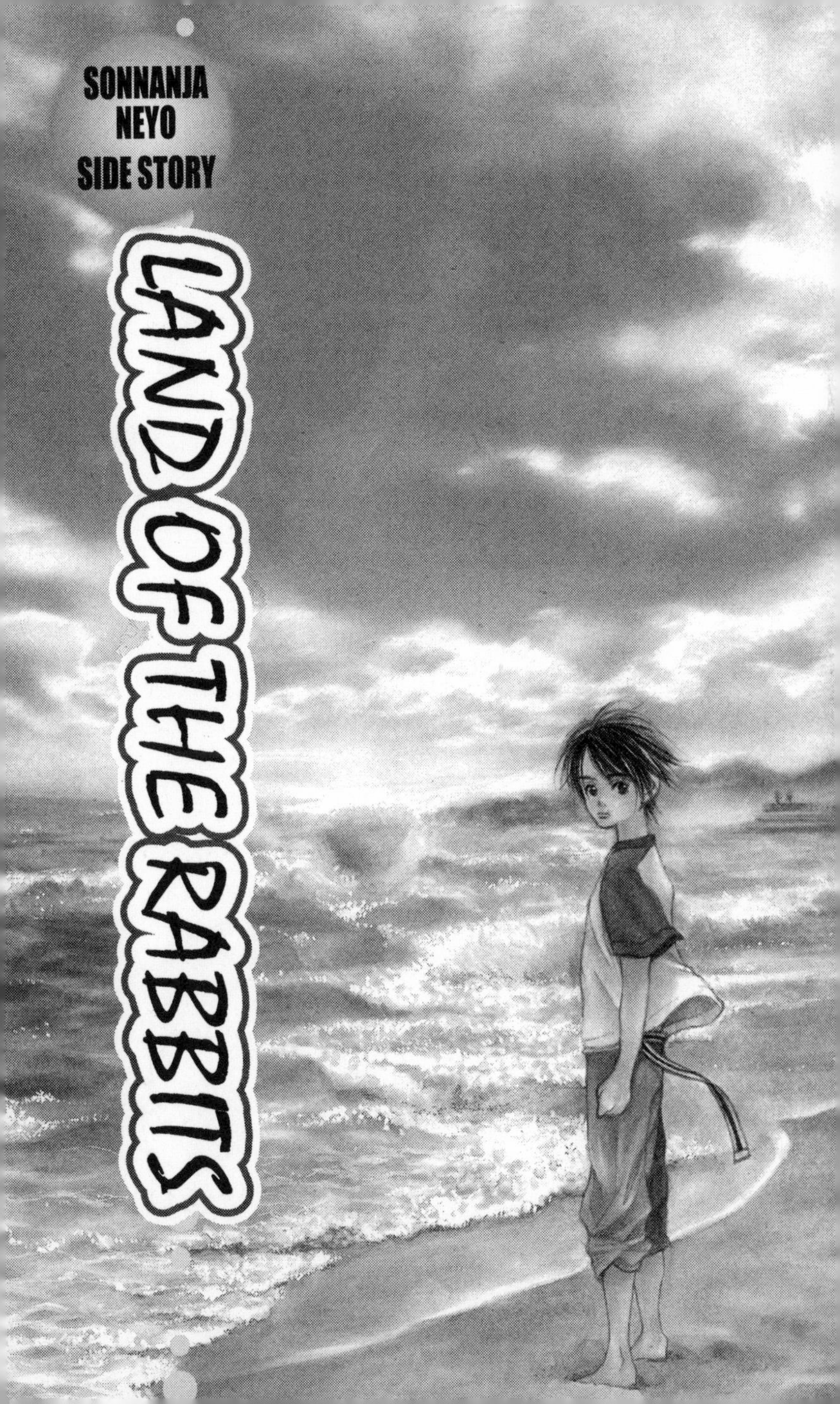
SONNANJA NEYO SIDE STORY
LAND OF THE RABBITS

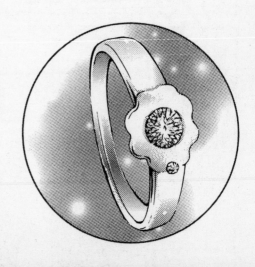

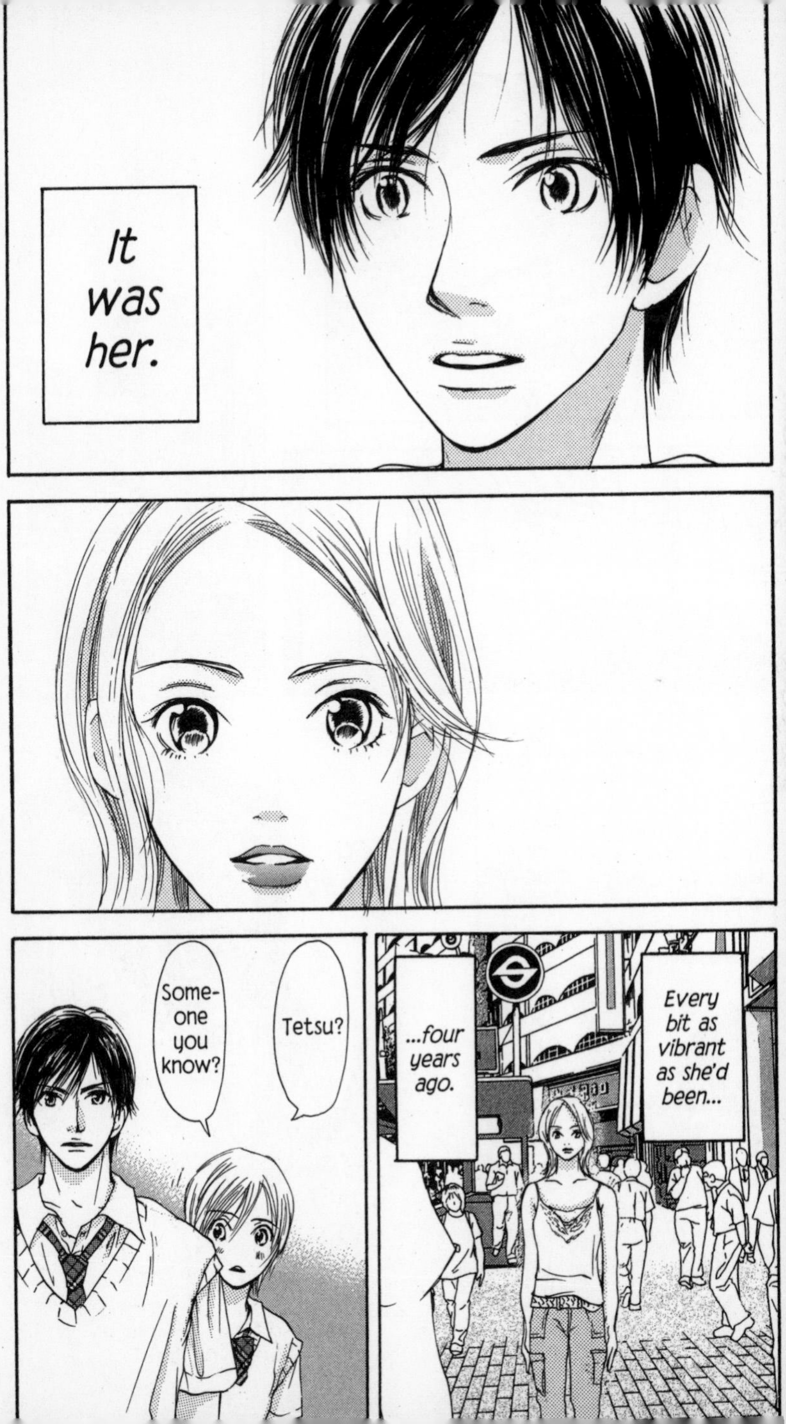
It was her.
Every bit as vibrant as she'd been...
...four years ago.
Tetsu?
Some-one you know?

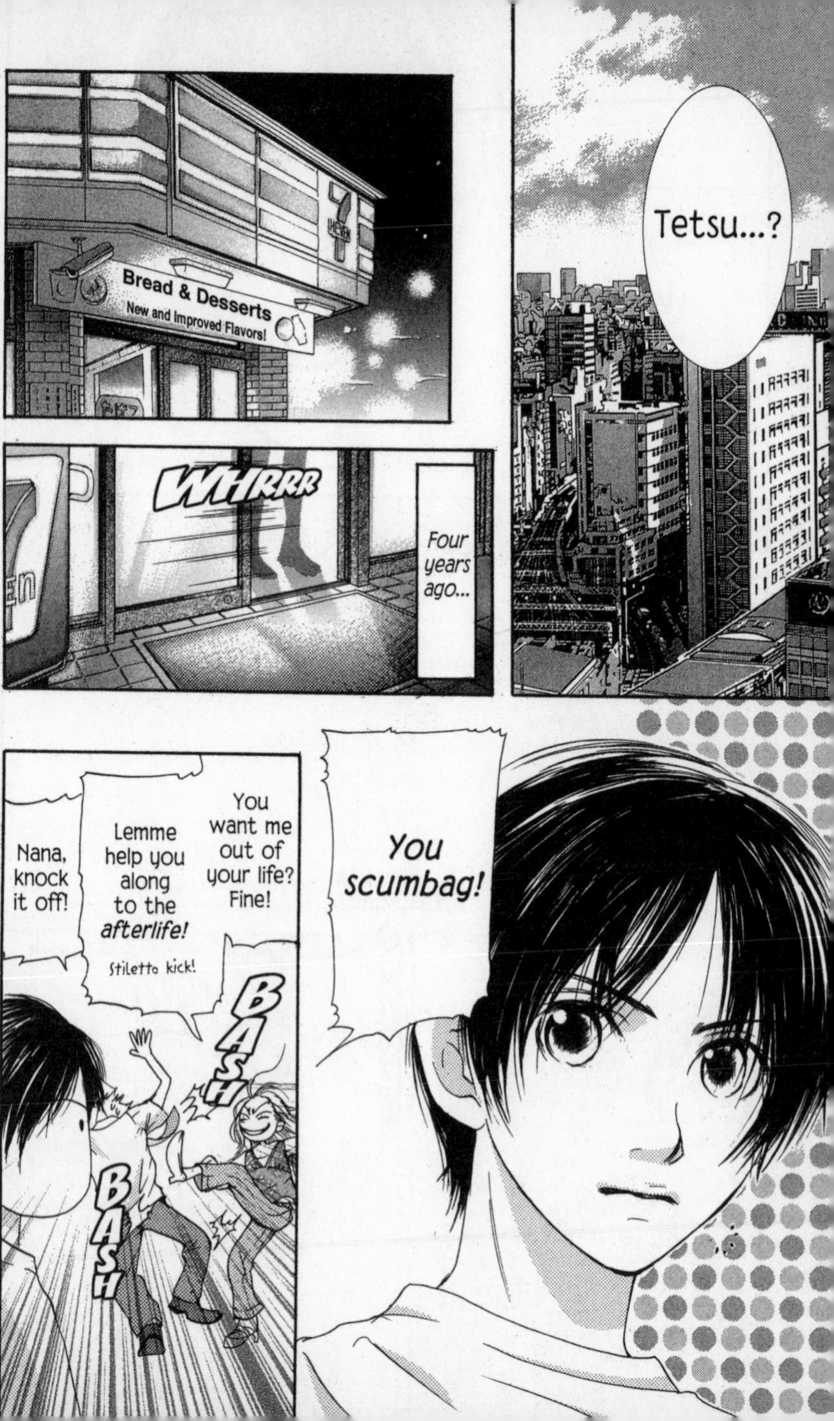
Tetsu...?
Bread & Desserts
New and Improved Flavors!
WHRRR
Four years ago...
You scumbag!
You want me out of your life? Fine!
Lemme help you along to the afterlife!
Nana, knock it off!
Stiletto kick!
BASH
BASH

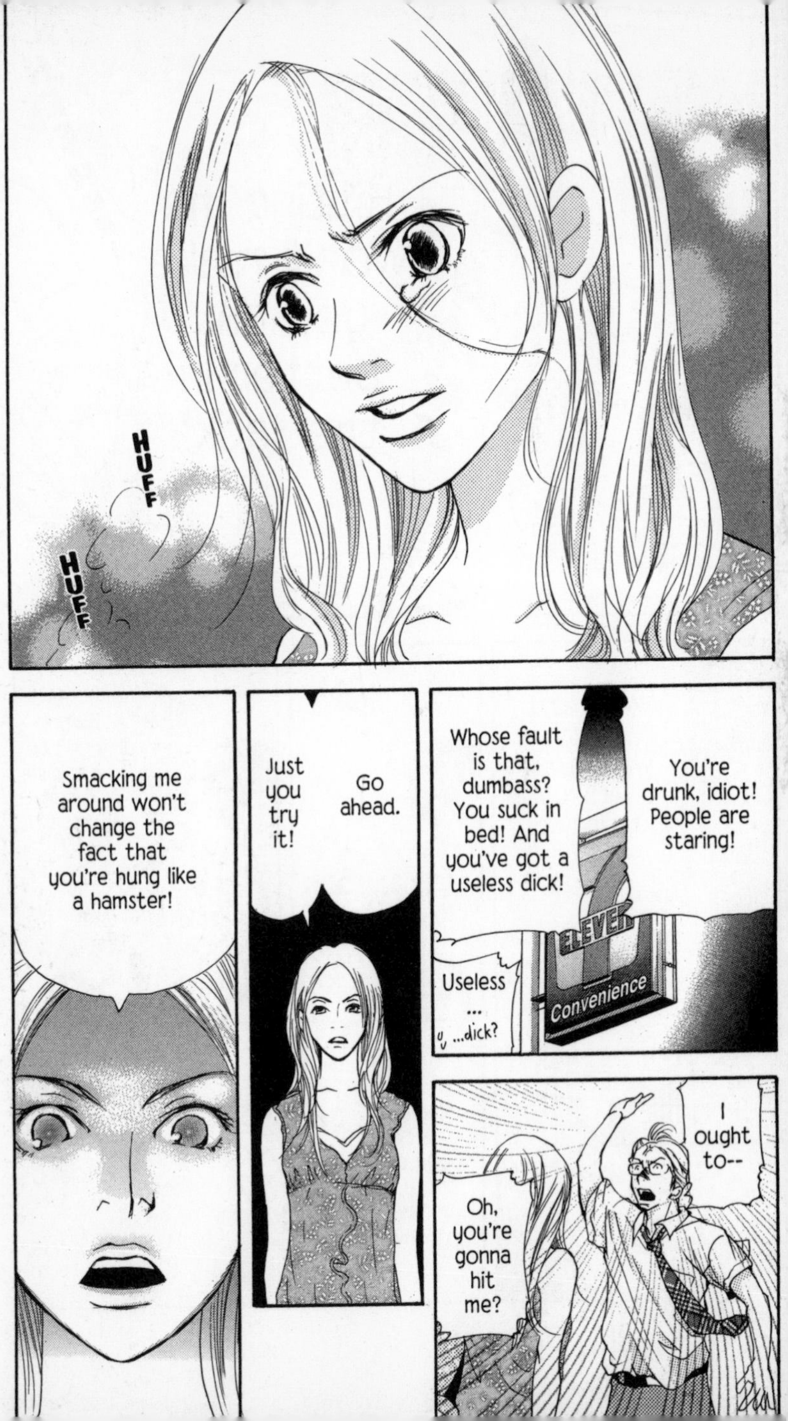
HUFF
HUFF
You're drunk, idiot! People are staring!
Whose fault is that, dumbass? You suck in bed! And you've got a useless dick!
Convenience
Useless ...
...dick?
I ought to--
Oh, you're gonna hit me?
Go ahead.
Just you try it!
Smacking me around won't change the fact that you're hung like a hamster!

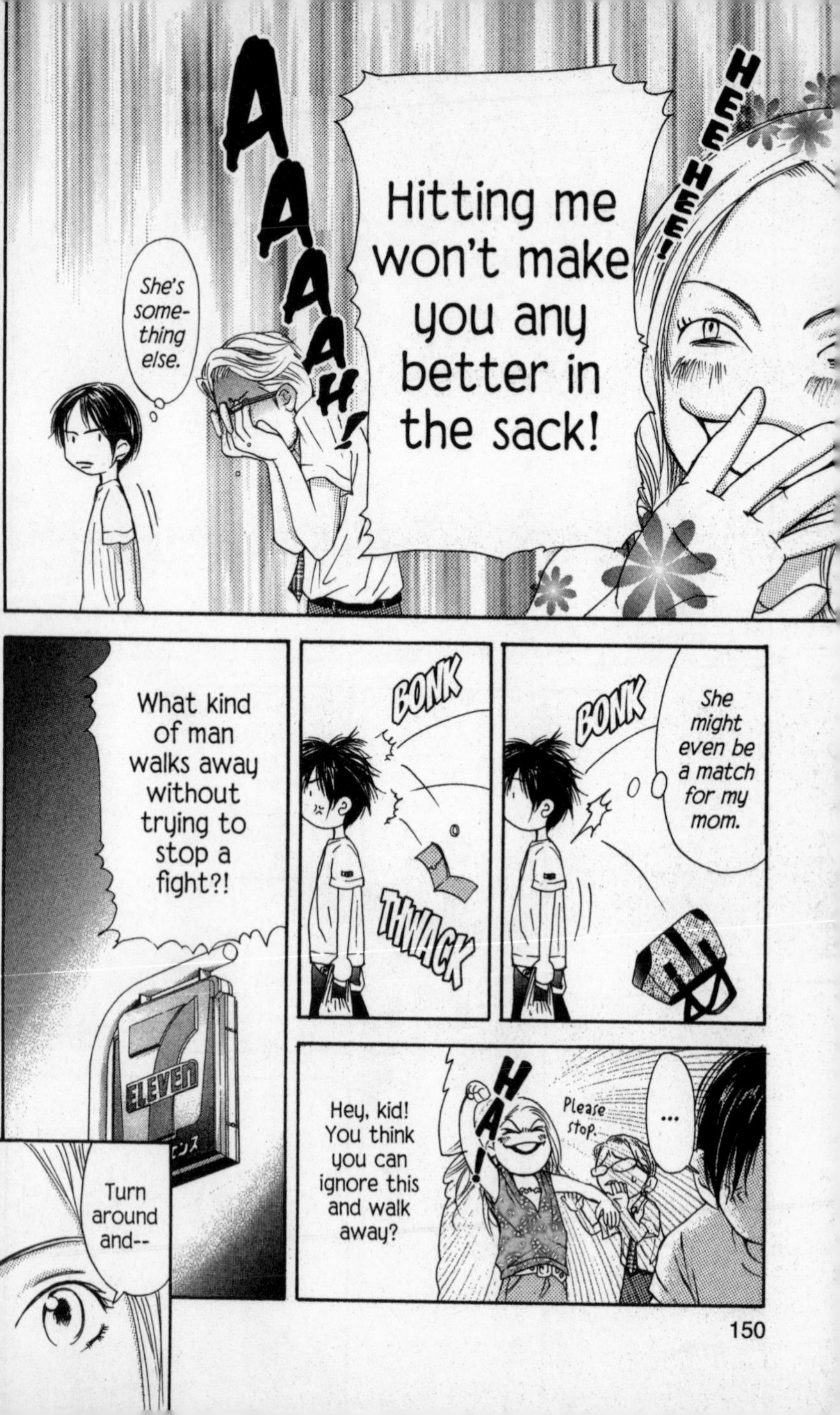
HEE HEE!
Hitting me won't make you any better in the sack!
AAAAH!
She's some-thing else.
She might even be a match for my mom.
BONK
BONK
THWACK
...
Please stop.
HA!
Hey, kid! You think you can ignore this and walk away?
What kind of man walks away without trying to stop a fight?!
ELEVEN
Turn around and--

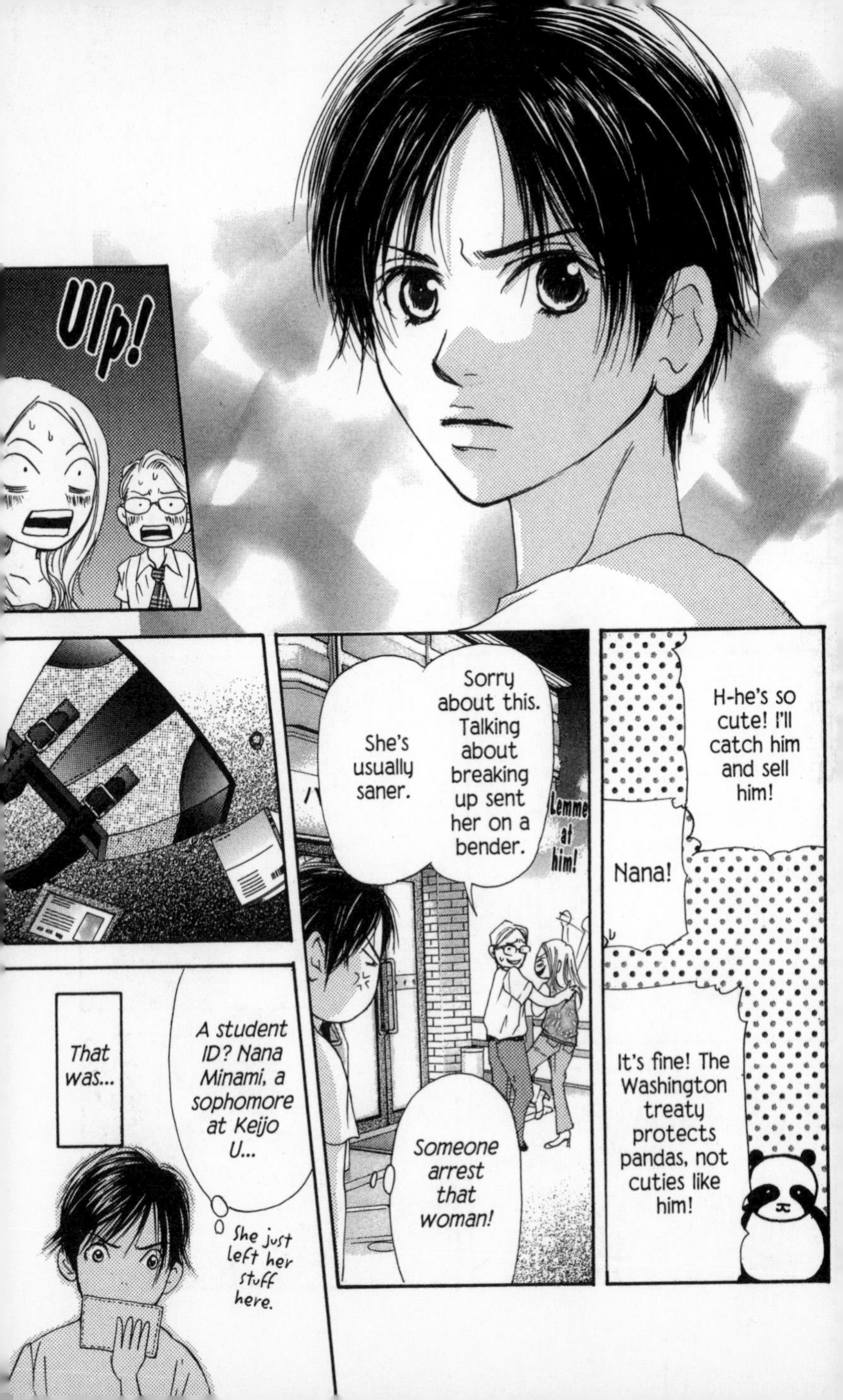
Ulp!
H-he's so cute! I'll catch him and sell him!
Nana!
It's fine! The Washington treaty protects pandas, not cuties like him!
Sorry about this. Talking about breaking up sent her on a bender.
She's usually saner.
Lemme at him!
Someone arrest that woman!
That was...
A student ID? Nana Minami, a sophomore at Keijo U...
She just left her stuff here.

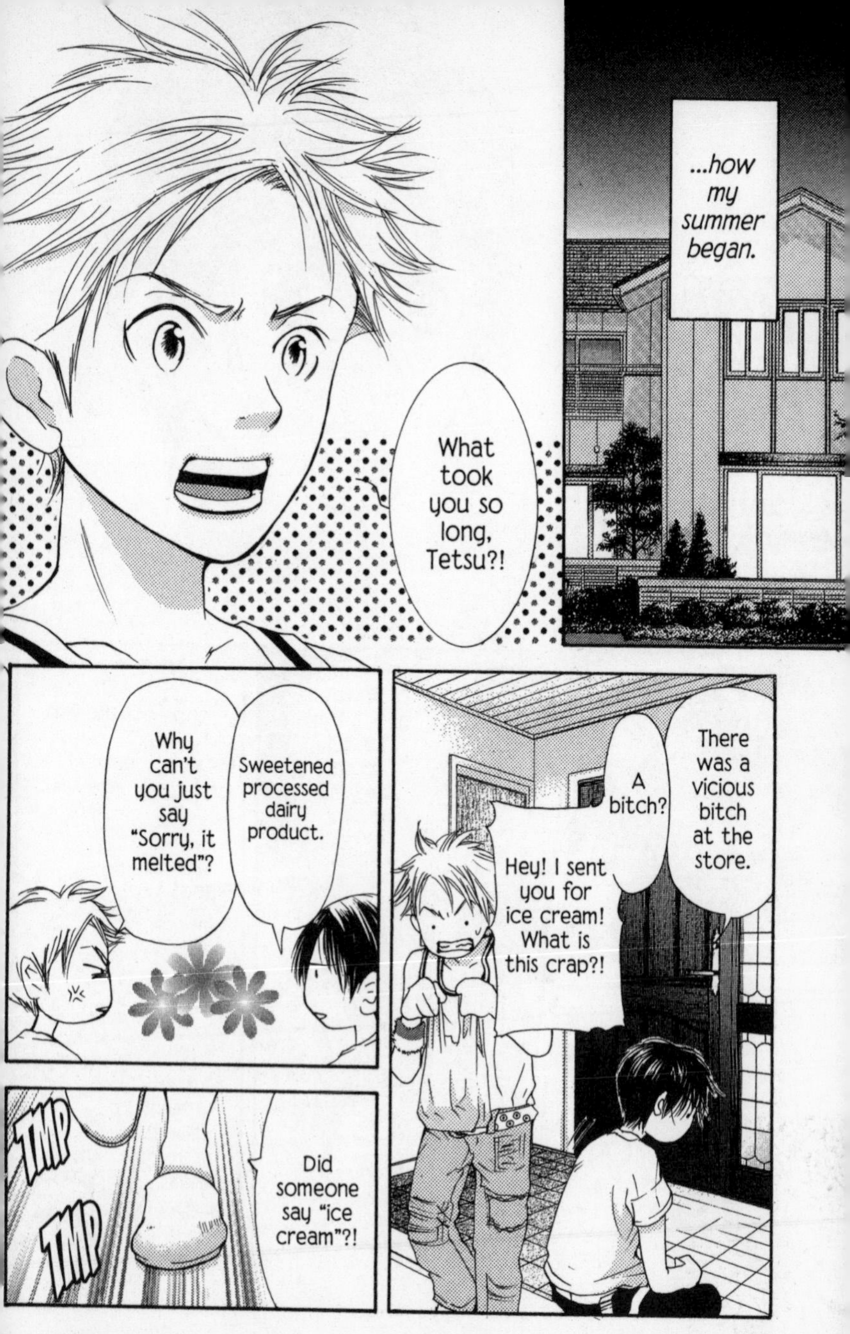
...how my summer began.
What took you so long, Tetsu?!
There was a vicious bitch at the store.
A bitch?
Hey! I sent you for ice cream! What is this crap?!
Sweetened processed dairy product.
Why can't you just say "Sorry, it melted"?
Did someone say "ice cream"?!
TMP
TMP

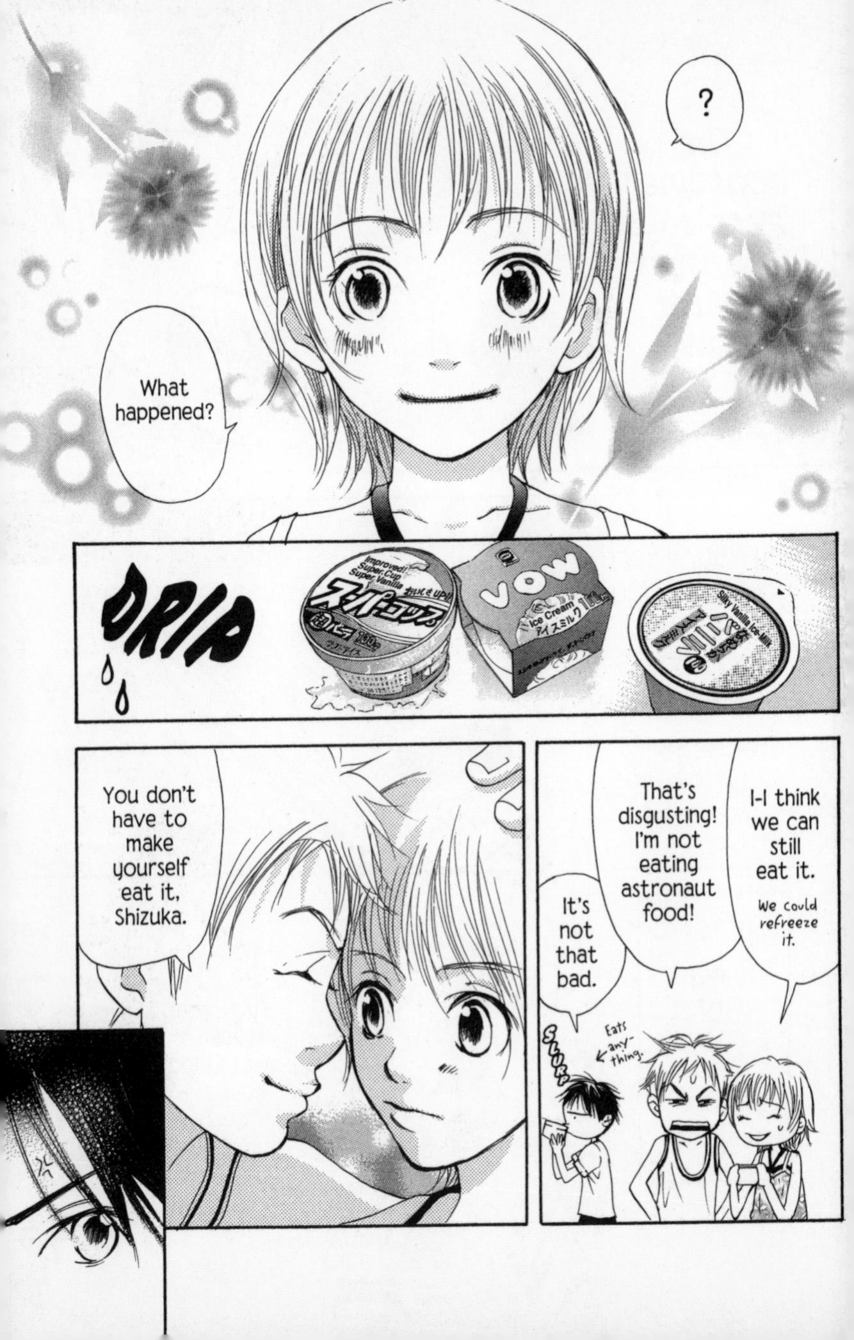
?
What happened?
DRIP
Improved! Super Cup Super Vanilla
VOW
Ice Cream
Silky Vanilla Ice Milk
I-I think we can still eat it.
We could refreeze it.
That's disgusting! I'm not eating astronaut food!
It's not that bad.
SLURP
Eats any-thing.
You don't have to make yourself eat it, Shizuka.

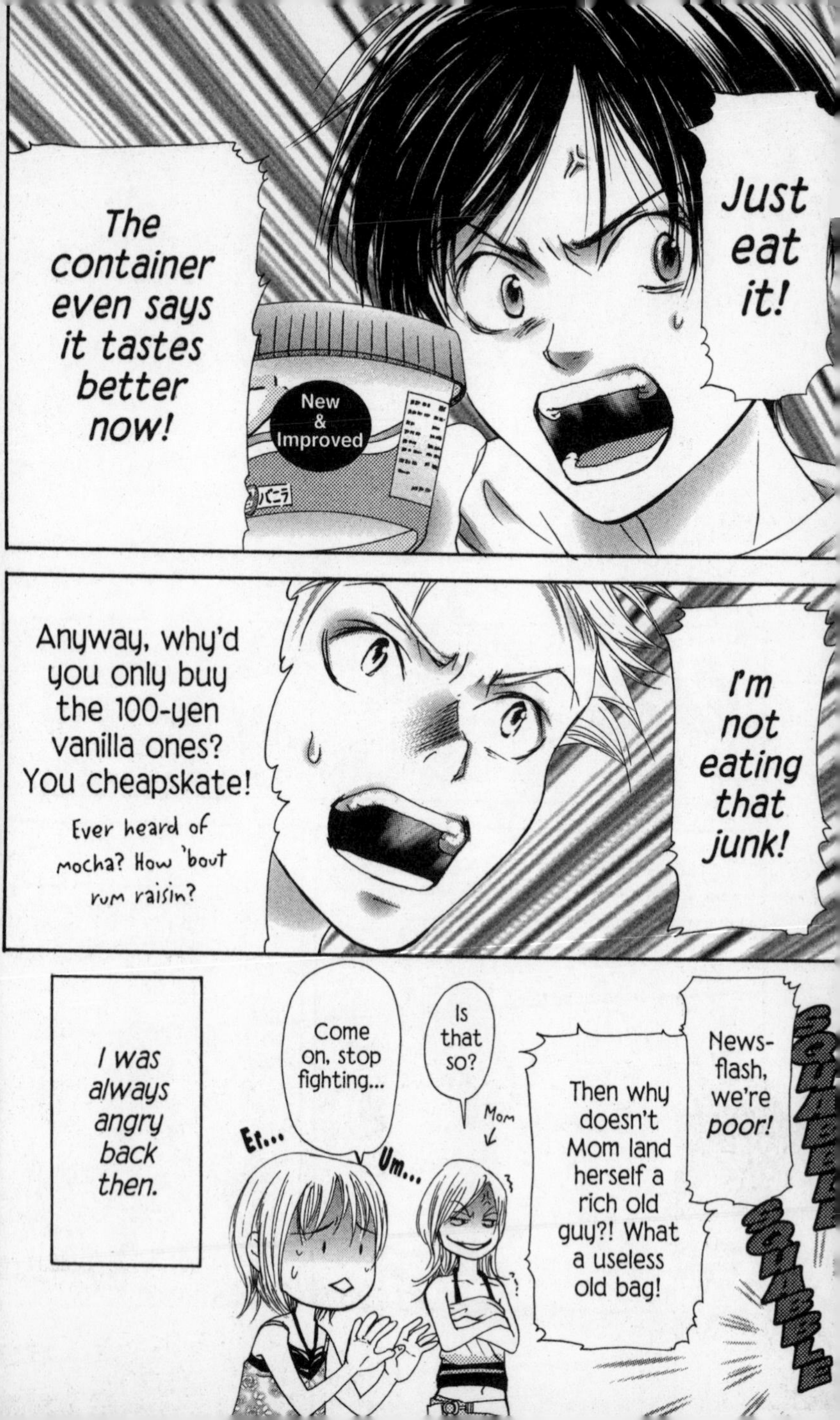

Just eat it!
The container even says it tastes better now!
New & Improved
バニラ
I'm not eating that junk!
Anyway, why'd you only buy the 100-yen vanilla ones? You cheapskate!
Ever heard of mocha? How 'bout rum raisin?
News-flash, we're poor!
Then why doesn't Mom land herself a rich old guy?! What a useless old bag!
Is that so?
Mom
Um...
Come on, stop fighting...
Er...
I was always angry back then.

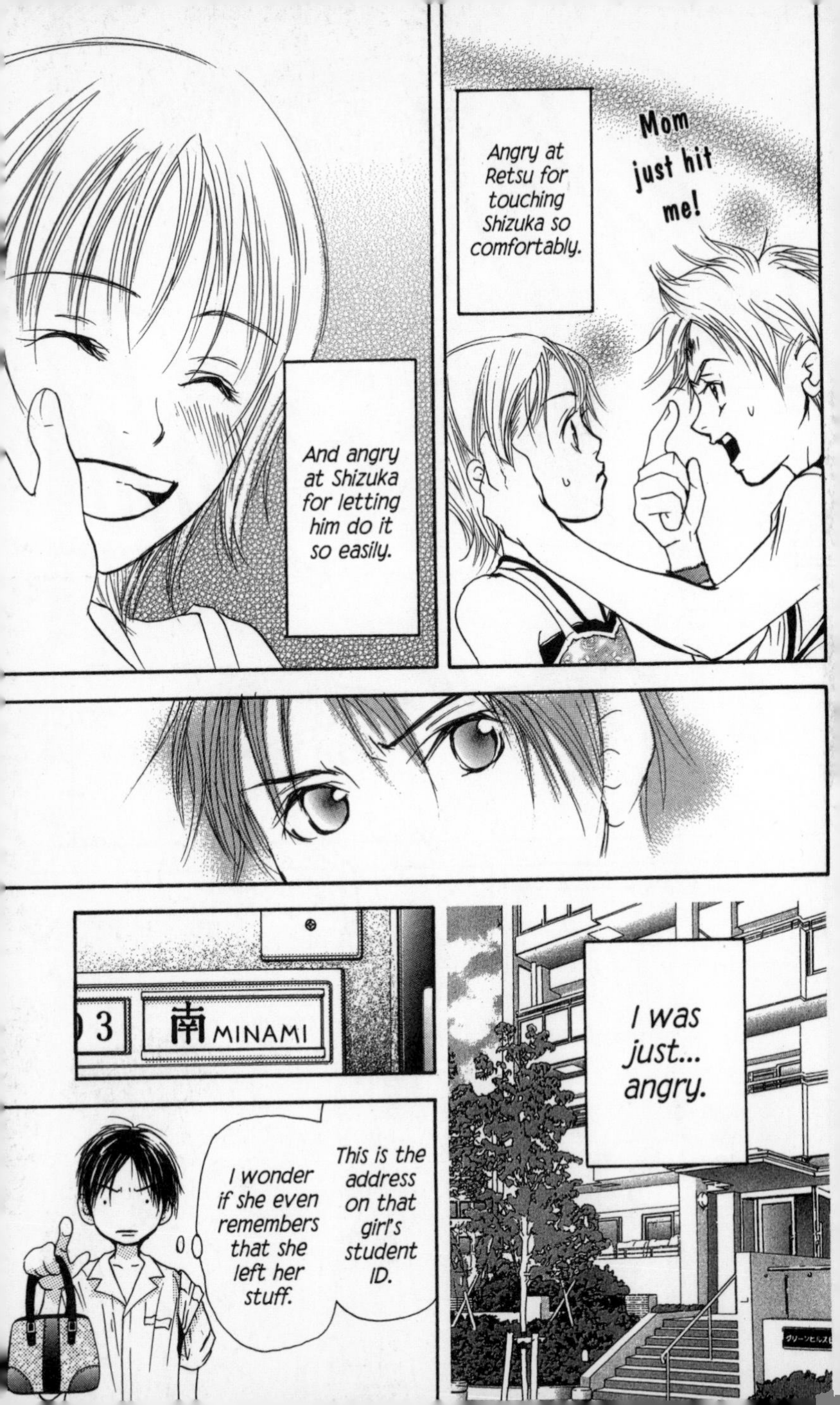

Angry at Retsu for touching Shizuka so comfortably.
Mom just hit me!
And angry at Shizuka for letting him do it so easily.
I was just... angry.
3
南 MINAMI
This is the address on that girl's student ID.
I wonder if she even remembers that she left her stuff.

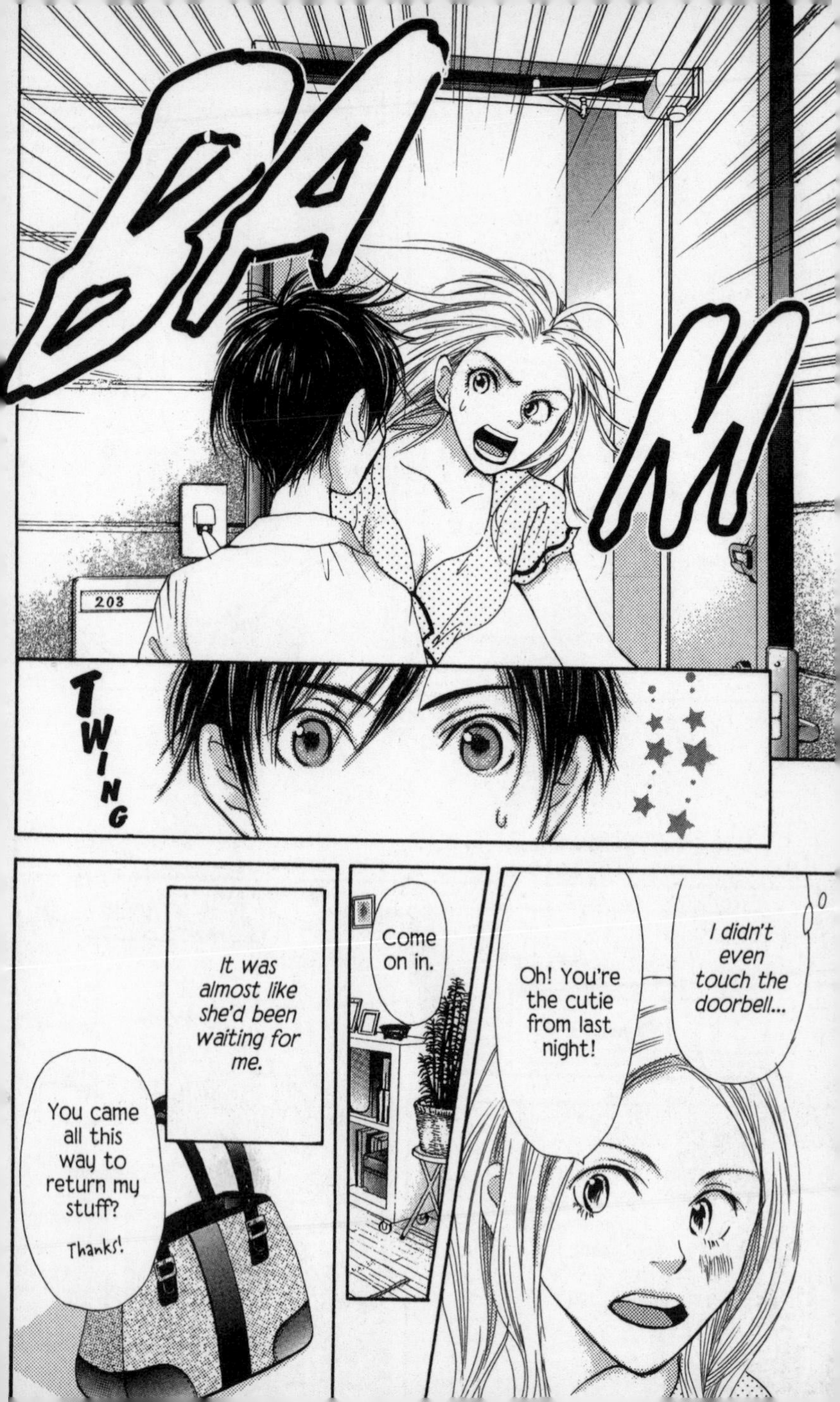
BAM
TWING
I didn't even touch the doorbell...
Oh! You're the cutie from last night!
Come on in.
It was almost like she'd been waiting for me.
You came all this way to return my stuff?
Thanks!

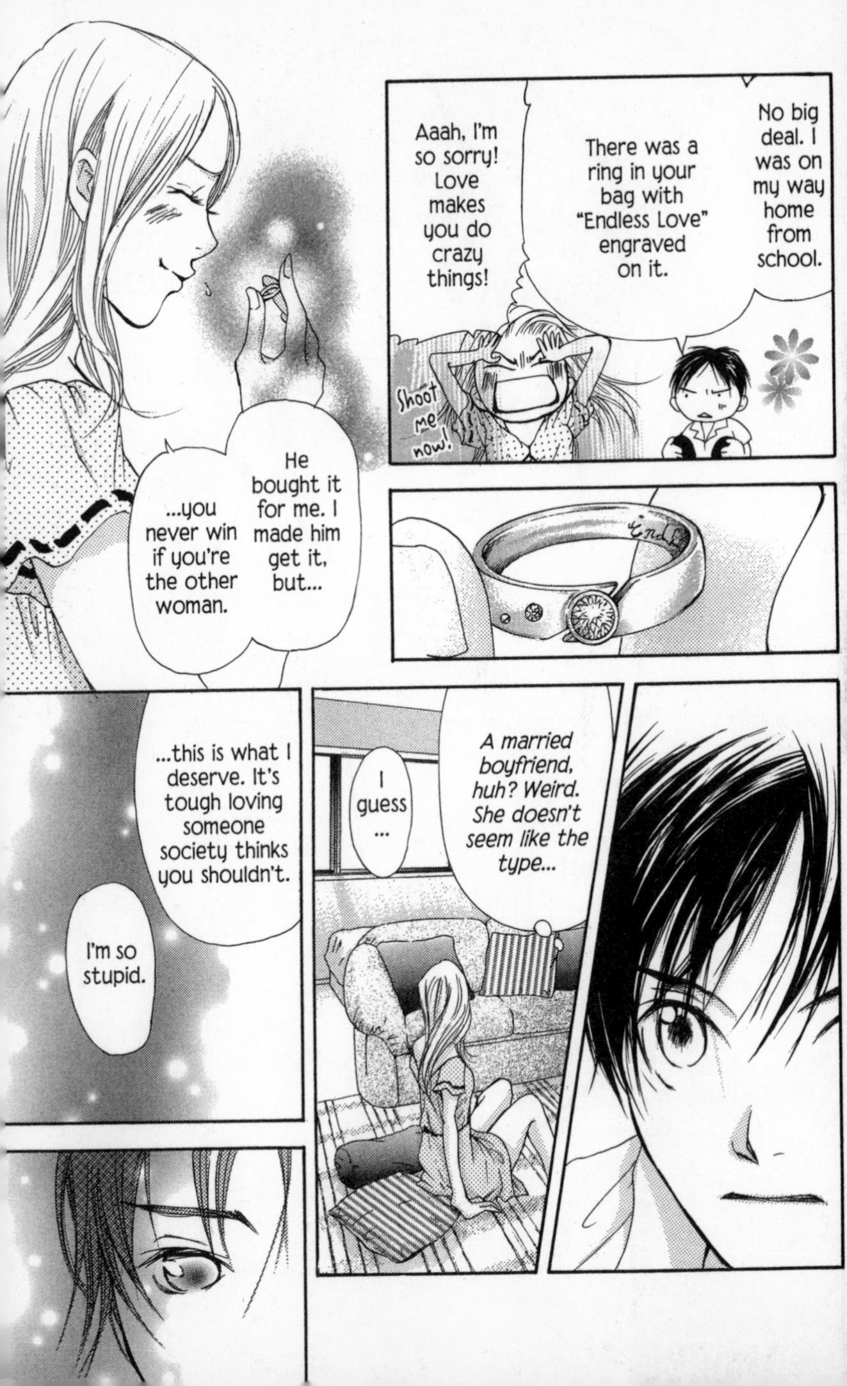
No big deal. I was on my way home from school.
There was a ring in your bag with "Endless Love" engraved on it.
Aaah, I'm so sorry! Love makes you do crazy things!
Shoot me now!
He bought it for me. I made him get it, but...
...you never win if you're the other woman.
A married boyfriend, huh? Weird. She doesn't seem like the type...
I guess...
...this is what I deserve. It's tough loving someone society thinks you shouldn't.
I'm so stupid.

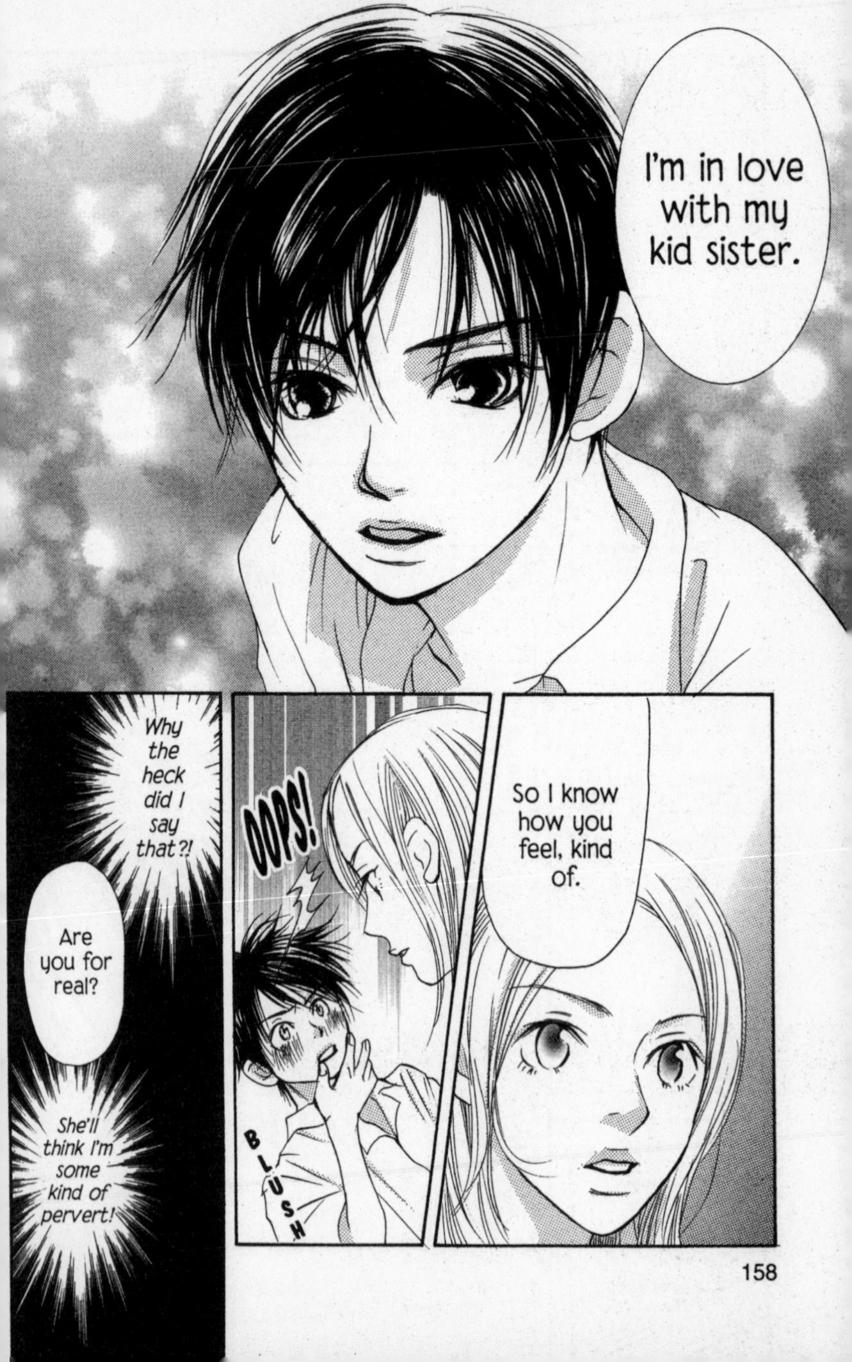
I'm in love with my kid sister.
So I know how you feel, kind of.
OOPS!
BLUSH
Why the heck did I say that?!
Are you for real?
She'll think I'm some kind of pervert!

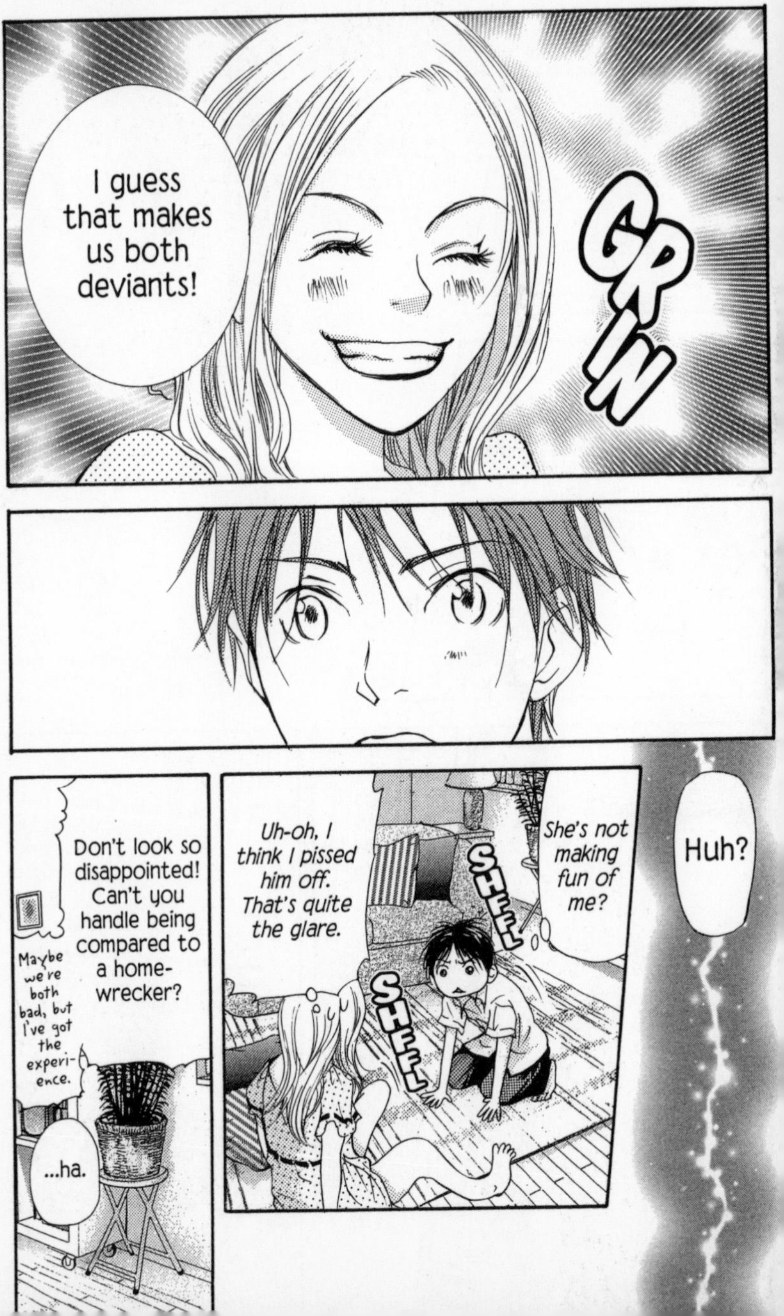
I guess that makes us both deviants!
GRIN
Huh?
She's not making fun of me?
SHFFL
Uh-oh, I think I pissed him off. That's quite the glare.
SHFFL
Don't look so disappointed! Can't you handle being compared to a home-wrecker?
Maybe we're both bad, but I've got the experience.
...ha.

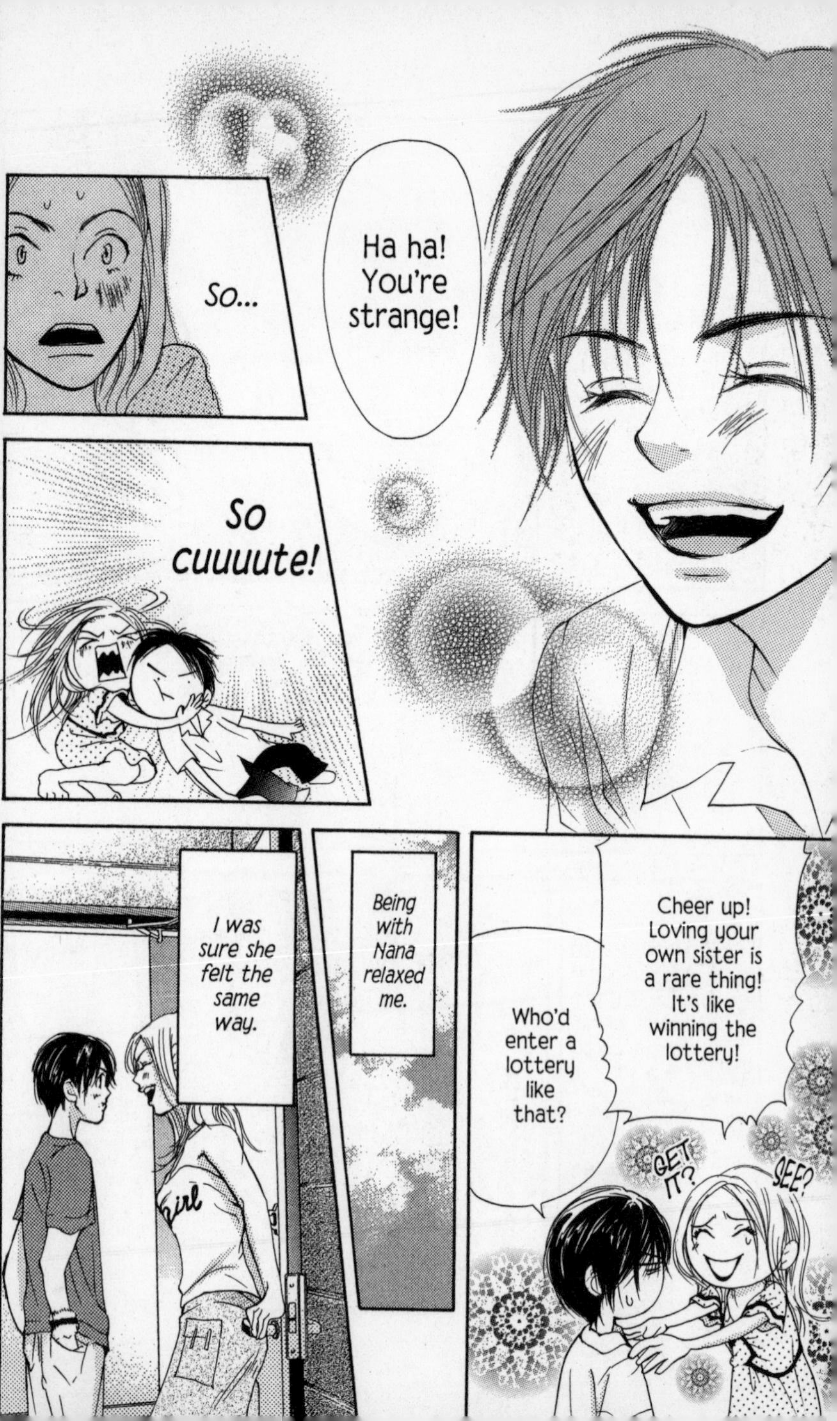
Ha ha! You're strange!
So...
So cuuuute!
Cheer up! Loving your own sister is a rare thing! It's like winning the lottery!
Who'd enter a lottery like that?
SEE?
GET IT?
Being with Nana relaxed me.
I was sure she felt the same way.

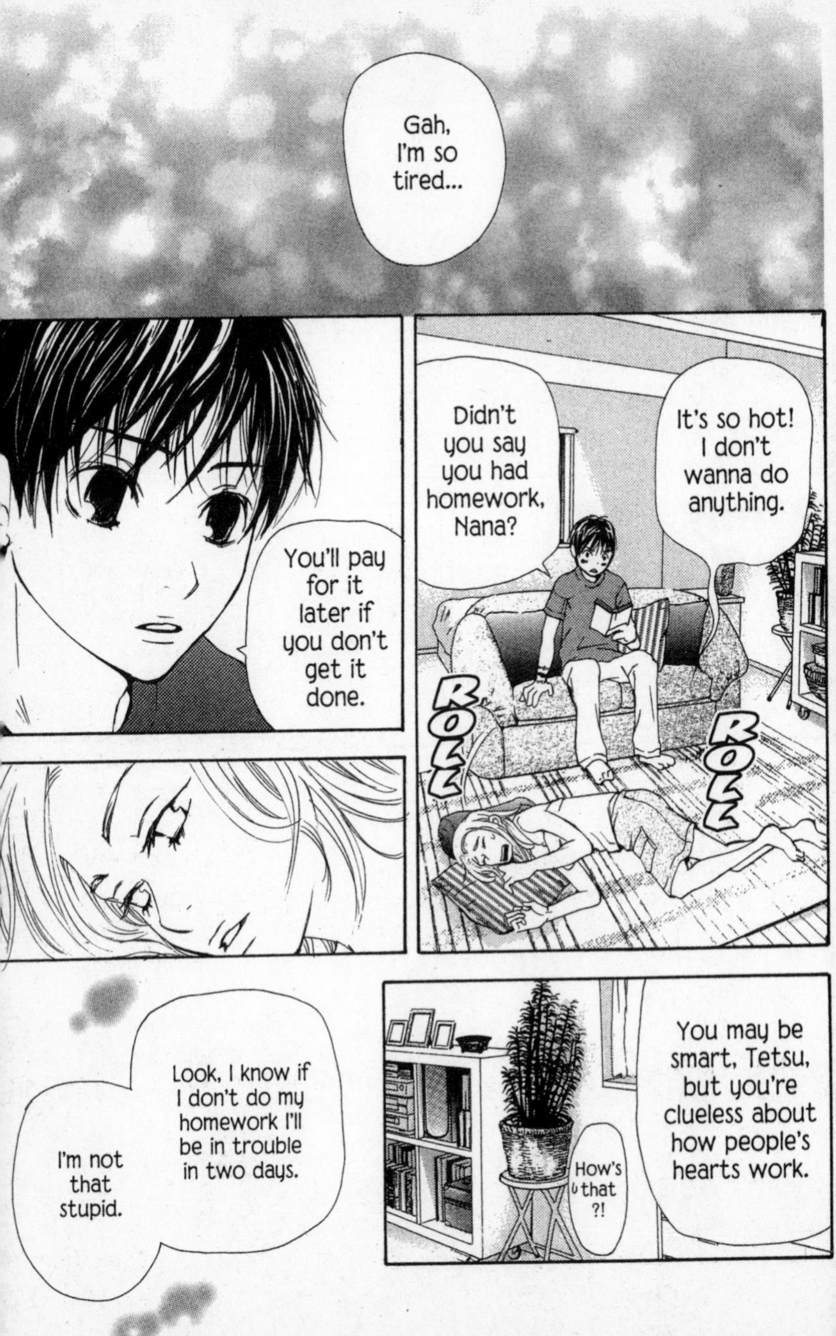
Gah, I'm so tired...
It's so hot! I don't wanna do anything.
Didn't you say you had homework, Nana?
ROLL
ROLL
You'll pay for it later if you don't get it done.
You may be smart, Tetsu, but you're clueless about how people's hearts work.
How's that?!
Look, I know if I don't do my homework I'll be in trouble in two days.
I'm not that stupid.

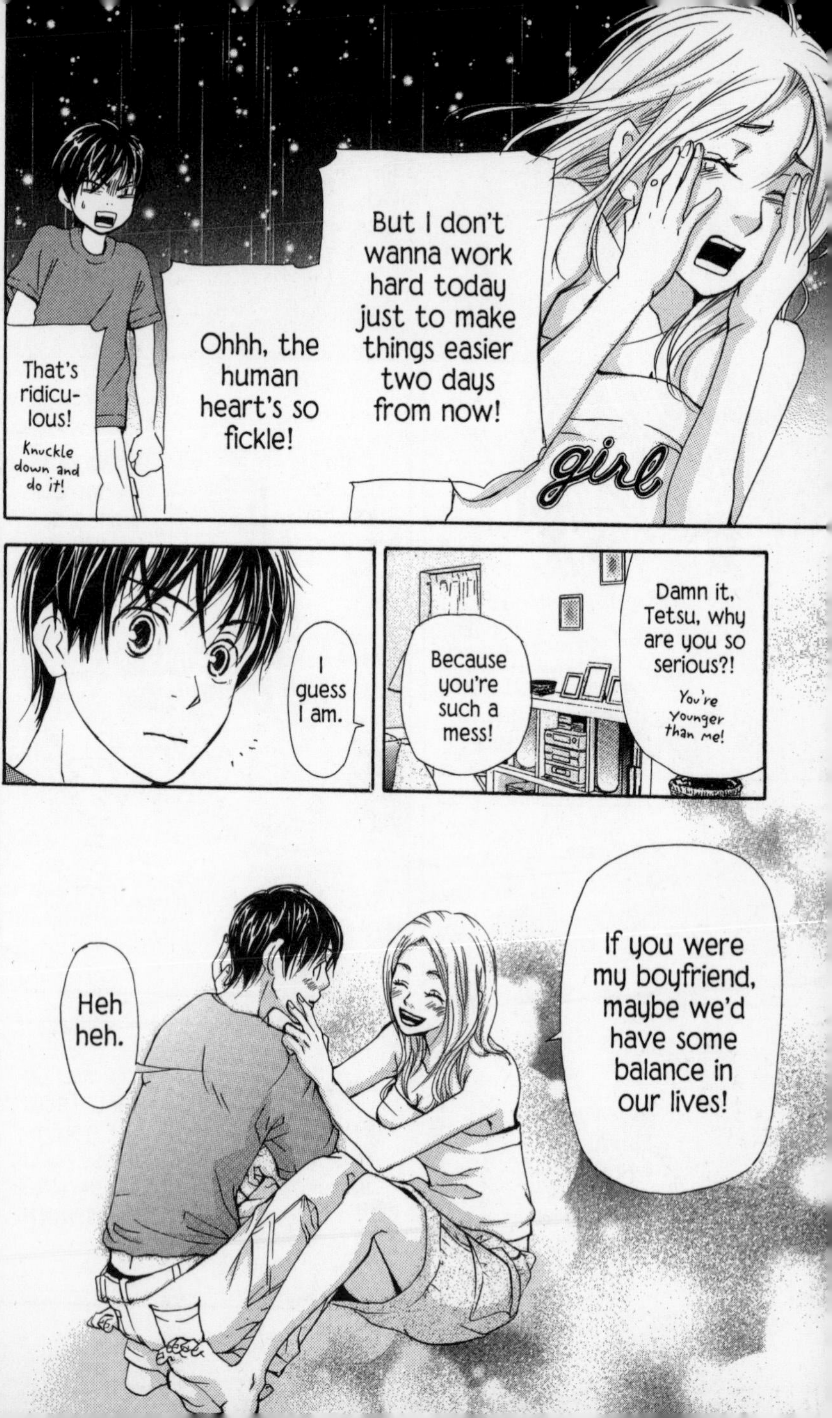
But I don't wanna work hard today just to make things easier two days from now!
Ohhh, the human heart's so fickle!
That's ridicu-lous!
Knuckle down and do it!
Damn it, Tetsu, why are you so serious?!
You're younger than me!
Because you're such a mess!
I guess I am.
If you were my boyfriend, maybe we'd have some balance in our lives!
Heh heh.

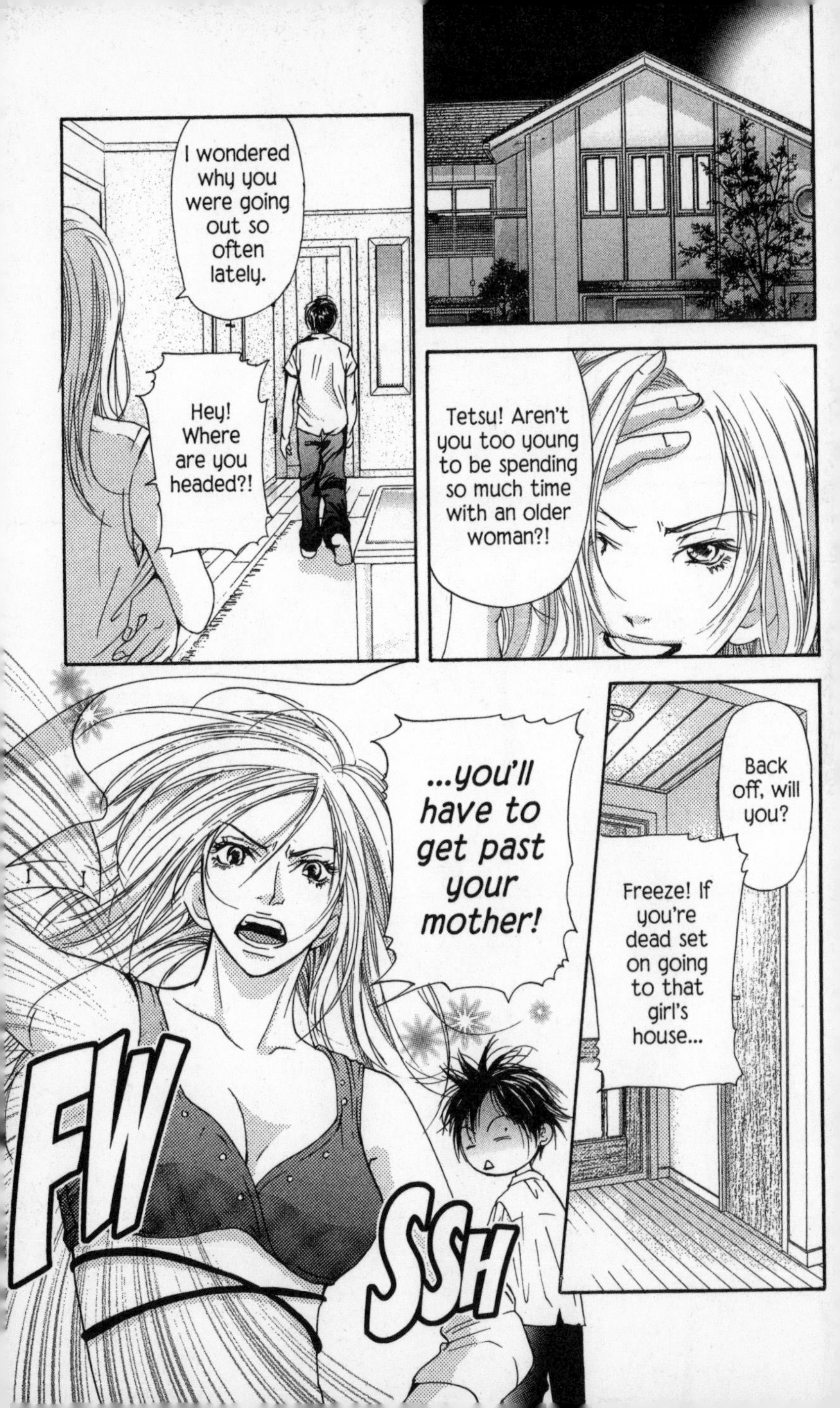
Tetsu! Aren't you too young to be spending so much time with an older woman?!
I wondered why you were going out so often lately.
Hey! Where are you headed?!
Back off, will you?
Freeze! If you're dead set on going to that girl's house...
...you'll have to get past your mother!
FW
SSH

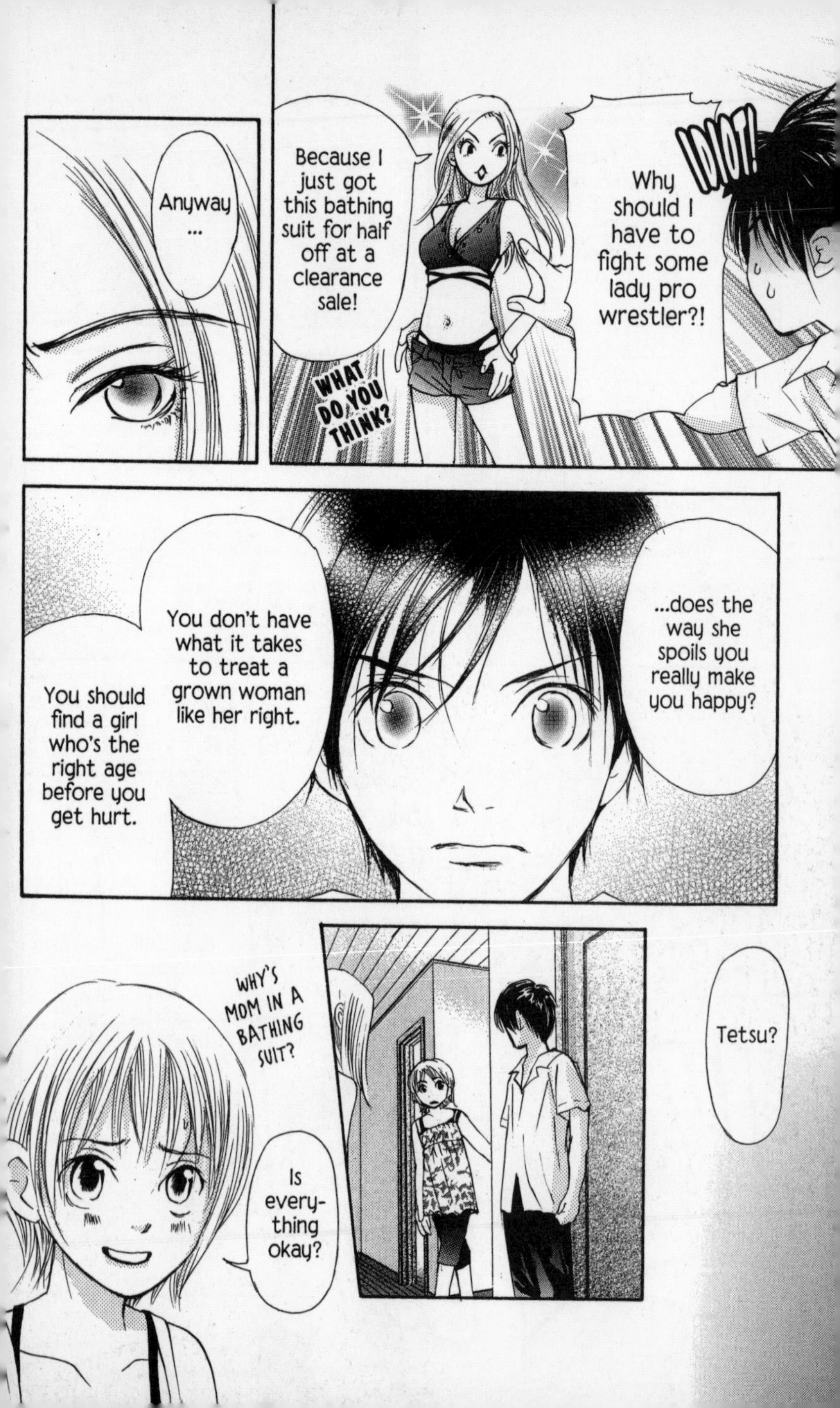
IDIOT!
Why should I have to fight some lady pro wrestler?!
Because I just got this bathing suit for half off at a clearance sale!
WHAT DO YOU THINK?
Anyway ...
...does the way she spoils you really make you happy?
You don't have what it takes to treat a grown woman like her right.
You should find a girl who's the right age before you get hurt.
Tetsu?
WHY'S MOM IN A BATHING SUIT?
Is every-thing okay?

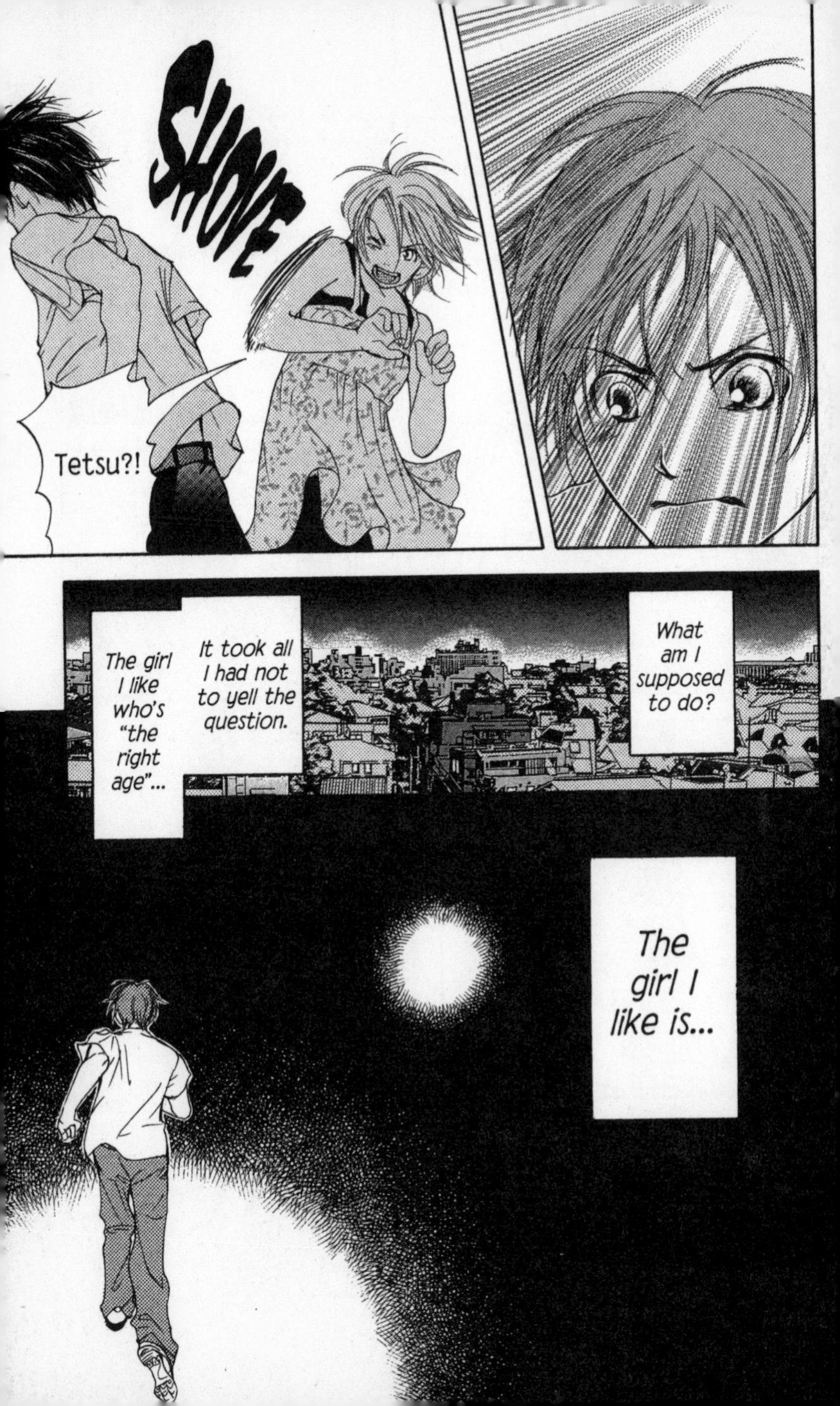
SHOVE
Tetsu?!
What am I supposed to do?
It took all I had not to yell the question.
The girl I like who's "the right age"...
The girl I like is...

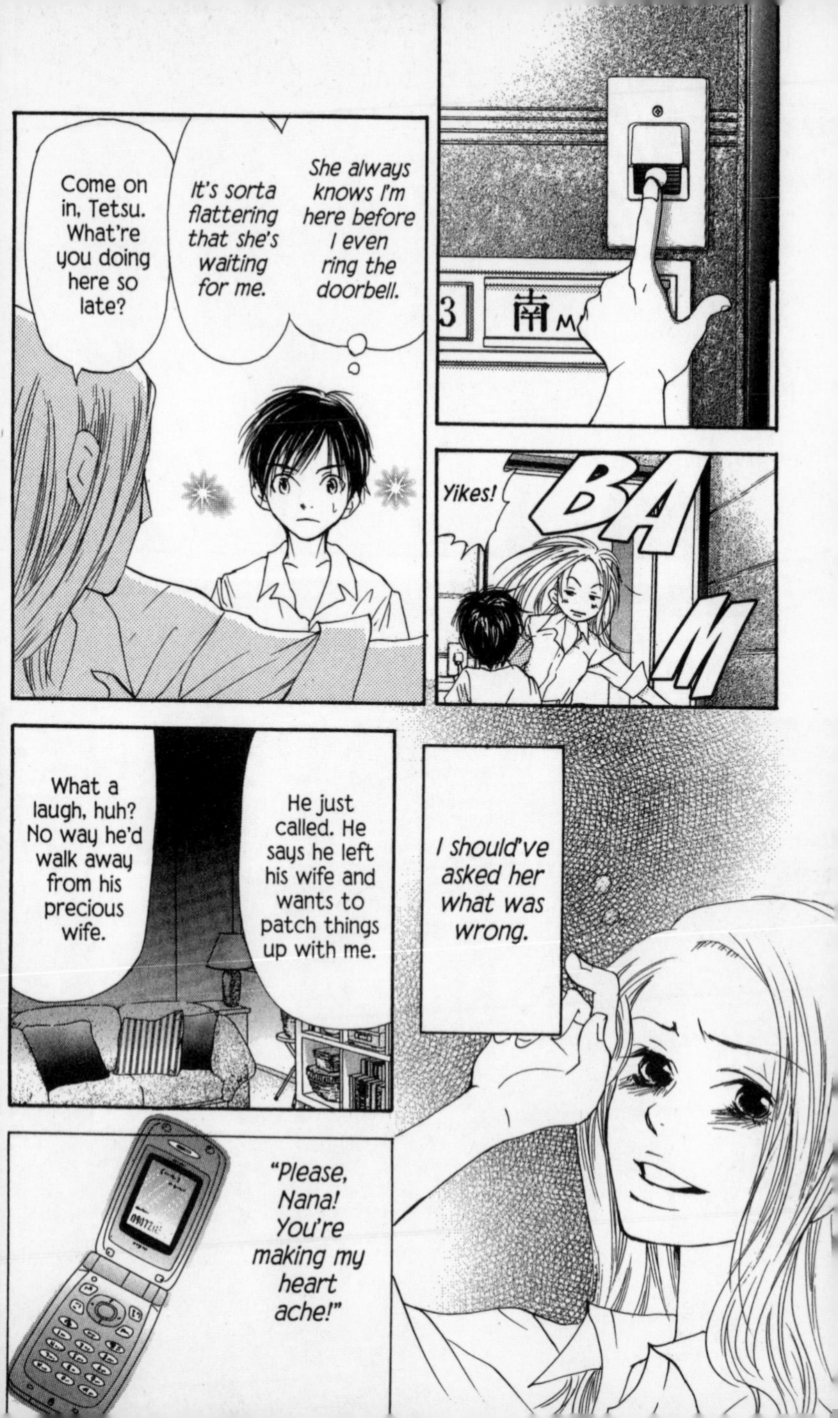
BAM
Yikes!
She always knows I'm here before I even ring the doorbell.
It's sorta flattering that she's waiting for me.
Come on in, Tetsu. What're you doing here so late?
I should've asked her what was wrong.
He just called. He says he left his wife and wants to patch things up with me.
What a laugh, huh? No way he'd walk away from his precious wife.
"Please, Nana! You're making my heart ache!"

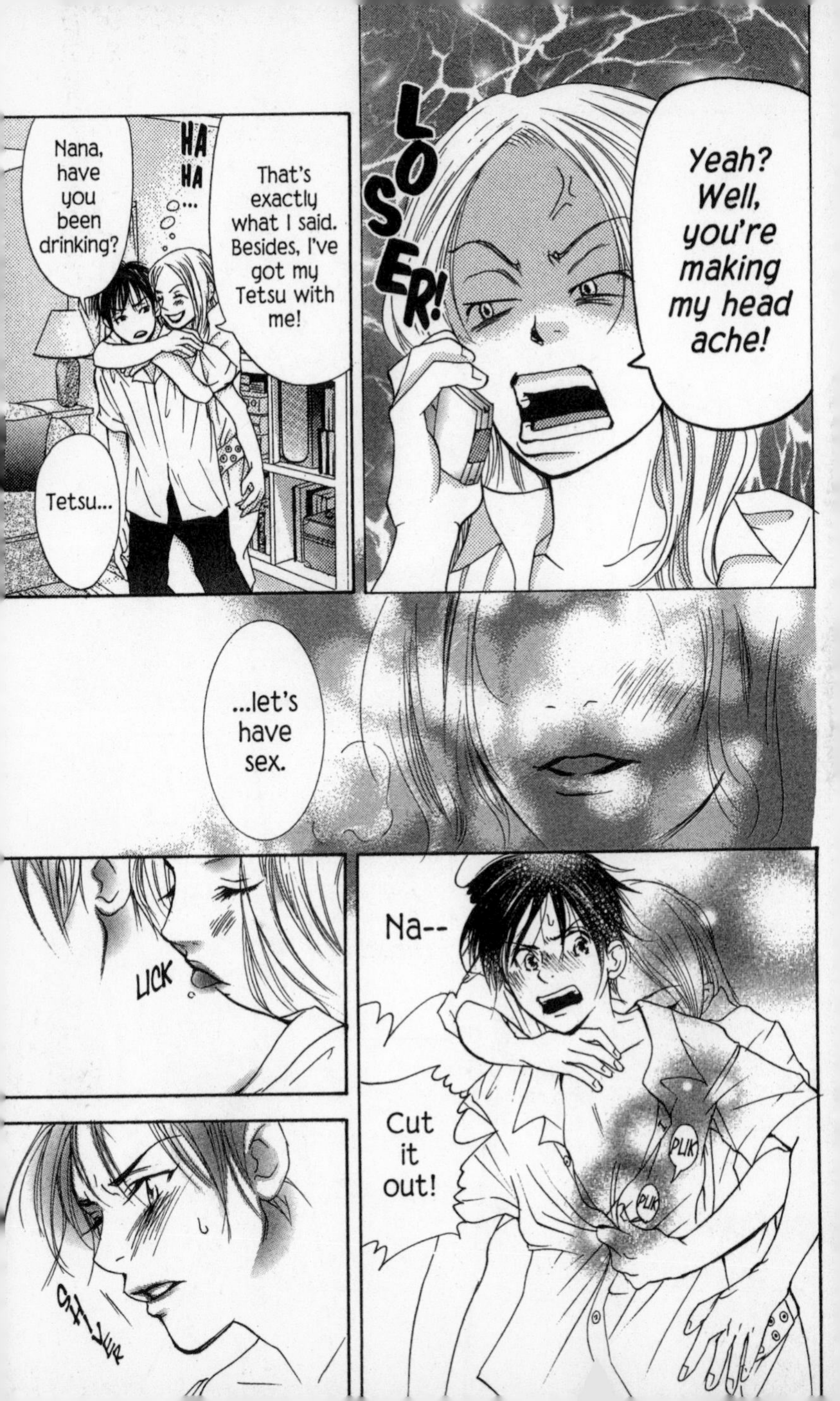
LOSER!
Yeah? Well, you're making my head ache!
That's exactly what I said. Besides, I've got my Tetsu with me!
HA HA...
Nana, have you been drinking?
Tetsu...
...let's have sex.
Na--
Cut it out!
PLIK
PLIK
LICK

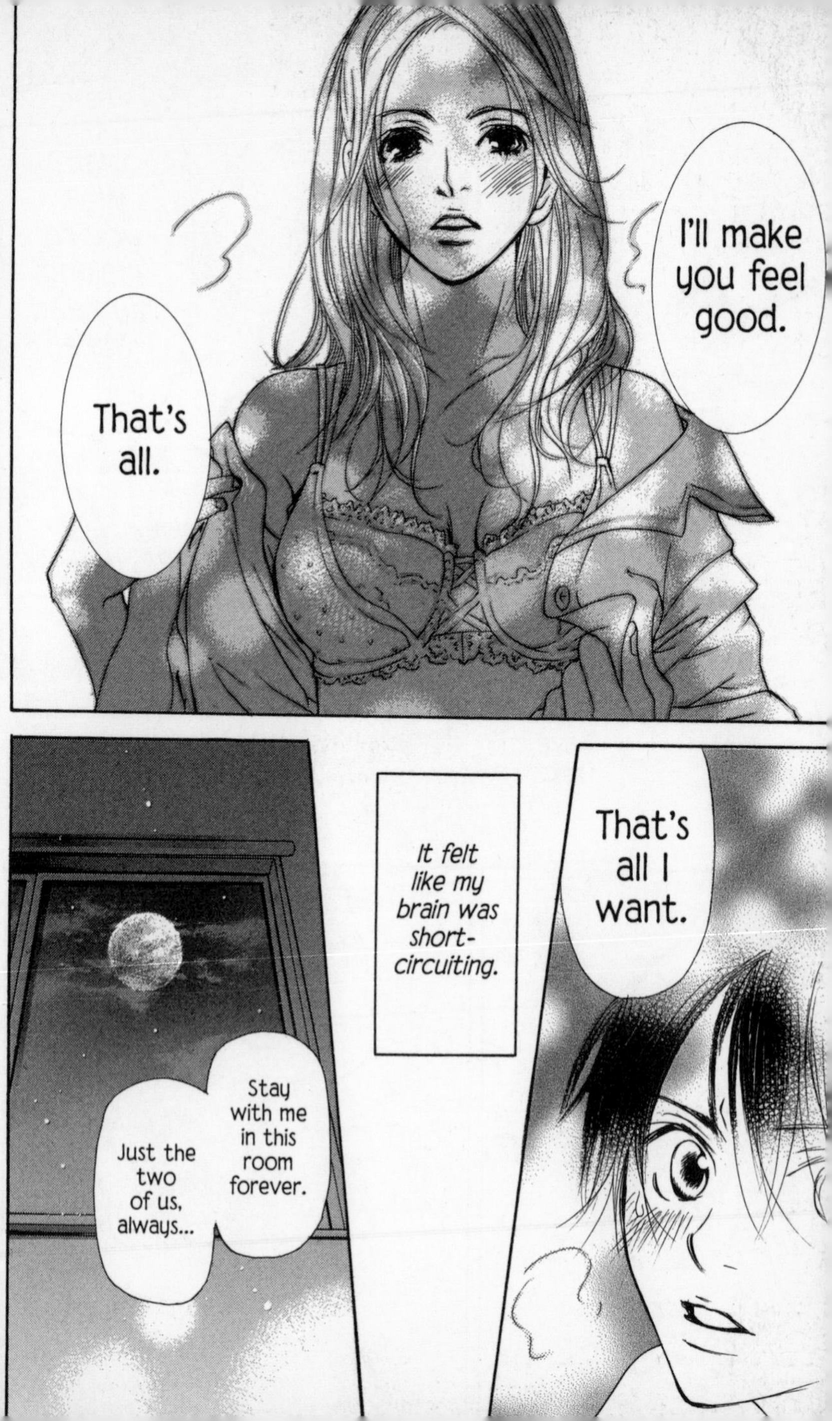
I'll make you feel good.
That's all.
That's all I want.
It felt like my brain was short-circuiting.
Stay with me in this room forever.
Just the two of us, always...

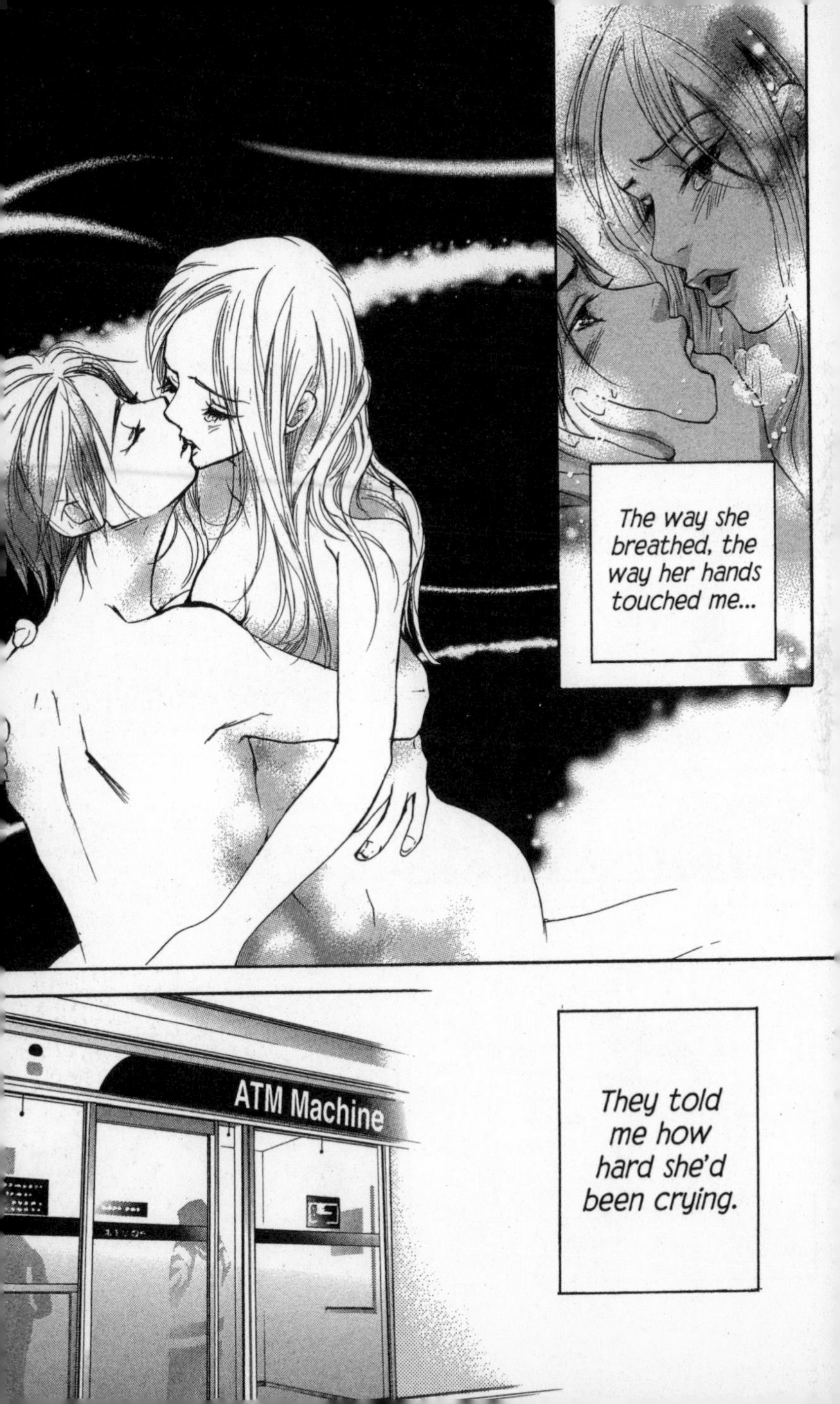
The way she breathed, the way her hands touched me...
They told me how hard she'd been crying.
ATM Machine

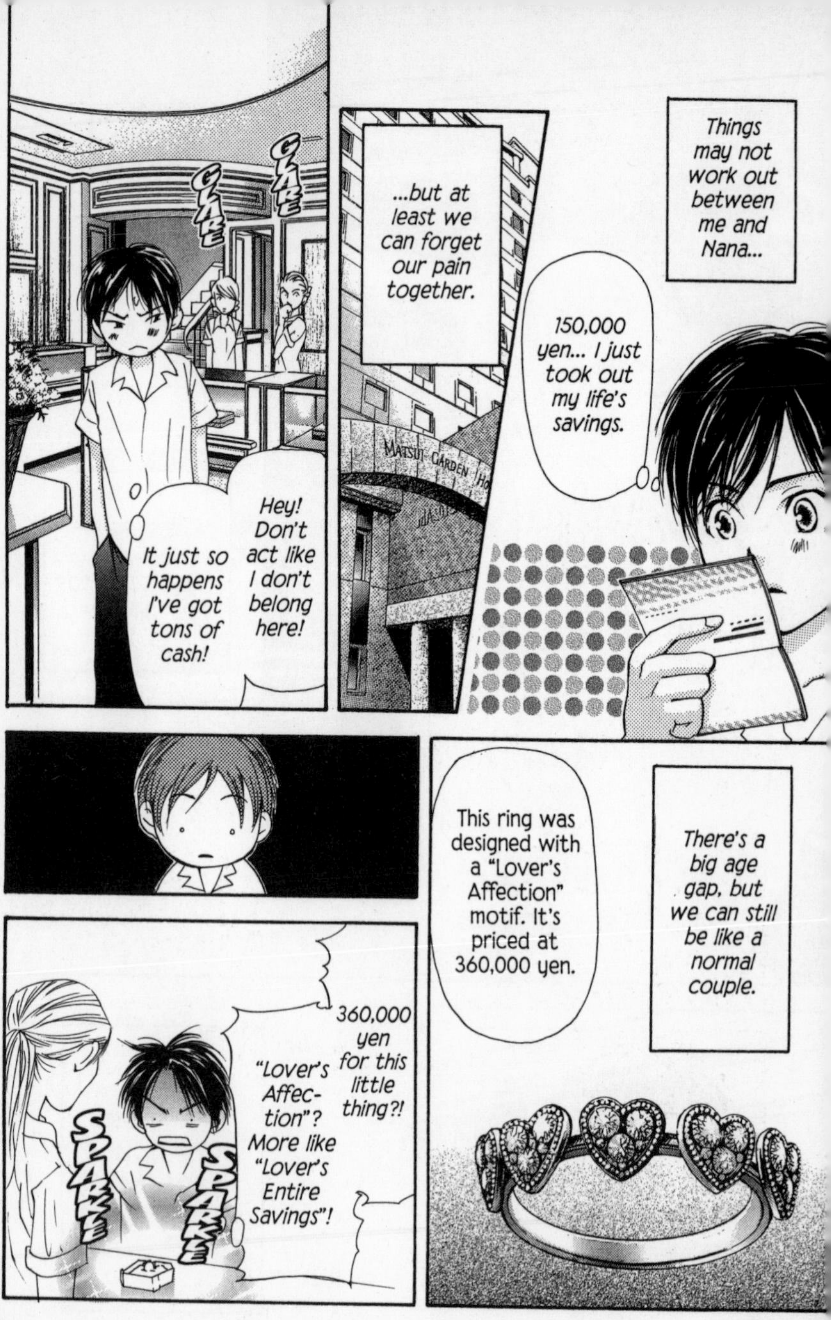

Things may not work out between me and Nana...
150,000 yen... I just took out my life's savings.
...but at least we can forget our pain together.
MATSUI GARDEN Ho
GLARE
GLARE
Hey! Don't act like I don't belong here!
It just so happens I've got tons of cash!
There's a big age gap, but we can still be like a normal couple.
This ring was designed with a "Lover's Affection" motif. It's priced at 360,000 yen.
360,000 yen for this little thing?!
"Lover's Affection"? More like "Lover's Entire Savings"!
SPARKLE
SPARKLE

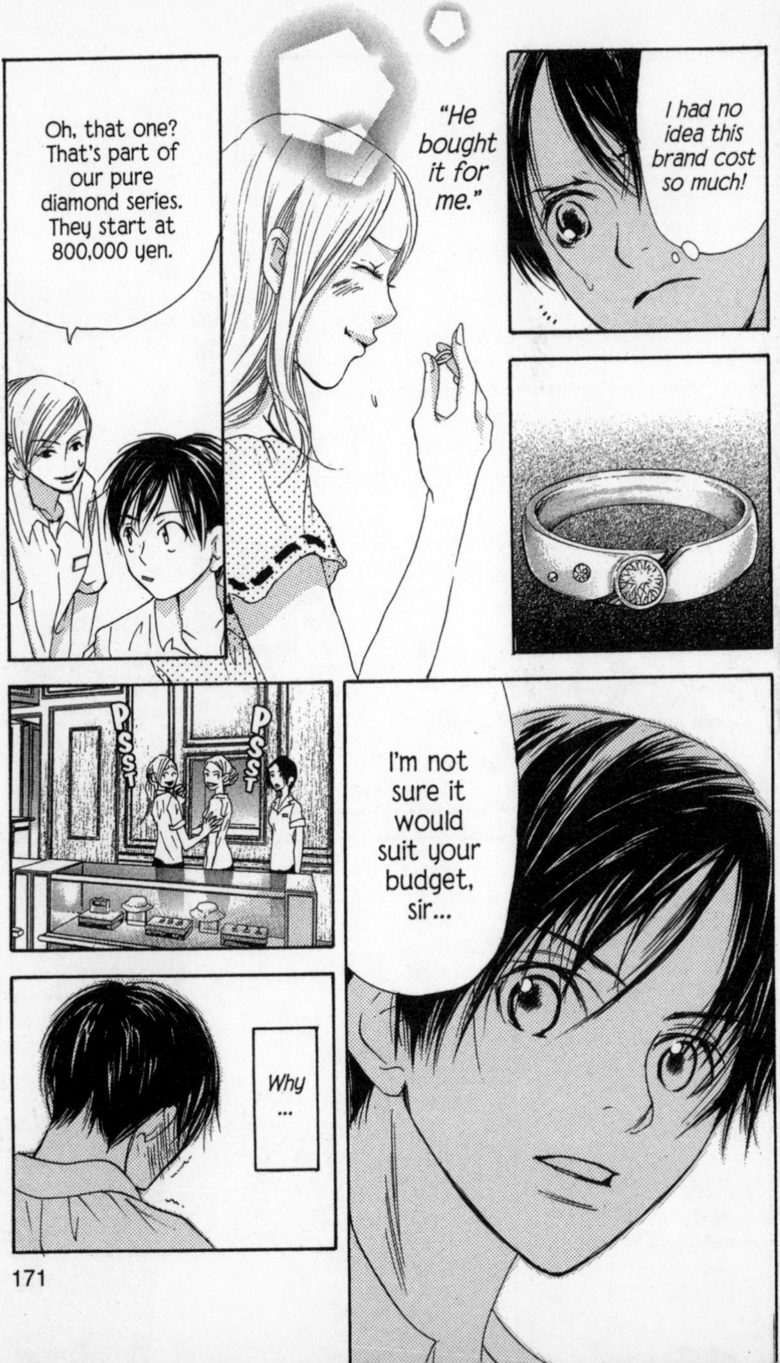
I had no idea this brand cost so much!
"He bought it for me."
Oh, that one? That's part of our pure diamond series. They start at 800,000 yen.
I'm not sure it would suit your budget, sir...
PSST
PSST
Why ...

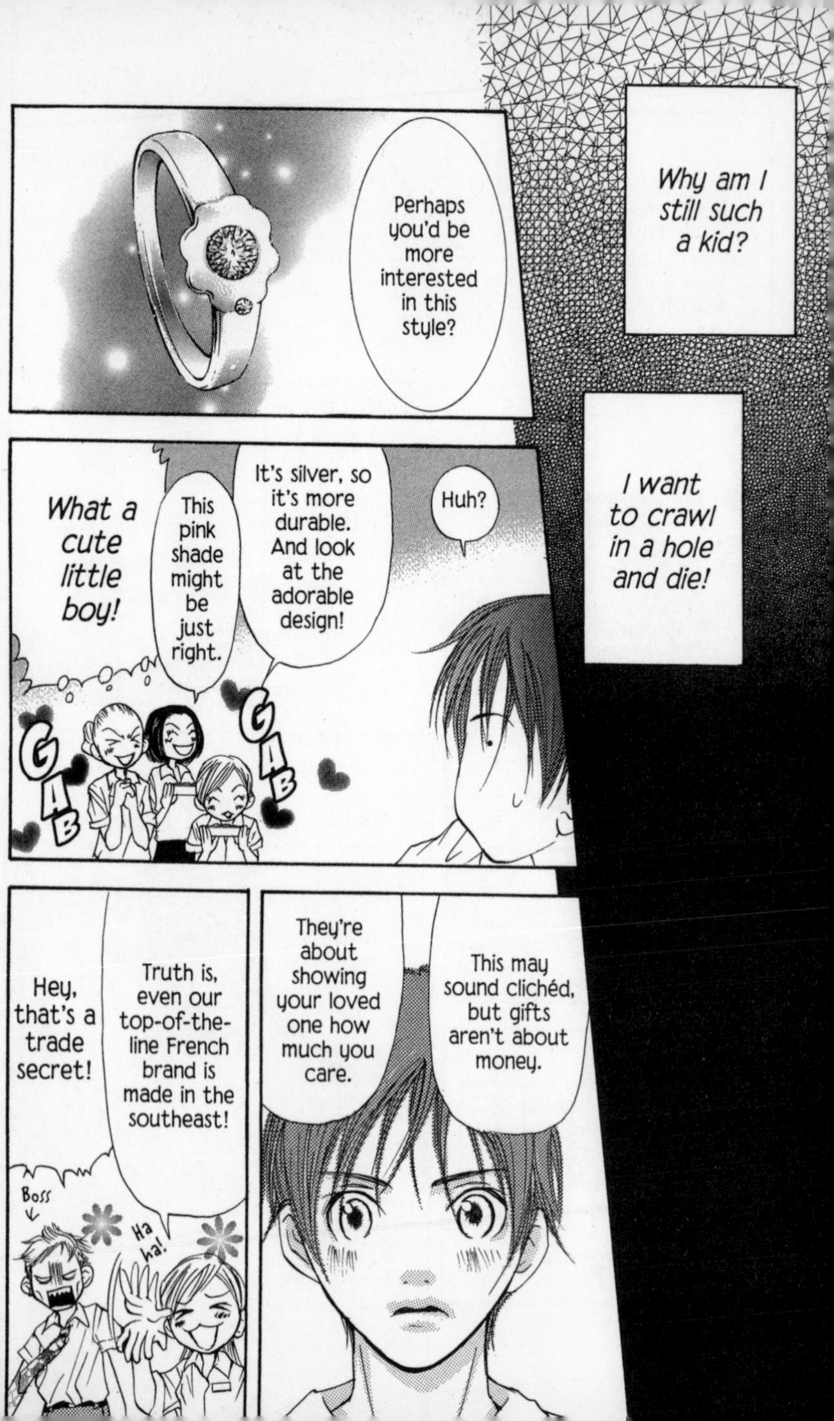
Why am I still such a kid?
I want to crawl in a hole and die!
Perhaps you'd be more interested in this style?
Huh?
It's silver, so it's more durable. And look at the adorable design!
This pink shade might be just right.
What a cute little boy!
GAB
GAB
This may sound clichéd, but gifts aren't about money.
They're about showing your loved one how much you care.
Truth is, even our top-of-the-line French brand is made in the southeast!
Hey, that's a trade secret!
Boss
Ha ha!

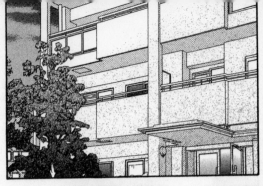

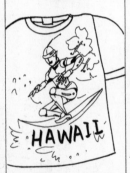

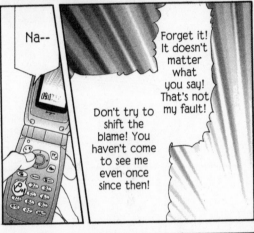

Forget it! It doesn't matter what you say! That's not my fault!
Don't try to shift the blame! You haven't come to see me even once since then!
Na--
Just stop.
It's too late now.

1/3
Half-Assed Space Filler

Introducing gifts I don't appreciate!

#4
From: Hawaii

T-Shirt

HAWAII

Sooo...for some reason it's a futuristic **mech** on a surfboard but...
(Pause for 20 seconds)

Come on! Obviously it'd get rusty doing that!

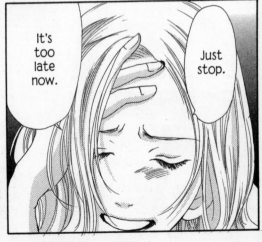

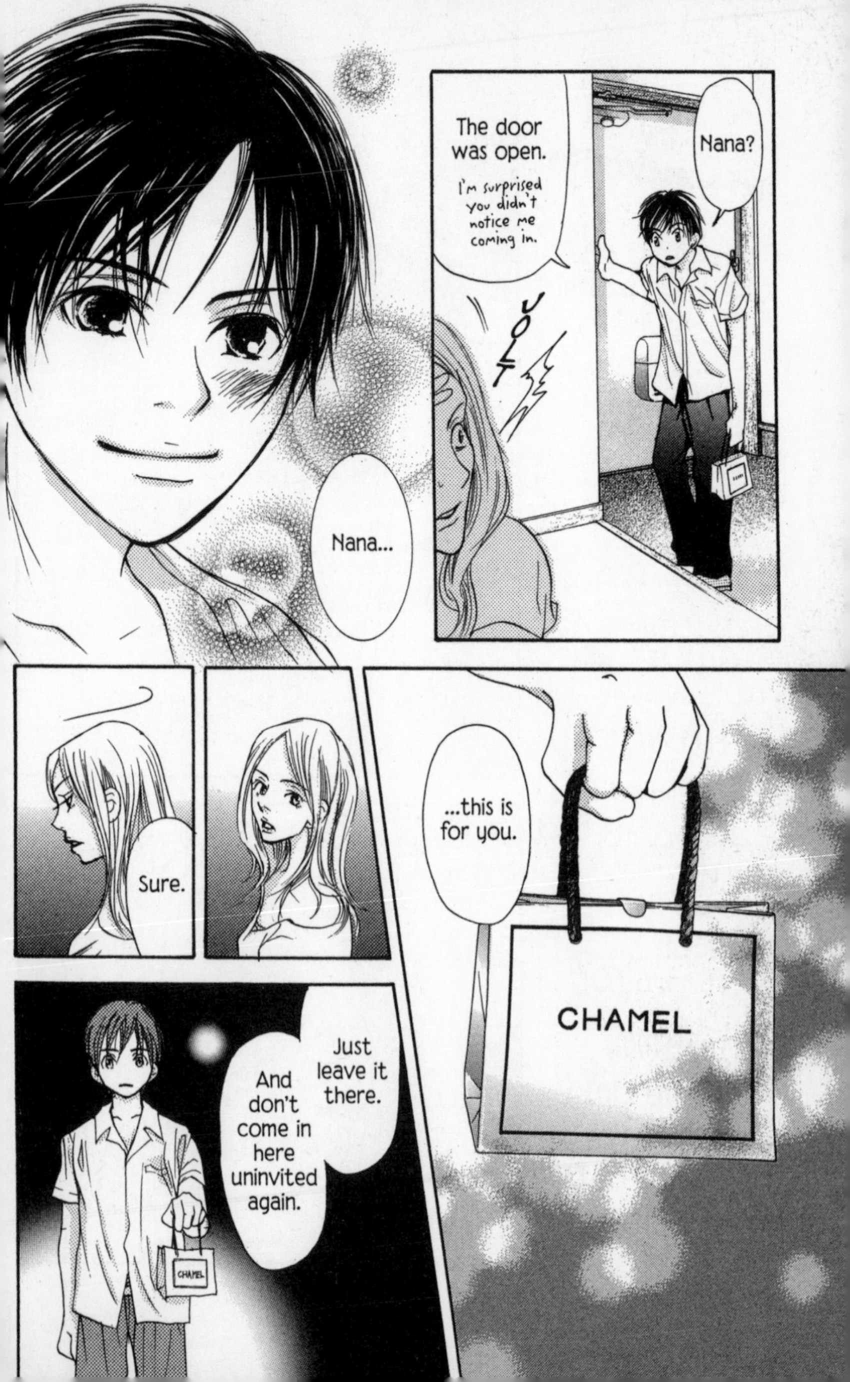
Nana?
The door was open.
I'm surprised you didn't notice me coming in.
JOLT
Nana...
...this is for you.
CHAMEL
Sure.
Just leave it there.
And don't come in here uninvited again.
CHAMEL

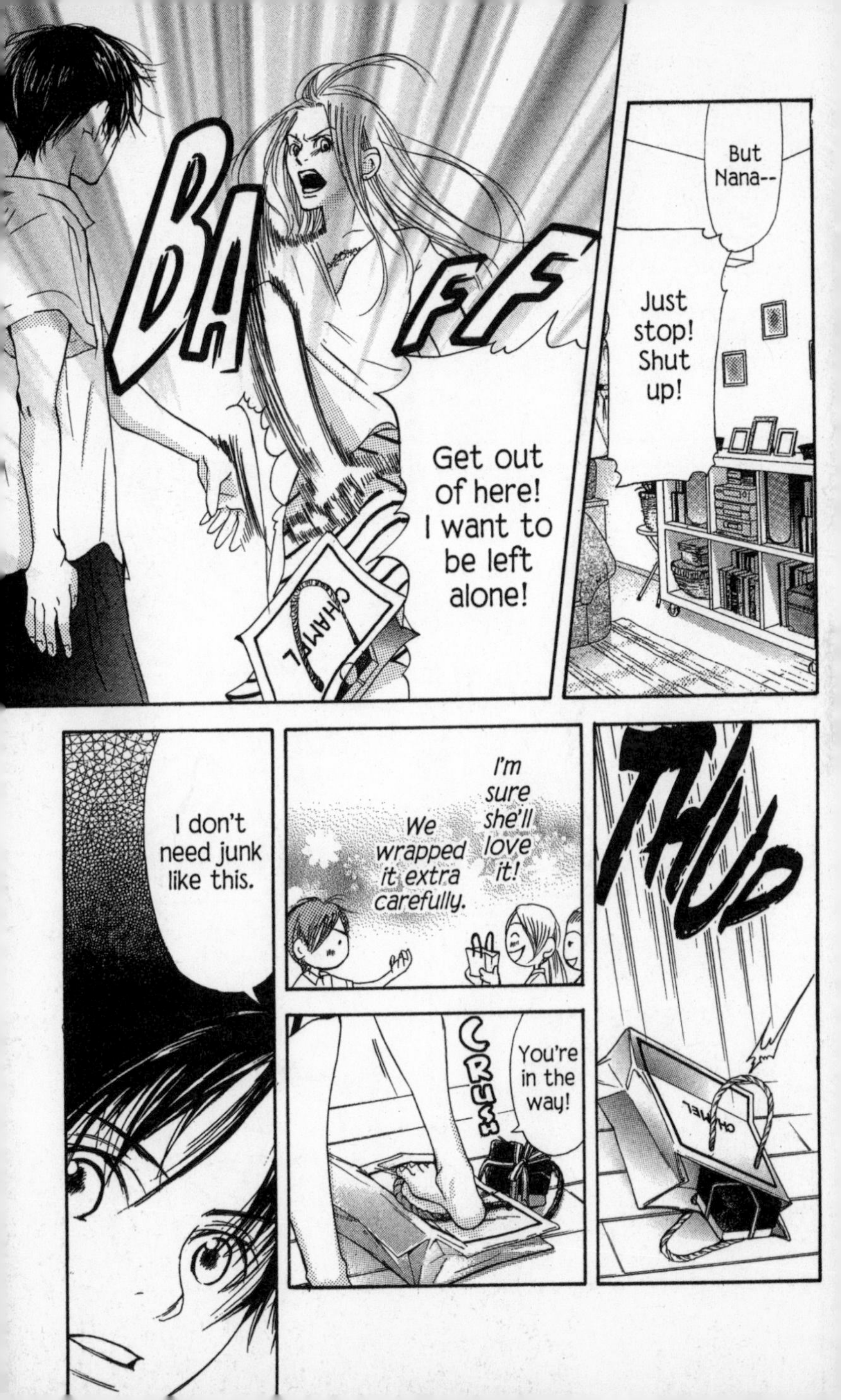
But Nana--
Just stop! Shut up!
BAFF
Get out of here! I want to be left alone!
THUD
I'm sure she'll love it!
We wrapped it extra carefully.
You're in the way!
CRUSH
I don't need junk like this.

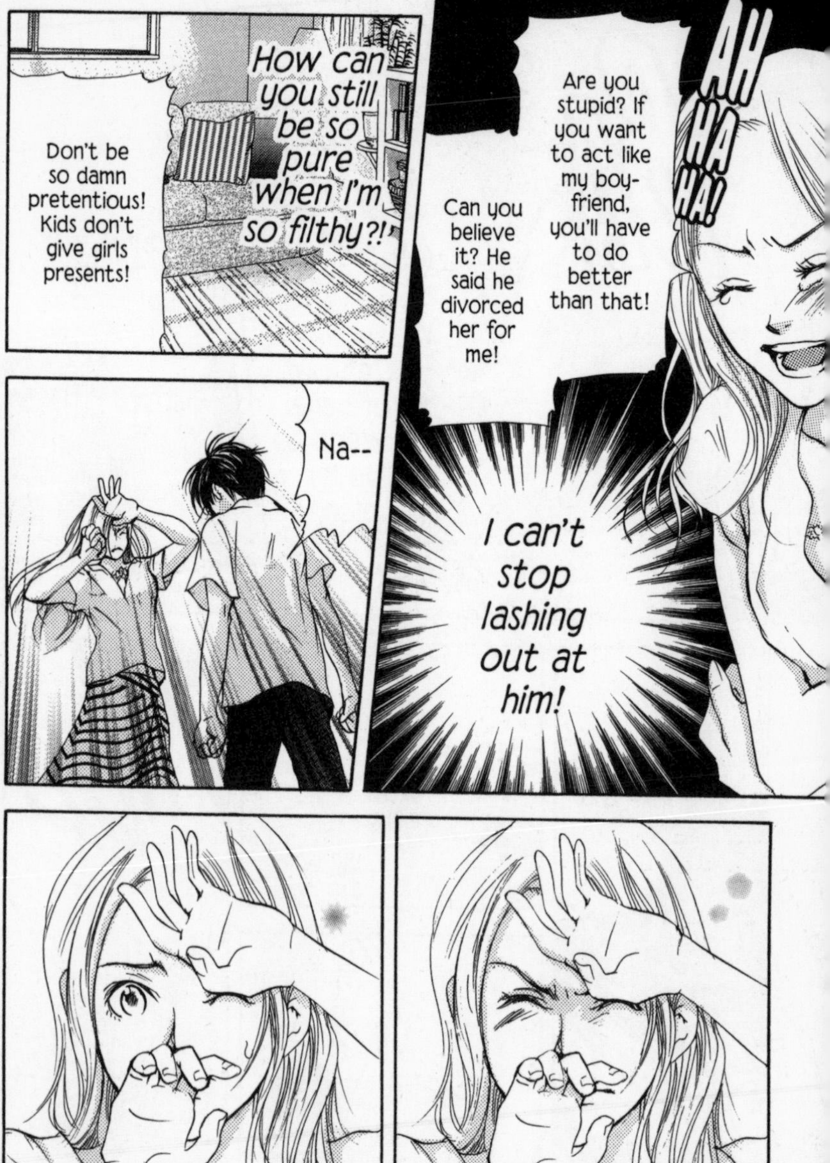
AH HA HA HA!
Are you stupid? If you want to act like my boy-friend, you'll have to do better than that!
Can you believe it? He said he divorced her for me!
I can't stop lashing out at him!
How can you still be so pure when I'm so filthy?!
Don't be so damn pretentious! Kids don't give girls presents!
Na--

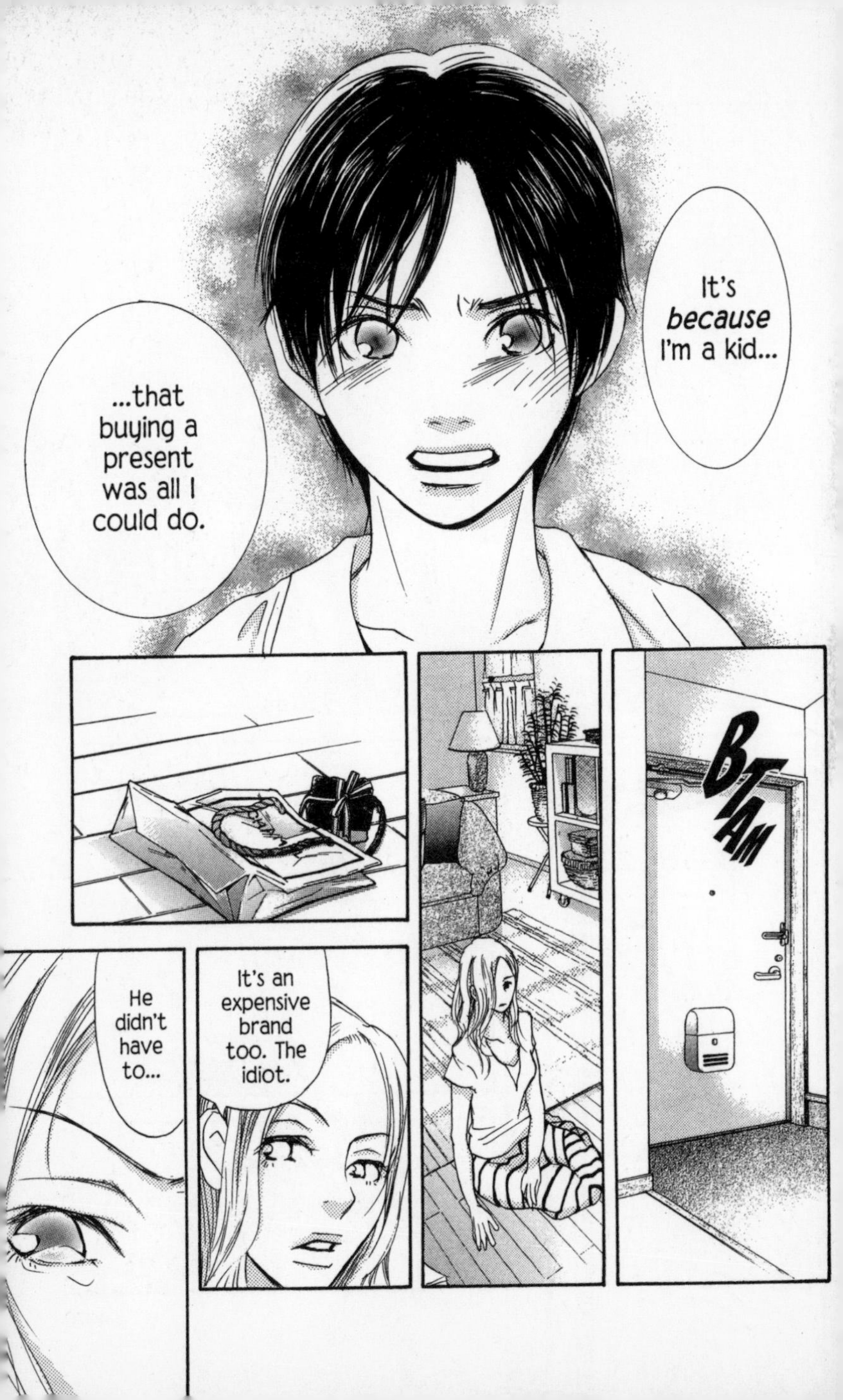
It's *because* I'm a kid...
...that buying a present was all I could do.
BTAM
It's an expensive brand too. The idiot.
He didn't have to...

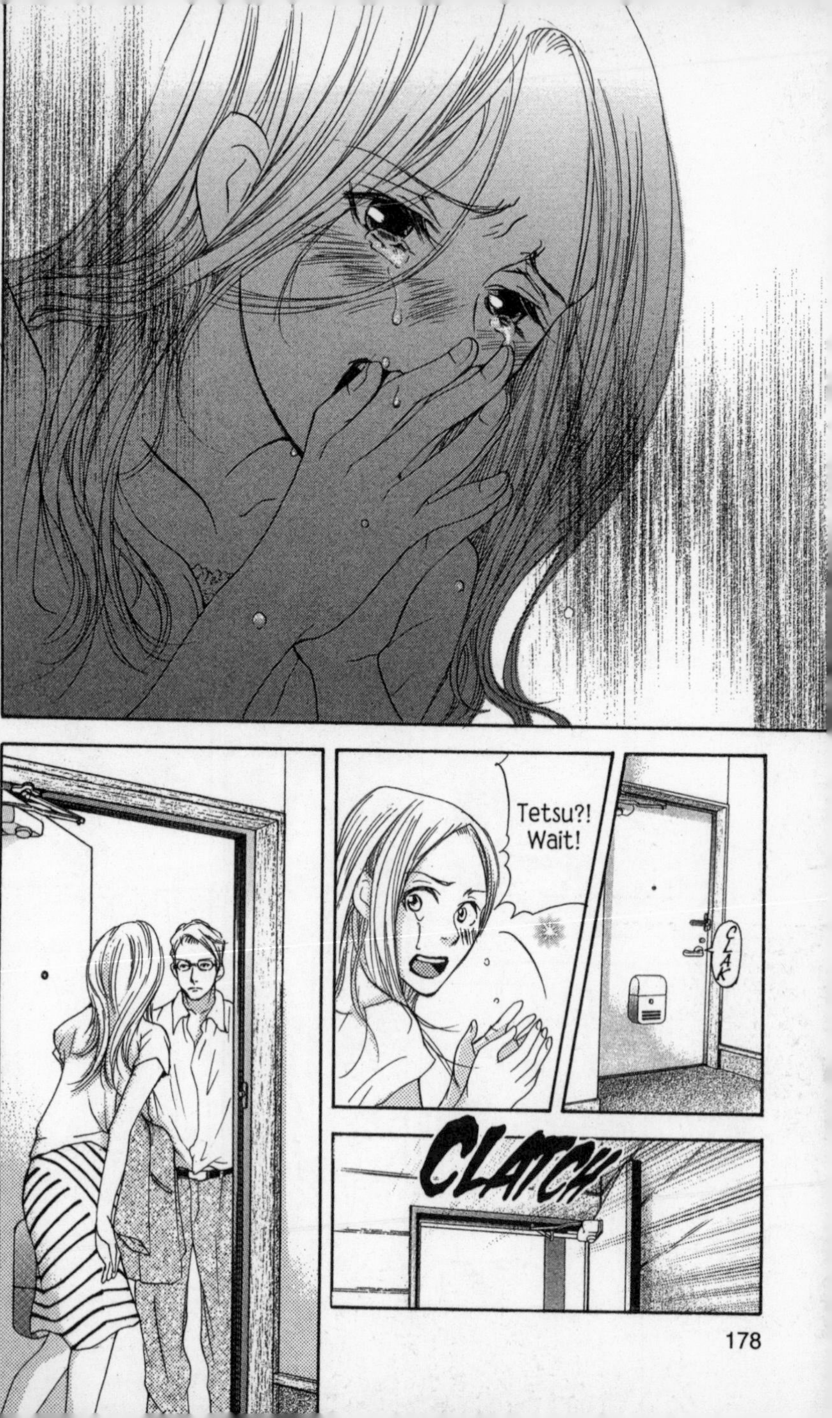
CLAK
Tetsu?! Wait!
CLATCH

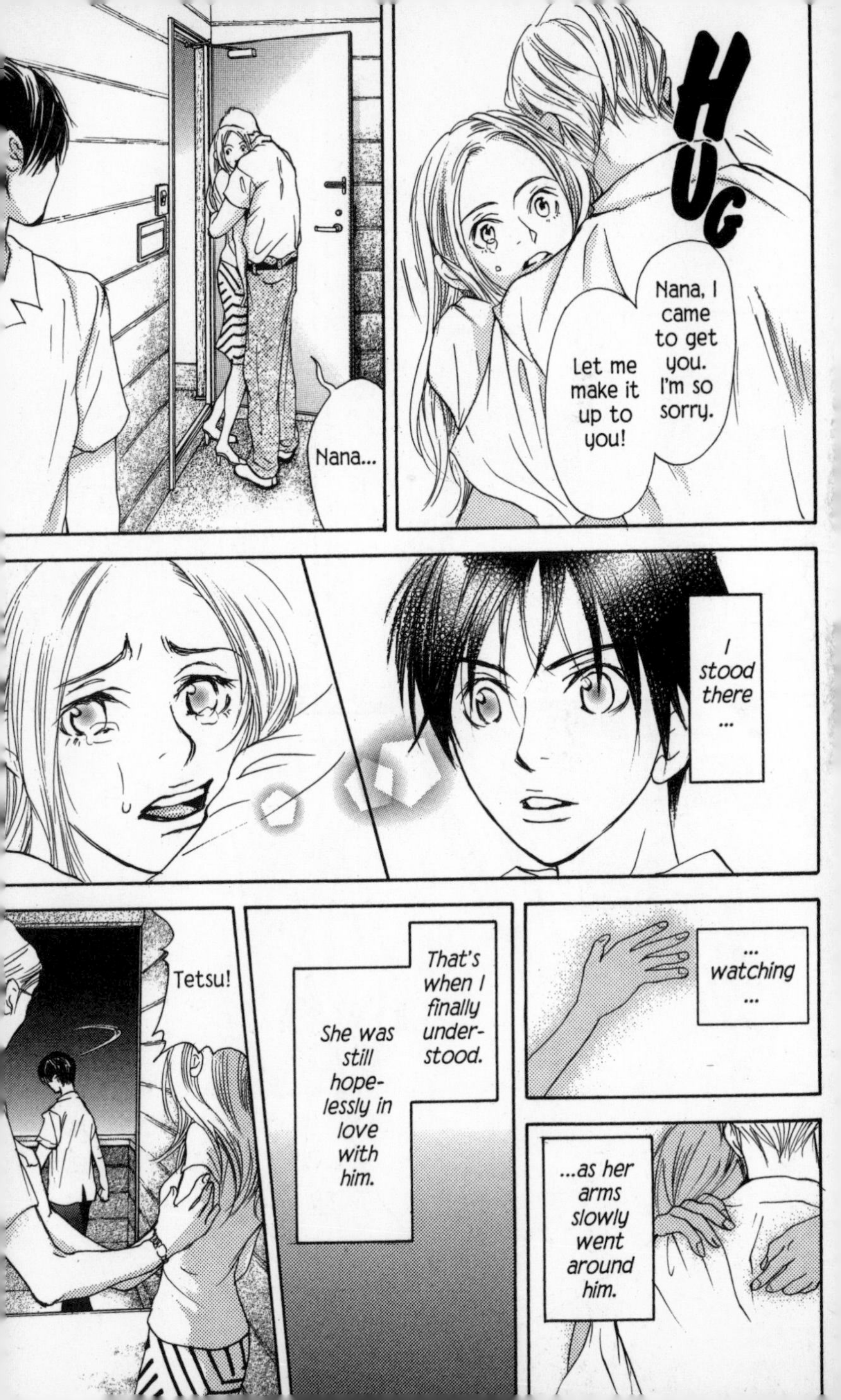
HUG
Nana, I came to get you. I'm so sorry.
Let me make it up to you!
Nana...
I stood there ...
... watching ...
...as her arms slowly went around him.
That's when I finally understood.
She was still hopelessly in love with him.
Tetsu!

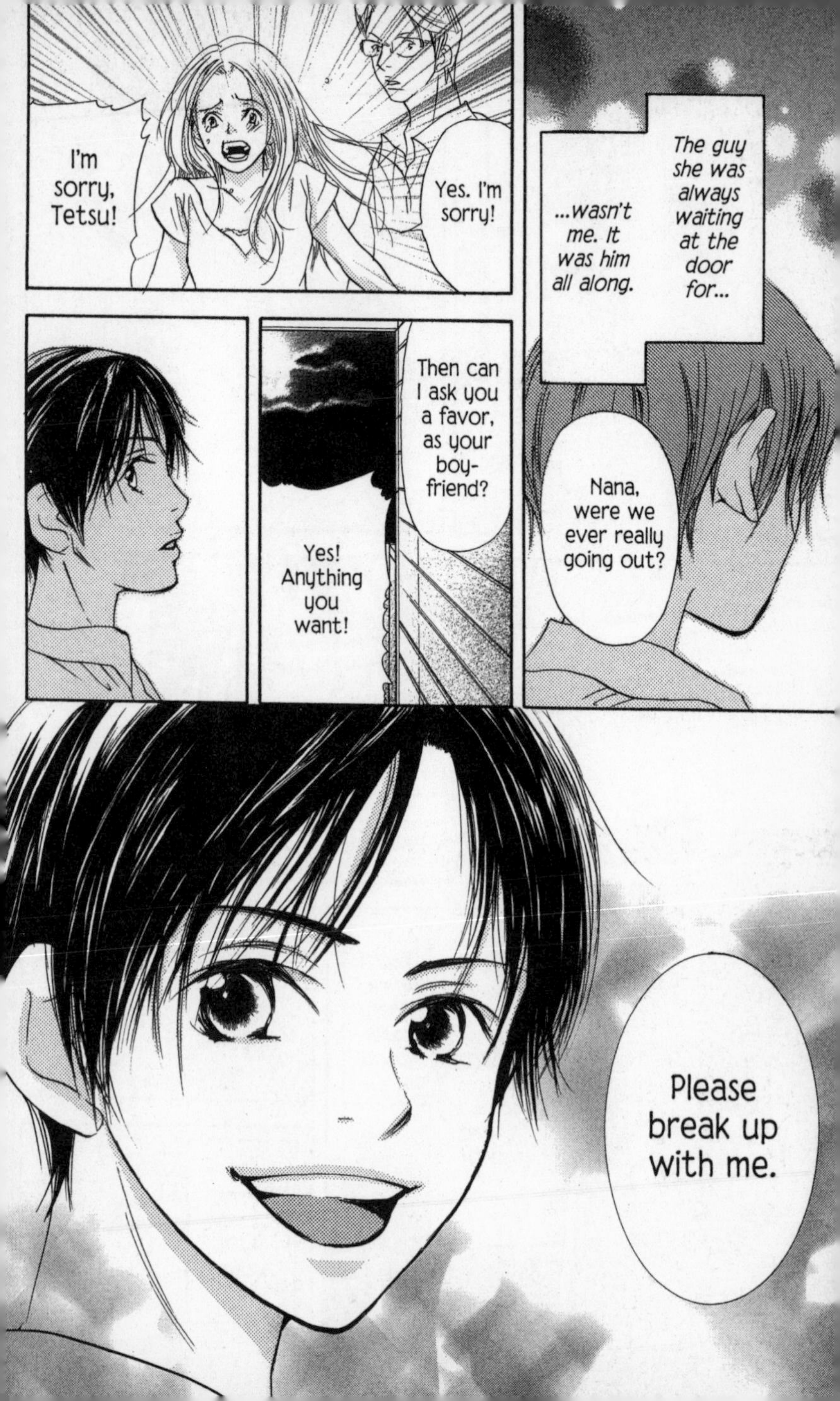
The guy she was always waiting at the door for...
...wasn't me. It was him all along.
Nana, were we ever really going out?
Yes. I'm sorry!
I'm sorry, Tetsu!
Then can I ask you a favor, as your boy-friend?
Yes! Anything you want!
Please break up with me.

I'm sorry... I'm so sorry!

Thank you...

Tetsu...

I'd always been alone anyway.

And I wasn't lonely.

SPLASH

I wasn't particularly sad.

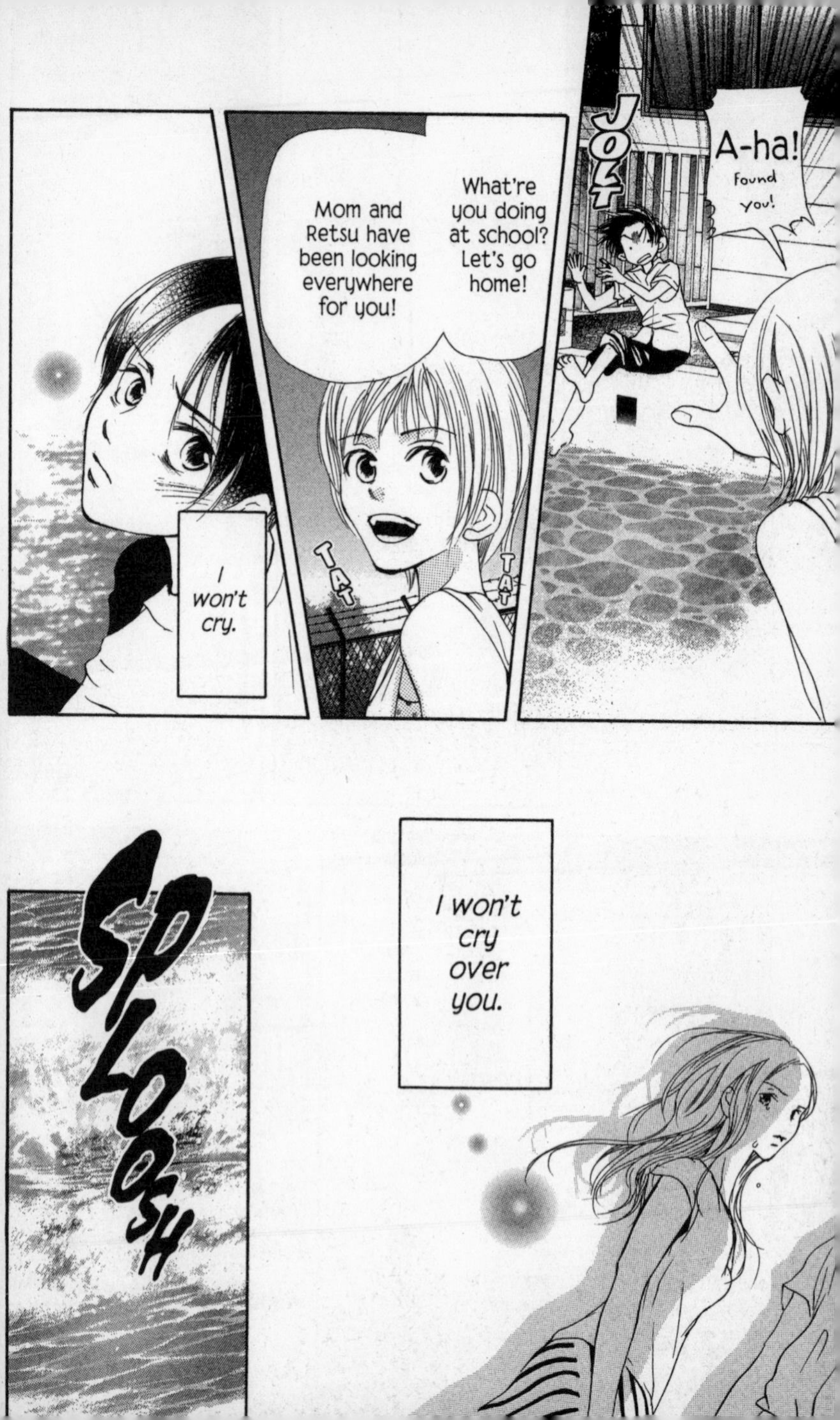
A-ha! Found you!
JOLT
What're you doing at school? Let's go home!
Mom and Retsu have been looking everywhere for you!
TAT
TAT
I won't cry.
I won't cry over you.
SPLOSH

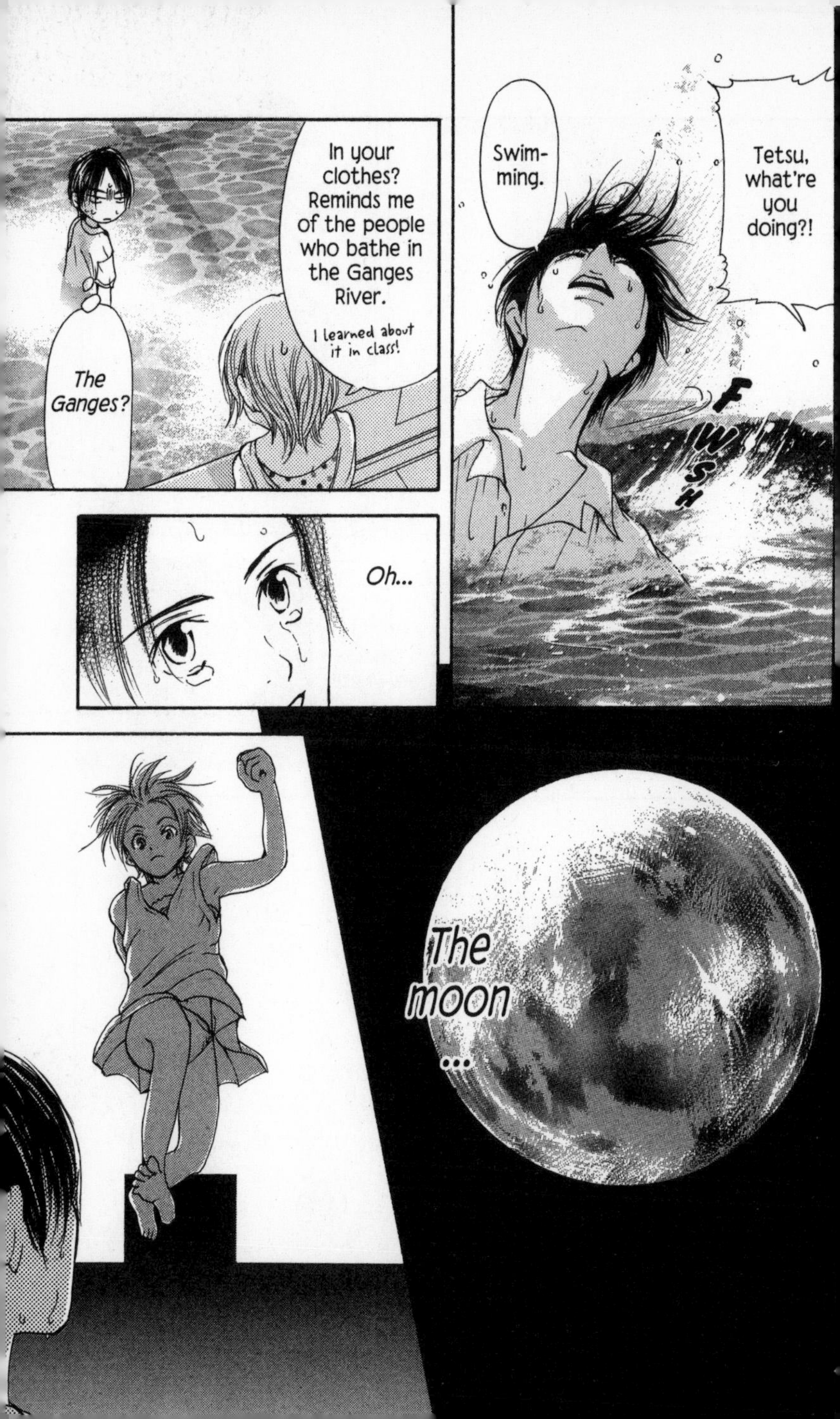
Tetsu, what're you doing?!
Swim-ming.
FWSH
In your clothes? Reminds me of the people who bathe in the Ganges River.
I learned about it in class!
The Ganges?
Oh...
The moon ...

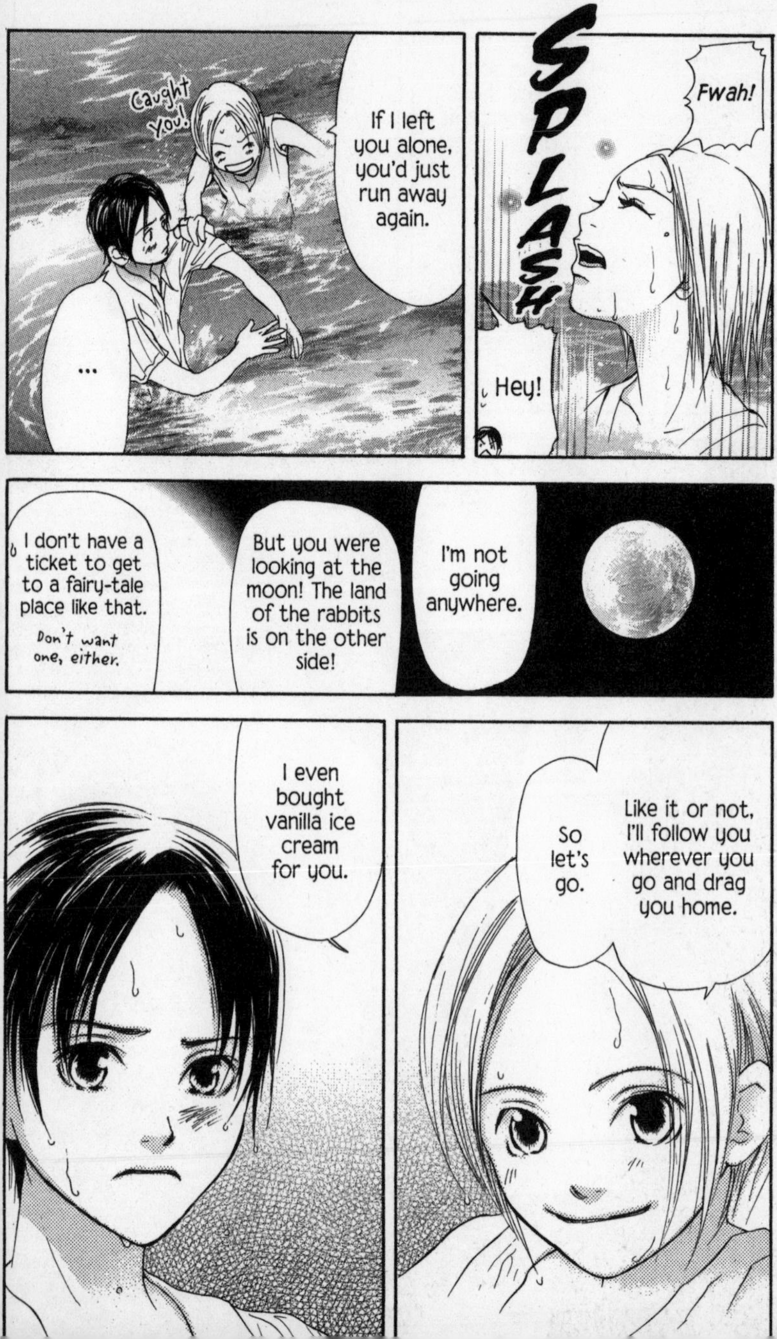

Fwah!
SPLASH
Hey!
If I left you alone, you'd just run away again.
Caught You!
...
I'm not going anywhere.
But you were looking at the moon! The land of the rabbits is on the other side!
I don't have a ticket to get to a fairy-tale place like that.
Don't want one, either.
Like it or not, I'll follow you wherever you go and drag you home.
So let's go.
I even bought vanilla ice cream for you.

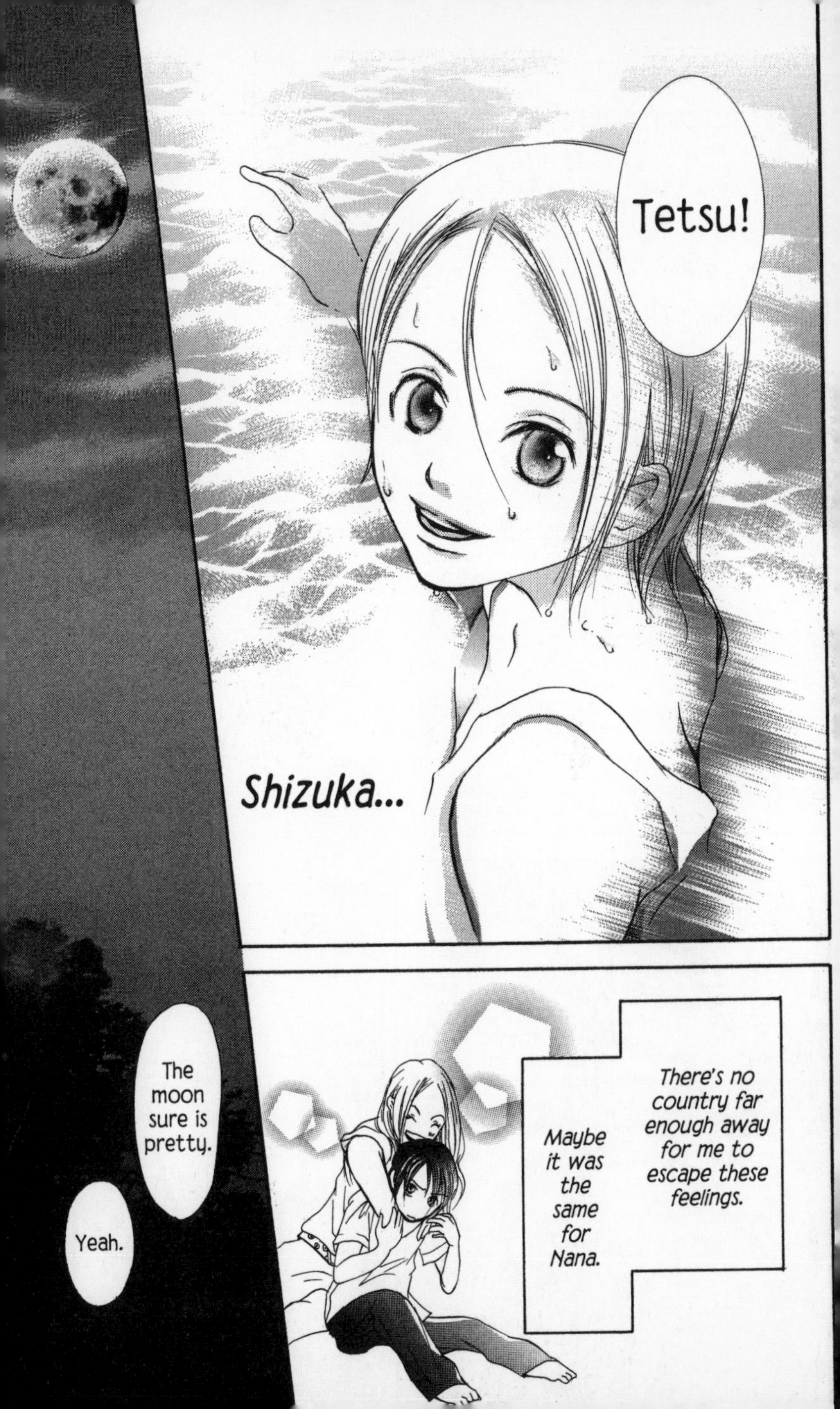
Tetsu!
Shizuka...
There's no country far enough away for me to escape these feelings.
Maybe it was the same for Nana.
The moon sure is pretty.
Yeah.

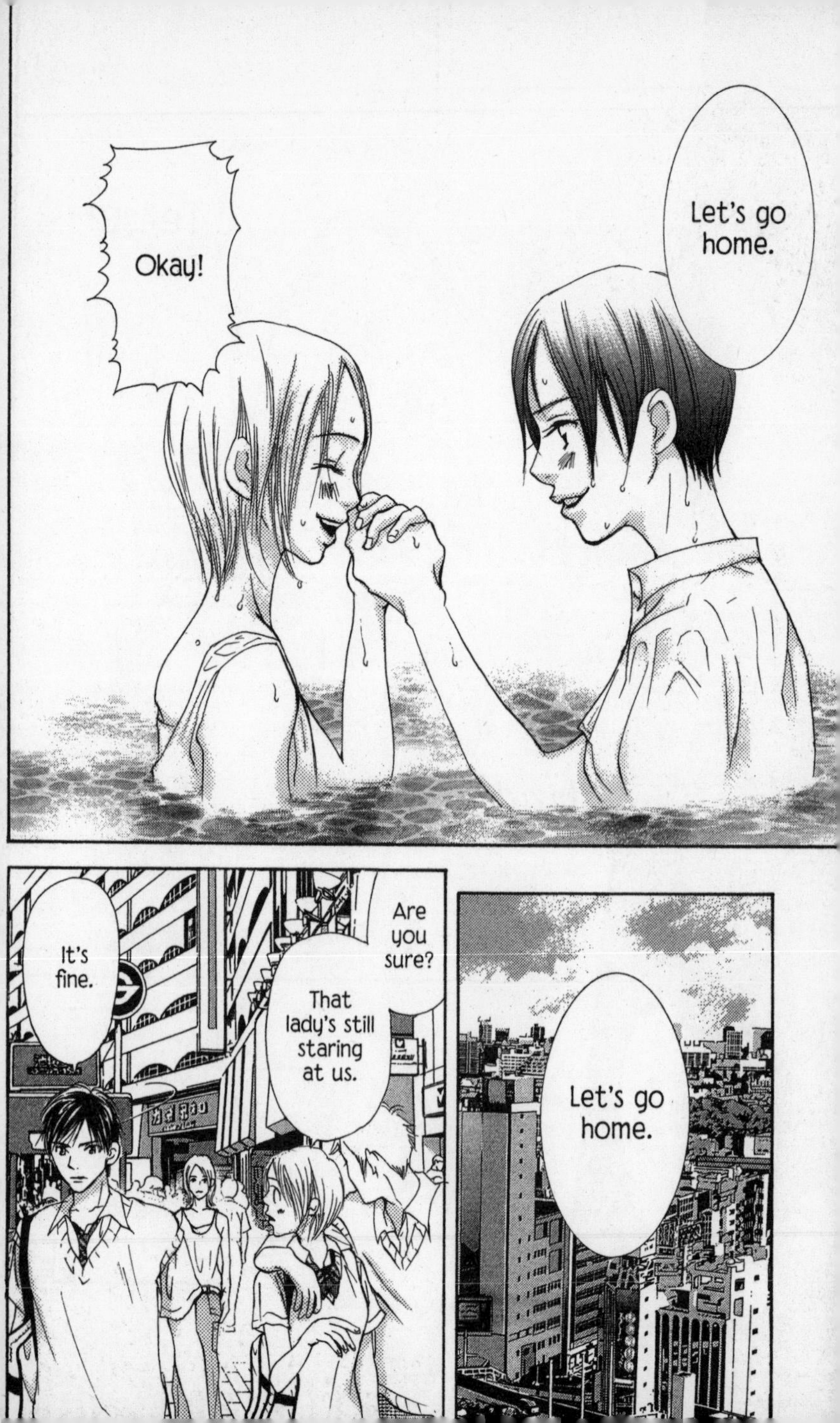
Let's go home.
Okay!
Let's go home.
Are you sure?
That lady's still staring at us.
It's fine.

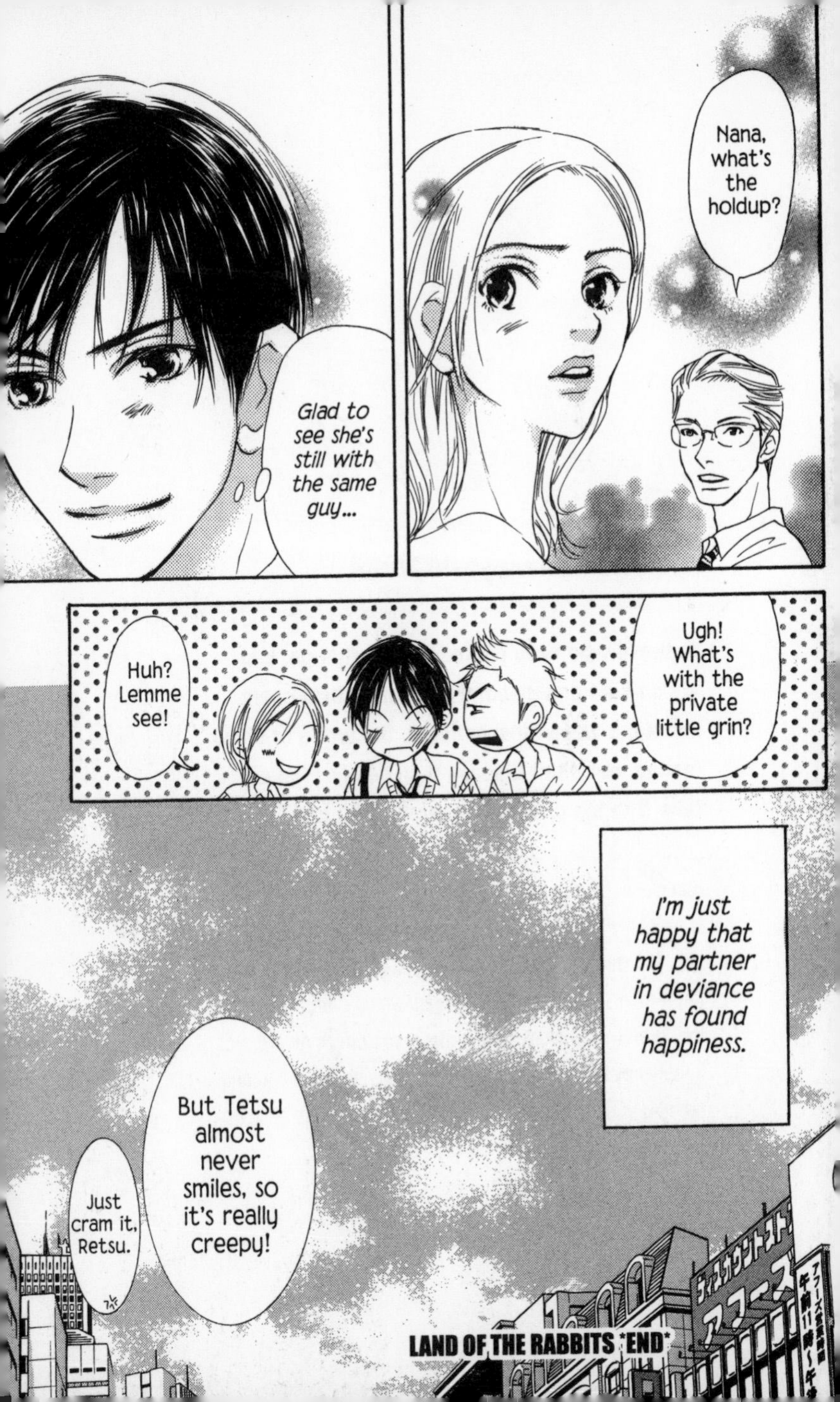
Nana, what's the holdup?
Glad to see she's still with the same guy...
Ugh! What's with the private little grin?
Huh? Lemme see!
I'm just happy that my partner in deviance has found happiness.
But Tetsu almost never smiles, so it's really creepy!
Just cram it, Retsu.
LAND OF THE RABBITS *END*

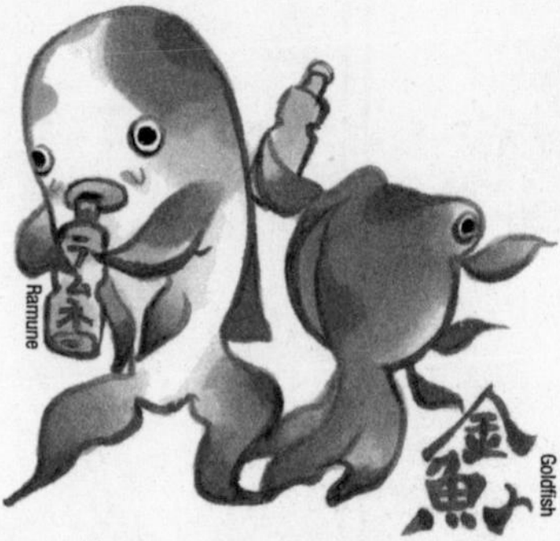
Ramune
Goldfish

Kaneyoshi Izumi

To those who have picked up this manga, you are so kind and sweet. This manga may seem like a big weed blossoming in the world of shojo manga, but don't dismiss it so easily. Please, take it to the cashier. Sincerely, with love.

Kaneyoshi Izumi's birthday is April 1, and her blood type is probably type A (but she hasn't actually had it checked yet). Her debut story "Tenshi" (Angel) appeared in the September 1995 issue of *Bessatsu Shojo Comic* and won the 36th Shogakukan Shinjin (newbie) Comics Award. Her hobbies include riding motorcycles, playing the piano and feeding stray cats, and she continues to work as an artist for *Betsucomi.*

SEIHO BOYS' HIGH SCHOOL
Volume 1
Shojo Beat Edition

STORY AND ART BY
KANEYOSHI IZUMI

© 2007 Kaneyoshi IZUMI/Shogakukan
All rights reserved.
Original Japanese edition "MEN'S KOU"
published by SHOGAKUKAN Inc.

English Adaptation/Ysabet MacFarlane
Translation/Katherine Schilling
Touch-up Art & Lettering/Kelle Han
Design/Hidemi Sahara
Editor/Alexis Kirsch

VP, Production/Alvin Lu
VP, Sales & Product Marketing/Gonzalo Ferreyra
VP, Creative/Linda Espinosa
Publisher/Hyoe Narita

Printed in the U.S.A.

Published by VIZ Media, LLC
P.O. Box 77010
San Francisco, CA 94107

10 9 8 7 6 5 4 3 2 1
First printing, August 2010

www.viz.com

www.shojobeat.com

A Beauty Who Feels Like a Beast!

To overcome an embarrassing past, teenage Ai gets a makeover and attends a new high school. Soon, the hottest guy at school is chatting her up! But beauty is only skin deep, and Ai learns that fresh makeup and new clothes can't hide her insecurities or doubts.

A tale of high school neurosis at its finest—start your graphic novel collection today!

doubt!!™

www.viz.com
store.viz.com

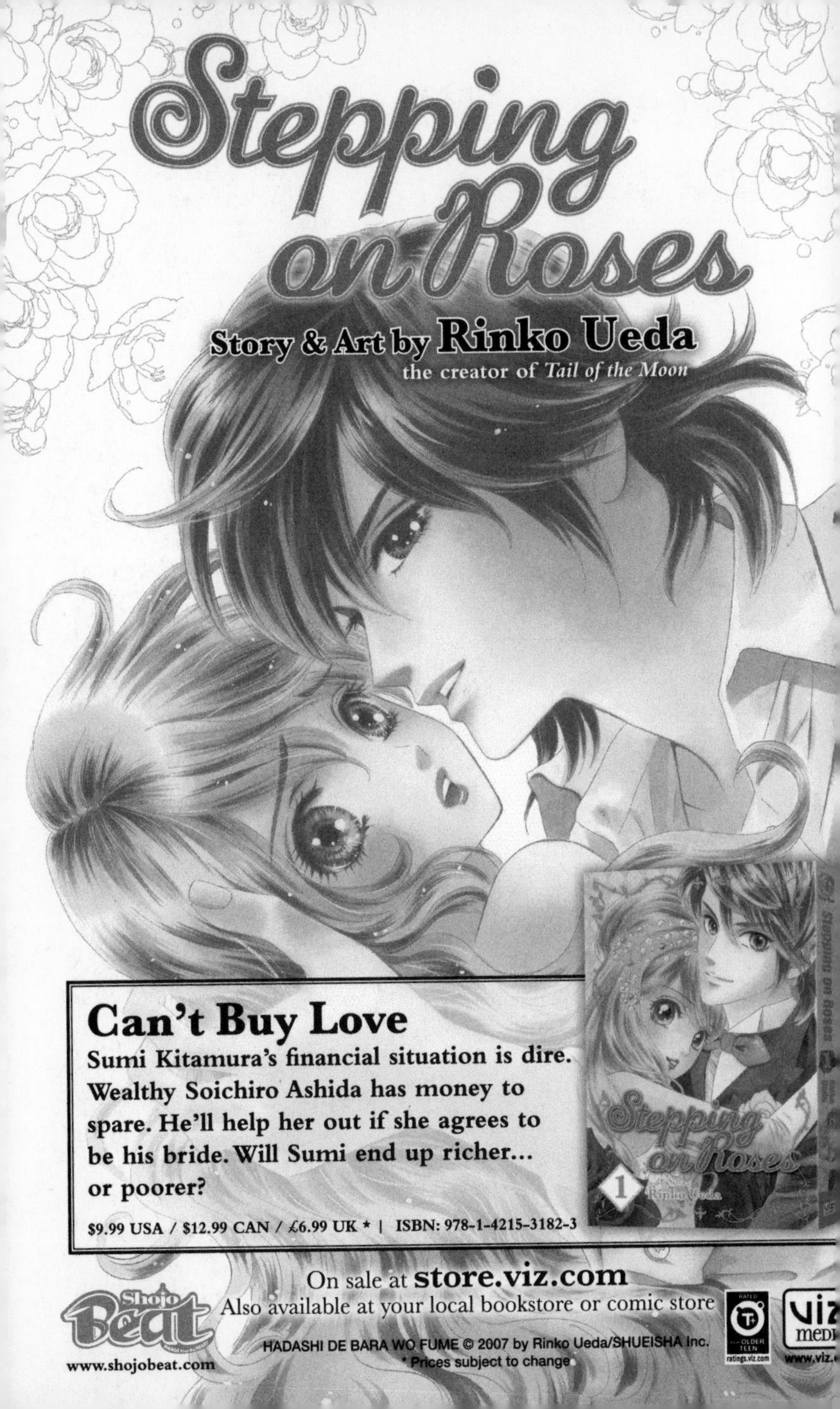
Stepping on Roses
Story & Art by Rinko Ueda
the creator of *Tail of the Moon*
Can't Buy Love
Sumi Kitamura's financial situation is dire. Wealthy Soichiro Ashida has money to spare. He'll help her out if she agrees to be his bride. Will Sumi end up richer... or poorer?
$9.99 USA / $12.99 CAN / £6.99 UK * | ISBN: 978-1-4215-3182-3
On sale at store.viz.com
Also available at your local bookstore or comic store
HADASHI DE BARA WO FUME © 2007 by Rinko Ueda/SHUEISHA Inc.
* Prices subject to change
Shojo Beat
www.shojobeat.com
RATED OLDER TEEN
ratings.viz.com

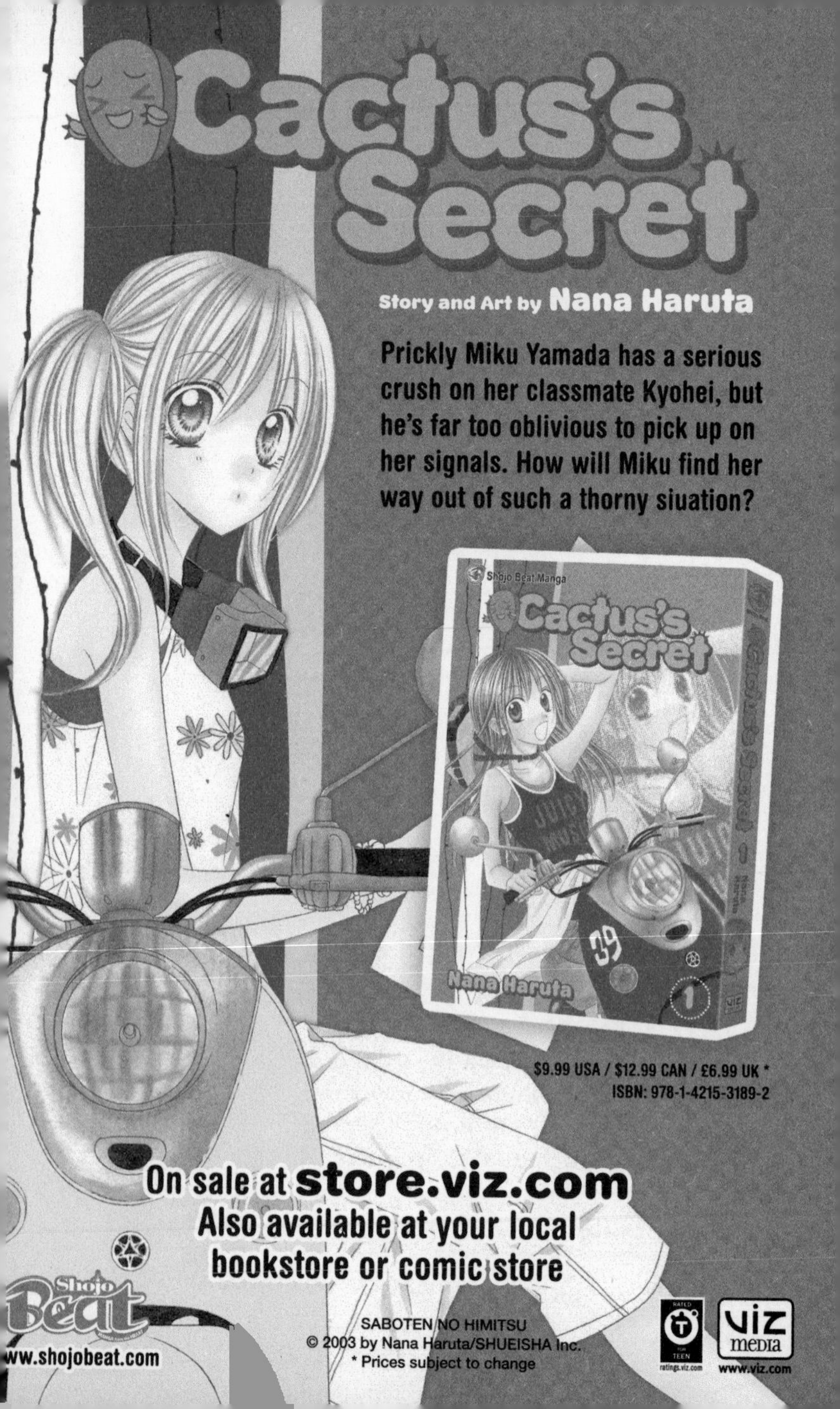
Cactus's Secret
Story and Art by Nana Haruta
Prickly Miku Yamada has a serious crush on her classmate Kyohei, but he's far too oblivious to pick up on her signals. How will Miku find her way out of such a thorny siuation?
Shojo Beat Manga
Cactus's Secret
Nana Haruta
1
$9.99 USA / $12.99 CAN / £6.99 UK *
ISBN: 978-1-4215-3189-2
On sale at store.viz.com
Also available at your local bookstore or comic store
Shojo Beat
www.shojobeat.com
SABOTEN NO HIMITSU
© 2003 by Nana Haruta/SHUEISHA Inc.
* Prices subject to change
RATED T TEEN
ratings.viz.com
VIZ media
www.viz.com